Advances in Culture and Psychology

Advances in Culture and Psychology

Oxford University Press
ISSN 2155-2622

Advances in Culture and Psychology

Volume One

Edited by

Michele J. Gelfand
Chi-yue Chiu
Ying-yi Hong

OXFORD
UNIVERSITY PRESS
2011

OXFORD
UNIVERSITY PRESS

Oxford University Press, Inc., publishes works that further
Oxford University's objective of excellence in research, scholarship, and education.

Oxford   New York
Auckland   Cape Town   Dar es Salaam   Hong Kong   Karachi
Kuala Lumpur   Madrid   Melbourne   Mexico City   Nairobi
New Delhi   Shanghai   Taipei   Toronto

With offices in
Argentina   Austria   Brazil   Chile   Czech Republic   France   Greece
Guatemala   Hungary   Italy   Japan   Poland   Portugal   Singapore
South Korea   Switzerland   Thailand   Turkey   Ukraine   Vietnam

Published by Oxford University Press, Inc.
198 Madison Avenue, New York, New York 10016

www.oup.com

Library of Congress Cataloging-in-Publication Data

Advances in culture and psychology
ISSN 2155-2622
ISBN-10: 0-19-538039-8
ISBN-13: 978-0-19-538039-2

_____

9 8 7 6 5 4 3 2 1

Printed in the United States of America on acid-free paper

CONTENTS

FOREWORD

The publication of *Advances in Culture and Psychology* is of historic importance. The buzz surrounding research on culture and psychology reemerged in the 1980s and has been reverberating through several disciplines ever since, including social, developmental, and cognitive psychology, anthropology, and linguistics. There are now first-rate textbooks, handbooks, and journals on the topic. A growing literature on psychic pluralism versus psychic unity across cultural groups is rich with inspiring philosophical and theoretical manifestos, eye-opening empirical studies, and informative review essays. Now happily there is *Advances in Culture and Psychology*. The editors of the series invite leading scholars to give an overview of their mature research programs. *Advances in Culture and Psychology* is sure to become an ongoing canonical vehicle for the revival of psychological research that is both comparative and sensitive to cultural realities.

Research programs in comparative psychology can, of course, be traced back to the late nineteenth century and early decades of the twentieth century. In the late 1890s a young psychologist, William McDougall, participated in the famous pioneering interdisciplinary Cambridge University Torres Straits expedition and established an experimental laboratory in New Guinea to assess similarities and differences in sensory perception across cultural groups. In the early 1930s a young anthropologist, Margaret Mead, returned from a field trip to the Admiralty Islands and told a young Jean Piaget that Swiss children in Geneva were distinctively Western and that he had wildly overgeneralized about the universal development of animistic thinking in children. Concerns and debates of that sort—attentive to the population-based boundary conditions for generalizations about human mental functioning and the global representativeness of the samples and evidence supporting "fundamental psychological processes"—have never been entirely absent from the psychological, semiotic, and behavioral sciences. Nevertheless they were largely set to the side in "mainstream psychology" in the decades immediately following World War II. Fortunately researchers in Europe and North America are beginning, once again, to become self-conscious about the possibility that the findings they publish might be significantly (and interestingly) culture-bound. And today research on culture and psychology is one of the growth sectors in the psychological, semiotic, and behavioral sciences.

One looks forward to the day when the recurrence of interest in culture and psychology has been systematically documented. Any such history, one imagines, will point to events and processes both inside and outside the academy that have created a favorable environment for a field that is concerned with questions of cultural influence. Concerning outside events, I have in mind, for example, changes in the U.S. immigration laws in the 1960s that prepared the way for increased levels of Asian, African, and South and Middle American migration; the international pendulum swing in the direction of economic globalization, which eroded national barriers to the flow of goods, information, capital, and labor (including students and scholars) all over the world; the emergence of identity politics, social justice concerns, and affirmative action policies and their beneficial consequences for funding research or researcher training with regard to ethnic and racial minority groups; and the various and numerous conflicts and competitions between nations and groups over the past decades (from the Japanese success in the world economy to the wars in Iraq and Afghanistan and the tensions between Islam and Christianity in Europe). These conflicts and competitions have made it increasingly apparent that cultural influences and group differences in human goals, values, and pictures of reality are not only here to stay but need to be understood for the sake of domestic and international tranquility, and for everyone's general well-being. Concerning events inside the academy, I have in mind scholarly institutions, including, for example, this publication series, which will regularly publish and make visible the advances that mark progress in the disciplined investigation of the ways culture and psyche make each other up.

Breadth of coverage is a positive thing for a publication series on culture and psychology, if for no other reason than the diversity of existing research program on mental states among human beings on a global scale. Most researchers who work this field have more than just a general interest in cultural influences on behavior. For some the aim of research on culture and psychology is to guard against the hazards of parochialism and to ensure the general truth or universal validity of any proposed psychological theory (including theories of psychological development) by grounding any claims about psychic unity in evidence that is representative of the diverse populations of the world. For others the (closely related) aim of culture and psychology is to establish comparability or equivalence for measuring instruments across different populations (and to be especially alert to the hazards of misunderstanding or miscommunication or mistranslation across cultural and linguistic worlds). For still others the aim is to construct a credible theory of psychological pluralism and to give priority to the study of the distinctive mental characteristics of various peoples. Here the aim of research in culture and psychology is to document and explain differences in what people want, think, know, feel, and value (and hence do) by virtue of growing up in a particular cultural group. It is the study of human diversity in emotional functioning, self-organization, moral evaluation, social cognition, and pathways of development. *Advances in Culture and Psychology* will be a lively and welcoming home to a multiplicity of such aims.

Richard A. Shweder
William Claude Reavis Distinguished Service Professor
Department of Comparative Human Development
University of Chicago

Introduction

The launching of the *Advances in Culture and Psychology* series is the result of a confluence of events that happened at the right place and the right time. Like many ideas, the germ of the conception of the series was quite serendipitous. It was December of 2006, during a conference on culture sponsored by the Hong Kong University of Science and Technology, that we were reflecting on the achievements of the culture field over a coffee break. After days of very stimulating presentations that energized and connected culture scholars from across the field, we had the collective recognition that the state of the science of culture and psychology was far deeper, far broader, and far more impactful than anyone at the conference had even begun to acknowledge. It was a recognition that a cultural revolution is beginning to take form throughout the discipline, with culture research infiltrating all of psychology—from neuroscience, cognitive, developmental, clinical, and counseling, to social and organizational and beyond. Far from being the "exception," culture research in the discipline was becoming more of the norm. Over our coffee break, we also had another collective realization: While culture research pervades the discipline, the disciplinary structure of the field inhibits this very recognition and synergy. Much of the culture work in psychology remains within its own disciplinary walls, rarely breaking out to be found in its sister disciplines. Additionally, with few exceptions, there is little institution building that organizes, disseminates, and marks the collective contributions of the culture and psychology field. The *Advances in Culture and Psychology* series seeks to do just that.

In this series, we seek to showcase highly influential research programs on topics related to culture and psychology, broadly defined. The series is a source for students, researchers, and practitioners who want to find comprehensive, critical, and state-of-the-art reviews on mature research programs in culture and psychology. The *Advances* series is committed to showcasing culture research that represents a wide variety of theoretical, epistemological, and methodological perspectives, including research from cross-cultural, cultural, indigenous, computational, linguistic, among many other traditions; work that spans many levels of analysis; and work from psychology as well as our sister disciplines, including linguistics, sociology, anthropology, political science, economics, among others. Of note, we deliberately chose the title *Culture and Psychology* to communicate the breadth and depth with which we view the intellectual terrain of the series.

With this series, we hope to develop an intellectual home for culture and psychology research programs and to foster bridges among culture scholars from across the discipline and beyond. We aim to provide a space to display our collective knowledge, to take stock of the best that our field has to offer, and to push the cultural envelope even farther and deeper into the discipline of psychology. We also envision the series as a mechanism to translate our knowledge into practical relevance for managing interdependence in an increasingly "flat" world. In a world of global threats and global opportunities, knowledge about cultural processes is critical for dealing with pressing universal concerns, from terrorism to globalization to the preservation of the environment.

Scholars from across the discipline will be invited to contribute articles on a yearly basis so that the volume reflects diverse contributions across the fields of culture and psychology. Authors are also encouraged to submit their work to be considered for publication. Target articles for the *Advances in Culture and Psychology* series are scholars' own mature research programs—comprehensive reviews of the cumulative knowledge that has been gained through one's programmatic work (similar to the high-profile *Advances in Experimental Social Psychology* series). We will also consider manuscripts that describe up-and-coming research programs that have already shown promise on cutting-edge topics, as well as manuscripts that describe new data from large-scale empirical research projects. We envision the *Advances in Culture and Psychology* series to also showcase work from other disciplines, given that culture research is inherently interdisciplinary.

We extend our sincere gratitude to many people who have helped in the design and implementation of the series. First, we thank members of the *Advances in Culture and Psychology* Advisory board, which provides advice and ideas for the series, including Patricia Greenfield (University of California, Los Angeles), Yoshi Kashima (University of Melbourne), Shinobu Kitayama (University of Michigan), Mark Schaller (University of British Columbia), Richard Shweder (University of Chicago), and Colleen Ward (Victoria University of Wellington). We are grateful to Mark Zanna (University of Waterloo), the editor of the *Advances in Experimental Social Psychology* series, for his sage advice on the structure of the series. We thank Oxford University Press, and Lori Handleman in particular, for their support in launching the series. We also thank our respective institutions, the University of Maryland, the University of Illinois, and Nanyang Technological University, for their support. Finally, we thank Harry Triandis, a pioneer in the field, who has inspired us throughout the years with his wisdom and his friendship.

Michele J. Gelfand
College Park, Maryland

Chi-yue Chiu
Singapore

Ying-yi Hong
Singapore

CHAPTER 1

Human Culture in Evolutionary Perspective

MICHAEL TOMASELLO
Max Planck Institute for Evolutionary Anthropology

I. INTRODUCTION

Many animal species are "cultural" in the sense that individuals acquire important behaviors and skills from groupmates via social learning. Thus, whales socially learn some foraging techniques from others, capuchin monkeys socially learn some grooming-type behaviors from others, and chimpanzees acquire the use of some tools by observing the tool-use activities of others in their social group (see Laland & Galef, 2009, for an overview).

But human culture is clearly different. The challenge from an evolutionary perspective is to specify the nature of this difference. The proposal here is that nonhuman primate (and other animal) culture is essentially individualistic, or maybe even exploitative. That is to say, when a chimpanzee individual observes another using a tool and then learns something that facilitates her own use, she is simply gathering information that is useful to her—much as she might gather information from the inanimate world. The one being observed may not even know that the observer is gathering information from her actions.

In contrast, human culture and cultural transmission are fundamentally cooperative. Synchronically, humans engage in much more cooperative behavior in terms of such things as collaborative problem solving and cooperative (or even conventional) communication. Moreover, human individuals live in a world in which the group expects them to conform to its particular conventions and social norms—or else! The result is a society structured by cooperatively created and enforced conventions and norms for how to behave as one of "us," resulting ultimately in rule-governed social institutions. Diachronically, this cooperative way of living translates into established members of the group teaching things to youngsters and novitiates, who not only learn but actively conform. Teaching and conformity are main contributors to the stability of cultural practices in a group and—precisely because of this stability—to the unique ways in which human cultural practices ratchet up in complexity over historical time. The result is human artifacts and symbol systems with "histories," so-called cumulative cultural evolution (Tomasello, Kruger, & Ratner, 1993).

Underlying humans' uniquely cooperative lifeways and modes of cultural transmission are a set of species-unique social-cognitive processes, which we may refer to collectively as skills and motivations for shared intentionality (Tomasello, Carpenter, Call, Behne, & Moll, 2005). These involve such things as the ability and motivation to form shared goals and intentions with others in collaborative activities, and the ability and motivation to share experience with others via joint attention, cooperative communication, and teaching. Skills and motivations of shared intentionality arose as part of a coevolutionary process in which humans evolved species-unique ways of operating, indeed cooperating, within their own self-built cultural worlds (Richerson & Boyd, 2006).

In this chapter, we attempt to characterize human culture in evolutionary perspective. We do this, first, by specifying some of the most important ways in which human social life is more cooperatively structured than that of other primates. Second, we detail how this more cooperative mode of living transforms the process of cultural transmission across generations. And third, we look at the underlying social-cognitive skills and motivations that make it possible for developing children to come to participate in the culture into which they are born—which then leads them to construct still further, culturally specific cognitive skills. We conclude with some speculations about how this all might have come about in the process of human evolution.

II. APE AND HUMAN COOPERATION

The vast majority of primate species live in social groups and so are cooperative in a very general way. But what we are concerned with here are more specific, and arguably more complex, forms of cooperation such as collaborative problem solving; coalitions, alliances, and group defense; active food sharing; cooperative communication; conventions and social norms for cooperation;

and so forth. These are all things that characterize human cultural life, and our question here is the degree to which they are shared by other primates. To answer this question, we focus, in the case of humans, on small-scale societies, as cooperation in modern technological societies has some special properties. In the case of nonhuman primates, we focus on our nearest great ape relatives who, despite some species differences, are basically similar on the dimensions of interest here—with special attention to the species for whom most is known, chimpanzees, one of humans' two closest living relatives. We proceed by reviewing in fairly broad strokes what is known about humans and their great ape relatives in six domains of cultural life: subsistence; economy; childrearing and prosocial behavior; communication and teaching; politics; and norms and institutions.

A. Subsistence

Great apes basically forage for food individually. They may travel in groups or small bands and sit together while eating—and may even vocalize upon finding food, which attracts others (perhaps as protection against predation)—but there are almost no habitual foraging activities in which great apes actively collaborate in the acquisition of food. Upon entering a patch of fruit, for example, individuals typically take a piece of fruit and then move away a certain distance from others to eat it. (This can be observed on a daily basis in captive settings in pretty much all great apes when highly desirable food is involved.) Some great apes are more tolerant than others in feeding contexts, perhaps especially bonobos, but even they do not actively share food often (there is some exchange of food for services; see later section on "Economy").

The one major exception is the group hunting of monkeys by chimpanzees. Not all chimpanzee groups engage in this activity, and there are major differences among the groups that do. In some groups the hunt resembles a kind of helter-skelter chase in which multiple individuals attempt to capture the monkey with little if any coordination (e.g., at Gombe: Stanford, 1998; Ngogo: Watts & Mitani, 2002). In the Tai Forest, however, the canopy is continuous, and the monkeys are quite agile, and so such uncoordinated chasing will not get the job done. In the account of Boesch (e.g., Boesch, 2005; Boesch & Boesch, 1989; Boesch & Boesch-Achermann, 2000), hunting chimpanzees have a common goal and take complementary roles in the hunt. In this account, one individual chases the prey in a certain direction while others climb the surrounding trees and prevent the prey from escaping, at which point one or more individuals pounce. But a less rich characterization of this activity is the following (see Tomasello et al., 2005). One chimpanzee begins by chasing the monkey, given that others are around (which he knows is necessary for success). Each other chimpanzee then goes, in turn, to the most opportune spatial position still available at any given moment in the emerging hunt. In this process, each participant is attempting to maximize its own chances of catching the prey, without any kind of prior joint goal or joint plan or assignment of roles. This kind of hunting event clearly is a group activity of some complexity in which individuals are mutually responsive to one another's spatial position as they encircle the prey. But wolves and lions do something very similar, and most researchers do not attribute to them any kind of joint goals and/or plans (Cheney & Seyfarth, 1990; Tomasello & Call, 1997). It is perhaps also important that bonobos do not hunt in groups in the wild (nor other apes), suggesting that the chimpanzee version and the human version may have arisen independently, based on different underlying psychological processes.

This interpretation of chimpanzee hunting is supported by what happens after the kill. When a group of chimpanzees captures a monkey, the participants in the hunt typically all get meat—more than late-arriving chimpanzees who did not participate in the hunt. However, recent research by Gilby (2006) elucidates the basically individualistic mechanisms involved in this "sharing." Gilby notes, first of all, that chimpanzees who possess meat after the kill often attempt to avoid others by stealing away from the kill site, by climbing to the end of a branch to restrict the access of other chimpanzees, or by chasing beggars away. Nevertheless, meat possessors are typically surrounded by beggars. The possessor usually allows the beggars to take some of their meat, but this is a direct result of the begging and harassment: the more a beggar harasses, the more food he gets. The logic is that if the possessor actually fights the harasser for the meat actively, he will likely lose the rest of it to either the harasser or others nearby in the melee—so the best strategy is to eat quickly and allow others to take some meat to keep them happy (the so-called tolerated theft, or harassment, model of food sharing). Tomasello et al. (2005) suggest the further possibility that hunters obtain more meat than latecomers because they are the first ones immediately at the carcass and begging, whereas latecomers are relegated to the second ring.

This general account is supported by a recent experimental study. Melis, Hare, and Tomasello (2006a) presented pairs of chimpanzees with out-of-reach food that could only be obtained if they each pulled on one of the two ropes available (attached to a platform with food on it) and did so simultaneously. When there were two piles of food, one in front of each participant, there was a moderate amount of synchronized pulling. However, when there was only one pile of food in the middle of the platform, making it difficult to share at the end, coordination fell apart almost completely. Moreover, Melis et al. also found that there was more synchronized pulling from pairs of individuals previously identified as tolerant of one another than from less tolerant pairs (and generally more tolerant bonobos do better in this task as well; Hare, Melis, Woods, Hastings, & Wrangham, 2007). The point is that chimpanzees only coordinate synchronized activities when there is likely to be no squabbling over the food at the end. Thus, while it is relatively easy for hunting chimpanzees to collaborate in the "large carcass" scenario in which each individual has a reasonable probability of capturing the monkey and even unsuccessful participants can still harass the capturer and get some meat, this strategy does not generalize easily to other hunting contexts.

Humans, as compared with apes and other primates, engage in an extremely wide array of collaborative activities, many of these on a very large scale with non-kin (and many under the aegis of social norms in the context of symbols and formal institutions; see later discussion). And different cultural groups collaborate in different activities: some in hunting, some in fishing, some in house building, some in playing music, some in governing, and on and on, which testifies to the flexibility of the underlying cognitive skills involved. In foraging activities in particular, the prototypical situation is one in which a small group establishes the joint goal of capturing a certain prey or extracting a certain plant. Then they plan their various roles and how they should be coordinated ahead of time—or else those roles are already common knowledge based on a common history of the practice (see Hill & Hurtado, 1996, for a review).

From the point of view of other primates, the distinguishing characteristic of these collaborative foraging activities is their highly cooperative nature. In addition to the joint planning and execution, during the foraging itself individuals help others in their roles with regularity. For example, Hill (2002) documents the following cooperative activities that take place during group foraging in the Ache of South America: cutting a trail for others to follow; making a bridge for others to cross a river; carrying another's child; climbing a tree to flush a monkey for another hunter; allowing another to shoot at a prey instead of self; allowing another to extract honey or larvae that self has found; vocalizing to locate escaping prey for others; calling the location of the resource for another to exploit while self continues searching for something else; waiting for others to join a pursuit, even when this lowers probability of success;

carrying game shot by another hunter or the palm fiber that others have gathered; climbing tree to knock down fruit for others to gather; bringing weapons and giving to others for their hunting; spending time instructing others in the best technique; lending bow or ax to other when self could use it; helping look for others' lost arrows; helping repair others' broken arrows; going back on trail to warn others of wasp nest or poisonous snake; removing dangerous obstacles from trail before others arrive; and so forth. Hill (2002) documents that the Ache spend from about 10% to 50% of their foraging time engaged in such altruistic activities—pretty much all of which would be unthinkable for nonhuman primates.

When a large prey is caught, the norm in most forager societies is that the participants carry the carcass back to some home base and share the catch with others, not only in their immediate families but also more broadly in the social group at large. Indeed, they are typically under strict social norms to do so, as those who do not share are harshly sanctioned (Hill & Hurtado, 1996). This propensity to share the fruits of collaborative labor in a "fair" way is extremely strong in humans; people in almost all cultural groups have internalized norms for sharing and fairness (see Fehr & Fischbacher, 2003, for a review). In a study similar to that reported earlier by Melis et al. (2006a), Warneken et al. (in press) found that young children cooperate just as eagerly regardless of whether the rewards are already divided for them or they must find a way to divide them themselves; they continue to cooperate in either case, trusting that they will be able to work out a satisfactory solution.

In general, then, great apes forage in basically the same manner as other social mammals: traveling and eating together, presumably as protection against predation, with very few collaborative foraging activities. The group hunting of chimpanzees very likely operates in the same manner as that of social carnivores, although perhaps based on more flexible cognitive mechanisms. In contrast, humans forage cooperatively, helping others as needed and sharing the spoils at the end in a "fair" manner (see Fig. 1.1). That is to say, great apes forage individualistically, whereas humans forage (and farm—but that is another story) cooperatively.

B. Economy

Like many animal species, each of the great ape species may be said to participate in a "biological market." In chimpanzees, the "commodities" exchanged are such things as grooming, support in fights, sex, and meat, with most of the activity involving males (Muller & Mitani, 2005). Many other animal species

FIGURE 1.1: Group foraging in the Hadza. (Photograph courtesy of Frank Marlowe.)

have analogous biological markets in the various social behaviors and resources important in their lives (see Noe, Van Hooff, & Hammerstein, 2001).

But human markets are different. In addition to reciprocity of various behaviors, humans trade items that they own. Although apes may have some respect for a physical possession, physical possession is not ownership. Thus, for example, if one ties a valuable object onto a string and then onto an individual macaque, others will not take it if the string is very short and so the object is close to the individual, but they will take it if the string is long so the object is far from its "possessor" (Kummer & Cords, 1991). This kind of respect for possession is presumably based on fear of retaliation for taking an object another physically holds. Human ownership of various kinds of property, on the other hand, is a fundamentally cooperative arrangement in which everyone agrees to respect others' rights. "Claims to property only makes sense in a social context where there is some level of cooperative behavior: if any given subject is to have control over any given object, others must understand the signals of ownership and acquiesce in them" (Rose, 2007, pp. 3–4). For example, when driftwood washes onto the beach after a storm, people who desire it often go and collect it and pile it in a pile, sometimes leaving a personal object beside it to mark that they have collected it and so claim ownership. Others naturally respect this and do not attempt to take that wood, but only wood not already in piles (Rose, 2007). On the other hand, when captive chimpanzees encounter large numbers of small pieces of food spread out over an area, they grab as much as they can and hold it as close as they can to their body (or perhaps sit right next to it), but there are no reported instances, to our knowledge, of them using anything like this piling strategy as a way of claiming ownership—presumably because no other chimpanzees would recognize or respect it if they did.

Another obstacle to real ownership and trade is that chimpanzees do not really trust others in the trading situation (typically with good reason). Thus, captive chimpanzees can learn to trade objects with humans—for example, tokens for food—but when they themselves have a valuable object, such as a grape, they have an extremely difficult time letting go of it in trade even for something obviously much more valuable, such as a whole bunch of grapes. Brosnan, Grady, Lambeth, Schapiro, and Beran (2008, abstract) speculate that "Chimpanzees lack ownership norms, and thus have limited opportunity to benefit from the gains of trade, and [the] risk of defection is sufficiently high that large gains must be imminent to justify the risk." In stark contrast, human foragers are often said to live in a kind of "primitive communism," in which the sharing of many things, especially food, is the norm ("no one starves unless we all starve"). In a systematic review, Gurven (2004) documents how widespread the sharing and trading of food among humans is in small-scale societies. In assessing possible hypotheses to explain this pattern of widespread food sharing, Gurven concludes that it is probably multiply determined, but he also opines that the big picture is not tit-for-tat reciprocity, but rather "more complicated social arrangements, including those whereby important social support is provided only if one adheres to socially negotiated sharing norms" (p. 559). And, of course, in many small-scale societies a large role is played by the gift (Mauss, 1954), which serves to establish and cement social bonds as well as create obligations of reciprocation.

The general conclusion is that chimpanzees and other great apes are fairly similar to many other animal species in terms of their biological markets—based mainly on kinship or some kind of close reciprocity. But in the human market reciprocity is structured by a cooperative regime in which ownership rights are cooperatively recognized and enforced by all. Food sharing is much more widespread in humans than in other primates, at least partly because there is more trust in reciprocity. One speculation is that humans' unique forms of food sharing arose originally in the context of cooperative foraging, with the "fair" division of spoils (see earlier discussion) now extended to other contexts.

C. Child Care and Prosocial Behavior

The special cooperativeness with which humans, as compared with other great apes, deal with food comes out again when we look at their prosocial behavior in general. In recent experiments it has been found that chimpanzees will help others achieve their goals when all that is required is expending a little energy. But they are not so helpful in supplying others with food.

Warneken and Tomasello (2006, 2007) had 1-year-old human infants and three human-raised chimpanzees confront a human adult needing help with 10 simple problems such as fetching an out-of-reach object or opening cabinet doors with hands full. Almost all of the infants helped at least once, and they basically did so immediately. Although they did not help in the other tasks, the chimpanzees did help humans to fetch out-of-reach objects. Because there may be many reasons that human-raised chimpanzees would help a human, in another study, Warneken, Hare, Melis, Hanus, and Tomasello (2007) gave mother-raised chimpanzees the opportunity to help humans, which they did, and then also the opportunity to help one another. The latter situation was that one chimpanzee watched while another struggled to open a door into a room. The observing ape knew from previous experience that the door could be opened by removing a pin. The surprising finding was that the chimpanzee observers did indeed remove the pin and help their groupmate gain access to the room (and there was no evidence that they expected any reward themselves).

But despite their helpful attitude in providing services for others, chimpanzees do not seem to be motivated to provide food for others—even at no cost to themselves, and even when the recipient is their child. In a recent set of experiments by Silk et al. (2005) and Jensen, Hare, Call, and Tomasello (2006), chimpanzee subjects were faced with the choice of pulling in one of two boards, on each of which was two reward trays—one tray accessible to the subject and one tray accessible to another individual in an adjoining room. In the simplest situation, one of the boards contained one piece of food for the subject and none for the partner, whereas the other board contained one piece of food for each. Thus, the energy that a subject needed to expend was identical in the two cases, and the reward for the subject (one piece of food) was identical in the two cases. And so the question was whether the chimpanzees would go ahead and pull the board that would also deliver some food to the partner—at absolutely no cost to themselves. The answer in both studies was that they did not. And in a control condition in which the other room was empty and the door to it open—so that the pulling chimp could quickly go get the food designated for the other room—the subjects in Jensen, Call, and Tomasello (2007a) demonstrated that they knew that the food was indeed going to the other room. Fehr, Bernhard, and Rockenbach (2008) have recently shown that school-age children in a very similar paradigm pull the equitable option more often than the selfish option, and Brownell, Svetlova, and Nichols (2009) found the same thing with children at 25 months of age.

Even more startling, in a recent study, Ueno and Matsuzawa (2004) looked systematically at food sharing among three chimpanzee mothers and their infants. They recorded many attempts by the infant to get food from the mother, approximately 60% of which were rejected. More active transfers of food by the mothers to the infants were rare, and when they did occur the mothers always—100% of the time—transferred to their infants the less palatable part of the food they were eating, that is, the peeling, the husk, or the shell. This is more than they would do for other adults, of course, and so there are clearly some maternal instincts at work here. But human mothers, obviously, actively provision their infants at a much higher and more generous rate (Hrdy, 2009).

The way that human mothers actively provision their children with food reflects a larger pattern. Humans are so-called cooperative breeders, which basically means that children are cared for not only by their mothers but also by other adults, including the father and maternal grandmother, of course, but also other mothers in cooperative arrangements. These other caretakers not only help the children in various ways but also actively provision them with food (Hrdy, 2009). Although there are some New World primate species who are also cooperative breeders, among the four species of great apes, mothers provide basically 100% of the child care themselves. In humans, across both traditional and modern industrial societies, the figure is closer to 50%. Hrdy (2009) speculates that cooperative breeding is the evolutionary context within which humans began down their distinctively cooperative way of living. A related speculation that would fit especially well with the current account is that cooperative foraging creates the need for some way of managing the children so that mothers may forage more efficiently and effectively. Help from otherwise idle grandmothers, or cooperative child-care arrangements among mothers, would clearly be beneficial for maximizing foraging efficiency as a whole.

As part of this whole complex, another unique aspect of human social life (i.e., among great apes) is of course the family in general. Male and female humans form pair bonds, sometimes exclusively, and males are partially responsible for their children's provisioning and care. One consequence of this familial pattern is that human children and fathers form strong bonds, as do siblings, which is not true in other great ape species. Chapais (2008) spells out some of the many implications of stronger familial (especially paternal) bonds, not the least of which is that when females immigrate to neighboring groups (characteristic of chimpanzees, bonobos, and humans) human males still retain ties with their sisters and daughters, and these kinship bonds serve to dampen aggression between neighboring groups (see section on "Politics").

D. Communication and Teaching

It comes so naturally to humans that we do not think of it as cooperative behavior at all, but the free exchange of information in humans is premised on the cooperative assumption that a communicative act provides useful or relevant information not for the speaker but for the listener (Grice, 1957). Thus, humans routinely inform others of things that they believe will help them, even when the speaker is just a bystander and gains no benefit at all—like giving directions or pointing to something that the other person dropped. True, the energy or cost associated with an informative communicative act is low. But that makes it all the more mysterious why, apparently, even our closest primate relatives do not seem to offer up information to others helpfully in this same way.

Virtually all animal communication, including that of great apes, involves one individual getting the other to do what he wants him to. The apparent exceptions are food calls and alarm calls. But, in recent interpretations, even these vocalizations are considered mainly self-serving. Thus, when chimpanzees find food, they call so that they can have company while eating, as protection against predators; and when they spy a predator, they vocalize as a way of recruiting allies for defense, or as a way of signaling the predator that he has been spotted (Owren & Rendall, 2001). Importantly, these vocalizations are given even when the entire group is already there and so not in need of any information about the situation; thus, their function is not to inform. Seyfarth and Cheney (2003, p. 168) say about nonhuman primates: "Listeners acquire information from signalers who do not, in the human sense, intend to provide it"; and Zuberbühler (2005, p. 126) says: "Nonhuman primates vocalize in response to important events, irrespective of how potential recipients may view the situation." Even when chimpanzees communicate with a human (e.g., by pointing), they are virtually always attempting to get him to do something for them, as are language-trained great apes (over 95% imperatives in various studies; Tomasello, 2008).

In contrast, even from their earliest, prelinguistic attempts at intentional communication, human infants inform others of things helpfully. Thus, when 12-month-old infants see an adult searching for an object, they will direct her to it with a pointing gesture, if they know where it is (Liszkowski, Carpenter, Striano, & Tomasello, 2006). Variations on this basic situation establish that the infants do not want the object for themselves (e.g., they quit pointing as soon as the adult has fetched it), and they are not just eager for the adult to perform an activity with the object (e.g., they point preferentially to objects whose location the adult is ignorant of; Liszkowski, Carpenter, & Tomasello, 2008). Cooperative informing comes naturally to even very young, prelinguistic human infants (see Fig. 1.2).

FIGURE 1.2: Human infant pointing to coordinate a collaborative activity.

Perhaps surprisingly, great apes do not even *comprehend* pointing when it is used in an informative manner. Apes follow gaze and pointing direction to visible targets, but they do not seem to understand an informative communicative intent. Thus, many different studies have found that when apes are searching for hidden food and a human points to a cup to inform them of its location, they do not understand. They do not ask themselves why the pointer wanted them to attend to the cup; they do not seek relevance (Tomasello, 2006). This makes perfect ape sense, of course, as in their everyday lives apes do not experience someone pointing out food for them helpfully—they compete with others for food—and so they do not assume an altruistic intent here. Human infants, on the other hand, understand informative pointing and make the appropriate relevance inference in such situations prelinguistically, at 12–14 months of age (Behne, Carpenter, & Tomasello, 2005). In this situation, infants appear to ask themselves the question: Why does *she* think that my attending to that cup will be helpful or relevant for *me*? This self-question is based on the cooperative assumption that others are trying to be helpful. Chimpanzees do not operate with anything like this Gricean principle of cooperation, and thus they have no basis for making the appropriate relevance inference.

A special application of this kind of cooperative communication is teaching, in which one individual, often an adult, cooperatively informs another, often a child, of how things work. Gergely and Csibra (2006) argue that teaching is especially important in the human case because the existence of relatively "opaque" cultural conventions (there is no causal structure or else it is difficult to see this structure) requires that human adults be specifically adapted for pedagogy toward children and that human children be specifically adapted for recognizing when adults are being pedagogical toward them (what Tomasello, Kruger, & Ratner 1993, called instructed learning). Though it varies greatly in form across cultures (some employing very little formal instruction beyond teaching children appropriate behavior in public and various kin relations), teaching in one form or another would seem to be universal across human cultures (Kruger & Tomasello, 1996). There have been no reported observations of chimpanzees engaged in anything resembling teaching since the two observations of Boesch (1991), and these have multiple interpretations not involving informing or teaching.

The overall point is that humans seem to have evolved a system of communication premised on cooperation, whereas other great apes have not. One possible explanation is that humans evolved this informative communicative function in the context of collaborative activities such as collaborative foraging, where helping the other typically helps us both toward our common goal, whereas chimpanzees do not engage in the appropriate kind of collaborative activities (Tomasello, 2008). The extension to situations aimed at instructing the young just contributed further to the cooperative structure of the group.

E. Politics

Politics is about social power, and the lines of social power are relatively clear for all four great ape species. In gorillas and orangutans, dominant males do whatever they want whenever they want, and they mainly stay clear of one another. In chimpanzees, multiple males live in the same group and they have a fairly clear dominance hierarchy, with all males dominating all females, though less dominant chimpanzee males may form coalitions and alliances and so increase their power. Bonobos have taken this strategy to the extreme, as bonobo females use coalitions and alliances to dominate males (who are actually individually physically stronger). Coalitions and alliances are a fairly common political strategy in various mammalian species (Harcourt & de Waal, 1992).

The main mechanism for keeping the peace among great apes is that if one individual harms another (e.g., by stealing its food or baby), the victim will quite often retaliate (within the constraints of any dominance relations at play). Indeed, the retaliation motive is so strong in chimpanzees that if one individual steals food from a victim in an experimental setting, this victim will knock that food away from the thief even if that means no one, including the victim, will get it (Jensen, Call, & Tomasello, 2007a). After conflicts are over, great ape combatants, like many mammals, quite often reconcile with various species-typical behaviors, often including touching (de Waal, 1989). De Waal (1989) has also claimed that in great apes third parties sometimes console losers in fights, but recent research suggests that the "consolers" are actually just trying to keep from being the targets of aggression themselves (Koski & Sterck, 2009). The same interpretation may also be given to so-called policing in the group by dominant individuals (e.g., Flack, Girvan, de Waal, & Krakauer, 2006), as dominants have a direct interest in keeping the peace (and breaking up emergent coalitions) as well. And so, in the group, chimpanzees and other apes retaliate against transgressors, and sometimes individuals intervene in fights in an attempt to keep themselves safer.

In terms of "foreign policy," chimpanzees are particularly hostile to individuals from neighboring groups (bonobos apparently less so). Even though chimpanzee and bonobo females immigrate to neighboring groups as adolescents (and so there is much kinship between neighboring groups), because there is no recognition of paternity, males do not know they have relatives next door. Chimpanzees in particular have violent, sometimes deadly, encounters with their neighbors, and indeed males often go on so-called border patrol to check for any foreigners that might be encroaching on their territory (Watts & Mitani, 2001). While humans clearly have an ingroup bias, and engage in intergroup conflict with some regularity, they are often more friendly with immediately neighboring groups, perhaps partly because potentially aggressive and hostile males recognize their sisters and daughters next door (Chapais, 2008). This then sometimes leads to a kind of tribal structure in which neighboring groups with high levels of kinship among one another trade goods and services with each other reciprocally and are natural allies against more distant groups (Johnson & Earle, 2000).

Internally, human forager groups have traditionally been considered highly egalitarian. Dominance plays a much less powerful role than in other great ape societies, as the group exercises a kind of cooperative power in making sure that no individual becomes too powerful (Boehm, 1999; Leach, 2003; Wrangham & Pilbeam, 2001). Indeed, in human small-scale societies the most powerful individuals often obtain and retain their power not by dominating resources directly in the manner of other great apes, but by demonstrating both their ability to control resources and their cooperative propensities by distributing resources generously to others (Mauss, 1954). In human small-scale societies peace is kept not only by retaliation for harms done, and reconciliation after fights, but also by third-party enforcement. That is, human observers punish perpetrators who victimize others, sometimes at a cost to themselves, whereas there is no solid evidence of such third-party punishment in other great apes. Third-party punishment may be thought of as a kind of cooperative enforcement of peace and well-being in the group, and it plays a critical role in the creation and maintenance of social norms in general.

F. Norms and Institutions

In many ways the most distinctive feature of human social organization is its normative structure. Human beings do not just have statistical expectations about what others *will* do—which all apes have—they also have normative expectations about what others *should* do. These vary across different cultures, of course, and form a continuum from moral norms (typically concerning harm to others) to mere conventions. Social expectations gain normative force from the fact that they are shared, mutual expectations in the group. Thus, we all know and expect that people in our society should dress sedately for a funeral, and so anyone who wears a red shirt cannot plead ignorance and thus may be thought of as flaunting our norm for his own individual purposes. We may reasonably respond to this flaunting with disapproval, gossip, and, in egregious cases, by social ostracism—which means that individuals must be ever vigilant about their reputations as norm followers (leading to various impression management strategies; Goffman, 1959). If the glue of primate societies is individual social relationships, the super glue of human societies is generalized social norms.

In great apes, as noted earlier, dominant individuals sometimes intervene in fights to break them up—and this has sometimes been called "policing" (Flack et al., 2006)—but nondominant individuals do not do this, and dominants do not do it for behaviors other than aggression which threatens to escalate. These interventions may thus be evolutionary precursors of third-party punishment and social norms, but they do not, by all appearances, involve mutual expectations and cooperative enforcement. With respect to norms of fairness, Brosnan, Schiff, and de Waal (2005) claimed that some nonhuman primates, including chimpanzees, have a normative sense of fairness, for example, in food distribution. In their study, chimpanzees rejected food they otherwise would have accepted if they observed others receiving better rewards. But subsequent research has shown that what is at work here is a simple contrast effect in which seeing a better food makes the one I have now appear less palatable. There is no social comparison here, only food comparison, and so there is nothing in the direction of norms of fairness either (Bräuer, Call, & Tomasello, 2006, 2008). Moreover, in experimental studies using, for example, the ultimatum game, humans in all cultures show some kinds of social norms in distributing resources (Henrich et al., 2005), whereas chimpanzees in an ultimatum game behave in an almost totally self-centered manner (Jensen, Call, & Tomasello, 2007b).

Humans live in a sea of social norms that govern pretty much all aspects of their lives. Just to take the cases of most direct interest to biologists, individual humans living in a society cannot just take food or have sex whenever and wherever they wish. In human small-scale societies the distribution of food is governed by strict social norms, and basically all human societies have some form of marriage contract, or something similar, that regulates who can mate with whom and when. In terms of the psychology of social norms, people respect and follow norms for two basic reasons (Tomasello, 2009). The first is that it is prudent to do so, because breaking social norms often leads to one or another kind of sanction, ranging from physical punishment to disapproval with gossip to social ostracism. The second is that social norms are part of the social identity of the group: This is the way we dress; this is the way we behave at weddings or at funerals. If you do not follow these norms, you are in an important sense not one of us. Humans have also evolved social emotions of guilt and shame to self-punish for norm violations—perhaps to forestall punishment by others and also to signal to others in the group that the violator knows the norm, and so is one of us, even if he did not follow it on this particular occasion.

The group mindedness of social norms is most clearly displayed not in conformity to them—which is typically in the individual's self-interest—but in their enforcement. As many theorists have noted, punishing others, even by simply gossiping about them, is either costly or risky, and others in the group benefit as much as the punisher (thus making it a kind of collective action problem). This is especially true when the norm violation does not involve a moral norm concerning harm, but merely a convention. Nevertheless, even young children go to some trouble to admonish others that they are doing something the "wrong" way if they do not conform. For example, Rakoczy, Warneken, and Tomasello (2008) showed 3-year-old children how to play a game. When a puppet then entered later and announced it would play the game also, but then did so in a different way, most of the children objected, sometimes vociferously. Importantly, the children's language when they objected demonstrated clearly that they were not just expressing their personal displeasure at a deviation; they said generic, normative things like "It doesn't work like that," "One can't do that," and so forth. It is not just that they do not like the puppet's playing the game in his own way; he is playing it the *wrong* way. Importantly, this is not a moral wrongness—it's only a game after all—but simply not doing it like "we" do it. The motivation for enforcing such nonconsequential norms in this way presumably stems from some kind of identity with the group and its constitutive norms.

The ultimate outcome of social norms in human groups is the creation of social institutions, whose existence is constituted by the collective agreement of all group members that things should be done in a particular way. Institutions create both joint goals and individual social roles (for both persons and objects). Searle (1995) refers to the creation of these roles as the creation of status functions, because as individual people and objects assumed these roles they acquire deontic powers. For example, in the process of trade, some objects (e.g., pieces of gold, special pieces of paper) have acquired in some societies the status of money and so play a special role in the trading process. And while nonhuman primates have some understanding of familial relatedness, humans assign special status to social roles such as "spouse" and "parent," which everyone recognizes and which create certain entitlements and obligations. The main point here is that human social institutions represent both a unique form of collaborative activity and also a unique form of cooperative agreement in which we, together, normatively stipulate the way particular roles are to be played and the kinds of deontic powers that each role should be granted.

G. Summary

Thus, while most primates live in complex social groups, humans live in cultures premised on normative expectations that they will participate in many different collaborative activities. Distinctively, human collaboration involves shared goals and a division of labor (often organized via cooperative communication), with contributions by all participants and a sharing of spoils at the end. And human cooperation has a distinctly normative structure in which individuals do not just cooperate themselves; they expect others to cooperate and sanction those who do not. People are expected to do their share in cooperative foraging, to divide the spoils fairly at the end, to respect others' property, to participate in child care and teaching, to communicate truthfully, to help control bullies and norm violators, and to play their roles in institutions. Many of these forms of collaborative activity, and the norms that govern them, very likely either evolved or were culturally constructed in the context of foraging for food.

By way of summarizing this overall account of ape and human cooperation, Table 1.1 characterizes the chimpanzee version (as generally representative of nonhuman great apes) and the human version (especially in small-scale societies) of social participation in the various domains of activity reviewed in this section.

III. APE AND HUMAN CULTURAL TRANSMISSION

Behavioral biologists tend to think of culture as the social (rather than genetic) transmission of information across generations. In earlier work, I and others have claimed that this transmission is more powerful in the case of humans, as compared with other primates, mainly because humans are much better imitators than other great apes, and humans intentionally teach their young

TABLE 1.1: **Chimpanzee and Human Social Participations**

	Chimpanzees	Human Small-Scale Societies
Subsistence	• Individual foraging • Sharing under harassment	• Cooperative foraging • Sharing spoils "fairly"
Economy	• Biological markets • Individual possession	• Cooperative markets • Cooperative property
Child care and prosocial	• Maternal child care • Reciprocal food sharing	• Cooperative child care • Cooperative food sharing
Communication and teaching	• Intentional communication • No intentional teaching	• Cooperative communication • Intentional teaching
Politics	• Dominance • No third-party punishment	• Cooperative power • Cooperative enforcement
Norms and institutions	• No mutual expectations • No institutions	• Social norms • Institution + status functions

(e.g., Tomasello, Kruger, & Ratner, 1993; Tomasello, 1999). This perspective is still valid, although it may be that the gap between great apes and humans in skills of imitation is not as great as it once seemed (e.g., Whiten & van Schaik, 2007). A perspective that was underplayed in this earlier work is the role that cooperation plays in human cultural transmission. Teaching is obviously a cooperative activity, and it can even be normative if parents expect their children to learn or be sanctioned. In turn, children not only learn from teaching and normative expectations, but they actively conform to them. Teaching and normative conformity play a critically important role in generating the so-called ratchet effect, which leads to cumulative cultural evolution in human but not other primate societies.

A. Chimpanzee Behavioral Traditions

Whiten et al. (1999) report the results of discussions among the major chimpanzee fieldworkers relevant to the question of chimpanzee culture. These fieldworkers reported observations of interesting chimpanzee behaviors and checked whether they occurred at other field sites. Based on these discussions, and some systematic published data, several dozen population-specific behavioral traditions were identified as "cultural"—meaning that they were used by most members of a population, not used by most other populations, and most likely due to social learning (because not due to ecological factors). Van Schaik et al. (2003) report a very similar set of observations for orangutans, though based on less data and fewer populations.

Perhaps the most difficult issue in these data is how to deal with behaviors that are widespread in some but not all populations, with these populations being widely dispersed so that there seem to be multiple origins for the behavior. This turns out to be characteristic of two of the best-known and best-studied chimpanzee traditions. First, the so-called grooming hand clasp (McGrew & Tutin, 1978) has arisen in several populations independently, including at least one in captivity not even on the African continent (de Waal & Seres, 1997). Second, nut cracking was always thought to occur only in West Africa on the west side of the Sassandra River, but it has recently been found 1700 kilometers to the east, with many non-nut-cracking populations in between (Morgan & Abwe, 2006). The most plausible explanation is that we are dealing here with behaviors that are inventable by individuals, and they spread within groups by some form of social learning—with the within-group spreading being facilitated in some way by the ease of individual invention (see Tennie, Call, & Tomasello, 2009, on the "zone of latent solutions" for explaining such patterns).

A very telling study in this connection is that of Humle and Matsusawa (2002) on ant dipping in a community of chimpanzees in Bossou. Ant dipping was at one time used by many fieldworkers as the best example of chimpanzee "culture" because it involved different groups engaging in the same basic foraging activity—poking sticks into ant nests to capture and eat ants—but done differently. Chimpanzees at Tai and at Gombe, for example, dip for the same species of ant using different techniques: At Tai they use shorter wands and bite the ants off the wand directly (Boesch & Boesch, 1990), whereas at Gombe they use longer wands and typically (though not always) pull the ants off it with their other hand before eating them (McGrew, 1974). Humle and Matsusawa observed that the chimpanzees at Bossou sometimes used both techniques. The choice of technique was driven in the first instance by the length of the wand: biting from shorter ones, and pulling ants off with longer ones. In turn, the length of the wand was driven mainly by the aggressiveness of the ants—with different species of ants being differentially aggressive, and all ants being more aggressive at the nest than when on the move—such that longer tools were used (to avoid being bitten) when the ants were more aggressive. What seemed originally to be cultural transmission, then, would seem also to have a large component of individual learning about the behavior of ants and how best to avoid painful bites. Further support for this interpretation comes from the fact that when investigators compared the ant-dipping techniques used by three mother–infant pairs in different situations at Bossou, no relationship was found.

Another important method for characterizing the nature and source of chimpanzee behavioral traditions is exposing captive individuals to materials from the wild and seeing what they do with them. Thus, Huffman and Hirata (2004) found that giving medicinal leaves, whose use was thought to be socially transmitted in the wild, to naive individuals in captivity resulted in their using them in ways similar to wild chimpanzees, thus undermining the social transmission hypothesis. Tennie, Hedwig, Call, and Tomasello (2008) did something very similar for gorillas and their supposedly culturally transmitted nettle-feeding behaviors and found that again the captive animals—some with almost no relevant experience—used techniques very similar to those in the wild. And so, again, individual learning (or even "prepared learning") would seem to be at work.

It is also interesting and important that behavioral traditions of this same general type have now been reported by fieldworkers investigating many other animal species, both primate and nonprimate, for example, capuchin monkeys (Perry et al., 2003), whales and dolphins (Rendell & Whitehead, 2001), among others. This raises the question of how the naturally occurring behavioral traditions of chimpanzees compare with these others, and whether the chimpanzee and orangutan versions are any closer to human cultural traditions than are those of other mammalian species.[1]

B. Chimpanzee Social Learning

Another source of information to help characterize the nature of chimpanzee behavioral traditions is experimental work on their social learning. The most systematic program of research over the past dozen years or so is that of

---

[1] The textbook example of nonhuman primate culture is the potato washing of a group of human-provisioned Japanese macaques (Imanishi, 1965). But this is a poor example for myriad reasons that have been amply documented. For example, the human provisioning may have influenced the behavior, the spread in the group was relatively slow (and did not accelerate exponentially as would be expected if individuals were socially learning from one another), new individuals may have learned the behavior by following others into the water and discovering it themselves, the behavior was isolated and died out after a few years, and so on (Galef, 1992; Tomasello, 1990).

Whiten and colleagues. Whiten, Custance, Gomez, Teixidor, and Bard (1996) showed that chimpanzees will choose the way of opening a box they observe, rather than some other plausible way of opening it, and Whiten, Horner, and de Waal (2005) even showed that other observing chimpanzees will follow the original learner in a "transmission chain" across individuals (see also Horner, Whiten, Flynn, & de Waal, 2006). These studies thus demonstrate the social transmission of behavioral traditions in captive chimpanzee populations. But two facts about these experiments are important. The first is that they leave open the possibility that individuals are learning about how the box works— perhaps supplemented by an understanding of the demonstrator's goal— without attending much or at all to the behavioral techniques used (so-called emulation learning). Indeed, in the Whiten et al. (1996) study, clear results emerged only when investigators looked at the demonstrator's and learner's behavior in terms of the result it produced on the box, not in terms of particular modeled actions. It is thus an open question whether the apes would have learned the same thing if they had simply observed the box opening itself in a particular way without any demonstrator, and indeed Tennie, Call, and Tomasello (2006) found no difference in learning between individuals exposed to this so-called ghost control and those exposed to a full demonstration (although see Hopper, Lambeth, Schapiro, & Whiten 2008, for some different results).

The second important fact is that the Whiten et al. (1996) study also had a comparison group of 3-year-old human children, and they produced the demonstrated actions much more faithfully than did the chimpanzees. This result was corroborated by Call, Carpenter, and Tomasello (2005), who found that chimpanzees preferentially focused on the outcomes of problem-solving activities, whereas human children preferentially focused on the actions of the demonstrator. Most importantly, Horner and Whiten (2005) found that observer chimpanzees tended to ignore irrelevant actions on a box when their causal ineffectiveness was clear, but they tended to produce them when their causal effectiveness was unclear. Again, this suggests that chimpanzees are focused mainly on the desired outcome (the goal) of the demonstrator in assessing what they themselves should do to solve the problem. But in this study, as well as in Nagell, Olguin, and Tomasello (1993), the human children paid much more attention to the actions of the demonstrator, even ignoring the apparent causal relations governing the problem to imitate the adult—not an intelligent strategy, perhaps, but simply one more focused on demonstrator actions. In all of the studies in which chimpanzees and human children have been compared, the clear result is that the human children are much more focused on the actual actions of the demonstrator, whereas the chimpanzees are much more focused on the outcome of her actions—either the actual outcome (the result) or the desired outcome (her goal). As an important addendum, Tomasello and Carpenter (2005) found that young, enculturated chimpanzees reproduce only intended and not accidental actions, and they produce a demonstrator's desired outcome even when the demonstration was of a failed attempt. Being raised by humans may facilitate chimpanzees' skills of social learning.

Help in interpreting these results comes from studies in another behavioral domain, namely, gestures. Tomasello et al. (1997) systematically compared the gestures of two different groups of captive chimpanzees (with extensive longitudinal data on one group available as well). In brief, there was no evidence for the social transmission of gestures within groups, as there were just as many differences among individuals within each group as between the two groups. In addition, Tomasello et al. (1997) reported an experiment in which one chimpanzee was taught a novel gesture and put back in the group to demonstrate it (on two different occasions using two different gestures and demonstrators). The other members of the group did not acquire this gesture, suggesting that chimpanzees do not socially transmit their gestures, but rather they learn them individually via ritualization. It is possible that individuals raised or trained by humans might imitate gestural actions, as Custance, Whiten, and Bard (1995) were able to train individuals over a several-month period to reproduce some demonstrated actions in the so-called do-as-I-do paradigm, and Tomasello, Savage-Rumbaugh, and Kruger (1993) found that enculturated apes were better at following demonstrations of actions on objects than were unenculturated apes.

A reasonable hypothesis is thus that chimpanzees are able to understand to some degree the goal of a demonstrator's action, and as observers they tend to focus on that goal, or else the actual outcome, with little attention to the actions designed to achieve that goal. Being raised and/or trained by humans can lead chimpanzees to focus more on actions, but human children naturally focus much more readily on the actions involved. It is important to note, however, that children also focus quite a bit on outcomes in concrete problem-solving situations (Call et al., 2005; Nagell et al., 1993), and so one might actually say it this way. In observing instrumental actions, apes in general, including humans, tend to focus on the outcome, either produced or intended, but in some cases they analyze the action backward to the behavioral technique used to see how that outcome was achieved; human children engage in such analysis more naturally and perhaps more skillfully than do chimpanzees.

C. Human Cultural Learning and Cumulative Culture

In addition to their special focus on actions in social learning situations involving concrete instrumental goals, human children also imitate for purely social reasons: to be like others (Uzgiris, 1981). The tendency of humans to follow fads and fashions and to conform are well known and well documented, and indeed Carpenter (2006) argues that this represents a different and important motivation for social learning that may produce qualitatively different behaviors. For example, human infants have a greater tendency than do chimpanzees for copying the unnecessary "style" of an instrumental action (Tomasello & Carpenter 2005), and of course human children naturally acquire linguistic symbols and other cultural conventions whose use cannot be discovered on one's own. This analysis would also explain why children in the studies cited earlier sometimes tended to imitate poor demonstrators when it would have been to their advantage to ignore them, and, in general, why children copy the actual actions of others more readily than do other apes. This so-called social function of imitation—simply to be like others—is clearly an important part of human culture and cultural transmission, including language acquisition (Tomasello, 2003).

Moreover, as already noted, human cultural learning is different because humans also engage in teaching, whereas there is no evidence for systematic teaching in any great ape species (Hoppitt et al., 2008). Teaching is especially important in the human case because of cultural conventions that cannot be invented on one's own but only imitated (Gergely & Csibra, 2006; see earlier discussion). Teaching is a key manifestation of the cooperative way in which humans transmit information across generations, and it contributes to the faithfulness with which such information transmission occurs in human societies.

Finally, as also noted earlier, human culture persists and has the character it does not just because human children do what others do but also because adults expect and even demand that they behave in a certain way. Children understand that this is not just the way that something *is* done but rather the way it *should* be done. This normative dimension to human cultural traditions serves to further guarantee their faithful transmission across generations. Nothing like normative learning has been observed in any nonhuman primate species.

The result of all this is that human cultural traditions are qualitatively different from those of other primates in readily observable ways. Most importantly, virtually all of humans' complex cognitive practices and products have arisen not instantaneously; rather, they are cumulative products that have arisen gradually across generations, ratcheting up in complexity as individuals work to improve on what they have inherited from their forebears to meet current needs (Tomasello Kruger, & Ratner, 1993). A critical component of this ratcheting effect is the faithful transmission of traditions across generations, which keeps the tradition stable until further improvements come along. Human social imitation, teaching, and normativity—for all the reasons listed earlier—are mainly responsible for this extraordinary stability and cumulativity over historical time. Importantly, social imitation, teaching, and normativity are not just three unrelated human behaviors, but rather they are all manifestations of humans' uniquely cooperative way of life. And so, humans are not only more cooperative in their daily interactions, but their cooperative way of life also leads to different forms of cultural transmission across generations, leading to humans' unique version of culture in the form of cumulative cultural evolution.

IV. APE AND HUMAN SOCIAL COGNITION

To cooperate with one another in all of the ways just elaborated, human beings must be born with a certain set of social-cognitive skills and motivations, or at least have the ability to construct such skills and motivations during early ontogeny. They must be capable and motivated to do such things as understand the intentional actions of others in terms of its underlying goals and intentions; form with others shared goals and intentions; locate and identify the attentional focus of others; direct and even share others' attention to outside entities; and learn or create shared conventions and symbols. We will argue that while humans share many social-cognitive capacities with other apes, the unique skills and motivations that enable their unique form of culture all fall under the general rubric of what we may call shared intentionality.

A. The Human Adaptation for Culture

Evidence for the general hypothesis that humans are specially adapted for cultural life comes from a large-scale study comparing a wide range of cognitive abilities in human children and two great ape species. Herrmann, Call, Lloreda, Hare, and Tomasello (2007) administered a comprehensive battery of cognitive tests to large numbers of chimpanzees ($n = 106$), orangutans ($n = 32$), and 2.5-year-old human children ($n = 105$). The test battery consisted of 16 different nonverbal tasks assessing all kinds of cognitive abilities involving both physical and social problems relevant to primates in their natural environment. The tests relating to the physical world consisted of problems concerning space, quantities, tools, and causality. The tests relating to the social world consisted of problems requiring subjects to imitate another's solution to a problem, communicate nonverbally with others, and read the intentions of others from their behavior. If the difference between human and ape cognition is a difference in something like "general intelligence," then the children should have differed from the apes uniformly across all the different tasks. But this was not the case. The finding was that the children and apes had very similar cognitive skills for dealing with the physical world; but the children—old enough to use some language but still years away from reading, counting, or going to school—already had more sophisticated cognitive skills than either ape species for dealing with the social world.

Examining the correlational structure of individual differences in this large range of cognitive tasks, neither the children nor the chimpanzees showed a factor structure including a factor of general intelligence (Herrmann, Hernandez-Lloreda, Call, Hare, & Tomasello, 2010). This means that individual differences in the species' cognitive performance on the various physical and social-cognitive tasks cannot be explained by one underlying general factor for either species. The main specific commonality was that for both species a similar factor of spatial cognition was found. But the main difference was that for the chimpanzees there was only one additional factor comprising various physical and social-cognitive tasks, whereas the children showed distinct, separate factors for physical cognition and social cognition. The suggestion is that this species-unique adaptation for social cognition then enables children to culturally learn from others in ways that then "bootstrap" their understanding of the physical world—in its spatial, causal, and quantitative structure—through language, instruction, and other cultural and educational interactions, so that as adults they will have more cognitive skills than other apes across the board.

Together, these findings suggest that the differences between human and ape cognition are not based on humans being generally more intelligent. Instead, they suggest that humans share many cognitive skills with their closest living relatives, especially for dealing with the physical world, but in addition they have evolved some specialized and more integrated social-cognitive skills. One hypothesis is that humans have evolved a kind of species-specific cultural intelligence for living and exchanging information in cultural groups, and this then bootstraps their cognitive skills in all other domains as well. This very general study does not help us to specify in detail, however, the nature of this species-specific cultural intelligence. For that we need more targeted experimental investigations.

B. Understanding Intentions and Attention

One obvious candidate for a uniquely human social-cognitive skill is the understanding of others as intentional agents, which is clearly necessary for human cultural learning and cognition (Tomasello, 1999). But recent research has demonstrated beyond a reasonable doubt that great apes also understand much about how others work as intentional, perceiving agents. Specifically, recent research has demonstrated that great apes understand something of the goals and perceptions of others and how these work together in individual intentional action—in ways very similar to young human children (see Call & Tomasello, 2008, for a review; see Povinelli & Vonk, 2006, for a different view).

First, great apes (most of the research is with chimpanzees) understand that others have goals. Evidence is as follows:

- When a human passes food to a chimpanzee and then fails to do so, the ape reacts in a frustrated manner if the human is doing this for no good reason (i.e., is unwilling), whereas she waits patiently if the human is making good-faith attempts to give the object but failing or having accidents (i.e., is unable) (Call, Hare, Carpenter, & Tomasello, 2004; see Behne, Carpenter, Call, & Tomasello, 2005, for similar findings with human infants).
- When a human or conspecific needs help reaching an out-of-reach object or location, chimpanzees help them in a way very similar to human infants—which requires an understanding of the other's goal (Warneken & Tomasello, 2006; Warneken et al., 2007).
- When a human shows a human-raised chimpanzee an action on an object that is marked in various ways as a failed attempt to change that object's state, the ape, in her turn, actually executes the intended action (and not the action actually demonstrated, e.g., hands slipping off the object) (Tomasello & Carpenter, 2005; based on Meltzoff's 1995 study with human infants).
- When a human shows a human-raised chimpanzee a series of two actions on an object, one of which is marked in various ways as

accidental, the ape, in her turn, usually executes only the intended action (Tomasello & Carpenter, 2005; based on Carpenter, Akhtar, & Tomasello's 1998 study with human infants; see also Call & Tomasello, 1998, for further evidence).

The conclusion is thus that apes and young human children both understand in the same basic way (in simple situations) that individuals pursue a goal in a persistent manner until they have reached it. Furthermore, they understand the goal not as the result produced in the external environment, but rather as the actor's internal representation of the state of the world she wishes to bring about.

Second, great apes (most of the research is again with chimpanzees) also understand that others have perceptions. Evidence is as follows:

- When a human peers behind a barrier, apes move over to get a better viewing angle to look behind it as well (Bräuer et al., 2006; Tomasello, Hare, & Agnetta, 1999; see Moll & Tomasello, 2004, for a similar study with human infants).
- When a human's gaze direction is toward a barrier and there is also an object further in that same direction, apes look only to the barrier and not to the object—unless the barrier has a window in it, in which case they look to the object (Okamoto-Barth, Call, & Tomasello, 2007; see Caron, Butler, & Brooks, 2002, for similar findings with human infants).
- When apes beg a human for food, they take into account whether the human can see their gesture (Kaminski, Call, & Tomasello, 2004; Liebal, Pika, Call, & Tomasello, 2004).
- When chimpanzees compete with one another for food, they take into account whether their competitor can see the contested food (Hare, Call, Agnetta, & Tomasello, 2000, Hare, Call, & Tomasello, 2001), and even on occasion attempt to conceal their approach from a competitor (Hare, Call, & Tomasello, 2006; Melis, Hare, & Tomasello, 2006b).

The conclusion is thus that apes and young human children both understand in the same basic way (in simple situations) that individuals perceive things in the world and react to them, and they understand that the content of the other's perception is something different from their own.

Understanding others as intentional agents is almost certainly a necessary condition for participating in a human-like culture. But it is not sufficient.

Current research demonstrates that chimpanzees and other great apes understand much about intentional action, but they still have not created cultural artifacts, practices, and symbols of the human kind. Something else is needed.

C. Sharing Intentions and Attention

Tomasello et al. (2005) proposed that this something else is skills and motivations for shared intentionality. Beyond just understanding others as intentional agents and responding to them—often in competition—humans also understand others as potential cooperative agents, and this requires some additional skills and motivations.

According to a number of philosophers of action, shared intentionality refers to behavioral phenomena that are both intentional and irreducibly social, in the sense that the agent of the intentions and actions is the plural subject "we." For example, Gilbert (1989) looks at extremely simple collaborative activities such as taking a walk together—as opposed to walking down a sidewalk in parallel to an unknown person—and concludes that the agent of the social activity is "we." The difference can be clearly seen if one person simply veers off in another direction unannounced. If we just happen to be walking in parallel, this deviation means nothing; but if we are walking *together*, my veering off is some kind of breach and you may rebuke me for it (since we have made a joint commitment to take a walk together and so certain social norms now apply). Scaled up, we may even get to phenomena in which "we" intend things together in such a way that they take on new powers—such as when pieces of paper become money, and ordinary people are transformed into presidents within institutional realities (Searle, 1995). The proposal is that because humans are able to engage with one another in acts of shared intentionality—everything from a joint walk together to joint participation in transforming people into institutional officials—their social interactions take on new qualities.

For current purposes, the key expression of shared, or "we," intentionality is collaborative activities in which the participants have both a joint goal and individual roles (Bratman, 1992). This dual-level structure is apparent even in the early collaborative interactions of young children. As evidence of a joint goal, to which both participants are jointly committed, Warneken, Chen, and Tomasello (2006) found that if an adult partner suddenly stopped interacting with a young child in the middle of a collaborative activity, the child quite often made active attempts to reengage the adult. Human-raised chimpanzees tested in a similar situation never, not once, attempted to reengage their human partner. Graefenhain, Behne, Carpenter, and Tomasello (2009) found that human children attempted to reengage even when they could easily continue the activity successfully to the goal on their own. Moreover, from about 3 years of age if the child herself wanted to opt out of the activity, she engaged in some kind of "leave taking" as a direct acknowledgment that she wished to break her commitment to the joint goal. And Hamann et al. (in press) even found that when a peer partner needed help in the middle of a collaborative activity—like that supplied by human foragers in the observations of Hill (2002)—many 3-year-old children stopped and helped their partner, including after they had already retrieved their part of the spoils. And they helped the partner much more in the context of this collaborative activity than they did in more neutral contexts—which was not true of chimpanzees in a similar study—suggesting a normative commitment to the joint goal.

In addition to a joint goal, a fully collaborative activity requires that there be some division of labor and that each partner understand the other's role. In another study, Carpenter, Tomasello, and Striano (2005) engaged in a collaborative activity with very young children, around 18 months of age, and then took over their role on the next turn—forcing them into a role they had never before played. Even these very young children readily adapted to the new role, suggesting that in their initial joint activity with the adult they had somehow processed her perspective and role. Three young, human-raised chimpanzees did not reverse roles in the same way (Tomasello & Carpenter, 2005). One interpretation is that this role reversal signals that the human infants understood the joint activity from a "bird's-eye view," with the joint goal and complementary roles all in a single representational format (similar to Nagel's [1986] "view from nowhere"). In contrast, the chimpanzees understood their own action from a first-person perspective and that of the partner from a third-person perspective, but they did not have a bird's-eye view of the activity and its roles. Human collaborative activities thus have in them, from the perspective of both participants, generalized roles potentially fillable by anyone, including the self, what some philosophers call agent-neutral roles.

As individuals coordinate their actions with one another in collaborative activities with agent-neutral roles, they also coordinate their attention to things relevant to their joint goal—so-called joint attention (Bakeman & Adamson, 1984). Children thus monitor the adult and her attention, who is of course monitoring them and their attention. No one is certain how best to characterize this potentially infinite loop of me monitoring the other, who is monitoring my monitoring of her, and so forth (called recursive mindreading by Tomasello, 2008), but it seems to be part of infants' experience—in some nascent form—from before the first birthday. In addition to this shared attention on things, participants in these interactions each have their own perspective on things as well. Indeed, Moll and Tomasello (2007) argue that the whole notion of perspective depends on us first having a joint attentional focus, as topic, that we may then view differently (otherwise we just see completely different things). This dual-level attentional structure—shared focus of attention at a higher level, differentiated into perspectives at a lower level—is of course directly parallel to the dual-level intentional structure of the collaborative activity itself—joint goal with individual roles—and ultimately derives from it.

To coordinate their complex collaborative and joint attentional activities, humans have evolved some species-unique forms of communication. Most obvious is of course language, but even before this complex form of conventional communication humans engage in species-unique forms of gestural communication, specifically, pointing and pantomiming. Pointing and pantomiming express communicative intentions to refer others' attention to something in the external world. For pointing and pantomiming to communicate in the complex ways that they do, the communicator needs to use them in the context of joint attention with the recipient, and the recipient needs to be capable of comprehending communicative intentions (i.e., intentions about the other's intentional states). Comprehending communicative intentions requires complex inferencing (Sperber & Wilson, 1986), what Tomasello (2008) calls cooperative reasoning in which each participant attempts to infer what the other is intending toward him or her recursively (recursive mindreading).

Collaborative activities with joint goals and joint attention take place within the context of prosocial motives for helping and sharing with others. From early in ontogeny, human infants seem motivated to share psychological states with others, first just in emotion sharing episodes (often called proto-conversations; Trevarthen, 1979), but then more actively in cooperative communication involving pointing, pantomiming, and language. Beginning at around their first birthdays infants communicate not just to get what they want (imperatives) but also to provide others with information that is useful to them (informative declaratives) and to simply share attention with them to interesting phenomena (expressive declaratives) (Tomasello, Carpenter, & Liszkowski, 2007). Human communication is thus cooperative to the core, and it helps in coordinating collaborative activities as well.

The most sophisticated outcome of all this, as noted earlier, is creation of and participation in social institutions, whose existence is constituted by—and only by—the collective agreement of all group members that things should be done in a particular way. Institutions create both joint goals and individual social roles with deontic powers. Perhaps surprisingly, we can even see this kind of thinking and acting in children's early pretend play. For example, when two children agree to treat this stick as a horse, this is the assignment of a status function (Wyman, Rakoczy, & Tomasello, 2009). Stipulations of deontic status—in either pretense or institutional reality—go beyond normal social norms governing overt social behavior in that they begin with a conventionally created symbolic reality—the pretend or institutional scenario—and then collectively assign deontic powers to the relevant roles and entities within that symbolic scenario.

Overall, then, human children from very early in ontogeny collaborate with others in unique ways. They participate with adults and one another in interactions in which they commit themselves to a joint goal and each takes his or her agent-neutral role. In the process, they also share attention with the other to things and take unique perspectives (while still understanding the other's perspective) as well. Young children's communication is also a cooperative activity—both participants collaborating to get the message across for prosocial reasons—and the cooperative inferencing involved enables unique forms of communicative activity. They also create in their pretense the forerunners of institutional reality in the form of joint agreements to confer special deontic status to otherwise ordinary people and entities. And so from fairly early in ontogeny young children socially engage with others in unique ways—involving skills and motivations for shared intentionality—and this enables them to participate in unique forms of collaboration, communication, and social learning.

D. Cross-Cultural Differences

An obvious question in all of this is whether these skills and motivations of shared intentionality are universal in the children of all human cultures, and at the same age. Despite much research on the role of different cultural settings on cognitive development in school-age and older children, very little is known about how different parenting and socialization practices in different cultures might affect the kinds of early emerging social-cognitive skills and motivations of concern here. To our knowledge, there is only one relevant large-scale study.

Callaghan et al. (unpublished data) report a series of eight studies in which they systematically assessed the social-cognitive skills of 1- to 3-year-old children in three different cultural settings. One group of children was from a typical Western, middle-class cultural setting, while the other two were from more traditional, small-scale cultures in rural Peru and India. In a first group of studies they assessed 1-year-old children's most basic social-cognitive skills for understanding the intentions and attention of others: imitation, helping, gaze following, and communicative pointing. Children's performance in these tasks was mostly similar across cultural settings. In a second two studies, they assessed 1-year-old children's skills in participating in interactive episodes of collaboration and joint attention. Again in these studies the general finding was one of cross-cultural similarity. In a third pair of studies, they assessed 2- to 3-year-old children's skills with pretense and graphic symbols. Here they found that the Western children, who had had much more experience with such symbols, showed skills at a significantly earlier age.

The overall conclusion was that young children in all cultural settings get sufficient amounts of the right kinds of social experience to develop their most basic social-cognitive skills for interacting with others and participating in culture at around the same age. In contrast, young children's acquisition of more culturally specific skills for use in culturally specific practices involving culturally specific artifacts and symbols is more dependent on particular learning experiences.

E. The Ontogeny of Cultural Cognition

Humans are thus clearly biologically adapted for culture. Another piece of evidence for this claim is children with autism. Children with autism are born with a biological deficit for some aspects of shared intentionality (along with other things), and so they cannot take advantage of the cultural world into which they are born and do not develop normal social-cognitive skills (Hobson, 1993). However, it is also clear that no human could do any of the complex things he or she does with a biological predisposition alone; that is to say, no human could invent any of the complex cognitive practices and products of the species without a preexisting cultural world within which to grow and learn. A biologically intact human child born outside of any human culture— with no one to imitate, no one to teach him or her things, no language, no preexisting tools and practices, no symbol systems, no institutions, and so forth—also would not develop normal social-cognitive skills. Both biology and culture are necessary parts of the process.

Since organisms inherit their environments as much as they inherit their genes (albeit in different ways), perhaps it is most appropriate to say that human beings biologically inherit the cognitive skills necessary for developing in a cultural environment. Obviously some kind of social environment is also important in the ontogeny of other primate species for developing species-typical behaviors of all kinds, and cultural transmission may even play some role as well. But for humans the species-typical social-cultural environment is an absolute necessity for youngsters to develop the cognitive skills required for survival in the many very different, and sometimes harsh, environments that humans inhabit. And so the point is simply that ontogeny plays an especially large and important role in the cognitive development of *Homo sapiens* as compared with other primates.

Indeed, Tomasello (2009) argues that participating in collaborative activities with joint goals, joint attention, and normative structuring creates new and species-unique forms of cognitive representation. Specifically, participating in joint attention leads to the taking of perspectives, and consequently to perspectival cognitive representations in which the same entity can be construed in different ways depending on one's perspective. Using conventionally created symbols—that can be used either correctly or incorrectly from the point of view of the group—leads to normative cognitive representations. The argument is that perspectival, symbolic, and normative cognitive representations are only possible for individuals growing up in a cultural world interacting with others who are symbolically communicating different perspectives on things—indeed, the "correct" perspective on things—to them in the first place. These perspectival and normative cognitive representations will then be used by children in different cultures to acquire the particular skills of cultural cognition characteristic of their group.

F. Summary

Great apes function in social groups—perhaps we could call them cultural groups—that have some behavioral traditions. But these result basically from one individual exploiting the experience and hard work of others by observing their successes in instrumental situations and trying to profit from them. In contrast, groups of human individuals cooperate together to create cultural artifacts and practices that accumulate improvements (rachet up in complexity) over time, thus creating ever-new cognitive niches, including even complex social institutions with normatively defined roles. Children must be equipped to participate during ontogeny in this huge groupthink process by means of species-unique cognitive skills for collaboration, communication, and cultural learning, which coevolved with human cultural organization during relatively recent evolutionary history. These basic skills are universal across all cultural settings, and indeed, in an important sense, make human culture possible in the first place.

V. AN EVOLUTIONARY FAIRY TALE

Where did humans' ultra-cooperativeness come from? Although we are a long way from a full account, one hypothesis is that somewhere along the line, for some reason (changing climactic conditions, new competitor species, new prey species, etc.), humans were forced to become cooperative foragers or perish (see Sterelny, 2008). There had to have been, in our view, three basic steps along this road to obligate cooperative foraging (Hare & Tomasello, 2005; Tomasello, 2009).

First, for humans to become truly cooperative foragers, there must have been an initial step that broke them out of the great ape pattern of strong food competition, low tolerance for food sharing, and almost no food offering at all. This great ape pattern may be clearly seen in the experiment of Melis et al. (2006a) in which pairs of chimpanzees had trouble collaborating if the food reward was not predivided for them (whereas human children had no such trouble). Relatedly, on another dimension of primate temperament, when human children were directly compared with chimpanzees and orangutans on their response to novelty, children were found to be especially uncertain when encountering novel people and objects. This quite often led to their seeking reassurance from parents and peers in ways that might often provide opportunities for social referencing, social learning, teaching, and coordinating activities (Herrmann et al., 2007). The proposal is thus that changes in human temperament—toward greater tolerance and social comfort seeking, among other things—were prerequisite for humans beginning down their ultra-cooperative pathway (Hare, 2007; Hare & Tomasello, 2005).

The temperamental change in humans may have occurred in any one of several possible ways (or in some combination). One possibility is that humans evolved an especially tolerant and prosocial temperament through a process of self-domestication in which aggressive and despotic individuals within a group were systematically punished or shunned—a pattern commonly seen in small-scale societies (Boehm, 1999). Another possibility is that changes in human temperament in a prosocial direction were brought about by cooperative breeding (Hrdy, 2009). In humans, unlike other apes, mothers get the support of alloparents who contribute to basic child-care activities and also engage in a variety of active prosocial behaviors such as active food provisioning of the infant and teaching of the child as well. In this context, selection presumably favored more tolerant and prosocial individuals for playing the role of helper (who presumably benefits in many ways, from kin selection to direct and indirect reciprocity). It is of course possible that both of these factors—self-domestication and cooperative breeding—may have played a role. The important point is that there was some initial step in human evolution away from great apes involving the emotional and motivational side of things that propelled humans into a new adaptive space in which complex skills and motivations for collaborative activities and shared intentionality could be selected.

The second step toward humans' ultra-cooperativeness was that in this new social context, these tolerant and prosocial individuals would be more likely to be doing the kinds of things together in which cognitive skills for forming joint goals, joint attention, cooperative communication, and social learning and teaching would be especially beneficial—such things as hunting animals together, gathering embedded plants together, and so forth. As Alvard (2001) argues, obligate cooperative foraging poses a basic coordination problem in which individuals have to negotiate a shared goal and somehow communicate about their respective roles. Tomasello (2008) argues that humans' unique skills of cooperative communication (including language) evolved originally to coordinate collaborative foraging activities. And so a more tolerant disposition led to the possibility of individuals acting together with one another in new ways, which set the conditions for selection for ever more complex cognitive skills of shared intentionality for collaborating and communicating in ever more complex ways.

The third step involved group-level processes, including the creation of group-enforced norms and group-constituted social institutions. These required significant social-cognitive skills of coordination for forming both mutual expectations and normative rules with others in the group (Tomasello, 2009). Then, in addition, human groups began to compete with one another, leading to processes of cultural group selection. That is, as Richerson and Boyd (2005) have argued, human groups at some point possessed different traditions—and even norms and institutions—for engaging in various activities, including for subsistence. Those groups that passed along culturally "better" traditions, norms, and institutions did better in competition with other groups. And in the new context of obligate cooperative foraging, "better" could easily mean more cooperative. This could then lead to a kind of runaway selection involving a new process of coevolution between culture and cognition: Cultural artifacts, norms, and institutions create a new environment to which individuals must adapt. Thus, individuals who could most quickly learn to participate in various collaborative cultural practices and use various cultural artifacts and symbols—through special skills of communication and social learning supported by more sophisticated ways of reading and sharing the intentions of others—were at a selective advantage. Also advantaged were individuals who could most quickly identify with their group and negotiate its various social norms (expectations of judging and punishing groupmates) for how one interacts peaceably in the group (and so avoids being shunned).

Human evolution is thus characterized to an inordinate degree by niche construction, in the form of cultural practices and products (Odling-Smee, Laland, & Feldman, 2003), and gene–culture coevolution, as the species has evolved cognitive skills and motivations enabling them to function effectively in any one of their many different self-built cultural worlds (Richerson & Boyd, 2005). No one knows, but it is possible that these skills of cultural cognition were still absent in *Homo erectus* 1–2 million years ago. First of all, their relatively rapid brain growth during ontogeny resembled more closely that of modern apes than that of modern humans, and overall modern humans have significantly larger brains than *Homo erectus* (Coqueugniot, Hublin, Veillonm, Houët, & Jacob, 2004). In addition, most evidence suggests that at that time there were very likely not extensive cultural differences between different human groups (Klein, 1999). One hypothesis, then, is that humans' special skills of cooperation and shared intentionality—leading to all kinds of specialized cultural practices and products—arose for the first time in modern humans (or their immediate predecessors) in the last 100,000–200,000 years.

Interestingly, humans also have a species-unique physiological adaptation that might have emerged along with the emergence of their ultra-cooperativeness. Unlike other primates, humans have eyes with large white sclera, making it especially easy to follow their looking direction (Kobayashi & Kohshima, 1997). Indeed, whereas other great apes typically follow the head direction of other individuals when they are gazing somewhere, human children typically follow specifically their eye direction (Tomasello, Hare. Lehmann, & Call, 2007). A morphological adaptation such as this could only have evolved in cooperative social groups in which groupmates did not too often exploit the gaze direction of others for their own benefit, but rather more often used it in coordinating collaborative and communicative interactions involving joint attention. When this cooperative physical trait evolved in the species is currently unknown.

VI. CONCLUSION

As compared with their nearest great ape relatives, who all live in the vicinity of the equator, humans occupy an incredibly wide range of environmental niches covering almost the entire planet. To deal with everything from the Arctic to the Tropics, humans have evolved a highly flexible suite of cognitive skills and motivations for modifying the environments in adaptive ways. But these are not individual cognitive skills that enable them to survive alone in the tundra or rain forest, but rather they are cooperatively based social-cognitive skills and motivations that enable them to develop, in concert with others in their cultural groups, creative ways of coping with whatever challenges may arise. Humans have evolved not only skills of individual intentional action and cognition but also skills and motivations for sharing intentions and cognition with others in collaborative activities of all kinds.

As always, there are still many unanswered questions. With regard to apes, negative findings are of course never final, and so it may be that at some point we will find new methods that reveal skills in great apes that I have denied them here—in social cognition, communication, cooperation, and/or social learning. And the ways apes differ from human children in these different domains have not been specified as precisely as we might like. With regard to children, exactly how they acquire their various social norms is not totally clear, nor is it clear why they choose to enforce these norms on others when it would seem that they gain nothing concrete by doing this. Finally, in the context of the current volume we must note the most glaring lacuna of all in the data relevant to the evolutionary origins of human culture, and that is the almost complete lack of cross-cultural data on young children's early skills and motivations for social interaction, social learning, cooperation, teaching, and norm enforcement. In particular, one might expect that children who grow up in cultures in which they are socialized more through peer than adult interaction might have some special skills of cooperation and norm creation and enforcement. This would be an especially important question for future cross-cultural research.

It must be emphasized in closing that the evolutionary dimension of culture highlighted here is clearly only one aspect of the process. The specific cultural practices and products generated by individuals interacting with one another in cultural groups—everything from specific linguistic constructions to techniques for building kayaks or skyscrapers—can in no way be reduced to biology. Human cognitive and motivational adaptations for culture are simply psychological enabling conditions for the generation and maintenance of the specific cultural artifacts and practices created by specific cultural groups—which, by all appearances, are endlessly creative.

REFERENCES

Alvard, M. (2001). Mutualistic hunting. In C. Stanford & M. Bunn (Eds.), *The early human diet: The role of meat* (pp. 261–278). New York: Oxford University Press.

Bakeman, R., & Adamson, L. (1984). Coordinating attention to people and objects in mother–infant and peer–infant interactions. *Child Development*, *55*, 1278–1289.

Behne, T., Carpenter, M., Call, J., & Tomasello, M. (2005). Unwilling versus unable? Infants' understanding of intentional action. *Developmental Psychology*, *41*, 328–337.

Behne, T., Carpenter, M., & Tomasello, M. (2005). One-year-olds comprehend the communicative intentions behind gestures in a hiding game. *Developmental Science*, *8*, 492–499.

Boehm, C. (1999). *Hierarchy in the forest: The evolution of egalitarian behavior*. Cambridge, MA: Harvard University Press.

Boesch, C. (1991). Teaching in wild chimpanzees. *Animal Behaviour*, *41*(3), 530–532.

Boesch, C. (2005). Joint cooperative hunting among wild chimpanzees: Taking natural observations seriously. *Behavioral and Brain Sciences*, *28*, 692–693.

Boesch, C., & Boesch, H. (1989). Hunting behavior of wild chimpanzees in the Tai Forest National Park. *American Journal of Physical Anthropology*, *78*, 547–573.

Boesch, C., & Boesch, H. (1990). Tool use and tool making in wild chimpanzees. *Folia Primatologica*, *54*, 86–99.

Boesch, C., & Boesch-Achermann, H. (2000). *The chimpanzees of the Tai Forest*. Oxford, England: Oxford University Press.

Bratman, M. (1992). Shared co-operative activity. *Philosophical Review*, *101*(2), 327–341.

Bräuer, J., Call, J., & Tomasello, M. (2006). Are apes really inequity averse? *Proceedings of Royal Society B*, *273*, 3123–3128.

Bräuer, J., Call, J., & Tomasello, M. (2008). Chimpanzees do not take into account what others can hear in a competitive situation. *Animal Cognition*, *11*, 175–178.

Brosnan, S. F., Grady, M., Lambeth, S. P., Schapiro, S. J., & Beran, M. J. (2008). Chimpanzee autarky. *PLoS ONE*, *3*(1), 1–5.

Brosnan, S. F., Schiff, H. C., & de Waal, F. (2005). Tolerance for inequity may increase with social closeness in chimpanzees. *Proceedings of the Royal Society B*, *272*, 253–258.

Brownell, C., Svetlova, M., & Nichols, S. (2009). To share or not to share: When do toddlers respond to another's need. *Infancy, 14*, 117–130.

Call, J., Carpenter, M., & Tomasello, M. (2005). Copying results and copying actions in the process of social learning: Chimpanzees *(Pan troglodytes)* and human children *(Homo sapiens)*. *Animal Cognition, 8*, 151–163.

Call, J., Hare, B., Carpenter, M., & Tomasello, M. (2004). Unwilling versus unable? Chimpanzees' understanding of intentional action. *Developmental Science, 7*(4), 488–498.

Call, J., & Tomasello, M. (1998). Distinguishing intentional from accidental actions in orangutans *(Pongo pygmaeus)*, chimpanzees *(Pan troglodytes)*, and human children *(Homo sapiens)*. *Journal of Comparative Psychology, 112*, 192–206.

Call, J., & Tomasello, M. (2008). Does the chimpanzees have a theory of mind: 30 years later. *Trends in Cognitive Science, 12*, 87–92.

Caron, A. J., Butler, S., & Brooks, R. (2002). Gaze following at 12 and 14 months: Do the eyes matter? *British Journal of Developmental Psychology, 20*, 225–239.

Carpenter, M. (2006). Instrumental, social, and shared goals and intentions in imitation. In S. J. Rogers & J. Williams (Eds.), *Imitation and the social mind: Autism and typical development* (pp. 48–70). New York: Guilford Press.

Carpenter, M., Akhtar, N., & Tomasello, M. (1998). 14-through 18-month-old infants differentially imitate intentional and accidental actions. *Infant Behavior and Development, 21*, 315–330.

Carpenter, M., Tomasello, M., & Striano, T. (2005). Role reversal imitation in 12 and 18 month olds and children with autism. *Infancy, 8*, 253–278.

Chapais, B. (2008). *Primeval kinship: How pair-bonding gave birth to human society.* Cambridge, MA: Harvard University Press.

Cheney, D. L., & Seyfarth, R. M. (1990). Attending to behaviour versus attending to knowledge: Examining monkeys' attribution of mental states. *Animal Behaviour, 40*, 742–753.

Coqueugniot, H., Hublin, J-J., Veillonm, F., Houët, F., & Jacob, T. (2004). Early brain growth in Homo erectus and implications for cognitive ability. *Nature, 431*, 299–302.

Custance, D. M., Whiten, A., & Bard, K. A. (1995). Can young chimpanzees *(Pan troglodytes)* imitate arbitrary actions? Hayes and Hayes (1952) revisited. *Behaviour, 132*, 837–859.

de Waal, F. (1989). *Peacemaking among primates.* Cambridge, MA: Harvard University Press.

de Waal, F. B. M., & Seres, M. (1997). Propagation of handclasp grooming among captive chimpanzees. *American Journal of Primatology, 43*, 339–346.

Fehr, E., & Fischbacher, U. (2003). The nature of human altruism. *Nature, 425*, 785–791.

Fehr, E., Bernhard, H., & Rockenbach, B. (2008). Egalitarianism in young children. *Nature, 454*, 1079–1083.

Flack, J. C., Girvan, M., de Waal, F. B. M., & Krakauer, D. C. (2006). Policing stabilizes construction of social niches in primates. *Nature*, *439*, 426–429.

Galef, B. (1992). The question of animal culture. *Human Nature*, *3*, 157–178.

Gergely, G., & Csibra, G. (2006). Sylvia's recipe: The role of imitation and pedagogy in the transmission of cultural knowledge. In N. J. Enfield & S. C. Levinson (Eds.), *Roots of human sociality: Culture, cognition and interaction* (pp. 229–255). Oxford, England: Berg Press.

Gilbert, M. (1989). *On social facts*. Princeton: Princeton University Press.

Gilby, I. C. (2006). Meat sharing among the Gombe chimpanzees: Harassment and reciprocal exchange. *Animal Behaviour*, *71*(4), 953–963.

Goffman, E. (1959). *The presentation of self in everyday life*. New York: Doubleday.

Graefenhain, M., Behne, T., Carpenter, M., & Tomasello, M. (2009). Young children's understanding of joint commitments. *Developmental Psychology*, *45*, 1430–1443.

Grice, P. (1957). Meaning. *The Philosophical Review*, *64*, 377–388.

Gurven, M. (2004). To give and to give not: The behavioral ecology of human food transfers. *Behavioral and Brain Sciences*, *27*, 543–583.

Hamann, K., Warneken, F., & Tomasello, M. (in press). Children's Developing Commitments to Joint Goals. Child Development.

Harcourt, A. H., & de Waal, F. B. M. (1992). *Coalitions and alliances in humans and other animals*. New York: Oxford University Press.

Hare, B. (2007). From nonhuman to human mind: What changed and why. *Current Directions in Psychological Science*, *16*, 60–64.

Hare, B., & Tomasello, M. (2005). Human-like social skills in dogs? *Trends in Cognitive Science*, *9*, 439–444.

Hare, B., Call, J., Agnetta, B., & Tomasello, M. (2000). Chimpanzees know what conspecifics do and do not see. *Animal Behaviour*, *59*, 771–785.

Hare, B., Call., J., & Tomasello, M. (2001). Do chimpanzees know what conspecifics know? *Animal Behaviour*, *61*, 139–151.

Hare, B., Call, J., & Tomasello, M. (2006). Chimpanzees deceive a human competitor by hiding. *Cognition*, *101*, 495–514.

Hare, B., Melis, A., Woods, V., Hastings, S., & Wrangham, R. (2007). Tolerance allows bonobos to outperform chimpanzees in a cooperative task. *Current Biology*, *17*, 619–623.

Henrich, J., Boyd, R., Bowles, S., Gintis, H., Fehr, E., Camerer, C., McElreath, R., Gurven, M., Hill, K., Barr, A., Ensminger, J., Tracer, D., Marlow, F., Patton, J., Alvard, M., Gil-White, F., & Henrich, N. (2005). "Economic man" in cross-cultural perspective: Ethnography and experiments from 15 small-scale societies. *Behavioral and Brain Sciences*, *28*, 795–855.

Herrmann, E., Call, J., Lloreda, M., Hare, B., & Tomasello, M. (2007). Humans have evolved specialized skills of social cognition: The cultural intelligence hypothesis. *Science*, *317*, 1360–1366.

Herrmann, E., Hernandez-Lloreda, M. V., Call, J., Hare, B., & Tomasello, M. (2010). The structure of individual differences in the cognitive abilities of children and chimpanzees. *Psychological Science*, *21*(1), 102–110.

Hill, K. (2002). Altruistic cooperation during foraging by the Ache, and the evolved human predisposition to cooperate. *Human Nature*, *13*, 105–128.

Hill, K., & Hurtado, A. M. (1996). *Ache life history: The ecology and demography of a foraging people*. New York: Aldine Press.

Hobson, R. P. (1993). *Autism and the development of mind*. Hove, England: Erlbaum.

Hopper, L. M., Lambeth, S. P., Schapiro, S. J., & Whiten, A. (2008). Observational learning in chimpanzees and children studied through "ghost" conditions. *Proceedings of the Royal Society B*, *275*, 835–840.

Hoppitt, W. J. E., Brown, G. R., Kendal, R., Rendell, L., Thornton, A., Webster, M. M., & Laland, K. N. (2008). Lessons from animal teaching. *Trends in Ecology and Evolution*, *23*, 486–493.

Horner, V., & Whiten, A. (2005). Causal knowledge and imitation/emulation switching in chimpanzees (*Pan troglodytes*) and children (*Homo sapiens*). *Animal Cognition*, *8*, 164–181.

Horner, V., Whiten, A., Flynn, E., & de Waal, F. B. M. (2006). Faithful replication of foraging techniques along cultural transmission chains by chimpanzees and children. *Proceedings of the National Academy of Sciences, USA, 103*, 13878–13883.

Hrdy, S. (2009). *Mothers and others*. Cambridge, MA: Harvard University Press.

Huffman, M. A., & Hirata, S. (2004). An experimental study of leaf swallowing in captive chimpanzees: Insights into the origin of a self-medicative behavior and the role of social learning. *Primates*, *45*, 113–118.

Humle, T., & Matsuzawa, T. (2002). Ant-dipping among the chimpanzees of Bossou, Guinea, and some comparisons with other sites. *American Journal of Primatology*, *58*, 133–148.

Imanishi, K. (1965). Newly-acquired pre-cultural behavior of the natural troop of Japanese monkeys on Koshima islet. *Primates*, *6*, 1–30.

Jensen, K., Call, J., & Tomasello, M. (2007a). Chimpanzees are rational maximizers in an ultimatum game. *Science*, *318*, 107–109.

Jensen, K., Call, J., & Tomasello, M. (2007b). Chimpanzees are vengeful but not spiteful. *Proceedings of the National Academy of Sciences*, *104*, 13046–13050.

Jensen, K., Hare, B., Call, J., & Tomasello, M. (2006). What's in it for me? Self-regard precludes altruism and spite in chimpanzees. *Proceedings of the Royal Society of London*, Series B - Biological Sciences, *273*, 1013–1021.

Johnson, A. W., & Earle, T. (2000). *The evolution of human societies*. Palo Alto, CA: Stanford University Press.

Kaminski, J., Call, J., & Tomasello, M. (2004). Body orientation and face orientation: Two factors controlling apes' begging behavior from humans. *Animal Cognition*, *7*, 216–223.

Klein, R., (1999). *The human career*. Chicago: University of Chicago Press.

Kobayashi, H., & Kohshima, S. (1997). Unique morphology of the human eye. *Nature, 387*(6635), 767–768.

Koski, S. E., & Sterck, E. H. M. (2009). Third-party affiliation in chimpanzees—what's in it for the third party? *American Journal of Primatology, 71*, 409–418.

Kruger, A. C., & Tomasello, M. (1996). Cultural learning and learning culture. In D. R. Olson & N. Torrance (Eds.), *The handbook of education and human development: New models of learning, teaching and schooling* (pp. 369–387). Oxford, England: Blackwell.

Kummer, H., & Cords, M. (1991). Cues of ownership in *Macaca fascicularis*. *Animal Behavior, 42*, 529–549.

Laland, K. N., & Galef, B. G., Jr. (2009). *The question of animal culture*. Cambridge, MA: Harvard University Press.

Leach, H. (2003). Human domestication reconsidered. *Current Anthropology, 44*, 349–368.

Liebal, K., Pika, S., Call J., & Tomasello, M. (2004). To move or not to move: How apes alter the attentional state of others. *Interaction Studies, 5*(2), 199–219.

Lizskowski, U., Carpenter, M., Striano, T., & Tomasello, M. (2006). 12- and 18-month-olds point to provide information for others. *Journal of Cognition and Development, 7*, 173–187.

Liszkowski, U., Carpenter, M., & Tomasello, M. (2008). Twelve-month-olds communicate helpfully and appropriately for knowledgeable and ignorant partners. *Cognition, 108*, 732–739.

Mauss, M. (1954). *Forms and functions of exchange in archaic societies*. New York: Routledge & K. Paul Ltd.

McGrew, W. C. (1974). Tool use by wild chimpanzees in feeding upon driver ants. *Journal of Human Evolution, 3*, 501–508.

McGrew, W. C., & Tutin, C. E. G. (1978). Evidence for a social custom in wild chimpanzees. *Man, 13*, 234–251.

Melis, A., Hare, B., & Tomasello, M. (2006a). Engineering cooperation in chimpanzees: Tolerance constraints on cooperation. *Animal Behaviour, 72*, 275–286.

Melis, A., Hare, B., & Tomasello, M. (2006b). Chimpanzees recruit the best collaborators. *Science, 31*, 1297–1300.

Meltzoff, A. (1995). Understanding the intentions of others: Re-enactment of intended acts by 18-month-old children. *Developmental Psychology, 31*, 1–16.

Moll, H., & Tomaselo, M. (2004). 12- and 18-month-olds follow gaze to hidden locations. *Developmental Science, 7*, F1–F9.

Moll, H., & Tomasello, M. (2007). Co-operation and human cognition: The Vygotskian intelligence hypothesis. *Philosophical Transactions of the Royal Society, 362*, 639–648.

Morgan, B. J., & Abwe, E. E. (2006). Chimpanzees use stone hammers in Cameroon. *Current Biology, 16*, R632–R633.

Muller, M., & Mitani, J. (2005). Conflict and cooperation in wild chimpanzees. *Advances in the Study of Behavior*, 35, 275–331.

Nagel, T. (1986). *The view from nowhere*. Oxford University Press.

Nagell, K., Olguin, R., & Tomasello, M. (1993). Processes of social learning in the tool use of chimpanzees *(Pan troglodytes)* and human children *(Homo sapiens)*. *Journal of Comparative Psychology*, 107, 174–186.

Noë, R., Van Hooff, J., & Hammerstein, P. (2001). *Economics in nature: Social dilemmas, mate choice and biological markets*. Cambridge, England: Cambridge University Press.

Odling-Smee F. J., Laland, K. N., & Feldman, M. W. (2003). Niche construction: The neglected process in evolution. *Monographs in Population Biology*, 37. Princeton, NJ: Princeton University Press.

Okamoto-Barth, S., Call, J., & Tomasello, M. (2007). Great apes' understanding of other's line of sight. *Psychological Science*, 18, 462–468.

Owren, M. J., & Rendall, D. (2001). Sound on the rebound: Bringing form and function back to the forefront in understanding nonhuman primate vocal signaling. *Evolutionary Anthropology*, 10, 58–71.

Perry, S., Baker, M., Fedigan, L., Gros-Louis, J., Jack, K., MacKinnon, K., Manson, J., Panger, M., Pyle, K., & Rose, L. (2003). Social conventions in wild white-faced capuchin monkeys: Evidence for traditions in a neotropical primate. *Current Anthropology*, 44, 241–268.

Povinelli, D. J., & Vonk, J. (2006). We don't need a microscope to explore the chimpanzee's mind. In S. Hurley (Ed.), *Rational animals* (pp. 385–412). Oxford, England: Oxford University Press.

Rakoczy, H., Warneken, F., & Tomasello, M. (2008). The sources of normativity: Young children's awareness of the normative structure of games. *Developmental Psychology*, 44(3), 875–881.

Rendell, L. E., & Whitehead, H. (2001). Culture in whales and dolphins. *Behavioral and Brain Sciences*, 24(2), 309–382.

Richerson, P., & Boyd, R. (2005). *Not by genes alone*. Chicago: University of Chicago Press.

Richerson, P., & Boyd, R. (2006). *Not by genes alone: How culture transformed human evolution*. Chicago: University of Chicago Press.

Rose, C. M. (2007). The moral subject of property. *William and Mary Law Review*, 48, 1897.

Searle, J. R. (1995). *The construction of social reality*. New York: Free Press.

Seyfarth, R. M., & Cheney, D. L. (2003). Signalers and receivers in animal communication. *Annual Review of Psychology*, 54, 145–173.

Silk, J. B., Brosnan, S. F., Vonk, J., Henrich, J., Povinelli, D. J., Richardson, A. S., Lambeth, S. P., Mascaro, J., & Schapiro, S. J. (2005). Chimpanzees are indifferent to the welfare of unrelated group members. *Nature*, 437, 1357–1359.

Sperber, D., & Wilson, D. (1986). *Relevance: Communication and cognition*. Cambridge, MA: Harvard University Press.

Stanford, C. B. (1998). *Chimpanzee and Red Colobus*. Cambridge, MA: Harvard University Press.

Sterelny, K. (2008). *Nicod lectures*. Retrieved Month DD, YYYY from the Jean Nicod Institute Web site.

Tennie, C., Call, J., & Tomasello, M. (2006). Push or pull: Emulation versus imitation in great apes and human children. *Ethology*, *112*, 1159–1169.

Tennie, C., Call, J., & Tomasello, M. (2009). Ratcheting up the ratchet: On the evolution of cumulative culture. *Philosophical Transactions of the Royal Society B*, *364*, 2405–2415.

Tennie, C., Hedwig, D., Call, J., & Tomasello, M. (2008). An experimental study of nettle feeding in captive gorillas. *American Journal of Primatology*, *70*, 584–593.

Tomasello, M. (1990). Cultural transmission in the tool use and communicatory signaling of chimpanzees? In S. Parker & K. Gibson (Eds.), *"Language" and Intelligence in Monkeys and Apes: Comparative Developmental Perspectives*, (pp. 333–358). Cambridge University Press.

Tomasello, M. (1999). *The cultural origins of human cognition*. Cambridge, MA: Harvard University Press.

Tomasello, M. (2003). *Constructing a language: A usage-based theory of language acquisition*. Cambridge, MA: Harvard University Press.

Tomasello, M. (2006). Why don't apes point? In N. Enfield & S. Levinson (Eds.), *Roots of human sociality* (pp. 506–524). Wenner-Grenn.

Tomasello, M. (2008). *Origins of human communication*. Cambridge, MA: MIT Press.

Tomasello, M. (2009). *Why we cooperate*. Cambridge, MA: MIT Press.

Tomasello, M., & Call, J. (1997). *Primate cognition*. New York: Oxford University Press.

Tomasello, M., Call, J., Warren, J., Frost, T., Carpenter, M., & Nagell, K. (1997). The ontogeny of chimpanzee gestural signals: A comparison across groups and generations. *Evolution of Communication*, *1*, 223–253.

Tomasello, M., & Carpenter, M. (2005). The emergence of social cognition in three young chimpanzees. *Monographs of the Society for Research in Child Development*, *70*(279).

Tomasello, M., Carpenter, M., Call, J., Behne, T., & Moll, H. (2005). Understanding and sharing intentions: The origins of cultural cognition. *Behavioral and Brain Sciences*, *28*, 675–691.

Tomasello, M., Carpenter, M., & Lizskowski, U., (2007). A new look at infant pointing. *Child Development*, *78*, 705–722.

Tomasello, M., Hare, B., & Agnetta, B. (1999). Chimpanzees follow gaze direction geometrically. *Animal Behaviour*, *58*, 769–777.

Tomasello, M., Hare, B., Lehmann, H., & Call, J. (2007). Reliance on head versus eyes in the gaze following of great apes and human infants: The cooperative eye hypothesis. *Journal of Human Evolution*, *52*, 314–320.

Tomasello, M., Kruger, A., & Ratner, H. (1993). Cultural learning. *Behavioral and Brain Sciences, 16*, 495–552.

Tomasello, M., Savage-Rumbaugh, S., & Kruger, A. (1993). Imitative learning of actions on objects by children, chimpanzees and enculturated chimpanzees. *Child Development, 64*, 1688–1705.

Trevarthen, C. (1979). Instincts for human understanding and for cultural cooperation: Their development in infancy. In M. von Cranach, K. Foppa, W. Lepenies, & D. Ploog (Eds.), *Human ethology: Claims and limits of a new discipline* (pp. 107–131). Cambrdige: Cambridge U. Press.

Ueno, A., & Matsuzawa, T. (2004). Food transfer between chimpanzee mothers and their infants. *Primates, 45*, 231–239.

Uzgiris, I. (1981). Two functions of imitation during infancy. *International Journal of Behavioral Developmental*, 4, 1–12.

van Schaik, C. P., Ancrenaz, M., Borgen, G., Galdikas, B., Knott, C. D., Singleton, I., Suzuki, A., Utami, S. S., & Merrill, M. Y. (2003). Orangutan cultures and the evolution of material culture. *Science, 299*, 102–105.

Warneken, F., & Tomasello, M. (2006). Altruistic helping in human infants and young chimpanzees. *Science, 31*, 1301–1303.

Warneken, F., & Tomasello, M. (2007). Helping and cooperation at 14 months of age. *Infancy, 11*, 271–294.

Warneken, F., Chen. F., & Tomasello, M. (2006). Cooperative activities in young children and chimpanzees. *Child Development, 77*, 640–663.

Warneken, F., Hare, B., Melis, A., Hanus, D., & Tomasello, M. (2007). Spontaneous altruism by chimpanzees and young children. *PLOS Biology, 5*(7), e184.

Warneken, F., Lohse, A., Melis, A., & Tomasello, M. (in press). Young children share resources equally after collaboration

Watts, D., & Mitani, J. C. (2001). Boundary patrols and intergroup encounters among wild chimpanzees. *Behaviour, 138*, 299–327.

Watts, D., & Mitani, J. C. (2002). Hunting behavior of chimpanzees at Ngogo, Kibale National Park, Uganda. *International Journal of Primatology, 23*, 1–28.

Whiten, A., Custance, D. M., Gómez, J. C., Teixidor, P., & Bard, K. A. (1996). Imitative learning of artificial fruit processing in children (Homo sapiens) and chimpanzees (Pan troglodytes). *Journal of Comparative Psychology, 110*, 3–14.

Whiten, A., Horner, V., & de Waal, F. B. M. (2005). Conformity to cultural norms of tool use in chimpanzees. *Nature, 437*(7059), 737–740.

Whiten, D. A., Goodall, J., McGew, W. C., Nishida, T., Reynolds, V., Sugiyama, Y., et al. (1999). Cultures in chimpanzees. *Nature, 399*, 682–685.

Whiten, A., & van Schaik, C. P. (2007). The evolution of animal "cultures" and social intelligence. *Philosophical Transactions of the Royal Society of London Series B, 362*(1480), 603–620.

Wrangham, R. & Pilbeam, D. (2001). African apes as time machines. In B. F. F. Galdikas, N. Erickson Briggs, L. K. Sheeran, G. L. Shapiro, & J. Goodall (Eds.), *All apes great and small* (pp. 5–17). New York: Kluwer Academic/Plenum.

Wyman, E., Rakoczy, H., & Tomasello, M. (2009). Normativity and context in young children's pretend play. *Cognitive Development*, *24*, 146–155.

Zuberbühler, K. (2005). The phylogenetic roots of language: Evidence from primate communication and cognition. *Current Directions in Psychological Science*, *14*(3), 126–130.

CHAPTER 2

Culture, Emotion, and Expression

DAVID MATSUMOTO

San Francisco State University and Humintell, LLC

HYI SUNG HWANG

San Francisco State University and Humintell, LLC

I. INTRODUCTION

Emotion and culture have been studied for centuries, and they were central topics to many individuals influential to modern psychology, such as Freud, Erikson, Piaget, and Bowlby. Contemporary studies of emotion and culture, however, find their roots in the work of Darwin. One reason for this was that Darwin inspired work on the expression of emotion, offering scientists a platform with which to measure emotions objectively. Darwin's thesis, summarized in *The Expression of Emotion in Man and Animals* (Darwin, 1872), suggested that emotions and their expressions had evolved across species, were evolutionarily adaptive, biologically innate, and universal. According to Darwin, all humans, regardless of race or culture, possessed the ability to express emotions in the same ways, primarily through their faces and other nonverbal behaviors.

Although compelling, Darwin's work was not without limitation, the largest of which was the lack of scientific data to support his claims. Between the time of Darwin's original writing and the 1960s, only seven studies examined his ideas concerning emotion and expression. These studies, however, were methodologically flawed (Ekman, Friesen, & Ellsworth, 1972), so that unequivocal data speaking to the issue of their possible universality did not emerge until the early 1960s when Sylvan Tomkins, a pioneer in modern studies of human emotion, joined forces independently with Paul Ekman and

Carroll Izard to conduct what has become known today as the universality studies. They obtained agreement in judgments of faces thought to express emotions from individuals in many literate cultures (Ekman, 1972; Izard, 1971). Ekman and his colleague Wallace Friesen also demonstrated that judgments by members of preliterate cultures were consistent with those from literate cultures, and that expressions posed by members of preliterate cultures were reliably judged by westerners (Ekman & Friesen, 1971; Ekman, Sorenson, & Friesen, 1969). They also showed that the same expressions were spontaneously produced in reaction to emotion-eliciting films across cultures (Friesen, 1972). These findings demonstrated the existence of six universal expressions—anger, disgust, fear, happiness, sadness, and surprise—as judges around the world agreed on what emotion was portrayed in the faces.

Another important development during this time was the concept of *cultural display rules* (Ekman & Friesen, 1969; Friesen, 1972). These are culturally prescribed rules, learned early in life, that dictate the management and modification of the universal expressions depending on social circumstance. The existence of these display rules was demonstrated in Friesen's (1972) study of American and Japanese participants viewing stressful films alone and in the presence of an experimenter. When alone, they displayed the same expressions of disgust, anger, fear, and sadness. When with the experimenter, however, there were dramatic differences. While the Americans tended to continue to show their negative feelings, many Japanese smiled. Ekman and Friesen reckoned that cultural display rules were operating, which prevented the free expression of negative emotions in the presence of another person in the Japanese culture. Today, the existence of both universality and cultural display rules is well accepted in mainstream psychology.

The universality findings had an enormous impact on contemporary psychology, as expressions provided an objective and reliable signal of emotion. Subsequently, methods of measuring facial behaviors were developed (Ekman & Friesen, 1978; Izard, 1983). In particular, the Facial Action Coding System (FACS; Ekman & Friesen, 1978) is recognized as the most comprehensive tool to analyze facial movements, involving the identification of the appearance changes associated with over 40 separate and functionally independent anatomical units. Using it, researchers can code the muscles involved in any facial expression, along with their timing characteristics (onset, apex, offset), intensity, and laterality.

The development of techniques like FACS, along with the theoretical contributions of universal emotions, led to a plethora of new research, theory, and application in psychology in the past 40 years. For instance, studies using facial expressions of emotion as markers have addressed decades-old questions concerning the role and function of physiology in emotion. We now know that each of the universal emotions is associated with a distinct and unique physiological pattern (Ekman, Levenson, & Friesen, 1983; Levenson, Ekman, Heider, & Friesen, 1992). Studies involving faces and emotions have also made substantial contributions to clinical, forensic, industrial, and organizational psychology. An increasing number of universities are offering programs that specialize in the study of emotion, and funding sources are increasing to provide specialized training to pre- and postdoctoral candidates to develop further research in the area. All of this has been made possible through the contributions of the original cross-cultural research on emotional expressions, which literally opened the door to contemporary affective sciences.

II. A THEORETICAL PREVIEW: THE CULTURAL CALIBRATION OF EMOTION

It was against this historical backdrop that we began our research program in the early 1980s. In this chapter we summarize our research in this space over the past nearly three decades. This line of research has generated many findings over the years that have contributed to an integrated view of the relationship between culture, emotion, and expression. While a comprehensive presentation is beyond the scope of this chapter, here we provide a brief overview of the theoretical framework generated by this line of research so that readers can preview and integrate the work reported later in this chapter. This framework begins by an understanding of the role and function of culture.

Human social life is complex. Individuals are members of multiple groups, with multiple social roles, norms, and expectations. And people move rapidly in and out of the multiple groups of which they are members. This creates the enormous potential for social chaos, which can easily occur if individuals are not coordinated well and relationships not organized systematically. One of the important functions of culture is to provide this necessary coordination and organization. Doing so allows individuals and groups to negotiate the social complexity of human social life, thereby maintaining social order and preventing social chaos. Culture does this by providing a meaning and information system to its members, which is shared by a group and transmitted across generations, and which allows the group to meet basic needs of survival, pursue happiness and well-being, and derive meaning from life. We define culture as a meaning and information system, transmitted across generations (Matsumoto & Juang, 2007).

Because one of the major functions of culture is to maintain social order, cultures create rules, guidelines, values, and norms concerning the regulation of emotion, because emotions serve as primary motivators of behavior (Tomkins, 1962, 1963) and have important social functions (Keltner & Haidt, 1999). For instance, cultural value orientations concerning interpersonal relationships (e.g., Individualism, Egalitarianism, Power Distance, Embeddedness, and Hierarchy) and emotions (Affective Autonomy) help to create and enforce norms concerning emotion regulation and behavioral expectations. Norms concerning emotion regulation in all cultures serve the purpose of maintaining social order by ensuring the engagement of culturally appropriate behavior mediated by culturally appropriate emotional responding (Fig. 2.1) (Matsumoto, Yoo, Nakagawa, et al., 2008).

How does culture aid this process? First, we believe that humans come to the world with an emotion system that helps people adapt to problems in the social and natural environment that have immediate consequences for welfare. This emotion system is an archaic, biologically based universal, developed in our evolutionary history, and it exists in all humans. There are two ways in which cultures regulate emotion and expression via the calibration

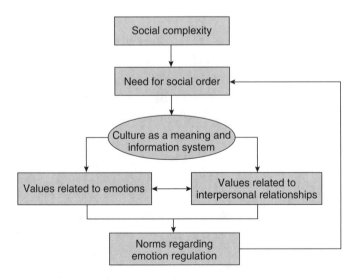

FIGURE 2.1: Social order and emotion regulation.

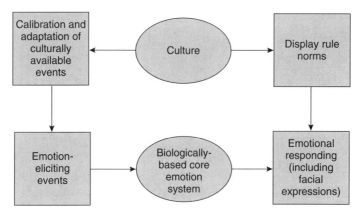

FIGURE 2.2: Cultural influences on the core emotion system. (From "Culture and emotional expression," *Problems and solutions in cross-cultural theory, research, and application,* by D. Matsumoto, 2009 by Taylor and Francis Group, LLC Books. Reproduced with permission of Taylor and Francis Group.)

and adaptation of the core, biologically based emotion system to culturally available events. One way this is accomplished is via front-end calibration of the emotion system to culturally available events (Fig. 2.2). In our development, we learn to have emotions to events in our lives, many of which are specific to our cultures (producing cultural differences) and to ourselves (producing individual differences). Although the core emotion system that produces universal facial configurations is biologically based, we view it as an entirely flexible system that is adaptable to many different contexts and events, allowing humans to have emotional reactions that color life and serve as a motivational basis for behavior.

Culture also influences emotion and expression via back-end calibration of emotional responses to cultural norms via cultural display rules. That is, once the emotion system is activated, individuals learn to modulate their emotional reactions, including expressions, according to learned rules and norms of what is appropriate in any given circumstance.

The emotion system is akin to the core computer processor inside the most elemental chip found in computers; individuals and groups certainly use their computers in ways that are both similar and different; they all are based, however, on the same core processing system. Human cultures, as meaning and information systems, elaborate the use and meaning of the emotion system, allowing for a multiplicity of uses. Cultures calibrate the emotion system to allow culture-constant and culture-specific events to be encoded with emotional meaning; regulate the type of expressive, verbal, and motor behaviors people should show depending on social situations; give culture-constant and specific meaning to attitudes, values, beliefs, and concepts about emotion; and provide the motivational basis for culture-constant and specific normative behaviors with regard to interpersonal and intergroup functions. Cultural calibration and adaptation of the core, biologically based emotion system, therefore, refers to front-end cultural influences on the core emotion system, while display rules refer to back-end influences. Both are cultural and involve the coordination and calibration of a biologically innate system.

This framework can explain not only universality and cultural differences in expression but also in judgment. That is, cultures also calibrate how we perceive and interpret the emotions of others. Cultures first influence the degree to which emotional stimuli in the environment are attended to, by influencing perceptual processes (gaze direction, eye contact during inter-action, etc.). For example, cultures that discourage direct eye contact among interactants may be discouraging the perception of emotion, at least from facial expressions, because there is likely to be less direct visual scanning of the face, and encouraging the reading of emotional cues from context. Once perceived, the recognition of emotion is likely to be universal and perhaps tied to biologically innate structures and systems, because of the universal production of emotional expressions. The interpretation of the meaning of the recognition, however, is likely to be culture specific, because of differences in display rules, values about emotion and its expression, and the meaning of expression, all of which are culturally based. Cumulatively, these form the basis for what we can term *cultural decoding rules* (Matsumoto & Ekman, 1989), which produce cultural differences in judgments.

Collectively, therefore, the cultural calibration of the evolved, biologically innate emotion and expression system allows for the regulation of culturally appropriate emotional responses to culturally available events, which in turn allows for culturally appropriate behavioral responding. This in turn allows for social coordination and prevents social chaos, thereby allowing human cultures to live and flourish.

III. OVERVIEW OF THE RESEARCH PROGRAM

Our research program involves a series of studies that can be loosely grouped into two major categories. The first involves *judgment studies*, in which observers are shown emotional stimuli, typically consisting of facial expressions, and are asked to make judgments or ratings about them. The independent variables in such studies are the stimuli presented and their characteristics, while the dependent variables are the judgments or ratings made by the observers. The second is known as *production studies*. These studies involve researchers eliciting emotions from participants, who then spontaneously react to those elicitations. The independent variable in these studies is the emotion elicitation; the dependent variable is the spontaneous behaviors of the participants as they react to the elicitation, which requires the use of a system to measure the behaviors that are produced (which is why measurement systems such as FACS have been useful to the field).

Next we present a review of our research program, following the division of judgment and production studies. Within each, we review the major research we have conducted according to the specific topic, further subdividing their findings into those with implications for universal and culture-specific processes.

IV. JUDGMENT STUDIES

Much of our early work focused on judgment studies. Although previous research demonstrated universality in emotion recognition, our work has documented both universal and culture-specific ways in which people of different cultures judge facial expressions of emotion. Next we describe our research, first focusing on emotion recognition, and then on attributions of intensity of emotional expressions. Within both of these sections we review research that has led to our understanding of universal as well as culture-specific processes. We also review some work we have done on attributions of personality based on smiles, judging faces in context, and training individuals to read facial expressions of emotion.

A. Emotion Recognition

1. Universal Processes

Universal Emotions—Contempt. The original universality research (cited earlier) documented the universal recognition of six emotions. In the past two decades, however, a number of studies have reported the existence of a seventh universal facial expression of emotion: contempt. Initial evidence supporting the universal recognition of contempt obtained from 10 countries, including West Sumatra (Ekman & Friesen, 1986; Ekman & Heider, 1988), was later replicated by Matsumoto (1992b) in four countries, three of which were different from Ekman and Friesen's original 10 countries. This finding received considerable attention and criticism (Izard & Haynes, 1988;

Russell, 1991a, 1991c). Russell (1991b, 1991c), for example, suggested that the presentation context in which the expression was shown influenced results in favor of universality. In his study, the expression reported as contempt by Ekman and Matsumoto was more often labeled as either disgust or sadness when shown either alone or after an expression of sadness or disgust. Ekman, O'Sullivan, and Matsumoto (1991a, 1991b), however, reanalyzed their data, which included a much broader test of the context effect suggested by Russell, and found no effect of context. Biehl et al. (1997) also tested and found no effects for other methodological confounds, and Rosenberg and Ekman (1995) suggested that people understand the emotional connotations of the expression even if they do not freely produce an emotion label for it.

Controversies concerning the universality of the contempt expression were subsequently laid to rest in a series of definitive studies that demonstrated that observers reliably associated the face of contempt with descriptions of situations that elicited contempt (Matsumoto & Ekman, 2004). That is, instead of using single emotion labels as response alternatives, observers were presented with short stories associated with each of the seven emotions and matched the faces with the stories. Also, observers had difficulties labeling the situations as "contempt," just as observers in previous studies had difficulties labeling faces, demonstrating that the lower agreement recognition rates for contempt previously observed were not limited to faces, but had to do with the label or concept of contempt. Thus, today we are fairly confident that contempt is a seventh universally recognized emotion.

Universal Recognition of Spontaneous Facial Expressions of Emotion. One major limitation of this area of research, including ours, was that the bulk of judgment studies had not utilized spontaneously produced faces, a criticism levied years ago (Russell, 1994). One of the reasons for this was the lack of studies examining the *production* of spontaneous facial expressions of emotion by individuals of different cultures that could be used as stimuli. Fortunately, a recent study of ours examining the spontaneous expressions of Olympic athletes solved this problem (Matsumoto & Willingham, 2006; described later). We took the expressions generated in that study—immediately at the end of a match for a medal (Match Completion) and later during the award ceremonies (Medal Ceremonies)—and showed them to 548 observers from four cultural groups: U.S.-born and raised Americans, immigrants to the United States, Japanese, and British. We then asked them to judge the emotion portrayed in each expression using a fixed-choice response task with the alternatives anger, contempt, disgust, fear, happiness, sadness, surprise, neutral, and other (Matsumoto, Olide, Schug, Willingham, & Callan, 2009). Observers in all countries recognized the emotions portrayed in the expressions at above chance levels most of the time. Moreover, when an expression was not judged at significantly greater than chance levels in one culture, it was generally not significant in all cultures. Observers in all four groups also reliably judged the expressions to portray the emotions predicted by the facial expression, commensurate with previous judgment and production studies. Correlations of the percentage of observers among the different countries selecting the intended emotion label across all expressions were all statistically significant and ranged from .74 to .97, indicating a very high level of cross-cultural agreement in relative emotion judgments.

However, percentage agreement rates for the intended emotions were lower than those reported for posed, prototypical expressions. We hypothesized that agreement rates would covary with signal clarity. To our knowledge, no measure of signal clarity in facial expressions existed; thus, we created one for use in this study (which in and of itself should be a useful technique for researchers in this area). The mean signal clarity across all Match Completion expressions was .53 (SD = .19); for Medal Ceremonies it was .65 (SD = .19), indicating substantial decrement in signal clarity from the prototypic expressions used in judgment studies. (The range for signal clarity according to the equation we developed was 0–1; prototypic expressions would have a signal clarity value of 1.0.) Across expressions we correlated each expression's signal clarity value with the percentage of observers who selected the predicted emotion label, separately for Match Completion and Medal Ceremonies. The correlations were significant for each of the four samples for both sets of expressions. Thus, the differences in percentage agreement in judgments were related to the signal clarity of the expressions in both conditions, and similarly for each culture. These findings were the first to document cross-cultural agreement in emotion judgments from facial expressions of emotion spontaneously produced by individuals of different cultures, addressed a major gap in the literature concerning emotion judgments, and provided additional evidence for the universality of emotion recognition in faces.

Second Mode of Response in Emotion Recognition. People of different countries agree on the secondary emotions portrayed in an expression. Observers in Ekman et al.'s (1987) study judged not only which emotion was portrayed in the faces but also the intensity of each of seven emotion categories. This task allowed observers to report multiple emotions, or no emotion, instead of being forced to select an emotion to describe the face.

While previous studies showed universality in the first mode of response, countries may have differed in which emotion is next most prevalent. Analyses supported cross-national agreement. For every country in Ekman et al.'s (1987) study, the secondary emotion for the disgust expressions was contempt, and for fear expressions, surprise. For anger, the second mode varied depending on the photo, with disgust, surprise, and contempt as the second responses. These findings have been replicated in numerous studies (Biehl et al., 1997; Matsumoto & Ekman, 1989; Yrizarry, Matsumoto, & Wilson-Cohn, 1998), suggesting pan-cultural agreement in the multiple meanings derived from universal faces. This agreement may exist because of overlap in the semantics of the emotion categories, antecedents and elicitors of emotion, or in the facial configurations themselves.

2. Culture-Specific Processes

Absolute Agreement Rates. Although the original universality research showed that subjects recognized emotions at well over chance rates, we were always fascinated by the fact that no study ever reported perfect cross-national agreement. And in fact, cross-cultural differences in the absolute levels of agreement in emotion recognition rates were often used to argue against the universality of facial expressions of emotion (Russell, 1991b, 1994), an argument that has been debated in the past (Ekman, 1994; Izard, 1994; Russell, 1995).

Today we know that facial expressions of emotion can be universal (and have biological sources), but that there can be cultural differences in absolute levels of agreement in recognizing them. Universality and cultural relativity are not mutually exclusive; the perception of emotion can be *both* universal as well as culture specific, depending on *what aspect* of perception we are talking about. Elsewhere (Yrizarry et al., 1998), we have suggested five sources that would produce cultural differences in emotion perception even though the expression judged is universal. They include the following: *(1)* semantic overlap in the linguistic categories and mental concepts related to emotion that are used in the judgment process—that is, overlap in the mental schemas associated with single emotion labels; *(2)* overlapping facial components in the expressions, such as the similarity in the facial muscles used in the expressions of surprise and fear, or the pulling down of the brows in disgust and anger; *(3)* cognitive overlap in events and experiences related to emotion, such as the fact that events that elicit fear are also often surprising; *(4)* personality biases in social cognition, including the individual differences in learned styles of perceiving emotion; and *(5)* differences in the specific meaning of the emotional labels used as response alternatives, or in the events that are associated with the expressions. That is, although the single-emotion labels used in studies may be translatable across cultures, they may refer to slightly different events or have slightly different cultural meanings, which may affect recognition rates.

Thus, cultural differences in emotion recognition rates are not only possible but expected. Matsumoto (1992a) examined this idea by testing Japanese and American judgments of emotion categories and found that recognition rates ranged from 64% to 99%, with Americans better at recognizing anger, disgust, fear, and sadness than the Japanese. These differences were in fact consistent with data reported in earlier universality studies (Ekman, 1972; Izard, 1971). Matsumoto (1992) suggested that the differences in recognition rates were due to cultural differences in socially learned rules about how emotions could be recognized. In Japan, emotions that threaten group harmony and conformity may be discouraged. Therefore, a Japanese person would be careful not to show negative emotions and would have a tendency not to recognize these expressions in others. In contrast, the United States, a country that encourages individuality, would encourage both the expression and perception of negative emotions. Biehl et al. (1997) also reported cross-national differences in emotion recognition agreement rates (and in intensity ratings). These differences could not be adequately explained according to a Western/non-Western dichotomy. Rather, Biehl et al. discussed these differences in terms of possible underlying sociopsychological variables, such as individualism versus collectivism, power distance, and the like.

What was equally important to uncovering cultural differences was the identification of the active ingredients of culture that produced such differences in the first place. As an initial exploration to this arena, Matsumoto (1989) selected recognition data from 15 cultures reported in four studies and ranked each country on Hofstede's (1980) dimensions. These included Power Distance (PD), the degree to which differences in power are maintained by culture; Uncertainty Avoidance (UA), the degree to which a culture develops institutions and rituals to deal with the anxiety created by uncertainty; Individualism (IN), the degree to which a culture encourages the sacrificing of group goals for the individual; and Masculinity (MA), the degree to which a culture emphasizes sex differences. The dimensions were then correlated with recognition accuracy levels. Individualistic cultures were better at recognizing negative emotions than collectivistic ones. These findings were also supported in a subsequent meta-analysis (Schimmack, 1996), supporting the notion that sociocultural dimensions account for differences in the perception of emotion, and that people of different cultures learn ways of perception management via cultural decoding rules.

Is There an Ingroup Advantage for Emotion Recognition? One type of cultural difference in emotion judgment that has received attention recently concerns the possibility of an *ingroup advantage* in emotion recognition (Elfenbein & Ambady, 2002). This refers to the tendency for individuals to recognize emotional expressions produced by members of their own culture more accurately than those produced by another. Researchers arguing for the existence of this effect have suggested that it occurs because of "emotion dialects"—culturally derived, minor variants of emotional expressions (Elfenbein, Beaupre,' Levesque, & Hess, 2007). Presumably, people are more accurate when judging such expressions because those expressions are differentially used in their culture (Elfenbein & Ambady, 2002; Elfenbein et al., 2007; Elfenbein et al., 2002). For instance, raising an eyebrow could be a sign of skepticism in one culture. If people of that culture judged expressions of encoders raising an eyebrow, they are likely to respond that the expression was one of skepticism. People from another culture, however, may not respond this way because the expression may not be used in that culture, or it may have a different meaning in that culture. Unfortunately, none of the research reported to date claiming to support the ingroup hypothesis has utilized spontaneous expressions that would support a dialect theory; instead, all of the research cited to support the hypothesis has involved expressions that were posed by members of different cultures, and that were not equivalent across cultural groups (Elfenbein & Ambady, 2002; Elfenbein et al., 2007; Elfenbein et al., 2002).

Recently, we tested the dialect theory of the ingroup effect using spontaneous expressions produced by members of different cultures in a naturalistic field setting (Matsumoto, Olide, & Willingham, 2009). The expressions came from Matsumoto and Willingham's (2006) study of expressions produced by athletes during the judo competition of the 2004 Athens Olympic Games. Expressions were captured using high-speed photography immediately at the end of a match determining gold, silver, bronze, or fifth place finish. American and Japanese observers judged expressions produced by American and Japanese athletes. Across all emotions studied, the ingroup advantage hypothesis was *not* supported, suggesting that the effect reported in previous studies may be localized to nonequivalent, posed expressions. That is, the cultural ingroup advantage hypothesis may not be ecologically valid because they have occurred only with posed mimes. Mimed expressions may not be valid analogs of actually occurring expressions when emotions are aroused because they may include extraneous muscle movements or not include muscle movements that spontaneously would occur. Innervated muscles may also be at different intensity levels or symmetries from spontaneous expressions. Any of these possible characteristics of posed, voluntarily expressions may be sufficient to produce the dialects proposed by Elfenbein and colleagues (2007) that in turn produced the ingroup effect in the past. Future studies need to examine whether the cultural dialects Elfenbein and colleagues suggest occur actually do occur in real life and whether these truly produce ingroup advantages in emotion recognition. The data to date suggest they do not.

Emotion Recognition in Bilinguals. If cultural differences in judgment are mediated by learned rules of emotion display and decoding, contextual activation of these rules should increase the likelihood of applying them. Recent work highlighting a dynamic constructivist approach to culture suggests that this may be true. In this approach, culture may be internalized as a loose network of domain-specific knowledge structures, including categories or implicit theories (Chiu, Morris, Hong, & Menon, 2000; Hong, Morris, Chiu, & Benet-Martinez, 2000). This perspective views culture as situated cognition (Oyserman & Lee, 2008), in which social norms, expectations, values, beliefs, attitudes, and opinions are held together in a loose but coordinated and organized network of schemas. This view suggests that individuals create different networks for different situational contexts, and that they switch networks as they move from one context to another to access context-relevant cultural information, priming culturally appropriate responses to culturally relevant environmental cues.

An important aspect of this approach is the notion that individuals can acquire more than one cultural meaning system (and thus more than one network of schemas), and that those multiple meaning systems can coexist, even if they are somewhat contradictory. This process may be at work when bilingual (bicultural) individuals judge emotion. If cultural decoding rules (Matsumoto & Ekman, 1989) are a type of cultural cognition situated in a network, and if bilinguals have multiple cultural networks, then it follows that bilingual individuals may be primed to judge emotions in one cultural framework or another. Matsumoto and Assar (1992) demonstrated this possibility by presenting facial expressions of emotion to bilingual Indians in either Hindi or English, and this showed that the participants were more accurate in judging the faces in English. These findings suggested that the terms used to label emotions may be more accessible in English than in Hindi, which is an interesting finding given that English was not the native language for these participants. If speaking English and activating the underlying cultural framework facilitates or even requires the increased labeling of emotions more than other languages, emotion recognition rates should be higher in English, which is what was observed.

But cultural decoding rules may affect other types of judgments differently. We tested the possibility that intensity ratings, particularly of the expressor's internal emotional states, may be more accessible in one's native language. A sample of bilingual Mexicans in an advanced English class was shown facial expressions of emotion and made three judgments of them: an emotion recognition judgment, rating of the intensity of the external display, and a rating of the intensity of the subjective experience of the expressor. They also completed a measure of emotion regulation that has been validated in English- and Spanish-speaking samples (Matsumoto, 2006; Matsumoto, et al., 2003). Emotion recognition scores were higher when the judgment task was in English compared to Spanish, although the observers were native Spanish speakers. This finding again highlighted the greater accessibility of emotion terms in English than in Spanish when labeling others' expressions, which was directly evidenced by a significant correlation between the students' end-of-semester grades in the advanced English class and emotion recognition scores in English but not Spanish. Ratings of the presumed subjective experience of the expressors, and ratings of emotion regulation, however, were higher in Spanish compared to English. This finding points to the greater accessibility of one's own emotional processes in one's native language. Finally, emotion regulation mediated the language differences in both emotion recognition and intensity ratings of subjective experience, but only when it was assessed in Spanish. This makes conceptual sense if one considers the Spanish ratings to be "truer" assessments of emotion regulation skills.

These findings contribute to a growing body of knowledge on the priming effects of language on the accessibility of various cognitive judgment tasks in bilinguals (Benet-Martinez, Lee, & Leu, 2006; Benet-Martinez, Leu, Lee, & Morris, 2002; Hong, Benet-Martinez, Chiu, & Morris, 2003), and they are commensurate with a dynamic, constructionist view of cognitive approaches to culture (Chiu et al., 2000; Hong et al., 2000). They demonstrate the greater accessibility of emotion-related processes in the self in one's native language, which has implications for social cognition. Lack of such access to knowledge of the emotions of others may serve as a basis for ethnocentrism and ingroup favoritism; improving such access may be a key to fostering mutual cross-cultural understanding.

B. Attributions of Intensity

1. Universal Processes

Relative Intensity Ratings. When comparing expressions, people of different countries agree on relative intensity differences among expressions. Ekman et al. (1987) compared intensity ratings between paired expressions of the same emotion across 10 countries, and they found that 92% of the time, the 10 countries in their study agreed on which was more intense. Matsumoto and Ekman (1989) extended this finding by including comparisons across different poser types, including Caucasian and Japanese posers. Looking separately for each emotion, within country across gender and then within gender across country, Americans and Japanese agreed on which photo was more intense 80% of the time. These findings suggested that observers from different cultures judge emotions on a similar basis, despite differences in facial physiognomy, morphology, poser race, poser sex, or culturally prescribed rules governing the expression and perception of faces.

The Association between Perceived Expression Intensity and Inferences about Subjective Experience. There is a strong, positive relationship between how strongly judges rate an expression and how much they believe the expressor is feeling that same emotion. Matsumoto, Kasri, and Kooken (1999) showed Japanese and American observers 56 expressions posed by Japanese and Caucasians. The observers judged what emotion the poser was expressing, and then the strength of both the external display and internal experience. Correlations between the two intensity ratings were computed twice, first across observers separately for each expression, and across expressions for each observer. The correlations for both were high and positive for both countries and all expressions, suggesting commonality in that linkage across cultures. This link is a topic of considerable importance in contemporary theories of emotion. Some authors have claimed that the linkage between expression and experience is unfounded (Feldman Barrett, 2006a, 2006b; Fernandez-Dols & Ruiz-Belda, 1997; Russell, 1997). Others, however, have argued that expressions and experience are linked with each other, but they need not always be coupled (Levenson, 1999; Matsumoto, 1987;

Rosenberg & Ekman, 1994; Winton, 1986). The data from Matsumoto et al. (1999) clearly support notions of linkage.

2. Culture-Specific Processes

Almost 25 years ago, Ekman et al. (1987) showed observers in 10 countries the universal facial expressions of emotion and asked them to not only judge which emotion was portrayed but also how intensely. Although the recognition data supported universality, there were cultural differences in the intensity ratings, with Asians giving significantly lower ratings on happiness, surprise, and fear. This was the first study to document cross-national differences in judgments of universal faces. These data suggested that the judges were acting according to culturally learned rules about how to perceive expressions. Given the fact that all posers were Caucasian, it could also have been that the Asians rated the Caucasian posers less intensely out of politeness or ignorance.

To pursue this finding, Matsumoto and Ekman developed a stimulus set comprised of Asian and Caucasian posers known as the Japanese and Caucasian Facial Expressions of Emotion (JACFEE; Matsumoto & Ekman, 1988) and presented them to judges in the United States and Japan (Matsumoto & Ekman, 1989). For all but one emotion, Americans rated the expressions more intensely than the Japanese, regardless of the ethnicity of the expressor. Because the differences were not specific to the expressor, Matsumoto and Ekman (1989) interpreted the differences as a function of *cultural decoding rules*. That is, people of all cultures may all have the ability, perhaps innate, to recognize which emotion is portrayed on a face; but people of different cultures may judge other aspects of faces differently, such as the intensity of the expression, according to culturally prescribed norms.

Matsumoto (1993) subsequently extended these findings to four ethnic groups in the United States. African Americans perceived anger more intensely than Asian Americans, and they perceived disgust more intensely than Caucasian and Asian Americans. Hispanic Americans perceived Caucasian faces more intensely than did Caucasian and Asian Americans. And African Americans perceived female expressions more intensely than did Asian Americans. Once again, Matsumoto (1993) argued that the observed differences resulted from cultural decoding rules, which members of the various ethnic groups learned vis-à-vis the decoding and interpretations of others' emotions.

Although Matsumoto and Ekman (1989) obtained intensity ratings by Americans and Japanese on multiple emotion scales, they only analyzed the ratings from the single scale corresponding to the emotion in the face. A subsequent study (Yrizarry et al., 1998) analyzed all ratings on all scales and found that members of both cultures saw multiple emotions in the universal expressions, and that the cultural differences in intensity ratings differed depending on the emotion scale rated. For example, Americans not only rated angry faces as expressing more anger; they also rated them as expressing more contempt and disgust. The Japanese rated angry faces as expressing more sadness than did the Americans.

While these findings demonstrated the existence of cultural differences in judgments, it was unclear as to what exactly the difference referred. This ambiguity occurred because the previous studies did not specify the source of the intensity being rated; thus, it was impossible to know whether the rating referred to the intensity of the expression itself or to the presumed underlying subjective experience of the expressor. It could be that cultural differences in intensity ratings existed for one but not the other. To tease out this effect, Matsumoto et al. (1999) compared American and Japanese judgments in which separate ratings were obtained for expression intensity and inferred subjective experience; they found that Americans rated external display more intensely than the Japanese, replicating previous findings. The Japanese, however, rated internal experience more intensely than Americans. Within-country analyses indicated no differences between the two ratings for the Japanese. Americans, however, consistently rated external display more intensely than subjective experience. These findings were totally unexpected. Previously, we suggested that American–Japanese differences occurred because the Japanese suppressed their intensity ratings, as they do their expressions. Contrarily, however, it was the Americans who exaggerated their external display ratings relative to subjective experience, not the Japanese who suppressed.

A subsequent study extended these findings further (Matsumoto et al., 2002). American and Japanese judges saw neutral, low-, high-, and very high–intensity expressions and made emotion judgments and intensity ratings. The data for the high and very high expressions replicated the previous findings; Americans rated external display significantly higher than internal experience, while there were no differences for the Japanese. Also, there were no differences between ratings for either Americans or Japanese on neutral expressions, which were expected. On low-intensity expressions, however, the findings were intriguing. While there was no difference between external and internal ratings for the Americans, the Japanese rated internal experience *higher* than external display. We suggested that, for weaker expressions,

Japanese may assume that a display rule is operating and may thus infer more emotion being felt than is actually displayed. When Americans see a weak expression, however, there need not be any such assumption; they interpret the same amount of emotion felt as expressed. For strong expressions, Japanese may assume that the context was such that the expression was justified; thus, they infer a level of emotion felt that is commensurate with what is shown. When Americans see a strong expression, however, they know that there is a display rule to exaggerate one's feelings; thus, they compensate for this display rule by inferring less emotion felt.

What aspect of culture can account for these findings? For many years (Matsumoto, 1989; Matsumoto & Yoo, 2006), we have contended that the mere documentation of cultural differences, especially in quasi-experimental designs operationalizing culture by country, is not sufficient to draw empirically justified conclusions concerning what active cultural ingredients may produce such differences. Instead, different methodologies are required to "unpackage" the cultural effects on psychological variables (Bond & Tedeschi, 2001; Poortinga, van de Vijver, Joe, & van de Koppel, 1987; van de Vijver & Leung, 1997). Unpackaging refers to the identification of specific, psychological dimensions of culture that may account for between-country differences in the variable of interest, their inclusion and measurement, and the statistical estimation of the degree to which they actually account for between-country differences. Thus, specific, measurable dimensions of culture on the psychological level replace the global, nonspecific construct we know of as "culture." There are several methodological paradigms that allow for such unpackaging to occur (Matsumoto & Yoo, 2006).

In fact, years earlier, we had conducted a preliminary investigation exploring the relationship between Hofstede's (1980) well-known dimensions of culture and emotion intensity ratings, on the cultural level. Two important findings emerged. First, there was a negative correlation between Power Distance and intensity ratings of anger, fear, and sadness, suggesting that cultures that emphasize status differences rate these emotions less intensely. Secondly, individualistic cultures rated anger and fear more intensely. These results suggested that understanding dimensions of culture could be a key to explaining cross-national differences in the perception of negative emotions.

In this vein, the study described earlier (Matsumoto et al., 2002) was unique in that not only did we obtain judgments of faces but also data assessing individual-level differences in two major cultural constructs—individualism versus collectivism (IC) and status differentiation (SD). Individualism versus collectivism has been used to explain many cross-national and cross-cultural differences in behavior, and it is arguably the most well-known, well-studied, and important dimension of culture that exists today (Triandis, 1995). Status differentiation refers to the degree to which cultures differentiate their behaviors toward others on the basis of the status differences that exist between them and their interactants; some cultures make large differentiations on the basis of status, affording people of higher status more power; others make smaller differentiations, treating people more or less the same regardless of status differences. To investigate the contribution of IC and SD to the cross-national differences in intensity ratings reported earlier, Matsumoto et al. (2002) compared the effect sizes associated with the differences between external and internal ratings separately for Americans and Japanese between analyses with and without the IC and SD ratings as covariates. Approximately 90% of the variance in the rating differences was accounted for by these two cultural variables. Subsequent follow-up analyses further indicated that IC contributed independent variance to this prediction. Thus, differences between Americans and Japanese on judgments of external and internal intensity may be almost entirely accounted for by higher individualism and lower status differentiation among Americans than Japanese. That makes sense, because cultures higher in individualism and lower in status differentiation would encourage greater expression of emotion with less modification or masking (which in fact has been documented in research on display rules reviewed later). These display rules would therefore correspond to decoding rules in these cultures that allowed members to interpret the emotions of others in ways that are commensurate with those display rules. Further research empirically documented that the cultural differences in intensity ratings were indeed mediated by cultural differences in display rules (Matsumoto, Choi, Hirayama, Domae, & Yamaguchi, unpublished data).

C. Attributions of Personality Based on Smiles

The smile is a common signal for greeting, acknowledgment, or for showing acceptance. It is also employed to mask emotions, and cultures may differ in the use of smiles for this purpose. This was the case in Friesen's (1972) study in which Japanese and American men watched disgusting video clips with an experimenter in the room. They used smiles to cover up their negative expressions much more often than the American men when with the experimenter, as opposed to when alone, when they showed the same negative emotions.

To further investigate the meaning of those differences, Matsumoto and Kudoh (1993) obtained ratings from Japanese and Americans on smiling versus nonsmiling (i.e., neutral) faces with regard to intelligence, attractiveness, and sociability. Americans rated smiling faces as more intelligent than neutral faces; the Japanese, however, did not. Americans and Japanese both found smiling faces more sociable than neutral faces, but for the Americans the difference was larger. These differences suggested that cultural display rules cause Japanese and Americans to attribute different meanings to the smile, and they serve as a good explanation for perceived major differences in communication styles across cultures.

D. Judging Faces in Context

Despite the fact that facial expressions always occur in context in real life, most mono- or cross-cultural judgment studies, including those described earlier, present them fairly acontextually. Writers have long debated the relative contribution of face and context in contributing to emotion messages by studying congruent and incongruent face-context combinations (Bruner & Tagiuri, 1954; Ekman & O'Sullivan, 1988; Fernberger, 1928; Russell & Fehr, 1987). One type of study in this genre is that which examines the linkage between an emotion eliciting context and a facial expression, which we have called *response linkage* (Matsumoto & Hwang, 2010). Studies involving congruent response linkages have found an additive effect (Bruner & Tagiuri, 1954; Knudsen & Muzekari, 1983), which probably occurred because of the increased signal clarity in the overall emotion message when two different signal sources provide the same message. Interestingly, studies involving incongruent response linkages have generally demonstrated a face superiority effect, indicating that the signals in the face tend to override the signals provided by the context (Ekman & O'Sullivan, 1988; Ekman et al., 1991a; Frijda, 1969; Goldberg, 1951; Nakamura, Buck, & Kenny, 1990).

But do these effects exist across cultures? We conducted two studies involving observers from three cultures (the United States, Japan, and South Korea) who judged facial expressions of anger, sadness, and happiness presented together with a congruent or incongruent emotion-eliciting context (Matsumoto, Hwang, & Yamada, in press). Analyses of the judgments of incongruent face-context pairs demonstrated face superiority in emotion judgments but also the simultaneous existence of cultural differences in the degree of influence of context, which moderated the face superiority effects. Japanese and South Korean observers were more influenced by context than Americans. The results provided a more nuanced view of how both culture and emotion moderate judgments of faces in context—by showing how face and context effects occur simultaneously—and how cultural differences existed in the judgments.

Moreover, analyses of congruent face-context pairs demonstrated that agreement rates in judgments were near perfect, with no cultural differences. This suggests that our (and others') previous work documenting cultural differences in emotion recognition rates may have been the result of methodological artifacts, at least partially, that is, of the fact that observers were asked to make judgments of emotion solely from faces. In reality, such judgments are made from multiple cues from both faces and contexts, and it makes sense that when multiple cues are given, cultural differences are eliminated.

E. Training Individuals to Read Facial Expressions of Emotion

In recent years we have turned our attention to developing ways of training individuals to recognize facial expressions of emotion when they occur. The development of such technologies is potentially useful in providing nonpharmacological interventions for such disorders as schizophrenia, autism, mental retardation, social conduct disorder, or acquired brain injuries. A decade ago we published the first valid and reliable individual difference measure of emotion recognition ability, known as the Japanese and Caucasian Brief Affect Recognition Test (JACBART; Matsumoto et al., 2000). Based on this test, Ekman, Matsumoto, and Frank (2003) created a CD-based, sequential, five-part, self-instructional training regimen called the Micro Expression Training Tool (METT v1). The first segment featured a 14-item pretest of ability based upon the JACBART items—that is, an image of a person in a neutral expression, followed by a one-fifteenth of a second flash of an image of the same person expressing one of the seven basic emotions, followed immediately by an image of the same person showing a neutral expression. The second segment was a training segment in which a series of rolling morphs were presented with commentary explaining how emotion was displayed for each of the seven emotions and highlighting the expressions most likely to be confused based upon appearance (e.g., anger and disgust, or fear and surprise). The third segment was also a training segment, in which 28 flash items like the pretest were shown, but this time the viewer was able to obtain feedback as to the accuracy of his or her judgment, view the item as many times as he or she would like, and freeze the one-fifteenth-second emotion expression image to study it. The fourth segment showed a different set of rolling morphs with commentary reviewing the similarities and differences among the different emotion expressions. The fifth segment was a 14-item posttest similar to the pretest, but it featured items that had not appeared in any previous segment and was designed to measure improvement in one's ability to accurately judge micro expressions.

Research using the METT v1 found that university students, Japanese business persons, and U.S. Coast Guard personnel significantly improved their ability to detect micro expressions with the naked eye in less than 30 minutes, regardless of occupation or culture (Frank, Matsumoto, Ekman, Kang, & Kurylo, unpublished data). Moreover, this training generalized to improved detection of real-time spontaneous micro expressions that occurred in deception situations. Other studies using METT v1 have shown that individuals afflicted with schizophrenia can improve their ability to read facial expressions of emotion (Russell, Chu, & Phillips, 2006) and improve their ability to focus attention on faces when doing so (Russell, Green, Simpson, & Coltheart, 2008).

Ekman and Matsumoto (2007) subsequently created a new version of the METT, which included faces from six different ethnic groups (Caucasian, African, Hispanic, Asian, South and Southeast Asian, and Middle Eastern). Using this new version of the METT (v2), we recently demonstrated that training the ability to read emotions produces a benefit in real-world situations, which heretofore had never been documented. Employees at a major retail department store near Seoul, South Korea, were randomly assigned to either a group that received training using METT v2 or a comparison group that received instruction about emotion but no training. Two weeks later, colleagues on the job who were blind to condition and assignment of the participants evaluated the trainees on a variety of scales measuring emotional competence on the job. Training produced higher scores in job-related emotional competence. The effect size differentiating the training and control groups on the outcome variables was large, and it survived when demographic variables associated with the outcomes were statistically controlled. Changes in the ability to read micro expressions of specific emotions were associated with the third-party outcome ratings, and a second study demonstrated that the ability to recognize emotions was retained a few weeks after initial training (Matsumoto & Hwang, unpublished data).

These findings open the door to new research and applications to help people see emotions better. This ability should aid groups to work collaboratively; colleagues to build better relationships, interpersonal trust, and rapport; bosses to communicate intent; and subordinates to read and interpret intent. The universality of facial expressions of emotion, and similarities in findings found with multiple groups of individuals from different cultures and professions, suggest that such training can benefit a wide range of people around the world. A current version of this tool can be found at http://www.humintell.com.

V. PRODUCTION STUDIES

Our research involving production studies have focused on five major themes: *(1)* the examination of spontaneous expressions in real-life situations, *(2)* the source of universal facial expressions of emotion, *(3)* cultural display rules, *(4)* the active cultural ingredients that influence and produce cultural differences, and *(5)* the temporal dynamics of culturally calibrated emotional expressions. Next we describe our major research findings in each of these areas.

A. Spontaneous Emotional Expressions in Real-Life, Naturalistic Contexts

Since Friesen's (1972) study, there have been at least 74 other studies that measured spontaneously produced facial behaviors that occurred in reaction to emotionally evocative situations; these studies found that the facial configurations originally posited by Darwin (1872) and verified (and somewhat modified) by Ekman (Ekman, 2003; Ekman & Friesen, 1975) actually occur (Matsumoto, Keltner, Shiota, Frank, & O'Sullivan, 2008). Despite this large number of studies, however, another glaring gap in this literature was the fact that all of these studies came from controlled, laboratory experiments. We closed this gap by examining the spontaneous facial expressions of the 84 gold, silver, bronze, and fifth place winners of the judo competition at the 2004 Athens Olympic Games, who came from 35 countries and six continents (Matsumoto & Willingham, 2006). As such they constituted a sample of the most culturally diverse individuals in whom spontaneous expressions that occurred in a highly charged, emotional event in three situations have been examined. Their expressions were coded using the Facial Action Coding System (FACS; Ekman & Friesen, 1978), and FACS codes were then compared to the Emotion FACS (EMFACS) dictionary to obtain emotion predictions (Ekman & Friesen, unpublished data; Matsumoto, Ekman, & Fridlund, 1991). EMFACS identifies action units (AUs) that are theoretically related to facial expressions of emotion posited by Darwin (1872) and later Tomkins (1962, 1963), and empirically verified by studies of spontaneous expression and judgments of expressions by Ekman and colleagues over 20 years (Ekman, Davidson, & Friesen, 1990; Ekman & Friesen, 1971; Ekman, Friesen, & Ancoli, 1980; Ekman, Friesen, & O'Sullivan, 1988; Ekman et al., 1969; Ekman et al., 1972).

The vast majority of the athletes produced expressions at match completion, and these corresponded to emotions predicted by EMFACS. Moreover, the expressions differentiated between victors and the defeated. Winners (gold and bronze medalists; bronze medalists were classified as winners because they had to win their last match to achieve the bronze medal) were much more likely to smile than the defeated, while the latter (silver medalists and fifth placers) were much more likely to display sadness, contempt, disgust, or no expressions (Fig. 2.3; for illustrative purposes only, these latter expressions were classified together). We tested for cultural differences in these expressions, but found none, providing evidence for the universality of the expressions.

An additional merit to the focus on medal matches was the fact that the medalists participated in the medal ceremony; thus, we had a chance to observe and measure their spontaneous behavior in two very different situations. Despite the fact that none of silver medalists had smiled when they lost their medal match, almost all (54 of 56) of the athletes who participated in the medal ceremonies smiled when they received their medal. When the specific type of smile was differentiated, however, differences emerged according to place finish. Gold and bronze medalists (i.e., those who had won their last

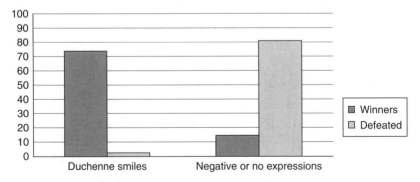

FIGURE 2.3: Proportion of athletes displaying different emotions at match completion. (From "Culture and emotional expression," *Problems and solutions in cross-cultural theory, research, and application,* by D. Matsumoto, 2009 by Taylor and Francis Group, LLC Books. Reproduced with permission of Taylor and Francis Group.)

match to take a medal) were much more likely to display Duchenne smiles, and especially uncontrolled Duchenne smiles,[1] than were the silver medalists (who lost their medal match). The silver medalists indeed did not display felt, enjoyable emotions as much as either the gold or bronze medalists (Fig. 2.4). Again, there were no cultural differences in these findings.

This study addressed a major limitation in the literature, demonstrating that spontaneous facial expressions of emotion are produced universally in naturalistic field settings when emotions are evoked. The expressions corresponded to those reported previously by Ekman (Ekman, 1972; Ekman & Friesen, 1971; Ekman et al., 1969; Ekman et al., 1972) and others, in Ekman and Friesen's (1975) *Unmasking the Face*, in their stimulus set *Pictures of Facial Affect* (Ekman & Friesen, 1976), and in Matsumoto and Ekman's (1988)

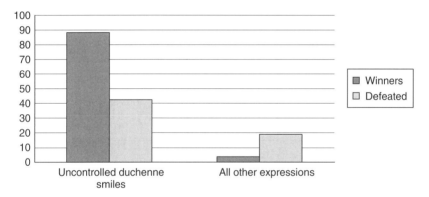

FIGURE 2.4: Proportion of athletes displaying different emotions during the medal ceremonies. (From "Culture and emotional expression," *Problems and solutions in cross-cultural theory, research, and application*, by D. Matsumoto, 2009 by Taylor and Francis Group, LLC Books. Reproduced with permission of Taylor and Francis Group.)

---

[1] Duchenne smiles are smiles that involve both the smiling muscle—zygomatic major—and the muscle surrounding the eye—orbicularis oculi. Non-Duchenne smiles do not involve the muscle around the eye. Duchenne smiles are associated with actual enjoyment or positive emotion, while non-Duchenne smiles are considered polite, social smiles (Frank & Ekman, 1993). Controlled smiles were those that co-occurred with buccinator (AU 14), sometimes in combination with mentalis and/or orbicularis oris (AUs 17 and 24). These lower face actions give the appearance that the expressor is making a conscious effort to control his or her facial behaviors and/or words, as though the expressor is "biting her [or his] lip." That they often occurred with both Duchenne and non-Duchenne smiles suggested that these facial actions qualified the meaning of the smile, adding information to the message of the smile beyond the signal of enjoyment.

Japanese and Caucasian Facial Expressions of Emotion (JACFEE) set. That there were no cultural differences in the first expressions at match completion was supportive of the universality of these expressions to occur when emotion is aroused. The expressions also clearly differentiated between victors and the defeated, indicating that emotions functioned in the same way across cultures. Finally, nearly all athletes spontaneously smiled during both periods of the medal ceremonies, probably due to the highly staged and public nature of the ceremonies. That this was true for the silver medalists, especially given the fact that *none* of them had smiled at match completion and nearly all had displayed a negative expression or no expression, demonstrates the powerful influence of social context on expressive behavior and the role of cultural display rules.

B. The Source of Universal Facial Expressions of Emotion

Universality in expression cannot inform us about the source of that universality. There are at least two such potential sources. One is culture constant learning, which would suggest that people all around the world learn to produce spontaneously the same facial configurations for the same emotions. The second is rooted in biology and evolution, and it suggests that the facial configurations for emotions are biologically innate and thus the same for everyone. One way to test which of these may be correct is to examine the spontaneous facial expressions of congenitally blind individuals. If congenitally blind individuals from different cultures produce the same facial configurations of emotion in the same emotionally evocative situations, this would be strong evidence for the biological basis of their source, because these individuals could not have possibly learned to produce these expressions through visual observation. Although there have been a number of studies that examined the expressions of the blind (Cole, Jenkins, & Shott, 1989; Dumas, 1932; Eibl-Eibesfeldt, 1973; Freedman, 1964; Fulcher, 1942; Galati, Miceli, & Sini, 2001; Galati, Sini, Schmidt, & Tinti, 2003; Goodenough, 1932; Thompson, 1941), unfortunately there was no study that directly compared the spontaneous facial configurations corresponding to emotion between blind and sighted individuals across cultures.

We addressed this gap by comparing the spontaneous facial expressions of blind judo athletes at the 2004 Athens Paralympic Games with the sighted athletes reported earlier (Matsumoto & Willingham, 2009). The athletes in this study came from 23 cultures, and the study was conducted in exactly the same manner as the study of sighted athletes reported earlier. The findings indicated near-perfect concordance between the blind and sighted. For example, correlations between the blind and sighted athletes individual FACS codes were $r(32) = .94$, $p < .01$; $r(32) = .98$, $p < .01$; and $r(32) = .96$, $p < .01$, for match completion, receiving medal, and on the podium, respectively. Moreover, the expressions of the blind athletes functioned in exactly the same ways as the sighted athletes. For example, winners displayed all types of smiles, especially Duchenne smiles, more frequently than the defeated athletes, who displayed more disgust, sadness, and combined negative emotions (Fig. 2.5). When receiving the medal, winners (gold and bronze) displayed all types of smiles and Duchenne smiles more frequently than did the defeated (silver medalists), who displayed more non-Duchenne smiles (Fig. 2.6). Thus, not only were the expressions comparable but similar types of expressions occurred at similar times and in reaction to similar events; thus, expressions functioned the same way for the blind individuals. (See Fig. 2.7 for example and comparisons.) These findings provided strong support for the notion that blind individuals produce exactly the same facial expressions of emotion as sighted individuals when emotions are spontaneously aroused. We believe that there is a biologically based emotion-expression linkage that is universal to all people of all cultures.

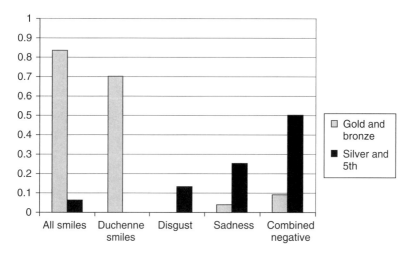

Figure 2.5: Proportion of occurrence of specific facial expressions at match completion. (From "Culture and emotional expression," *Problems and solutions in cross-cultural theory, research, and application*, by D. Matsumoto, 2009 by Taylor and Francis Group, LLC Books. Reproduced with permission of Taylor and Francis Group.)

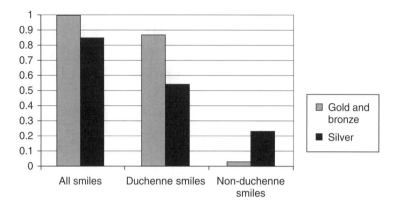

FIGURE 2.6: Proportion of occurrence of specific facial expressions when receiving medal. (From "Culture and emotional expression," *Problems and solutions in cross-cultural theory, research, and application,* by D. Matsumoto, 2009 by Taylor and Francis Group, LLC Books. Reproduced with permission of Taylor and Francis Group.)

FIGURE 2.7: Comparison of blind and sighted athletes who just lost a match for a medal. (Photographs courtesy of Bob Willingham.)

C. Cultural Display Rules

1. Early Work

After the inception of the concept of display rules, early research focused on the development of display rule knowledge in children (Cole, 1985, 1986; Saarni, 1979, 1988). But despite the fact that the concept of display rules was born from cross-cultural research, it was ironic that no cross-cultural studies were conducted for almost two decades since their original inception and documentation. This was unfortunate, because they are important parts of any culture, and information about them is important for knowledge in this area to continue to grow.

Some early research from my laboratory addressed this void. In fact, in Friesen's (1972) original display rule study, display rules were never measured; actual facial responses were measured, and differences between the two cultures were interpreted as occurring because of assumed display rule differences between the two cultures. Thus, in the first cross-cultural study since Friesen's (1972), we attempted to measure display rules directly by showing Americans and Japanese two examples of six universal facial expressions of emotion and obtaining ratings of the appropriateness of displaying each in eight social contexts (Matsumoto, 1990). Americans rated some negative emotions in ingroups, and happiness in outgroups, as more appropriate than did the Japanese. The Japanese, however, rated some negative emotions as more appropriate to outgroup members. These findings were interpreted within an individualism versus collectivism framework, reckoning that members of collectivisitic cultures (e.g., Japan) would be discouraged from expressing potentially threatening negative emotions to their ingroups, and potentially bonding positive emotions to their outgroups, while there would be no such tendency for members of individualistic cultures (e.g., the United States). Using a similar methodology, we obtained the same ratings from Americans, Poles, and Hungarians, and from four ethnic groups in the United States (Matsumoto, 1993; Matsumoto & Hearn, unpublished data).

These studies were important because they were the first cross-cultural studies since Friesen's (1972) on the concept of display rules. They also extended those findings by obtaining display rule ratings across a range of emotions and contexts, and they tested a theory that postulated display rule differences according to culture and social context (Matsumoto, 1991). But we were not satisfied with the measurement of display rules, and thus we turned our attention to the development of a more comprehensive and appropriate measure.

2. The Display Rule Assessment Inventory and Initial Research

We created the Display Rule Assessment Inventory (DRAI), in which participants choose a behavioral response when they experience different emotions in different social situations. The emotions were seven that previous research had shown to be universally expressed and recognized (Ekman, 1992b, 1993, 1999; Izard, 1992; Matsumoto, 2001)—anger, contempt, disgust, fear, happiness, sadness, and surprise—because universality served as a basis by which to examine display rules initially and by which comparisons across cultures would be meaningful. To build internal consistency, a synonym for each emotion label was also included—hostility, defiance, aversion, worry, joy, gloomy, and shock, respectively—resulting in 14 emotion terms. Participants were asked to consider what they would do if they felt each emotion in four social situations that were chosen because they represent a broad range of social categories with which people interact, and because previous research has demonstrated considerable variability in cultural values and attitudes across these social situations (Brewer & Kramer, 1985; Tajfel, 1982; Triandis, 1994). Participants were asked to complete the measure for two rating domains, once responding as to what they believe people *should* do and a second time responding to what *they actually* do. And, for each emotion, social situation, and domain, participants selected a response from a list of possible behavioral responses based on Ekman and Friesen's (1969, 1975) theoretical delineations of the possible ways in which expressions are modified and included the following:

1. Express the feeling as is with no inhibitions (Express)
2. Express the feeling, but with less intensity than one's true feelings (Deamplify)
3. Express the feeling, but with more intensity than one's true feelings (Amplify)
4. Try to remain neutral; express nothing (Neutralize)
5. Express the feeling, but together with a smile to qualify one's feelings (Qualify)
6. Smile only, with no trace of anything else, to hide one's true feelings (Mask)
7. Some other response (Other)

We used the DRAI and an individual-level measure of individualism-collectivism in a study examining cultural differences across the United States, Japan, South Korea, and Russia (Matsumoto et al., 1998). Russians exerted the highest control over their expressions, followed by South Koreans and Japanese; Americans had the lowest scores. These cultural differences were found across all rating domains, emotions, and social situations, as well as within both rating domains and each of the four social situations. Significant sex differences were also found, with females exerting more control on anger, contempt, disgust, and with family members, and males exerting more control on fear and surprise (Matsumoto et al., 1998).

The DRAI has also been used in a study examining the relationship between display rules and judgments of emotions (Matsumoto, Choi, et al., 2008). American and Japanese participants completed it and viewed a series of facial expressions of emotion portrayed at high and low intensities. They made three judgments for each face: a categorical judgment of which emotion was portrayed, and intensity ratings of the strength of the external display and the presumed subjective experience of the expressor. Cultural differences in the judgments were found, replicating findings reported earlier in this chapter. These differences were mediated by display rules assessed by the DRAI, suggesting that one's own rules for expression management influence one's judgments of expression management in others.

Considering the eventual need for a large, multinational study on cultural display rules, we then sought to establish further the psychometric properties of the DRAI and conducted two studies that did so (Matsumoto, Yoo, Hirayama, & Petrova, 2005). Because the structure of the DRAI allowed for multiple potential scoring procedures, the first study demonstrated the independence of the various response alternatives and established a scoring procedure. The second study documented the convergent and predictive validity of the DRAI by examining its correlations with two scales measuring emotion regulation and the Big Five personality traits. Internal and temporal reliabilities were also established. These findings allowed us to proceed confidently with a longtime goal of ours: a worldwide mapping of cultural display rules.

3. A Worldwide Mapping of Cultural Display Rules

Working with many collaborators, we (Matsumoto, Yoo, Fontaine, et al., 2008) administered the DRAI in over 30 countries, examining universal and culture-specific aspects to display rules, and linking the cultural differences to culture-level individualism-collectivism. Despite the larger potential range of scores, most countries' means on overall expression endorsement fell around the midpoint, and there was relatively small variation around this mean, suggesting a universal norm for expression regulation. And individuals of all cultures endorsed expressions toward ingroups more than toward outgroups, indicating another universal effect. Collectivistic cultures were associated with a display rule norm of less expressivity overall than individualistic cultures, suggesting that overall expressive regulation for all emotions is central to the preservation of social order in these cultures (Fig. 2.8). This finding is commensurate with the behavioral findings from both Friesen's (1972) original

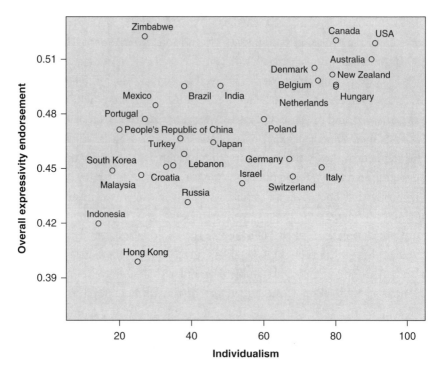

FIGURE 2.8: Graphical representation of the relationship between individualism and overall expressivity endorsement.

display rule study and Matsumoto and Kupperbusch's (2001) study (described later). Individualism was also positively associated with higher expressivity norms in general, and for positive emotions in particular. And it was positively associated with endorsement of expressions of all emotions toward ingroups, but negatively correlated with all negative emotions and positively correlated with happiness and surprise toward outgroups. Cumulatively, these findings suggest a fairly nuanced view of the relationship between culture and expression endorsement that varies as a function of emotion, interactant, and overall expressivity endorsement levels.

A secondary analysis of the DRAI data set allowed us to compute indices of variability according to context. We examined the relationships between these indices to Hofstede's (2001) and Schwartz's (2006) value dimensions. The findings indicated that context variability was positively correlated with Power Distance, Embeddedness, Hierarchy, and Mastery, and negatively with Individualism, Affective Autonomy, Egalitarianism, and Intellectual Autonomy (Matsumoto, Yoo, Fontaine, & Members of the Multinational Study of Cultural

Display Rules, 2009). Based on these findings, we coined the term *context differentiation* as a potential, stable dimension of variability, on both the cultural and individual levels.

D. The Search for Active Cultural Ingredients that Produce Cultural Differences in Expression and Display Rules

1. Individual-Level Culture and Emotional Expression

Despite the fact that the field got its start from a cross-cultural comparison (Friesen, 1972), studies comparing the spontaneous emotional expressions of people of different cultures were nonexistent. Matsumoto and Kupperbusch (2001) addressed this gap in the literature by unobtrusively videotaping individualistic and collectivistic participants as they watched films that elicited positive and negative emotion, first alone and then in the presence of an experimenter. Participants also rated their emotional responses. These procedures allowed us not only to replicate the original Friesen (1972) study but to extend it by including positive emotions, thus shoring up a major methodological limitation because his study did not include self-reports of emotion.

All participants experienced the films as intended, and there was no difference in their expressions when they viewed the stimuli alone. In the presence of the experimenter, however, the collectivists attenuated their negative expressions and more often masked them with smiles, replicating Friesen (1972). But the collectivists also attenuated their expressions of *positive* emotion in the presence of the experimenter; thus, the effects of culture on expression were not limited to negative emotions. Correlations between expressions and experience for all participants when viewing positive and negative films alone indicated coherence between them. Correlations from the second part of the experiment, however, were different. For individualists in both conditions and for collectivists in the control condition, expression and experience were coherent. But when collectivists were in the presence of the experimenter, coherence vanished. Thus, the collectivists still felt strong emotions, even though they did not show them in the presence of the experimenter, indicating a decoupling of the linkage between expression and experience.

This study, therefore, showed that the differences in emotional expressivity were indeed due to individualism-collectivism. The differences were found not only for negative emotions but also for positive emotions, suggesting cultural effects on overall expressivity. This latter finding is commensurate with research described earlier on the relationship between individualism-collectivism and cultural display rules. And the findings gave important clues about the nature of decoupling of the emotion system depending on culture and context, a topic that is important in the psychology of emotion regulation today (Matsumoto, Yoo, Nakagawa, et al., 2008; Mauss, Levenson, McCarter, Wilhelm, & Gross, 2005).

2. Possible Active Cultural Ingredients That Influence Cultural Display Rules

The work described earlier clearly demonstrated that cultural dimensions such as individualism-collectivism or context differentiation are related to cultural differences in display rules at a fairly high level of abstraction. Some of our more recent research has examined potential active ingredients that are more proximal to the ratings. For example, Koopmann-Holm and Matsumoto (in press) compared American and German display rules using the DRAI and also measured individual-level values using the Schwartz Value Scale. Americans valued Conservation and Self-Enhancement more than did Germans, who valued Openness to Change and Self-Transcendence more than did Americans. These differences were associated with differences in display rules; Americans endorsed contempt and disgust expressions more than did Germans, who endorsed anger and sadness expressions more than did Americans. Values mediated ("unpackaged") many of these country differences in display rules, indicating that cultural differences on display rules may be driven at least partially by individual-level values.

Searching for other potential cultural mediators, Chung and Matsumoto (unpublished data) examined the possibility that cultural differences in display rules were mediated by socially desirable responding (SDR), which is the tendency to present oneself in an overly favorable manner (Paulhus, 2002). Since its conception, SDR has been examined as a methodological artifact, a personal style, and evidence of measurement validity. Interestingly, some have suggested lately that response styles such as SDR should be considered part of an individual's cultural communication style; as such it should be related to cultural display rules (Lalwani, Shrum, & Chiu, 2009). Chung and Matsumoto (unpublished data) administered both the DRAI and the Balanced Inventory of Desirable Responding (Paulhus, 2002) to American and Japanese participants. Americans endorsed the expression of anger, contempt, disgust, fear, happiness, surprise, and overall emotion more than the Japanese; the Japanese endorsed the modification of fear and sadness more than the Americans.

Americans exhibited more self-deceptive enhancement (SDE) than the Japanese, and SDE partially mediated country differences on the endorsement of anger, disgust, happiness, and surprise, and on modification of sadness. This study broadens the display rule literature by examining the contribution of SDR as an individual difference factor to country differences in display rules.

E. Temporal Dynamics of Culturally Calibrated Emotional Expressions

Although it is known that facial expressions of emotion are both universal and culture specific, the consensus in the field is that when emotions are aroused, the displays are either universal *or* culture specific, depending on context. In our latest work, we investigated the idea that emotional displays can be both for the same person in the same context, if displays are examined *in sequence across time*. This possibility exists especially when intense emotions are aroused in a context that dictates individuals regulate their emotional behaviors, and because of the dual neural control of expressive displays. When emotions are aroused, impulses emanating from subcortical areas of the brain initiate the emotion response system, including expressive behavior (LeDoux, 2000; Panksepp, 2008). At the same time, the facial nerve receives stimulation from cortical areas under voluntary control (Matsumoto & Lee, 1993; Rinn, 1991), which would be associated with display rules (Ekman & Friesen, 1969). Thus, when intense emotions are aroused in a social context, the *initial and immediate* emotional responses may be universal (originating from the subcortex) and may appear first because their neural connections are lower and closer to the facial nerve. Culturally influenced emotional displays may occur subsequently because of the additional neural work necessary for regulatory needs to drive expressive behavior from the cortex.

To demonstrate this possibility, we went back to the study of Olympic athletes (Matsumoto, Willingham, & Olide, 2009). Recall that the previous study demonstrated that their first, immediate facial reactions upon match completion were universal (Matsumoto & Willingham, 2006). The subsequent expressions, however, were not analyzed. In this study, changes in the Olympic athletes' expressions after their initial reactions were examined and classified into one of several regulation strategies. We then examined the relationship between these expressive styles and cultural variables with Hofstede's (2001) cultural dimensions, and country demographics such as population density and affluence. Findings indicated that although the athletes' initial reactions were universal, their subsequent expressions were culturally regulated and reliably associated with population density, affluence, and individualism. Athletes from urban, individualistic cultures expressed their emotions more; athletes from less urban, more collectivistic cultures masked their emotions more.

These findings demonstrated that emotional expressions can be both universal and culture specific in the same individuals in the same context, provided that expressions are examined across time. They also indicated that expressive styles involving greater modification of the original initial reaction required more time for display than expressive styles involving relatively less modification, likely because the former recruit greater neurocognitive resources. Expressive modes that allow for the continued expression of the initial emotion or only slight modifications of its intensity (deamplification) require less such modification, and thus result in shorter elapsed times from initial response. Because Individualism-Collectivism was associated with expressive styles, it is no wonder that it was also correlated with elapsed time.

The fact that expressions change across time and are more culturally variable subsequent to an initial, immediate, universal emotional reaction explains why beliefs about the pervasiveness of cultural differences in expression exist. When intense emotions are aroused, attention is often drawn to the stimulus event and *not* the expressive behaviors of the individuals in that event. While attention is given to the eliciting event, immediate universal reactions occur but are missed. When attention returns to the individuals, they are already beginning to engage in culturally regulated behavior. Such a process may perpetuate beliefs about the cultural variability of expressive behavior. Because we tend to believe our experiences, it is easier to believe the existence of cultural differences in expressive behavior.

VI. CONCLUSION

We hope that the broad research program we have described in this chapter gives readers a sense of how we have approached our work for the past 30 years, and how the findings from that program have informed a cultural calibration theory of emotional expression and perception. In the future, we hope to expand this line of research into new areas of inquiry. To be sure, given the broad range of topics in which we are interested, it is difficult to predict with any certainty exactly what kinds of research we will be engaging in over the next few years. Nonetheless, we close this chapter by describing four potential areas of study we believe are important, and what we will likely be pursuing.

1. *The genetic bases of facial expressions of emotion*. The universality of facial expressions of emotion and their biological innateness lead naturally to questions concerning their exact location. Fortunately, research technologies in the area of family and genetics have advanced to the point where it may be possible in the future to isolate specific genetic correlates of the universal facial expressions of emotion, and we see our laboratory contributing to such efforts.

2. *Variations on the prototypic full-face facial expressions of emotion*. The vast bulk of the research on facial expressions of emotion have centered on full-face, prototypic expressions of emotion. Yet in real life these probably occur relatively infrequently, and what is relatively more frequent are more subtle expressions of emotion that involve either the full-face configurations at less intensity or components of the full-face configurations (i.e., partial expressions). There is very limited knowledge of these subtle and partial expressions, especially across cultures. Our hunch is that they differ depending on their method of elicitation, meaning, and subsequent instrumental behaviors. We envision future work aiding in the creation of elaborate dictionaries of facial emotions that flesh out these potentials.

3. *New expressions*. The universal facial expressions of emotion that have been studied until now are special because they convey emotional meaning in a single portrayal of the face; thus, they have snapshot capabilities, which have interesting implications to their importance in our evolutionary history. We do believe that other universal expressions of emotion do exist; they just likely do not exist in snapshot facial expressions. Instead, they are likely to involve combinations of face and other nonverbal channels such as gesture and voice. And there is the interesting possibility that multiple individual snapshots of an expressive state may collectively have universal meaning. We are excited to explore such possibilities in the future.

4. *Implications of training individuals to read facial expressions of emotion*. Finally, we are very interested in translating the scientific knowledge generated in this area of study into practical

and useful applications that can be used to improve people's lives around the world. Improving the ability to read facial expressions has the potential for providing nonpharmacological treatment interventions for millions of people afflicted with various disorders that impair social relations, such as schizophrenia or autism. And improving this ability can be useful for those involved in law enforcement, national intelligence and security, as well as to physicians and health-care providers, negotiators, and parents. So much of our everyday lives is based on reading others correctly, and we anticipate taking the knowledge base in this field to make a strong contribution here as well.

REFERENCES

Benet-Martinez, V., Lee, F., & Leu, J. (2006). Biculturalism and cognitive complexity: Expertise in cultural representations. *Journal of Cross-Cultural Psychology*, *37*(4), 386–407.

Benet-Martinez, V., Leu, J., Lee, F., & Morris, M. (2002). Negotiating biculturalism: Cultural frame-switching in biculturals with "oppositional" vs. "compatible" cultural identities. *Journal of Cross-Cultural Psychology*, *33*, 492–516.

Biehl, M., Matsumoto, D., Ekman, P., Hearn, V., Heider, K., Kudoh, T., et al. (1997). Matsumoto and Ekman's Japanese and Caucasian Facial Expressions of Emotion (JACFEE): Reliability data and cross-national differences. *Journal of Nonverbal Behavior*, *21*, 3–21.

Bond, M. H., & Tedeschi, J. (2001). Polishing the jade: A modest proposal for improving the study of social psychology across cultures. In D. Matsumoto (Ed.), *The handbook of culture and psychology* (pp. 309–324). New York: Oxford University Press.

Brewer, M. B., & Kramer, R. M. (1985). The psychology of intergroup attitudes and behavior. *Annual Review of Psychology*, *36*, 219–243.

Bruner, J. S., & Tagiuri, R. (1954). The perception of people. In G. Lindzey (Ed.), *Handbook of social psychology* (Vol. 2, pp. 634–654). Cambridge, MA: Addison-Wesley.

Chiu, C-Y., Morris, M. W., Hong, Y-Y., & Menon, T. (2000). Motivated cultural cognition: The impact of implicit cultural theories on dispositional attribution varies as a function of need for closure. *Journal of Personality*, *78*(2), 247–259.

Cole, P. M. (1985). Display rules and the socialization of affective displays. In G. Zivin (Ed.), *The development of expressive behavior* (pp. 269–290). New York: Academic Press.

Cole, P. M. (1986). Children's spontaneous control of facial expression. *Child Development*, *57*, 1309–1321.

Cole, P. M., Jenkins, P. A., & Shott, C. T. (1989). Spontaneous expressive control in blind and sighted children. *Child Development*, *60*(3), 683–688.

Darwin, C. (1872). *The expression of emotion in man and animals*. New York: Oxford University Press.

Dumas, F. (1932). La mimique des aveugles [Facial expression of the blind]. *Bulletin de l'Academie de Medecine*, *107*, 607–610.

Eibl-Eibesfeldt, I. (1973). The expressive behavior of the deaf-and-blind born. In M. von Cranach & I. Vine (Eds.), *Social communication and movement* (pp. 163–194). London: Academic Press.

Ekman, P. (1972). Universal and cultural differences in facial expression of emotion. In J. R. Cole (Ed.), *Nebraska Symposium on Motivation, 1971* (Vol. 19, pp. 207–283). Lincoln: Nebraska University Press.

Ekman, P. (1992). Facial expressions of emotion: New findings, new questions. *Psychological Science*, *3*(1), 34–38.

Ekman, P. (1993). Facial expression and emotion. *American Psychologist*, *48*(4), 384–392.

Ekman, P. (1994). Strong evidence for universals in facial expressions: A reply to Russell's mistaken critique. *Psychological Bulletin*, *115*, 268–287.

Ekman, P. (1999). Basic emotions. In T. Dalgleish & T. Power (Eds.), *The handbook of cognition and emotion* (pp. 45–60). Sussex, United Kingdom: John Wiley and Sons, Ltd.

Ekman, P. (2003). *Emotions revealed* (2nd ed.). New York: Times Books.

Ekman, P., Davidson, R. J., & Friesen, W. V. (1990). The Duchenne smile: Emotional expression and brain physiology: II. *Journal of Personality and Social Psychology*, *58*(2), 342–353.

Ekman, P., & Friesen, W. V. (1969). The repertoire of nonverbal behavior: Categories, origins, usage, and coding. *Semiotica*, *1*, 49–98.

Ekman, P., & Friesen, W. V. (1971). Constants across culture in the face and emotion. *Journal of Personality and Social Psychology*, *17*, 124–129.

Ekman, P., & Friesen, W. V. (1975). *Unmasking the face: A guide to recognizing emotions from facial clues*. Englewood Cliffs, NJ: Prentice-Hall.

Ekman, P., & Friesen, W. V. (1976). *Pictures of facial affect*. Palo Alto, CA: Consulting Psychologists Press.

Ekman, P., & Friesen, W. V. (1978). *Facial action coding system: Investigator's guide*. Palo Alto, CA: Consulting Psychologists Press.

Ekman, P., & Friesen, W. V. (1986). A new pan-cultural facial expression of emotion. *Motivation and Emotion*, *10*(2), 159–168.

Ekman, P., Friesen, W. V., & Ancoli, S. (1980). Facial signs of emotional experience. *Journal of Personality and Social Psychology*, *39*, 1125–1134.

Ekman, P., Friesen, W. V., & Ellsworth, P. (1972). *Emotion in the human face: Guidelines for research and an integration of findings*. New York: Pergamon Press.

Ekman, P., Friesen, W. V., & O'Sullivan, M. (1988). Smiles when lying. *Journal of Personality and Social Psychology*, *54*(3), 414–420.

Ekman, P., Friesen, W. V., O'Sullivan, M., Chan, A., Diacoyanni-Tarlatzis, I., Heider, K., et al. (1987). Universals and cultural differences in the judgments of facial expressions of emotion. *Journal of Personality and Social Psychology, 53*(4), 712–717.

Ekman, P., & Heider, K. G. (1988). The universality of a contempt expression: A replication. *Motivation and Emotion, 12*(3), 303–308.

Ekman, P., Levenson, R. W., & Friesen, W. V. (1983). Autonomic nervous system activity distinguishes among emotions. *Science, 221*(4616), 1208–1210.

Ekman, P., & Matsumoto, D. (2007). Microexpression Training Tool (METT), v2. On CD. http://www.humintell.com

Ekman, P., Matsumoto, D., & Frank, M. G. (2003). Microexpression Training Tool, v1. On CD. Oakland, CA.

Ekman, P., & O'Sullivan, M. (1988). The role of context in interpreting facial expression: Comment on Russell and Fehr (1987). *Journal of Experimental Psychology: General, 117*(1), 86–88.

Ekman, P., O'Sullivan, M., & Matsumoto, D. (1991a). Confusions about context in the judgment of facial expression: A reply to "The contempt expression and the relativity thesis." *Motivation and Emotion, 15*(2), 169–176.

Ekman, P., O'Sullivan, M., & Matsumoto, D. (1991b). Contradictions in the study of contempt: What's it all about? Reply to Russell. *Motivation and Emotion, 15*(4), 293–296.

Ekman, P., Sorenson, E. R., & Friesen, W. V. (1969). Pancultural elements in facial displays of emotion. *Science, 164*(3875), 86–88.

Elfenbein, H. A., & Ambady, N. (2002). On the universality and cultural specificity of emotion recognition: A meta-analysis. *Psychological Bulletin, 128*(2), 205–235.

Elfenbein, H. A., Beaupre', M. G., Levesque, M., & Hess, U. (2007). Toward a dialect theory: Cultural differences in the expression and recognition of posed facial expressions. *Emotion, 7*(1), 131–146.

Elfenbein, H. A., Mandal, M. K., Ambady, N., & Harizuka, S. (2002). Cross-cultural patterns in emotion recognition: Highlighting design and analytic techniques. *Emotion, 2*(1), 75–84.

Feldman Barrett, L. (2006a). Are emotions natural kinds? *Perspectives on Psychological Science, 1*(1), 28–58.

Feldman Barrett, L. (2006b). Solving the emotion paradox: Categorization and the experience of emotion. *Personality and Social Psychology Review, 10*, 20–46.

Fernandez-Dols, J. M., & Ruiz-Belda, M. A. (1997). Spontaneous facial behavior during intense emotional episodes: Artistic truth and optical truth. In J. A. Russell & J. M. Fernandez-Dols (Eds.), *The psychology of facial expression* (pp. 255–274). New York: Cambridge University Press.

Fernberger, S. W. (1928). False suggestions and the Piderit model. *American Journal of Psychology, 40*, 562–568.

Freedman, D. G. (1964). Smiling in blind infants and the issue of innate versus acquired. *Journal of Child Psychology and Psychiatry*, 5, 171–184.

Friesen, W. V. (1972). *Cultural differences in facial expressions in a social situation: An experimental test of the concept of display rules*. Unpublished PhD dissertation, University of California, San Francisco.

Frijda, N. H. (1969). Recognition of emotion. In L. Berkowitz (Ed.), *Advances in experimental social psychology* (Vol. 4, pp. 167–224). New York: Academic Press.

Fulcher, J. S. (1942). "Voluntary" facial expression in blind and seeing children. *Archives of Psychology*, 272, 5–49.

Galati, D., Miceli, R., & Sini, B. (2001). Judging and coding facial expression of emotions in congenitally blind children. *International Journal of Behavioral Development*, 25(3), 268–278.

Galati, D., Sini, B., Schmidt, S., & Tinti, C. (2003). Spontaneous facial expressions in congenitally blind and sighted children aged 8–11. *Journal of Visual Impairment and Blindness*, July, 418–428.

Goldberg, H. D. (1951). The role of "cutting" in the perception of the motion picture. *Journal of Applied Psychology*, 35, 70–71.

Goodenough, F. L. (1932). Expression of emotions in a blind-deaf child. *Journal of Abnormal and Social Psychology*, 27, 328–333.

Hofstede, G. H. (1980). *Culture's consequences: International differences in work-related values*. Beverly Hills, CA: Sage Publications.

Hofstede, G. H. (2001). *Culture's consequences: Comparing values, behaviors, institutions and organizations across nations* (2nd ed.). Thousand Oaks, CA: Sage Publications.

Hong, Y-Y., Benet-Martinez, V., Chiu, C-Y., & Morris, M. W. (2003). Boundaries of cultural influence: Construct activation as a mechanism for cultural differences in social perception. *Journal of Cross-Cultural Psychology*, 34(4), 453–464.

Hong, Y-Y., Morris, M., Chiu, C-Y., & Benet-Martinez, V. (2000). Multicultural minds: A dynamic constructivist approach to culture and cognition. *American Psychologist*, 55, 709–720.

Izard, C. E. (1971). *The face of emotion*. East Norwalk, CT: Appleton-Century-Crofts.

Izard, C. E. (1983). *The Maximally Discriminative Facial Movement Coding System*. Newark: Instructional Resources Center, University of Delaware.

Izard, C. E. (1994). Innate and universal facial expressions: Evidence from developmental and cross-cultural research. *Psychological Bulletin*, 115, 288–299.

Izard, C. E., & Haynes, O. M. (1988). On the form and universality of the contempt expression: A challenge to Ekman and Friesen's claim of discovery. *Motivation and Emotion*, 12, 1–16.

Izard, C. E. (1992). Basic emotions, relations among emotions, and emotion–cognition relations. *Psychological Review*, 99(3), 561–565.

Keltner, D., & Haidt, J. (1999). Social functions of emotion at four levels of analysis. *Cognition and Emotion, 13*(5), 505–521.

Knudsen, H. R., & Muzekari, L. H. (1983). The effects of verbal statements of context on facial expressions of emotion. *Journal of Nonverbal Behavior, 7*(4), 202–212.

Koopmann-Holm, B., & Matsumoto, D. (in press). Values and display rules for specific emotions. *Journal of Cross-Cultural Psychology.*

Lalwani, A. K., Shrum, L. J., & Chiu, C-Y. (2009). Motivated response style: The role of cultural values, regulatory focus, and self-consciousness in socially desirable responding. *Journal of Personality and Social Psychology, 96*, 870–882.

LeDoux, J. E. (2000). Emotion circuits in the brain. *Annual Review of Neuroscience, 23*, 155–184.

Levenson, R. W. (1999). The intrapersonal functions of emotion. *Cognition and Emotion, 13*(5), 481–504.

Levenson, R. W., Ekman, P., Heider, K., & Friesen, W. V. (1992). Emotion and autonomic nervous system activity in the Minangkabau of West Sumatra. *Journal of Personality and Social Psychology, 62*(6), 972–988.

Matsumoto, D. (1987). The role of facial response in the experience of emotion: More methodological problems and a meta-analysis. *Journal of Personality and Social Psychology, 52*(4), 769–774.

Matsumoto, D. (1989). Cultural influences on the perception of emotion. *Journal of Cross-Cultural Psychology, 20*(1), 92–105.

Matsumoto, D. (1990). Cultural similarities and differences in display rules. *Motivation and Emotion, 14*(3), 195–214.

Matsumoto, D. (1991). Cultural influences on facial expressions of emotion. *Southern Communication Journal, 56*, 128–137.

Matsumoto, D. (1992a). American-Japanese cultural differences in the recognition of universal facial expressions. *Journal of Cross-Cultural Psychology, 23*(1), 72–84.

Matsumoto, D. (1992b). More evidence for the universality of a contempt expression. *Motivation and Emotion, 16*(4), 363–368.

Matsumoto, D. (1993). Ethnic differences in affect intensity, emotion judgments, display rule attitudes, and self-reported emotional expression in an American sample. *Motivation and Emotion, 17*(2), 107–123.

Matsumoto, D. (2001). Culture and Emotion. In D. Matsumoto (Ed.), *The Handbook of Culture and Psychology* (pp. 171–194). New York: Oxford University Press.

Matsumoto, D. (2006). Are cultural differences in emotion regulation mediated by personality traits? *Journal of Cross-Cultural Psychology, 37*(4), 421–437.

Matsumoto, D., & Assar, M. (1992). The effects of language on judgments of universal facial expressions of emotion. *Journal of Nonverbal Behavior, 16*(2), 85–99.

Matsumoto, D., Consolacion, T., Yamada, H., Suzuki, R., Franklin, B., Paul, S., et al. (2002). American-Japanese cultural differences in judgments of emotional expressions of different intensities. *Cognition and Emotion*, *16*(6), 721–747.

Matsumoto, D., & Ekman, P. (1988). Japanese and Caucasian Facial Expressions of Emotion and Neutral Faces (JACFEE and JACNeuF). http://www.humintell.com

Matsumoto, D., & Ekman, P. (1989). American-Japanese cultural differences in intensity ratings of facial expressions of emotion. *Motivation and Emotion*, *13*(2), 143–157.

Matsumoto, D., & Ekman, P. (2004). The relationship between expressions, labels, and descriptions of contempt. *Journal of Personality and Social Psychology*, *87*(4), 529–540.

Matsumoto, D., Ekman, P., & Fridlund, A. (1991). Analyzing nonverbal behavior. In P. W. Dowrick (Ed.), *Practical guide to using video in the behavioral sciences* (pp. 153–165). New York: John Wiley & Sons.

Matsumoto, D., & Hwang, H.-S. (2010). Judging faces in context. *Social and Personality Psychology Compass, 3*, 1–10.

Matsumoto, D., Hwang, H.-S., & Yamada, H. (in press). Cultural Differences in the Relative Contributions of Face and Context to Judgments of Emotion. *Journal of Cross-Cultural Psychology*.

Matsumoto, D., & Juang, L. (2007). *Culture and psychology* (4th ed.). Belmont, CA: Wadsworth.

Matsumoto, D., Kasri, F., & Kooken, K. (1999). American-Japanese cultural differences in judgments of expression intensity and subjective experience. *Cognition and Emotion*, *13*, 201–218.

Matsumoto, D., Keltner, D., Shiota, M. N., Frank, M. G., & O'Sullivan, M. (2008). What's in a face? Facial expressions as signals of discrete emotions. In M. Lewis, J. M. Haviland & L. Feldman Barrett (Eds.), *Handbook of Emotions* (pp. 211–234). New York: Guilford Press.

Matsumoto, D., & Kudoh, T. (1993). American-Japanese cultural differences in attributions of personality based on smiles. *Journal of Nonverbal Behavior*, *17*, 231–243.

Matsumoto, D., & Kupperbusch, C. (2001). Idiocentric and allocentric differences in emotional expression and experience. *Asian Journal of Social Psychology*, *4*, 113–131.

Matsumoto, D., & Lee, M. (1993). Consciousness, volition, and the neuropsychology of facial expressions of emotion. *Consciousness and Cognition: an International Journal*, *2*(3), 237–254.

Matsumoto, D., LeRoux, J. A., Iwamoto, M., Choi, J. W., Rogers, D., Tatani, H., et al. (2003). The robustness of the Intercultural Adjustment Potential Scale (ICAPS). *International Journal of Intercultural Relations*, *27*, 543–562.

Matsumoto, D., LeRoux, J. A., Wilson-Cohn, C., Raroque, J., Kooken, K., Ekman, P., et al. (2000). A new test to measure emotion recognition ability: Matsumoto and Ekman's Japanese and Caucasian Brief Affect Recognition Test (JACBART). *Journal of Nonverbal Behavior, 24*(3), 179–209.

Matsumoto, D., Olide, A., Schug, J., Willingham, B., & Callan, M. (in press). Cross-Cultural Judgments of Spontaneous Facial Expressions of Emotion. *Journal of Nonverbal Behavior, 33*, 213–238.

Matsumoto, D., Olide, A., & Willingham, B. (2009). Is there an ingroup advantage in recognizing spontaneously expressed emotions? *Journal of Nonverbal Behavior, 33*, 181–191.

Matsumoto, D., Takeuchi, S., Andayani, S., Kouznetsova, N., & Krupp, D. (1998). The contribution of individualism-collectivism to cross-national differences in display rules. *Asian Journal of Social Psychology, 1*, 147–165.

Matsumoto, D., & Willingham, B. (2006). The thrill of victory and the agony of defeat: Spontaneous expressions of medal winners at the 2004 Athens Olympic Games. *Journal of Personality and Social Psychology, 91*(3), 568–581.

Matsumoto, D., & Willingham, B. (2009). Spontaneous facial expressions of emotion of congenitally and non-congenitally blind individuals. *Journal of Personality and Social Psychology, 96*(1), 1–10.

Matsumoto, D., Willingham, B., & Olide, A. (2009). Sequential dynamics of culturally-moderated facial expressions of emotion. *Psychological Science, 20*(10), 1269–1274.

Matsumoto, D., & Yoo, S. H. (2006). Toward a new generation of cross-cultural research. *Perspectives on Psychological Science, 1*(3), 234–250.

Matsumoto, D., Yoo, S. H., Fontaine, J. R. J., Anguas-Wong, A. M., Arriola, M., Ataca, B., et al. (2008). Mapping expressive differences around the world: The relationship between emotional display rules and individualism v. collectivism. *Journal of Cross-Cultural Psychology, 39*(1), 55–74.

Matsumoto, D., Yoo, S. H., Fontaine, J. R. J., & Members of the Multinational Study of Cultural Display Rules. (2009). Hypocrisy or maturity: Culture and context differentiation. *European Journal of Personality, 23*, 251–264.

Matsumoto, D., Yoo, S. H., Hirayama, S., & Petrova, G. (2005). Validation of an individual-level measure of display rules: The Display Rule Assessment Inventory (DRAI). *Emotion, 5*(1), 23–40.

Matsumoto, D., Yoo, S. H., Nakagawa, S., Alexandre, J., Altarriba, J., Anguas-Wong, A. M., et al. (2008). Culture, emotion regulation, and adjustment. *Journal of Personality and Social Psychology, 94*(6), 925–937.

Mauss, I. B., Levenson, R. W., McCarter, L., Wilhelm, F. L., & Gross, J. J. (2005). The tie that binds? Coherence among emotion experience, behavior, and physiology. *Emotion, 5*(2), 175–190.

Nakamura, M., Buck, R. W., & Kenny, D. A. (1990). Relative contributions of expressive behavior and contextual information to the judgment of the emotional state of another. *Journal of Personality and Social Psychology*, *59*(5), 1032–1039.

Oyserman, D., & Lee, S. W.-S. (2008). Does culture influence what and how we think? Effects of priming individualism and collectivism. *Psychological Bulletin*, *134*(2), 311–342.

Panksepp, J. (2008). The affective brain and core consciousness: How does neural activity generate emotional feelings? In M. Lewis, J. M. Haviland-Jones, & L. Feldman Barrett (Eds.), *Handbook of emotions* (3rd ed., pp. 47–67). New York: The Guilford Press.

Paulhus, D. L. (2002). Socially desirable responding: The evolution of a construct. In H. I. Braun, D. N. Jackson, D. E. Wiley, & S. Messick (Eds.), *The role of constructs in psychological and educational measurement*. Mahwah, NJ: Erlbaum.

Poortinga, Y. H., van de Vijver, F. J. R., Joe, R. C., & van de Koppel, J. M. H. (1987). Peeling the onion called culture: A synopsis. In C. Kagitcibasi (Ed.), *Growth and progress in cross-cultural psychology* (pp. 22–34). Berwyn, PA: Swets North America.

Rinn, W. E. (1991). Neuropsychology of facial expression. In R. Feldman & B. Rime (Eds.), *Fundamentals of nonverbal behavior* (pp. 3–70). New York: Cambridge University Press.

Rosenberg, E. L., & Ekman, P. (1994). Coherence between expressive and experiential systems in emotion. *Cognition and Emotion*, *8*(3), 201–229.

Rosenberg, E. L., & Ekman, P. (1995). Conceptual and methodological issues in the judgment of facial expressions of emotion. *Motivation and Emotion*, *19*(2), 111–138.

Russell, J. A. (1991a). The contempt expression and the universality thesis. *Motivation and Emotion*, *15*, 149–168.

Russell, J. A. (1991b). Culture and the categorization of emotions. *Psychological Bulletin*, *110*, 426–450.

Russell, J. A. (1991c). Negative results on a reported facial expression of contempt. *Motivation and Emotion*, *15*, 281–291.

Russell, J. A. (1994). Is there universal recognition of emotion from facial expression? A review of cross-cultural studies. *Psychological Bulletin*, *115*, 102–141.

Russell, J. A. (1995). Facial expressions of emotion: What lies beyond minimal universality? *Psychological Bulletin*, *118*, 379–391.

Russell, J. A. (1997). Reading emotions from and into faces: Resurrecting a dimensional-contextual perspective. In J. A. Russell & J. M. Fernandez-Dols (Eds.), *The psychology of facial expression* (pp. 295–320). New York: Cambridge University Press.

Russell, J. A., & Fehr, B. (1987). Relativity in the perception of emotion in facial expressions. *Journal of Experimental Psychology: General*, *116*(3), 223–237.

Russell, T. A., Chu, E., & Phillips, M. L. (2006). A pilot study to investigate the effectiveness of emotion recognition mediation in schizophrenia using the

Micro-Expression Training Tool. *British Journal of Clinical Psychology*, 45, 579–583.

Russell, T. A., Green, M. J., Simpson, I., & Coltheart, M. (2008). Remediation of facial emotion perception in schizophrenia: Concomitant changes in visual attention. *Schizophrenia Research*, 103(1–3), 248–256.

Saarni, C. (1979). Children's understanding of display rules for expressive behavior. *Developmental Psychology*, 15(4), 424–429.

Saarni, C. (1988). Children's understanding of the interpersonal consequences of nonverbal emotional-expressive behavior. *Journal of Nonverbal Behavior*, 3–4, 275–295.

Schimmack, U. (1996). Cultural influences on the recognition of emotion by facial expressions: Individualist or Caucasian cultures? *Journal of Cross-Cultural Psychology*, 27, 37–50.

Schwartz, S. H. (2006). Value orientations: Measurement, antecedents, and consequences across nations. In R. Jowell, C. Roberts, R. Fitzgerald, & G. Eva (Eds.), *Measuring attitudes cross-nationally—Lessons from the European social survey* (pp. 161–193). Long Beach, CA: Sage.

Tajfel, H. (1982). Social psychology of intergroup relations. *Annual Review of Psychology*, 33, 1–39.

Thompson, J. (1941). Development of facial expression of emotion in blind and seeing children. *Archives of Psychology*, 37, 1–47.

Tomkins, S. S. (1962). *Affect, imagery, and consciousness: Vol. 1. The positive affects*. New York: Springer.

Tomkins, S. S. (1963). *Affect, imagery, and consciousness: Vol. 2. The negative affects*. New York: Springer.

Triandis, H. C. (1994). *Culture and social behavior*. New York: McGraw Hill.

Triandis, H. C. (1995). *New directions in social psychology: Individualism and collectivism*. Boulder, CO: Westview Press.

Van de Vijver, F. J. R., & Leung, K. (1997). *Methods and data analysis for cross-cultural research*. Newbury Park, CA: Sage.

Winton, W. M. (1986). The role of facial response in self-reports of emotion: A critique of Laird. *Journal of Personality and Social Psychology*, 50, 808–812.

Yrizarry, N., Matsumoto, D., & Wilson-Cohn, C. (1998). American-Japanese differences in multiscalar intensity ratings of universal facial expressions of emotion. *Motivation and Emotion*, 22(4), 315–327.

CHAPTER 3

Infectious Disease and the Creation of Culture

MARK SCHALLER
University of British Columbia

DAMIAN R. MURRAY
University of British Columbia

I. INTRODUCTION

The study of cultural psychology is a massive scientific enterprise. Cultural psychology is defined by two conceptually distinct bodies of scientific research, each of which explores a different set of causal connections between psychology and culture.

One body of research examines the influence of psychology on culture. That is, it addresses questions about exactly how psychological processes (defined at an individual level of analysis) exert causal consequences on cultural outcomes (measured at a collective level of analysis). There are many different investigations that, in one way or another, fit into this broad program of research. In doing so, they provide many different insights into the effects of individual-level psychological processes on the rituals and norms and collective beliefs that define cultures in the first place (e.g., Conway & Schaller, 2007; Heath, Bell, & Sternberg, 2001; Latané, 1996; for an overview, see Schaller & Crandall, 2004). Of course, when people think about "cultural psychology," this is not typically the first body of research that comes to mind.

Rather, for most people, the concept of "cultural psychology" conjures up a rather different body of research, in which the arrow of causality reverses and the research questions pertain to the influence of culture on psychology. The results of these investigations describe the myriad ways in which individuals' cultural backgrounds influence the specific ways in which they perceive, think about, and respond to the world around them. The vast majority of empirical research in cultural psychology is this particular kind of cultural psychology: the study of cross-cultural differences. Indeed, for many people the phrase "cultural psychology" probably equates immediately to "cross-cultural psychology."

Research on cross-cultural differences typically begins with the recognition that cultures differ in many profound ways—some human populations are characterized by norms, values, and belief systems that are demonstrably different from the norms, values, and belief systems that define other human populations. For instance, it is recognized that some geographically defined populations (East Asians, for example, or aboriginal Native Americans) have relatively collectivistic ideologies, whereas other populations (Northern Europeans and the descendants of European immigrants to the Americas) tend to have more individualistic ideologies. Based on the assumption of cultural difference, specific empirical investigations proceed to examine specific ways in which those cultural differences manifest in the perceptions, thoughts, emotions, and actions of individuals. Thus, we witness flourishing literatures documenting specific ways in which East Asians and Euro-Americans differ in visual perception, logical reasoning, self-concept, and many other fundamental aspects of psychological functioning (Heine, Lehman, Markus, & Kitayama, 1999; Lehman, Chiu, & Schaller, 2004; Masuda & Nisbett, 2006; Nisbett, Peng, Choi, & Norenzayan, 2001). Of course, the study of cross-cultural differences in psychology is hardly limited to this one prototypical comparison between East Asians and Euro-Americans. There now exists a burgeoning psychological database documenting—across many small-scale societies as well as dozens and dozens of countries worldwide—substantial cross-cultural differences in all kinds of fundamental kinds of psychological phenomena, including behavioral decision making (Henrich et al., 2005), interpersonal attachment (Schmidt et al., 2004), sexual attitudes and behavior (Schmidt, 2005), personality traits (McCrae, Terracciano, & Members of the Personality Profiles of Cultures Project, 2005), and, of course, the sorts of attitudes, ideologies, and values implied by the individualism/collectivism distinction (Gelfand, Bhawuk, Nishii, & Bechtold, 2004).

However, despite this immense body of research on cross-cultural differences, a fundamental question of long-standing interest (e.g., Berry, 1979) remains largely unanswered: Exactly *why* do these cross-cultural differences exist in the first place?

In this chapter, we provide an overview of a program of research that identifies one possible answer to that question: Many contemporary cross-cultural differences may result from the fact that, historically, people living under ecological circumstances have been differentially vulnerable to the threat posed by infectious diseases. We begin with a very brief overview of previous work on the origins of cultural differences, emphasizing especially the ecological and evolutionary perspectives from which this particular research program has emerged. We then summarize the conceptual basis for predicting causal relations between (*a*) the prevalence of disease-causing pathogens in the local ecology and (*b*) cultural outcomes pertaining to dispositions, values, and behavior. This conceptual framework has provided the foundation for many hypotheses linking pathogen prevalence to specific kinds of cultural differences, including differences in social attitudes, personality traits (e.g., extraversion, openness to experience), value systems (e.g., individualism versus collectivism), and political ideologies. We summarize these hypotheses and review recent empirical evidence that tests (and supports) the hypotheses. Finally, we discuss additional research questions that are raised by these results, including important questions about the exact causal mechanisms through which the differential prevalence of infectious diseases might create cross-cultural differences.

A. Origins of Cross-Cultural Differences

There are many specific features that define any particular culture—its language and literature and religious practices, its arts and crafts, its folklore, its cuisine, and the countless numbers of popular beliefs, attitudes, expectations, and behavioral tendencies that distinguish its people from those in other cultures. Many of these diverse defining features may be attributable to quirky causes—ecological features unique to the local geography, singular events specific to the history of the local people, and a variety of other things that are idiosyncratic to a particular population and the particular place that they populate. These idiosyncratic causes may be revealed by intensive ethnographies or cultural histories, but they do not lend themselves to the systematic, quantitative, and comparative methods employed by psychological scientists. Any rigorous psychological inquiry into the origins of cross-cultural differences must rest upon the assumption (or hope, perhaps) that lurking within the noise of idiosyncratic cultural causes is some systematic signal of a causal process that applies widely across the entire human landscape.

Psychological inquiry into the origins of existing cross-cultural differences is also constrained by substantial methodological and inferential limitations. First of all, this kind of research is correlational. This is not to say that experimental methods are entirely off the menu. Experimental methods can certainly be used to test hypotheses, at an individual level of analysis, that bear *indirectly* on the roots of cultural differences. Illustrative examples include experiments showing that manipulations of perceptual context activate specific cultural identities (Hong, Morris, Chiu, & Benet-Martinez, 2000), and experiments showing that manipulations of social ecological circumstances can produce temporary psychological responses that mimic those of existing cultural differences (Chen, Chiu, & Chan, 2009). But any inquiry into the origins of already-existing cross-cultural differences is necessarily correlational (no one is randomly assigned to be, say, East Asian). Moreover, existing cultural differences are rarely of recent origin. Consequently, it is difficult to unambiguously measure a presumed causal variable that temporally precedes the cross-cultural difference itself. Therefore, even if one finds a strong correlation between a presumed causal variable and an existing cross-cultural difference, it is difficult to rule out alternative explanations based on reverse causal processes, or on the presumed existence of correlated third variables. Plus, of course, when we talk about causal processes through which cross-cultural differences might arise, we are talking about processes that presumably played out across a substantial chunk of historical time—the kind of longitudinal time scale that cannot be tracked with any typical psychological methodology.

So, while questions about the origins of cross-cultural differences in psychological functioning are of fundamental interest and importance, these questions are also perhaps fundamentally unanswerable. Or, at least, they cannot be answered with the degree of methodological rigor and inferential confidence to which psychological scientists (and other empirically minded scholars) typically aspire.

These constraints have not stopped scientists from speculating. Over the years, many types of explanations have been offered to explain the origins of contemporary cross-cultural differences. Some of these explanations may ultimately prove to be right. Of course, while they are typically compelling on logical grounds, given the substantial methodological problems that must be overcome to put them to empirical test, these hypotheses are typically buttressed by only modest smatterings of actual empirical results.

1. Migration-Based Perspectives

Across several different scholarly contexts, one can encounter suggestions that specific cross-cultural differences may be the result of specific human migrations. Within the economics literature, for example, it has been argued that contemporary regional differences in wealth and sociopolitical values associated with wealth (e.g., individual rights, democracy) have their roots in specific patterns of European migration and colonization over the past several hundred years (Acemoglu, Johnson, & Robinson, 2001).

A rather different—and more psychological—migration-based perspective has been offered by Kitayama and his colleagues to help explain geographical variation in individualistic versus collectivistic value systems (Kitayama & Bowman, 2010; Kitayama, Ishii, Imada, Takemura, & Ramaswary, 2006). They suggest that, compared to other people, individuals who choose voluntarily to migrate from their homeland to settle frontier regions are more likely to be characterized by independence of thought and nonconformist behavioral tendencies. Consequently, the cultures that emerge within frontier populations are also more likely to be characterized by individualistic (rather than collectivistic) values and ideologies. Consistent with this "voluntary settlement" hypothesis is evidence that, within one prototypically individualistic nation (the United States), especially high levels of individualism are observed in western regions that historically comprised the North American frontier (Vandello & Cohen, 1999). Similarly, within one prototypically collectivistic nation (Japan), the area that historically comprised the frontier (the northern province of Hokkaido) is characterized by a relatively "un-Japanese" tendency toward individualism in both thought and behavior (Kitayama et al., 2006).

A third migration-based perspective focuses not on human culture, nor even on human psychology, per se, but instead on genetic information that has been linked to human psychological outcomes. There is a particular variant of the DRD4 dopamine receptor gene that has been found, in some studies, to be predictive of novelty seeking (Bailey, Breidenthal, Jorgensen, McCracken, & Fairbanks, 2007; Schinka, Letsch, & Crawford, 2002). Intriguingly, the frequency of this DRD4 allele varies across different aboriginal populations in North and South America. The frequency is relatively low among populations living relatively close to the place (the now-submerged Bering land bridge) where humans first migrated out of Asia and into North America over 12,000 years ago, and the frequency is higher in places that represent further reaches of that migration, with the highest frequencies of all found among populations in the southernmost regions of South America (Chen, Burton, Greenberg, & Dmitrieva, 1999).

2. Ecological Perspectives

Another broad category of conceptual perspectives on the origins of cultural differences focuses on ecological diversity (Nettle, 2009). The basic idea is straightforward: Just as specific features of the natural and/or social ecology may incline people inhabiting those ecologies to engage in particular types of habitual behaviors (e.g., people populating coastlines will be especially likely to build boats and to cook fish; people populating deserts will not), specific features of the ecology may also incline people toward particular ways of perceiving, thinking, and interacting—and these differences may manifest in the behavioral norms, expectations, and value systems that define a culture (Berry, 1979; Cohen, 2001). Different ecological perspectives have focused on different kinds of ecological circumstances. Some work focuses on physical elements of the local ecology, such as ambient temperature and other variables pertaining to climate (e.g., Tavassoli, 2009; Van de Vliert, 2009). Other work emphasizes specific aspects of the local social ecology, such as the relative ease of residential and/or vocational mobility (e.g., Chen et al., 2009; Oishi, Lun, & Sherman, 2007).

A classic example is evidence that the perceptual susceptibility to the well-known Müller-Lyer optical illusion varies cross-culturally and may do so in part because of differences in the geometric properties of local architecture (Segall, Campbell, & Herskovits, 1963). Another well-known example links a specific set of social economic variables to the emergence of contemporary cultural differences in norms pertaining to honor and male violence (Cohen, Nisbett, Bowdle, & Schwarz, 1996; Nisbett & Cohen, 1996; see also Daly & Wilson, 2010). A third illustrative example focuses on ecological niches that constrain particular kinds of economic and social systems, and it suggests that these ecological differences may have contributed to the emergence of well-documented cultural differences in holistic perception and thought (Nisbett et al., 2001; Norenzayan, Choi, & Peng, 2007). This speculation is supported by evidence showing that, compared to herders, farmers and fishermen show a greater natural tendency toward holistic perception and thought (Uskul, Kitayama, & Nisbett, 2008).

More broadly, ecological variables have been conceptually linked to the potential for cultural variability of any kind. It has been suggested, for instance, that cultural diversity is especially likely to persist under conditions in which the ranges of cultural groups are geographically constrained, and that the size of these ranges is influenced by ecological variables pertaining to seasonality and temporal variation in food supply. This hypothesis is supported by evidence linking the mean length of the growing season within a region to that region's linguistic variability (Nettle, 1996, 1998).

3. Evolutionary Perspectives

Within the broad category of ecological approaches to cross-cultural variability, a subset of research has been informed by a conceptual approach that draws on the tools of evolutionary psychology (e.g., Gangestad, Haselton, & Buss, 2006; Nettle, 2009; Schmitt, 2005; Tooby & Cosmides, 1992). The program of research that we describe in detail later in this chapter fits within this evolutionary framework. The broad assumptions underlying this conceptual approach are explained next.

A culture is defined, in part, by the behavioral tendencies of the people who populate that culture. Those behavioral tendencies (and the psychological processes that produce them) are, to some extent, the product of evolutionary processes. Behavioral tendencies that inhibited reproductive fitness within ancestral ecologies would, over time, have become less prevalent within the population, whereas behavioral tendencies that promoted reproductive fitness within those ecologies would have become more prevalent. The consequence is that cross-cultural differences may emerge for any particular behavioral tendency (and the psychological processes that produce it) simply because that particular behavioral tendency has somewhat different implications for reproductive fitness under somewhat different ecological circumstances.

It is within this general framework that researchers with backgrounds in both the biological and psychological sciences have deduced, and empirically supported, hypotheses suggesting that that different kinds of cross-cultural differences (ranging from differences in food preparation and sexual behavior to differences in personality traits and value systems) may result from the fact that, in some places more than others, there has existed a greater prevalence of pathogens that cause debilitating infectious diseases.

B. The Evolutionary and Psychological Power of Pathogens

There are hundreds of different human infectious diseases, caused by hundreds of different pathogens. Some of these infectious diseases (e.g., human immunodeficiency virus [HIV]) have found their way into human populations only relatively recently, whereas other infectious diseases (e.g., malaria, tuberculosis, and many others) are of considerable antiquity (Ewald, 1993; Wolfe, Dunavan, & Diamond, 2007). Research on the antiquity of disease compels the inescapable conclusion that disease-causing pathogens have posed a threat to human (and prehuman) welfare and reproductive fitness throughout much of human evolutionary history.

Because pathogens have posed such a powerful threat to reproductive fitness, they have imposed an enormous force in guiding human evolution (McNeill, 1976; Ridley, 1993; Zuk, 2007). For instance, biologists have theorized that sexual reproduction itself emerged as an adaptation to the threat of disease, due to the disease-buffering benefits offered by the genetic and phenotypic diversity that is more readily promoted by sexual rather than asexual reproduction (Hamilton & Zuk, 1982; Zuk, 1992). The evolutionary power of pathogens is indicated also by the presence in humans (and across virtually all other species too) of anti-pathogen defense mechanisms that help to mitigate the threats posed by the presence of pathogens.

The most obvious form of anti-pathogen defense is the immune system. The immune system is comprised of a highly sophisticated set of mechanisms that are able to identify, and subsequently form a counterattack against, parasitic intruders within the body. This system, however, is far from perfect. Its detection mechanisms are prone to be outfoxed by pathogenic species that, because of their relatively short life cycle, evolve much faster than mammalian hosts (Ridley, 1993). In addition, for many pathogenic infections, activation of an immune response is initiated only after specific cells have detected its specific antagonist, by which time the invading pathogens may have already begun to cause considerable damage. Further, despite the benefits of defense against potentially deadly pathogens, the activation of an immune response is not without costs as well. It can be metabolically taxing to mount an immune response, robbing individuals of caloric resources that might otherwise be devoted to other fitness-promoting tasks such as caring for one's kin (Brown, 2003; Klein & Nelson, 1999). Specific features of an immune response, such as fever, may be even further debilitating. The logical upshot is that people (and other animals) benefit from the existence of their immune systems, but they are still better off when that immune system is engaged as infrequently as possible.

It follows logically that there would be additional adaptive benefits associated with a very different kind of anti-pathogen defense system—a system designed to promote behavioral avoidance of contact with pathogens in the first place. Consistent with this evolutionary speculation is evidence of anti-pathogen behavioral defense observed across the animal kingdom. Chimpanzees react aversively, and sometimes violently, to other chimpanzees infected with polio (Goodall, 1986). Rodents avoid mating with other rodents who produce olfactory cues connoting disease (Kavaliers & Colwell, 1995). Bullfrog tadpoles selectively avoid swimming in the vicinity of other tadpoles suffering from bacterial infections (Kiesecker, Skelly, Beard, & Preisser, 1999). Even whitefish *eggs* respond to waterborne cues of a virulent egg parasite from other infected eggs by hatching earlier than usual (Wedekind, 2002).

Humans too are characterized by a suite of mechanisms that serve to provide a first line of behavioral defense against pathogens—a sort of "behavioral immune system" (Schaller, 2006; Schaller & Duncan, 2007). These mechanisms are designed to detect the presence of infectious pathogens in the immediate environment, to trigger specific kinds of affective and cognitive responses, and to promote motor responses that facilitate avoidance of pathogen transmission. There is now a considerable body of evidence bearing on these mechanisms and their psychological implications, including implications for emotion (Oaten, Stevenson, & Case, 2009), person perception (Ackerman et al., 2009), interpersonal prejudice (Faulkner, Schaller, Park, & Duncan, 2004; Navarrete, Fessler, & Eng, 2007; Park, Faulkner, & Schaller, 2003, Park, Schaller, & Crandall, 2007), and interpersonal social contact in general (Mortensen, Becker, Ackerman, Neuberg, & Kenrick, 2010).

1. Flexibility and Context Contingency

One of the important general conclusions to emerge from this body of research is this: Not only are there a wide variety of everyday psychological responses that can have the functional consequence of inhibiting pathogen transmission, but these particular psychological responses are especially likely to be produced under conditions in which individuals perceive themselves to be especially vulnerable to pathogen transmission. For instance, it is postulated that the avoidance of pathogens is facilitated by aversive reactions to individuals characterized by gross morphological anomalies. Consistent with this conjecture, morphologically anomalous individuals are not only implicitly associated with disease-connoting semantic concepts, but these implicit associations tend to occur more strongly among perceivers who feel especially vulnerable to the potential transmission of infectious diseases (Park et al., 2003, 2007). Similarly, it is postulated that the avoidance of pathogens is facilitated by an avoidance of social interaction more generally. Consistent with this conjecture is recent research showing that when people feel more vulnerable to disease transmission, they report lower levels of extraversion and produce more socially avoidant motor responses (Mortensen et al., 2010).

The implication is that the behavioral immune system evolved not only to have the capacity to produce responses that inhibit contact with pathogens, but that it evolved in a way such that it produces these responses in a functionally flexible and context-contingent manner. These responses are especially likely to be produced under conditions in which people are (or merely perceive themselves to be) vulnerable to pathogen infections. They are less likely to be produced under conditions in which people are less vulnerable.

This implication—the context contingency of pathogen-relevant psychological responses—may play out not only at an individual level of analysis but also at a cultural level of analysis. In making this logical transition to a cultural (rather than individual) level of analysis, we must consider the fact that, just as there is variability in the perceptual contexts that influence individuals' cognitions and behaviors, so too there is variability in the ecological contexts that are home to entire human populations.

2. Ecological Variability in the Threat Posed by Pathogens

Pathogens—and the infectious diseases that they cause—may have been ubiquitous throughout human history, but that does not mean that they pose an equal threat to all people worldwide. Rather, there is considerable geographical and ecological variability in the distribution of human infectious diseases and in the burden they place on human welfare.

Many pathogens depend on warm, wet environments for survival and reproduction. Therefore, the prevalence of pathogens depends fundamentally on geographical and climatological variables (temperature, humidity, rainfall, etc.). Compared to cooler and drier climates, for instance, there is greater diversity and density of infectious pathogens in the tropics. More generally, the prevalence of pathogens is an inverse function of absolute distance from the equator (Guernier, Hochberg, & Guégan, 2004). Indeed, given the high correlation between absolute latitude and pathogen prevalence, and the precision with which absolute latitude can be measured, it could serve as a reasonable proxy for the prevalence of pathogens in a particular location.

This unequal distribution of pathogens has profound implications for predicting regional differences between human populations—differences not just in overt health outcomes but in psychological and behavioral outcomes as well.

II. PATHOGEN PREVALENCE AND THE PREDICTION OF CROSS-CULTURAL DIFFERENCES

The basic logical template is as follows: To the extent that a particular behavioral tendency increases the likelihood of pathogen transmission, that behavioral tendency has negative implications for reproductive fitness. Those fitness costs are likely to be greater within ecologies characterized by higher levels of pathogen prevalence. Therefore, all else being equal, to the extent that a particular behavioral tendency *increases* the likelihood of pathogen transmission, that particular behavioral tendency (and psychological characteristics associated with it) is expected to be *less* characteristic of human populations in geographical regions with historically higher levels of pathogen prevalence. Similarly, to the extent that a particular behavioral tendency *decreases* the likelihood of pathogen transmission, that particular behavioral tendency (and psychological characteristics associated with it) is expected to be *more* characteristic of human populations in regions with historically higher levels of pathogen prevalence. Therefore, any psychological or cultural characteristic that has consequences for pathogen transmission is likely to be predictably variable across human populations, as a function of pathogen prevalence within the local geographical region.

At this point, some readers might object and observe that, despite the fact that infectious diseases are relatively more prevalent in some places compared to others, infectious diseases have posed some threat everywhere. And so, therefore, one might argue that behaviors facilitating pathogen transmission should be inhibited within every culture, whereas behaviors inhibiting pathogen transmission should be celebrated and encouraged within every culture. This argument may seem sensible on the surface, but it ignores a very important point: Many behavioral tendencies that facilitate pathogen transmission (and so are costly in that one specific way) may actually be beneficial in other ways. These benefits may outweigh the relatively modest costs that occur in low-pathogen environments. But, as pathogen prevalence increases (along with the baseline likelihood of pathogen transmission), the costs are more likely to increase to the point that they outweigh the benefits. Similarly, behavioral tendencies that inhibit pathogen transmission (and so provide functional benefits of this very specific kind) may impose costs of other kinds. These costs may outweigh the modest benefits that are likely to emerge in environments with a low baseline level of pathogen transmission. But, as pathogen prevalence increases, the benefits are more likely to increase to the point that they outweigh the costs.

A. An Illustrative Example: Use of Spices in Food Preparation

The use of culinary spices offers a good example. Spices have natural disease-buffering properties; most culinary spices (such as garlic, onion, and rosemary) inhibit or kill foodborne bacteria (Billing & Sherman, 1998). Thus, the use of spices in food preparation is functionally beneficial specifically because of these antibiotic consequences. However, the use of spices can be costly as well. For instance, spices typically offer little nutritive value, and the resources (e.g., arable land) consumed in the cultivation or procurement of spices could presumably be used to cultivate or procure more nutritionally valuable foodstuffs. These costs are likely to outweigh the anti-pathogenic benefits of spice use under ecological circumstances in which there is a relatively low prevalence of foodborne bacterial diseases. But, under ecological circumstances characterized by a high prevalence of food-borne bacterial diseases, the anti-pathogenic benefits of spice use will be considerably greater, and are more likely to outweigh the costs. The logical upshot is a hypothesis specifying a relationship between pathogen prevalence and the use of culinary spices: The use of spices in food preparation should be a positive function of the prevalence of pathogens within the local ecology.

This hypothesis was tested by Sherman and Billing (1999). Sherman and Billing analyzed the contents of over 4500 meat-based recipes from traditional cookbooks in dozens of countries around the world. For each country, they computed mean annual temperature as a proxy measure indicating the threat posed by foodborne bacterial infections. The results were clear: In hotter, more tropical geographical regions, people traditionally employ a greater number of culinary spices. The same effect was also observed in analyses that examined regional differences within geographically vast countries such as the United States and China. Compared to cooler regions in northern China, for example, one finds spicier Chinese food in the hotter, more tropical regions of southern China.

Of course, a measure of temperature is just a measure of temperature. Does the same effect hold if one employs a more direct measure of pathogen prevalence? Yes. We reanalyzed these data using a country-level index of pathogen prevalence derived from old epidemiological data (we describe this pathogen prevalence index in more detail later). The results revealed that, compared to the correlation between temperature and spice use (reported by Sherman & Billing, 1999), the correlation between pathogen prevalence and spice use is, if anything, even stronger ($r = .58$; Murray & Schaller, 2010).

B. Another Illustrative Example: Mate Preferences

A more prototypically psychological illustration of this research strategy is offered by inquiry into the relation between pathogen prevalence and cross-cultural differences in mate preferences—specifically preferences for mates who are physically attractive. Physical attractiveness is universally prized, of course, but there are cross-cultural differences in the extent to which physical attractiveness is valued relative to other desirable traits (Buss, 1989). Why might this preference for physical attractiveness vary as a function of pathogen prevalence? The argument proceeds from two bodies of evidence. First, subjective appraisals of physical attractiveness are influenced by objective psychophysical characteristics such as feature prototypicality and bilateral facial symmetry (Rhodes, 2006; Thornhill & Gangestad, 1999). Second, these objective features, as well as subjective appraisals of attractiveness, appear to be somewhat useful indicators of an individual's health status, as well as their immunological functioning in general (Møller, 1996; Thornhill & Møller, 1997; Weeden & Sabini, 2005). The upshot is that another person's level of physical attractiveness may provide useful inferential information about the extent to which that person is *(a)* currently free from pathogenic infections, *(b)* likely to successfully fend off pathogen infections in the future, and *(c)* likely to produce offspring with the ability to fend off pathogen infections. A disease-free mate is beneficial to one's own reproductive fitness; and so, by implication, it is also reproductively beneficial to prefer mates who are physically attractive.

Of course, mate selection almost always involves trade-offs. To the extent that one places a high value on the physical attractiveness of a mate, one may place a relatively lower value on other traits (such as wealth, intelligence, or agreeableness) that are also desirable and functionally beneficial in a mate. Given these inevitable trade-offs, the underlying evolutionary logic implies that that individuals are most likely to place a high value on physical attractiveness under conditions in which the benefits signaled by attractiveness (good health and a strong immune system) are most especially beneficial: under conditions in which the threat from pathogens is especially high.

This leads directly to the hypothesis that pathogen prevalence within a region should predict the value placed on a mate's physical attractiveness.

And, in fact, it does. In a data set that included responses from 29 different countries, Gangestad and Buss (1993; see also Gangestad et al., 2006) found that the historical prevalence of pathogens within a country was positively correlated with the contemporary value that people within that country place on their mate's physical attractiveness. This effect occurred among both men and women and held when controlling for a variety of additional social and economic variables that also influence mate preferences.

C. Important Methodological and Inferential Issues

These examples illustrate not only the basic conceptual logic that links pathogen prevalence to the origin of cross-cultural differences, but they also illustrate some of the nontrivial methodological and inferential issues that must be addressed in pursuing this line of inquiry. We quickly summarize some of these issues here, so that readers might bear them in mind when evaluating the body of research evidence that we review later.

One issue arises from the use of contemporary geopolitical entities (e.g., countries) as units of analysis in research on cross-cultural differences. Almost no one would claim that country is synonymous with culture, and some scholars (e.g., many ethnographers and other cultural anthropologists) might strenuously object to the use of a country as a proxy for a culture. After all, many countries (especially those that are geographically vast and/or ethnically varied, such as China, India, Russia, and the United States) are home to multiple distinct cultures. These within-country cultural differences are possibly more profound than many differences between countries. But there are certain methodological advantages associated with the use of geopolitical entities as units of analysis. Political borders offer both a convenient and a geographically objective means of dividing up the worldwide human population into culture-like categories. Because of this, many important forms of worldwide cultural variability have been and continue to be categorized according to these geopolitical boundaries, such as documentation of worldwide differences in personality traits and cultural values. If one is to conduct empirical inquiries into the origins of these particular differences, one must employ the same unit of analysis. And, even if geopolitical borders are not truly identical to cultural boundaries, extensive empirical evidence suggests that they can still serve as useful proxies for cultural boundaries (e.g., Schwartz, 2004).

The use of countries as stand-ins for cultures also introduces a statistical issue: nonindependence of the units of analysis. Peoples move and migrate through geographical space, and aspects of their culture move with them. The closer that any two countries are in geographical space, the more likely those two countries are to have cultural elements in common, simply as a result of historical migrations and cultural borrowing. For highly focused forms of cross-cultural comparison (e.g., the prototypical study in which responses from a western European sample are compared to responses from an east Asian sample), this statistical nonindependence is a nonissue. But in the kinds of inquiries of the sort described here (exemplified by Sherman & Billing, 1999, and Gangestad & Buss, 1993), in which countries themselves are the units of analysis, one cannot easily ignore this statistical independence (which is sometimes referred to as autocorrelation or "Galton's problem"). Scholars in other disciplines that are accustomed to treating cultures and/or countries as units of analysis (e.g., anthropology, economics, political science) are highly sensitive to this issue, and they have developed a variety of statistically sophisticated strategies for dealing with it (e.g., Dow, 2007; Ross & Homer, 1976). At the very least, it can be inferentially informative to supplement analyses that treat countries as units of analysis with additional analyses that combine country-level data into a smaller set of geographical categories that correspond to regions of the world that have historically been culturally distinct (e.g., Eastern Eurasia, Western Eurasia, Africa, etc.; see Gupta & Hanges, 2004; Murdock, 1949).

Regardless of the units of analysis, this kind of inquiry is strictly correlational. From a positivist Popperian perspective, this poses no problem: A simple zero-order correlation is sufficient to empirically test (i.e., to potentially falsify) a conceptual hypothesis specifying the effect of pathogen prevalence on some specific kind of cross-cultural variability. But we typically aim a little higher than that, inferentially, and simple zero-order correlations are not completely compelling on their own. We must consider alternative explanations and control for additional variables that may produce entirely spurious correlations. For instance, in the case of culinary spicing, one must address the possibility that more culinary spices are used in tropical countries simply because more species of spices can be successfully cultivated in those countries (in fact, Sherman & Billing, 1999, do report data that addresses this alternative explanation). More broadly, within any particular investigation, one must consider a variety of alternative processes—which may have nothing to do with infectious diseases whatsoever—that might lead to the same cross-cultural differences, and one must ascertain whether variables bearing on those processes might covary with pathogen prevalence. If they do, they must be statistically controlled when testing whether pathogen prevalence actually predicts the cross-cultural difference of interest. Compelling support for any hypothesis about the effects of pathogen prevalence emerges only when pathogen prevalence uniquely predicts cross-cultural outcomes even when controlling for these additional variables.

These hypotheses about pathogen prevalence are clearly causal. But, of course, observation of correlation does not imply a particular direction of causality—at least not all by itself. Temporal precedence is therefore an important inferential ally in correlational studies. To infer that pathogen prevalence exerts a causal influence on culture (and not the reverse), it helps to obtain a measure of pathogen prevalence at a period of time substantially prior to the measure of the cultural outcome variable. Gangestad and Buss (1993) did exactly this. They employed old epidemiological atlases (documenting disease prevalence information from decades ago) to create a composite index of historical pathogen prevalence for the 29 countries included in their analyses. To further gain traction on this tricky inferential issue, it can be informative to also compute a measure of contemporary pathogen prevalence in exactly the same countries. If pathogen prevalence is a consequence (rather than a cause) of some cross-cultural difference, then the correlation with the contemporary pathogen prevalence measure would be expected to be greater than that with the historical pathogen prevalence measure. If not—if the historical measure predicts cross-cultural outcomes more strongly than the contemporary measure does—it lends credence to the argument that pathogen prevalence is the cause, rather than a consequence, of the cross-cultural difference.

D. Quantitative Indices of Pathogen Prevalence

How does one measure the historical prevalence of pathogens within a country? In our research, we employed a methodological strategy adapted from Gangestad and Buss (1993), who followed an approach used earlier by Low (1990) who focused not on countries, but on small-scale societies that are part of the Standard Cross-Cultural Sample employed in much comparative ethnographic research (Murdock &White, 1969, 2006). Low (1990) used old epidemiological atlases to estimate the prevalence of a handful of prototypical human infectious diseases within each small-scale population and combined these estimates into a single index indicating pathogen prevalence. This index has been proven to predict several cross-cultural differences observed in the ethnographic record, such as societal norms pertaining to marriage structures and parenting practices (Low, 1990; Quinlan, 2007). Similarly, in their study of mate preferences across 29 countries, Gangestad and Buss (1993) used old epidemiological atlases to estimate the country-level prevalence of seven specific kinds of prototypical pathogenic diseases. An overall index comprised by these prevalence estimates successfully predicts cross-cultural differences in the value accorded to physical attractiveness, as we described earlier, and differences in several additional kinds of mate preferences as well (Gangestad et al., 2006).

We extended this approach to cover a more complete set of 230 geopolitical regions worldwide (Murray & Schaller, 2010). Most of these regions are nations (e.g., Angola), whereas others are territories or protectorates (e.g., New Caledonia) or culturally distinct regions within a nation (e.g., Hong Kong). For the sake of expository ease, we use the word "country" to refer to all these regions. The nine diseases coded were leishmania, schistosoma, trypanosoma, leprosy, malaria, typhus, filaria, dengue, and tuberculosis. With one exception (tuberculosis), the prevalence of each disease was informed by epidemiological atlases and additional epidemiological information compiled in either the late nineteenth or early twentieth centuries. For the majority of countries (N = 160), prevalence data on all nine diseases were available, allowing the computation of a standardized nine-item index of historical pathogen prevalence. For all 230 countries, a standardized index of historical pathogen prevalence was computed based on data from either six or seven infectious diseases.

Given that that pathogenic diseases are generally more prevalent in the tropics (Epstein, 1999; Guernier et al., 2004), it is no surprise that the nine individual disease prevalence ratings were all positively correlated, and the composite indices have good internal reliability (e.g., for the nine-item index, Cronbach's alpha = .84). Additional results reported by Murray and Schaller, 2010) attest to the index's construct validity. (For example, this index correlates strongly with other indices of pathogen prevalence computed on more limited samples, and it correlates strongly with other variables—such as absolute latitude—that have previously been shown to predict both prevalence and diversity of infectious diseases.) Thus, although this numerical index is inevitably crude (given the nature of the source materials), it does appear to offer a reasonably valid and reliable indicator of the historical prevalence of pathogens within any particular contemporary country.

Historical pathogen prevalence scores for each of the 230 countries worldwide are summarized in an Appendix presented by Murray and Schaller (2010). These values are available to any researcher who wishes to test hypotheses linking pathogen prevalence to contemporary cross-national differences.

Complementing this measure of historical pathogen prevalence are measures based on contemporary epidemiological data. The Global Infectious Diseases and Epidemiology Online Network (GIDEON; http://www.gideononline.com) reports current distributions of infectious diseases in each country of the world and is updated weekly. Using this GIDEON database, Fincher and Thornhill (2008a, 2008b) computed two different indices. One index offers a measure of the contemporary variety of different pathogenic species within a country. As such, it assesses biodiversity rather than the actual threat to human health and welfare posed by those pathogenic species, and its implications for cross-cultural differences are not straightforward. The other index, however, is conceptually analogous to our index of historical pathogen prevalence. Focusing on seven classes of pathogens (leishmanias, trypanosomes, malaria, schistosomes, filariae, spirochetes, and leprosy), Fincher and Thornhill coded the relative prevalence of 22 specific pathogenic diseases. These 22 values were summed to create a composite index estimating the contemporary pathogen prevalence within each of 225 countries. (Actual country-level values on this measure of contemporary pathogen prevalence can be found in Appendix 2 of the online data supplement accompanying Fincher & Thornhill, 2008b.)

Armed with these measures, we have empirically tested a number of conceptual hypotheses specifying causal consequences of pathogen prevalence for the emergence of cross-cultural differences.

E. Pathogen Prevalence Predicts Cultural Differences in Sociosexual Attitudes

Epidemiologists define some human infectious diseases as sexually transmitted infections (STIs). The transmission of these pathogens depends upon (or, at least, is substantially facilitated by) human sexual intimacy. The more sexual partners one has, the greater the risk of disease transmission. Many other infectious diseases may not fit the epidemiological definition of an STI, but people are still more likely to contract those diseases if they engage in sexual contact with someone who is already infected—simply because of the prolonged interpersonal proximity that sexual contact entails. The implication is simple: To the extent that people tend to be sexually promiscuous or "unrestricted," those people are more likely to contract infectious diseases themselves and to transmit those diseases to others.

Of course, these specific fitness costs associated with unrestricted sexual behavior must be weighed against any potential fitness benefits that may accrue as a result of unrestricted mating strategies (e.g., among men, promiscuous mating strategies confer benefits through the production of more offspring). The cost/benefit ratio is likely to vary depending upon the prevalence of pathogens in the immediate ecology. In places where the prevalence of pathogens is relatively higher, the costs associated with unrestricted mating strategies are more likely to outweigh the benefits. This hypothesis for cross-cultural differences is clear: In places that historically have had a high prevalence of pathogens, one expects a less promiscuous, more "restricted" approach to sexual relations.

To test this hypothesis we (Schaller & Murray, 2008) employed the results of a cross-national study devoted to the assessment of attitudes and behaviors bearing on restricted versus unrestricted approaches to sexual behavior (Schmitt, 2005). Along with an international team of researchers, Schmitt collected responses on a Sociosexual Orientation Inventory (SOI; Simpson & Gangestad, 1991) from over 14,000 people in 48 different countries and reported mean standardized SOI scores (for both men and women separately) for each country. Higher SOI scores indicate a tendency toward more unrestricted sexual behavior. There is considerable worldwide variability in these country-level SOI scores. People in Argentina and Austria, for instance, on average have higher SOI scores (indicating a more unrestricted attitude toward sexual relations) than people in Bangladesh or Botswana.

Given the hypothesis, we expect to see a negative relation between pathogen prevalence and SOI. And, in fact, that is exactly what the results show: In places with a higher level of historical pathogen prevalence, both men and women report more restricted attitudes toward sexual relations (r's for men and women were $-.27$ and $-.62$, respectively; Schaller & Murray, 2008).

It is worth noting that this effect was substantially stronger for female SOI scores than for male SOI scores. And it was only on female SOI scores that the negative correlation remained statistically significant even after statistically controlling for other country-level variables (e.g., gross domestic product per capita, life expectancy). This sex difference in the effect sizes is consistent with the overall cost/benefit framework. Because of differential reproductive investment, the fitness benefits associated with unrestricted sexual behavior are likely to be considerably greater among men than among women. Therefore, for men only, these benefits may outweigh the costs (disease transmission) even at relatively high levels of pathogen prevalence. Among women, however, the benefits of unrestricted sexuality behavior are relatively minimal, and so they are more likely to be increasingly outweighed by the disease-related costs as pathogen prevalence becomes increasingly greater.

It is also worth noting that country-level SOI scores were more strongly predicted by historical pathogen prevalence than by contemporary pathogen prevalence. This pattern of findings is consistent with the hypothesized causal relation (in which pathogen prevalence is the cause, and cross cultural differences in sexual attitudes are the consequence) and is inconsistent with the reverse causal relation.

F. Pathogen Prevalence Predicts Cultural Differences in Extraversion and Openness

An individual's inclination toward restricted versus unrestricted sexual behavior is a kind of personality trait. But it is a highly specific trait, with implications for a relatively narrow domain of behavioral contexts. Might pathogen prevalence also predict cross-cultural differences in more fundamental personality traits, such as those that comprise the so-called Big Five (agreeableness, conscientiousness, extraversion, neuroticism, and openness to experience)?

Several cross-national investigations have documented important cultural differences along each of the Big Five personality traits. McCrae (2002) summarized results from multiple independent studies that used the NEO-PI-R questionnaire (Costa & McCrae, 1992) to assess the self-reported personality traits in 33 different countries. In a separate study, McCrae and an international team of collaborators obtained observer reports on the NEO-PI-R questionnaire from almost 12,000 individuals in 50 different countries (McCrae et al., 2005). And, in a third international study, Schmitt and his colleagues assessed self-reports on the Big Five Inventory (John & Srivastava, 1999) from almost 18,000 individuals in 56 different countries (Schmitt et al., 2007). Each investigation produced a set of country-level scores on each of the Big Five personality traits, documenting many different kinds of cross-cultural differences. For instance, on average, people in Norway and New Zealand report higher levels of extraversion than people in India or Ethiopia.

Given the questionnaire methodologies employed, some of the differences in country-level personality scores must surely be attributable to noise and/or methodological artifacts, such as nonequivalent linguistic translations or reference group effects. Indeed, some empirical evidence research suggests that country-level scores on conscientiousness in particular might be especially difficult to interpret (Heine, Buchtel, & Norenzayan, 2008). Nevertheless, to the extent that there is some validity associated with these country-level personality scores, they offer the potential to test conceptual hypotheses about the links between pathogen prevalence and cross-cultural differences in fundamental personality traits.

1. Extraversion

There is ample basis to expect a causal link between pathogen prevalence and cultural differences in extraversion. Being high in extraversion implies a wider circle of acquaintances and social contacts and an increased frequency of contact with those people. These social contacts have the potential to expose individuals to interpersonally transmitted pathogens. Indeed, there is empirical evidence that a dispositional tendency toward extraversion may be associated with an enhanced risk of disease transmission (Hamrick, Cohen, & Rodriguez, 2002; Nettle, 2005).

Of course, extraversion can be associated with many positive outcomes as well, including higher levels of leadership effectiveness, higher levels of happiness, and increased opportunities for sexual reproduction (Berry & Miller, 2001; Fleeson, Malanos, & Achille, 2002; Silverthorne, 2001). These benefits of extraversion are likely to outweigh the disease-related costs under conditions in which the disease-related costs are relatively minimal: in ecological settings characterized by low levels of interpersonally transmitted pathogens. However, as pathogen prevalence increases, there is increased likelihood that the disease-related costs of extraversion will begin to outweigh the benefits of extraversion. It is worth noting that these costs of extraversion are likely to accrue not only to extraverts themselves but also to anyone (even an introvert) in the local population who happens to interact with an extravert. Therefore, in places characterized by high pathogen prevalence, one might expect that individuals will not only be less extraverted themselves but will also devalue extraversion more generally. In any case, the hypothesis is straightforward: Regional variation in pathogen prevalence is expected to be inversely related to population-level variation in extraversion.

We (Schaller & Murray, 2008) conducted multiple tests of this hypothesis, using the results from the three different cross-national surveys of the

Big Five personality traits summarized earlier (McCrae, 2002; McCrae et al., 2005; Schmitt et al., 2007). As predicted, across every measure, cross-cultural differences in extraversion were negatively correlated with historical pathogen prevalence (see Table 3.1). These relationships remained even when controlling for a variety of additional country-level variables (e.g., gross domestic product, individualism/collectivism). In addition, consistent with the causal relation specified by the hypothesis, extraversion was more strongly predicted by historical pathogen prevalence than by contemporary pathogen prevalence.

2. Openness to Experience

A similar cost/benefit analysis implies a causal link between pathogen prevalence and cultural differences in openness to experience. Openness is associated with creativity, willingness to experiment, and attraction to novel experiences and unfamiliar stimuli (Larsen & Buss, 2005). These behavioral dispositions can be associated with certain kinds of fitness benefits, in that they encourage innovation and adaptive problem solving. But these dispositions also connote potential fitness costs specific to pathogen transmission. This is because many familiar ways of doing things—particular in domains such food preparation, personal hygiene, and public health—actually serve as buffers against pathogen transmission. To the extent that individuals deviate from these accustomed norms (e.g., experiment with novel methods of food preparation, or take a "creative" approach to hygiene), those individuals expose themselves—and others in their local community—to an increased risk of pathogen transmission. These particular kinds of costs, of course, are likely to be greater (and more likely to outweigh the benefits associated with dispositional openness) under conditions of greater pathogen prevalence. Thus, regional variation in pathogen prevalence is expected to be inversely related to population-level variation in openness to experience.

We conducted multiple tests of this hypothesis too, using exactly the same source materials as we used in our investigations into extraversion (Schaller & Murray, 2008). Again, across every measure, cross-cultural differences in openness to experience were negatively correlated with historical pathogen prevalence (see Table 3.1). These negative relationships remained even when controlling for additional country-level variables. And, consistent with the causal relation specified by the hypothesis, openness to experience was more strongly predicted by historical pathogen prevalence than by contemporary pathogen prevalence.

TABLE 3.1: **Correlations between Historical Pathogen Prevalence and Contemporary Cultural Outcomes Pertaining to Dispositions and Values**

Cultural Outcome Variable	Correlation with Pathogen Prevalence
Sociosexual attitudes (for details see Schaller & Murray, 2008)	
Female sociosexuality scores	−.62
Male sociosexuality scores	−.27
Extraversion (for details see Schaller & Murray, 2008)	
Extraversion scores from Macrae, 2002	−.67
Extraversion scores from Macrae et al., 2005	−.50
Extraversion scores from Schmitt et al., 2007	−.26
Three-sample composite	−.59
Openness to experience (for details see Schaller & Murray, 2008)	
Openness scores from Macrae, 2002	−.45
Openness scores from Macrae et al., 2005	−.34
Openness scores from Schmitt et al., 2007	−.24
Three-sample composite	−.59
Individualism (for details see Fincher et al., 2008)	
Individualism scores from Hofstede, 2001	−.69
Individualism scores from Suh et al., 1998	−.71
Collectivism (for details see Fincher et al., 2008)	
In-group collectivism practices	.73
Pronoun-drop indicator of collectivism	.63
Conformity pressure (Murray et al., unpublished data)	
Behavioral conformity effect sizes	.49
Percentage of people who prioritize obedience	.48
Tolerance for nonconformity (Murray et al., unpublished data)	
Dispositional variability	−.52
Percentage of left-handed people	−.73
Political ideologies (for details see Murray & Schaller, 2010)	
Restriction of individual rights and civil liberties	.55
Democratization	−.65

3. Negligible Effects on Other Big Five Traits

In addition to testing hypotheses linking pathogen prevalence to cross-cultural differences in extraversion and openness, we also conducted additional analyses to explore whether there might be any relationships with the other three Big Five factors: agreeableness, conscientiousness, and neuroticism (Schaller & Murray, 2008). No consistent patterns emerged across the various measures, although there was some evidence that pathogen prevalence may predict more narrowly defined facets of these additional factors. (For two of the three cross-national surveys—those that employed the NEO-PI-R questionnaire—facet scores were reported by McCrae, 2002, and by McCrae & Terraciano, 2008). For instance, at a cross-cultural level, pathogen prevalence was consistently positively correlated with measures of deliberation (a facet of conscientiousness) and negatively correlated with measures of impulsiveness (a facet of neuroticism).

It would probably be wise to be very careful about interpreting any results on these underlying facets. That said, it is perhaps worth noting that the findings on deliberation and impulsiveness fit neatly within the conceptual analysis that gave rise to the hypothesis pertaining to openness. However, there is some useful inferential value associated with the negligible relations between pathogen prevalence and these additional three Big Five factors (agreeableness, conscientiousness, and neuroticism). These negligible relations suggest that the conceptually interesting results on extraversion and openness cannot easily be attributed to response biases (e.g., acquiescence bias) or other methodological artifacts that affect all traits assessed by the personality questionnaires. This improves our confidence that the observed correlations involving pathogen prevalence and personality are truly meaningful.

G. Pathogen Prevalence Predicts Cultural Differences in Individualism and Collectivism

Just as pathogen prevalence is expected to predict worldwide cultural variability in personality style, it is also expected to predict variability in cultural values. There are many different kinds of cultural values (e.g., Hofstede, 2001; Schwartz, 2004), but there is one value construct in particular that has been the focus of an enormous amount of attention from cross-cultural researchers: values pertaining to individualism versus collectivism. This attention is warranted, as it has been suggested that individualism/collectivism "may ultimately prove to be the most important dimension for capturing cultural variation" (Heine, 2008, p. 189). Despite the attention that this dimension has received (including a limited number of attempts to explore possible antecedents of cultural differences along this dimension; e.g., Kitayama & Bowman, 2010), it still remains largely a mystery as to exactly *why* some cultures tend to be individualistic, whereas others tend to be more collectivistic. One solution to this mystery may lie in ecological variation in pathogen prevalence.

Why might pathogen prevalence have a causal influence on cultural inclinations toward individualism versus collectivism? There are several reasons, each related to a distinct definitional element of this multifaceted value construct.

According to most definitions of individualistic and collectivistic value systems (e.g., Gelfand et al., 2004), collectivist cultural values (as opposed to individualist values) are characterized in part by an expectation of prosocial behavior among family members and other individuals within a local social alliance. There are costs associated with the obligatory prosocial expenditure of resources. But there are benefits too, which may accrue whenever one (or one's immediate kin) is in need of assistance from others. These benefits are likely to be especially pronounced under conditions in which the local ecology is characterized by a high level of threat to health and welfare. Thus, because of the emphasis on obligatory prosociality within families and local alliances, collectivistic value systems are likely to be relatively more advantageous under conditions of greater pathogen prevalence (whereas individualism may be relatively more advantageous under conditions of lower pathogen prevalence).

Another defining feature of collectivistic (compared to individualistic) value systems is a relatively sharper psychological boundary between ingroup and outgroup (Gelfand et al., 2004). This manifests in higher levels of ethnocentrism and xenophobia (e.g., greater wariness of, and reduced contact with, foreigners and other outgroup members; Sagiv & Schwartz, 1995). Xenophobic attitudes come at some cost (e.g., reduced opportunities for trade, reduced exposure to exotic-but-useful ideas and technologies), but there are also benefits specific to the domain of disease transmission. Compared to ingroup members, outgroup members are more likely to host exotic pathogens. If introduced to the local population, exotic pathogens pose an especially virulent threat to individuals' health and reproductive fitness, given the immune system's proclivity to be most effective against local pathogens (Mayer, 2006). In addition, compared to ingroup members, outgroup members are more likely to be ignorant of, and thus to violate, local norms that serve as buffers against pathogen transmission. Thus, wariness and avoidance of outgroup members may be associated with disease-relevant benefits that must be weighed against the costs. These disease-relevant benefits are most likely to outweigh the costs under conditions of high pathogen prevalence. The implication is that, because of the emphasis on sharp ingroup/outgroup distinctions, collectivistic value systems are likely to be relatively more advantageous under conditions of greater pathogen prevalence, whereas individualism may be relatively more advantageous under conditions of lower pathogen prevalence.

A feature that accompanies collectivistic value systems is "tightness": a strong value placed on the upholding of cultural traditions and conformity to cultural norms, accompanied by a lack of tolerance for deviance from these established norms (Gelfand, Nishii, & Raver, 2006; Gelfand et al., 2004; Triandis, 1995). In contrast, individualist value systems are characterized by greater tolerance for deviation from established norms (Cukur, De Gusman, & Carlo, 2004; Oishi, Schimmack, Diener, & Suh, 1998). The cost/benefit implications are essentially identical to those for openness to experience, discussed earlier. While there are certain costs associated with values emphasizing tradition and conformity (decreased incidence of useful innovation), there are clear benefits specific to the domain of infectious diseases (decreased likelihood that individuals will violate the various norms and traditions that serve as buffers against pathogen transmission). These benefits are most likely to outweigh the costs under conditions of high pathogen prevalence. The implication is that, because of this emphasis on conformity and tradition, collectivistic value systems are likely to be relatively more advantageous under conditions of greater pathogen prevalence (whereas individualism may be relatively more advantageous under conditions of lower pathogen prevalence).

Thus, multiple complementary lines of deduction yield a single clear hypothesis linking pathogen prevalence to cultural values along the individualism/collectivism dimension: Regional variation in pathogen prevalence is expected to be inversely related to indicators of individualism and positively related to indicators of collectivism.

We conducted four tests of this hypothesis using two different country-level measures of individualism and two additional country-level measures of collectivism (Fincher, Thornhill, Murray, & Schaller, 2008). These measures included the following: *(a)* individualism scores reported by Hofstede (2001), which were based on extensive survey data along with a variety of additional observations; *(b)* individualism scores reported by Suh and colleagues (1998), which supplemented Hofstede's scores with the subjective assessments of a scholarly expert on worldwide differences in individualism and collectivism; *(c)* "in-group collectivism practices" scores reported by Gelfand et al. (2004), based on extensive survey data; and *(d)* a binary variable indicating whether it is acceptable to drop first- and second-person pronouns in spoken language (pronoun-drop is more prevalent in highly collectivistic cultures, and so serves as a linguistic indictor of collectivism; Kashima & Kashima, 1998). The sample of countries varied with each measure, but every analysis included a substantial number of countries from around the world (N's varied between 58 and 70). The results were clear and consistent across all four sets of analyses: Consistent with the hypothesis, geographical variation in the historical prevalence of pathogens was strongly negatively correlated with individualism (r's = −.69 and −.71) and strongly positively correlated with collectivism (r's = .73 and .63).

Fincher et al. (2008) also reported the results of analyses in which culturally distinct world regions (e.g., Western Eurasia, Eastern Eurasia), rather than individual countries, were treated as the units of analysis. The results were essentially the same. In fact, some of the correlations were even stronger when treating large cultural regions as units of analysis.

Additional analyses revealed that the predictive effect of pathogen prevalence remained even when controlling for a variety of additional country-level variables that might plausibly have a causal influence on individualistic/collectivistic value systems (e.g., gross domestic product, non-disease-related threats to health and morality). And, consistent with the causal relation specified by the hypothesis, individualism/collectivism was more strongly predicted by historical pathogen prevalence than by contemporary pathogen prevalence.

Overall, these results provide compelling evidence consistent with the hypothesized causal relation between pathogen prevalence and cultural value systems along the individualism/collectivism dimension. But recall that individualism and collectivism are multifaceted value systems, defined by a variety of more highly specific and conceptually distinct constructs. And recall that these different constructs are the foci of logically distinct conceptual analyses linking pathogen prevalence to individualism/collectivism. Evidence bearing on the broader value systems (individualism and collectivism) does not clearly indicate which—if any—of these more specific conceptual analyses might be right or wrong. In short, we still need to know about exactly what specific construct (or constructs) might be driving the effect. Do the individualism/collectivism findings reflect an effect of pathogen prevalence on obligatory prosociality? On ethnocentrism and/or xenophobia? On conformity pressures?

All of the above? Some of the above? None of the above? Answers to these questions require empirical analyses that focus more purely on indicators of these more specific underlying constructs.

Thus far, there is very little rigorous research addressing relations between pathogen prevalence and either obligatory prosociality, enthnocentrism or xenophobia. However, there are a couple of promising empirical beginnings. In one set of analyses, we examined the extent to which the prevalence of different categories of human-infecting pathogens (zoonotic, human-specific, multihost) might have differential relations with cross-cultural outcomes (Thornhill, Fincher, Murray, & Schaller, 2010). One finding that emerged is evidence that pathogen prevalence of all kinds (but especially the prevalence of human-specific and multihost pathogens) is positively correlated with cross-cultural differences in the strength of allegiance to one's immediate family (r's = .58 and .50 for human-specific and multihost pathogen prevalence, respectively; N = 78). Separately, in an analysis that employed data from the World Values Survey, we also found that pathogen prevalence is positively correlated with the percentage of people in a country who explicitly indicate that they would not want "people of a different race" as neighbors (r = .43, N = 67; Schaller & Murray, 2010). But these are just hints, at best. To our knowledge, no one has reported any comprehensive set of empirical analyses to test the hypothesized effects of pathogen prevalence on either of these two specific facets of collectivism.

In contrast, the hypothesized effect of pathogen prevalence on "tightness"—cultural conformity pressures—has recently been subjected to close empirical scrutiny, as will be discussed next.

H. Pathogen Prevalence Predicts Cultural Differences in Conformity Pressure

It has been previously documented that there are cross-cultural differences in the pressure to conform, and that these differences covary with the broader cultural differences in individualism and collectivism (Bond & Smith, 1996). We recently conducted a series of analyses designed to address the hypothesis that these cross-cultural differences in conformity pressure may result, in part, from regional differences in pathogen prevalence (Murray, Trudeau, & Schaller, in press data). We examined four different country-level outcome variables.

One of these measures was taken from Bond and Smith's (1996) meta-analysis of social psychological experiments (such as those designed originally by Asch, 1956) that assessed public conformity to majority behavior. In their results, they tabulated the effect sizes that emerged from over 100 experiments conducted in 17 different countries. For each of these countries it is possible to calculate the mean effect size. This mean effect size offers a crude, but direct measure of country-level behavioral conformity.

A second measure of conformity assesses not behavioral conformity per se, but rather the cultural value placed on a particular kind of conformity—obedience. This measure was obtained from the results of the World Values Survey (available at http://www.worldvaluessurvey.org). These results tabulate, for each of 83 countries, the percentage of survey respondents who indicated that obedience is a very important value for children to learn.

These two measures of within-country conformity pressures are complemented by two additional measures that, in different ways, provide indirect measures of tolerance for nonconformity. One of these measures follows from the logical implication that, in cultures characterized by stronger conformity pressure, there will be reduced tolerance for dispositional tendencies that deviate from dispositional norms within the culture (Gelfand et al., 2006). This in turn implies that tolerance for nonconformity may be indexed by within-country variability around mean values on basic personality traits. Exactly such an index was reported by McCrae (2002) who, in addition to reporting within-country means on the Big Five personality traits, also reported for each country (N = 33) the average standard deviation around mean values on the Big Five facet scores.

Finally, tolerance for nonconformity can also be measured indirectly by assessing the percentage of people within a country who are left-handed. In the words of Harry Triandis (1995, p. 56), "This works well because in all cultures the right hand is considered the correct one, but in cultures that are tight there is pressure for those who are naturally left-handed to become right-handed." And, in fact, evidence from many studies reveals that the percentage of left-handed people is greater—sometimes considerably so—within cultural contexts characterized by greater tolerance for nonconformity (e.g., Fagard, & Dahmen, 2004; Porac & Martin, 2007). Obtaining precise within-country estimates is not as straightforward as one might think. There are lots of different ways of measuring handedness, and these different measures sometimes produce rather different estimates. But, within the laterality literature, we were able to locate 20 different countries for which the same measurement techniques were employed to produce estimates of the percentage of people who are left-handed.

To what extent are these four variables (two measures of conformity pressure and the two measures of tolerance for nonconformity) predicted by pathogen prevalence? Substantially. The historical prevalance of pathogens correlated significantly positively with behavioral conformity effect sizes and the value placed on obedience (r's = .49 and .48), and significantly negatively with personality variation and the percentage of left-handers (r's = −.52 and −.73).

Of course, once again we must consider the possibility that these correlations are the spurious result of additional variables that covary with both pathogen prevalence and conformity. There are a variety of additional variables that have been linked either empirically or conceptually to conformity and/or nonconformity, including such things as non-disease-related threats, agricultural activity, and economic wealth (e.g., Berry, 1967, 1979; Griskevicius, Goldstein, Mortensen, Cialdini, & Kenrick, 2006). Additional regression analyses revealed, however, that the predictive impact of pathogen prevalence remained significant even when controlling for these additional variables. Furthermore, consistent with the causal relation specified by the hypothesis, these various measures of conformity (and tolerance for nonconformity) were more strongly predicted by historical pathogen prevalence than by contemporary pathogen prevalence. In addition, the relations hold—and are even stronger in magnitude—when treating world regions (the six world cultural regions identified by Murdock, 1949), rather than individual countries as units of analysis. Thus, the results are consistent with the hypothesis specifying a causal impact of pathogen prevalence on cultural values promoting obedience, conformity, and the conservation of existing cultural traditions.

I. Pathogen Prevalence Predicts Cultural Differences in Political Ideology

Thus far we have focused on the role that pathogen prevalence may have had in shaping the sorts of cultural outcomes that are of particular interest to psychologists—personality traits, behavioral dispositions, and value systems. But there are additional implications that matter to other kinds of social scientists as well, including implications for economists and political scientists.

Economic and political outcomes within a country are influenced substantially by political ideologies. These ideological outcomes are likely to be influenced by the traits, dispositions, and values of the people living within a country. For instance, within any culture that prizes tradition and conformity, specific kinds of individual rights and freedoms (e.g., freedom of speech) may be perceived to pose a threat. Consistent with this analysis is evidence that cultural tightness and collectivism are highly associated with the existence of authoritarian governments and legalized repression of civil liberties and individual freedoms (Conway, Sexton, & Tweed, 2006). An obvious implication is that these country-level differences in political ideology may have resulted, in part, from regional differences in pathogen prevalence.

Several empirical analyses provide preliminary support for this hypothesis. Thornhill, Fincher, and Aran (2009) found that contemporary pathogen prevalence was positively correlated with country-level measures that assess the repression of individual rights, negatively correlated with various additional measures of social and political liberalism, and negatively correlated with democratization in general. Further analyses (reported by Murray & Schaller, 2010) reveal that these ideological outcome variables are even more strongly predicted by historical pathogen prevalence (e.g., countries that historically have had a high prevalence of pathogens tend to be less democratic; see Table 3.1).

J. Pathogen Prevalence Predicts Cultural Diversity Itself

The results that we have discussed so far have documented a variety of ways in which regional differences in pathogen prevalence predict cultural differences between regions. Some of these effects have logical implications also for cultural diversity *within* regions.

The logic is as follows: To the extent that people are extraverted and open and willing to interact with outgroup members, they are more likely to engage in the kinds of cross-cultural interactions that allow for cultural accommodation and/or assimilation. In contrast, to the extent that people are cautious and introverted and wary of strangers, they are relatively unlikely to interact with people who are culturally distinct. And, as a result, their own cultural norms (their language, their religious rituals, their traditional beliefs and behaviors) are relatively unlikely to encroach upon other cultural norms, and also unlikely to be encroached upon by those outside influences. Thus, the lack of cross-group cultural interaction preserves cultural diversity. In a sense, just as specific kinds of physical barriers (waterways, mountain ranges) create island biogeographies, specific kinds of psychological traits (low levels of extraversion, low levels of openness to experience) and specific kinds of value systems (collectivism) create insular social geographies. And just as island biogeographies promote high levels of biodiversity within a geographical region, island social geographies promote high levels of cultural diversity within a geographical region. The logical upshot is that, because a high level of pathogen prevalence is associated with psychological traits and values that define island social geographies, it follows that a higher level of pathogen prevalence should also predict a higher level of cultural diversity within the broader region.

This appears to be the case. In two separate sets of analyses, Fincher and Thornhill (2008a, 2008b) examined the relationship between contemporary pathogen prevalence and two different indicators of cultural diversity: the number of different religions within a region, and the number of different languages spoken within a region. In both cases, as predicted, higher levels of pathogen prevalence were associated with higher levels of cultural diversity. These results suggest that not only might pathogen prevalence help to explain observed patterns in the contemporary record of worldwide cultural diversity, pathogen prevalence might also help to explain local cultural diversity.

K. Implications, Limitations, and Future Directions

Not only do these findings collectively support a variety of conceptually derived hypotheses specifying relations between pathogen prevalence and cultural outcomes, these findings also help to provide a more complete explanation for various previously documented relations between different kinds of country-level variables. We provide three examples.

First, at a cultural level of analysis, extraversion is associated with individualistic (rather than collectivistic) value systems. Consequently, cross-cultural researchers have speculated about the possible causal influence of personality dispositions on cultural values, and about the possible influence of values on dispositions (Hofstede & McCrae, 2004). It turns out, however, that the correlation between individualism and extraversion disappears when statistically controlling for pathogen prevalence (Fincher et al., 2008; Schaller & Murray, 2008). Rather than extraversion leading to individualism, or vice versa, it appears that the relation between these two constructs is largely spurious, resulting from the fact that both are cultural consequences of pathogen prevalence.

Second, there are well-documented relations between economic conditions and cultural characteristics. For instance, the mean level of economic affluence within a country (as indicated by gross domestic product per capita) is a powerful predictor of values along the individualism/collectivism dimension (Hofstede, 2001; Triandis, 1995). This relation is substantially diminished—although does not disappear entirely—when controlling for pathogen prevalence (Fincher et al., 2008). It appears, therefore, that the actual influence of economic conditions on cultural values may be considerably less substantial than has often been assumed. In fact, given that infectious diseases are powerful inhibitors of economic development (Sachs & Malaney, 2002), the indirect influence of pathogen prevalence may be lurking in the background behind even the unique effects of economic affluence on cultural outcomes.

Third, latitude is a strong statistical predictor of many different kinds of cross-cultural differences (Cohen, 2001; Hofstede, 2001; Kashima & Kashima, 2003). Of course, latitude is merely a cartographic abstraction; it cannot exert any direct causal influence on human behavior. The statistical effects of latitude require explanations that focus on more physically meaningful variables such as the higher temperatures, greater rainfalls, and other meteorological conditions associated with lower latitudes (e.g., Van de Vliert, 2009). Pathogen prevalence is profoundly influenced by these same meteorological variables, which is a major reason why the diversity and prevalence of pathogens is generally much greater in the tropics compared to higher latitudes (Epstein, 1999; Guernier et al., 2004). It appears likely that pathogen prevalence is an instrumental part of any complete causal explanation for the relation between latitude (and the meteorological variables that covary with latitude) and psychologically interesting cultural outcomes.

Of course, there are not only implications associated with this body of evidence but also limitations. It is important to bear these limitations in mind when interpreting the results that we have just reviewed and when proceeding with new research in the future.

One set of limitations arises from the fact that the units of analysis are countries, and not independent cultures per se. This analytic strategy raises the specter of Galton's problem, which we discussed at the outset of our review. To address this issue, some of the results summarized earlier were accompanied by additional analyses that focused not on countries as units of analysis, but instead on large world regions that, historically, have been culturally distinct. Reassuringly, the results from these additional analyses replicate those observed on the country-level data (e.g., Fincher et al., 2008). But not all the published findings have been accompanied by these additional analyses. For example, in our article reporting the effects of pathogen prevalence on personality traits (Schaller & Murray, 2008), we reported only country-level analyses, but no region-level analyses of the sort that might help address

Galton's problem. We are happy to report here that those region-level analyses have been done (we computed mean values on pathogen prevalence as well for each of the Big Five personality traits within each of the six world cultural regions identified by Murdock, 1949), and that the results do indeed replicate the primary effects by Schaller and Murray (2008): When treating world regions rather than countries as the units of analysis, the predictive effects of pathogen prevalence on extraversion and openness are identical in direction and even stronger in magnitude. More generally, across the various studies documenting relations between pathogen prevalence and cultural differences, there has emerged no evidence that the results—or conclusions—are compromised by the use of country as a unit of analysis.

Still, this inferential issue is a complicated one, and it would be unwise to dismiss it. There are a variety of methodological techniques that can be employed to address Galton's problem and the statistical issue of autocorrelation more generally (e.g., Dow, 2007; Mace & Holden, 2005). The issue itself might be minimized by inquiries that focus on cultural units of analysis that are more clearly independent, such as small-scale societies of the sort that have traditionally been the subject of ethnographic research in the anthropology literature. (It is worth noting, however, that even relatively isolated small-scale societies may not be as culturally independent as often assumed; Eff, 2004).

Another important inferential limitation arises from the twin facts that (a) the empirical methods are necessarily correlational, and (b) any one country-level variable is inevitably correlated with many other country-level variables. This is certainly the case for pathogen prevalence. In our research, we have drawn conclusions about the predictive effects of pathogen prevalence only when those effects remained after controlling for a variety of additional variables. But it is impossible to statistically control for every variable that might be correlated with pathogen prevalence. Any conclusion about the effects of pathogen prevalence on cultural outcomes must, logically, be accompanied by the familiar caveat that a causal inference cannot be claimed with absolute certainty.

Of course, this inferential issue applies equally to *any* investigation that tests hypothesized effects of any variable on cultural outcomes. Thus, regardless of whether a researcher has a conceptual interest in the effect of pathogen prevalence on culture, the results that we have reviewed suggest researchers must contend with the predictive effects of pathogen prevalence anyway. Before drawing conclusions about the alleged unique effects of other variables on cultural outcomes, researchers must show that those effects remain even after controlling for the historical prevalence of pathogens.

Ultimately, as evidence accumulates bearing on the potential causal relevance of various different kinds of ecological and economic variables, it will become important to articulate the complex causal relations between the multiple variables that predict contemporary cross-cultural differences. Only by rigorously pursuing multivariate and multicausal strategies of inquiry are we likely to arrive at a true reckoning of the possible role that pathogen prevalence may have played in the origin of contemporary cross-cultural differences.

It may be important also to consider the possibility that cultural consequences *of* pathogen prevalence may have reciprocal causal implications *on* pathogen prevalence, and that these implications may be especially complicated as ecological circumstances change over time. For instance, while collectivistic value systems can promote specific kinds of behavioral buffers against endemic pathogens (e.g., conformity to existing norms of culinary spicing inhibits the transmission of foodborne bacteria), these same value systems might be counter-productive in the context of exotic pathogens (conformity to existing norms inhibits the development of novel behavioral strategies that might effectively respond to the threat posed by novel diseases).

These are just a few of the ways that future research must build upon and extend the findings that we have reviewed here. Another agenda for future research is to illuminate the causal mechanisms through which pathogen prevalence might actually exert its effects on cultural outcomes. We believe that this particular agenda is of such fundamental importance—and of such wide-ranging scientific interest value—that we close this chapter with a detailed discussion of the diverse kinds of processes that might be implicated, and the diverse kinds of scientific methodologies that might be used to implicate them.

III. DEEPER CONSIDERATION OF UNDERLYING CAUSAL PROCESSES

Even if we allow ourselves to draw the tentative conclusion that many different kinds of cultural differences may indeed be the result, in part, of regional differences in pathogen prevalence, we must still contend with a huge question: Exactly how might this have occurred? What is the exact causal process—or set of processes—through which ecological variation in pathogen prevalence leads to cultural variation in human cognition and behavior?

There are at least four different kinds of processes through which pathogen prevalence might exert a causal influence on cross-cultural variability. These processes are all conceptually distinct—operating at four entirely different levels of analysis—and so they are not mutually exclusive. Each must be considered on its own terms and evaluated on the basis of both logical plausibility (which appears ample for all four) and available empirical evidence (which, thus far, is ample for none).

A. Cultural Evolution: Ecological Influence on Interpersonal Communication and Social Learning

Human beings have considerable cognitive capacities that allow them to recognize both the dangers and the opportunities in their local environments, to pragmatically adjust their behavior accordingly, and to communicate their pragmatic wisdom to others. Even in the absence of any knowledge about the pragmatic considerations that may have informed others' behavior, people learn from others' behavior, they imitate and reproduce that behavior, and thus they reify and perpetuate those behavioral norms. Through these processes of interpersonal communication and social learning, cultural norms evolve. And, under different ecological circumstances characterized by different kinds of perils and prospects and pragmatic considerations, cultural norms evolve differently.

On logical grounds alone, cultural transmission processes provide a highly compelling means through which ecological variability in pathogen prevalence might lead to cross-cultural variability in traits, values, and other behavioral norms (Schaller, 2006). Cultural transmission processes provide a speedy and efficient means through which human populations adapt sensibly to their ecological circumstances. Indeed, because of this speed, an explanation rooted in cultural evolutionary processes is entirely compatible with evidence documenting rapid-but-not-overnight changes in cultural values (i.e., changes observed over the course of a generation or two) associated with immigrant populations who migrate from countries characterized by high pathogen prevalence to countries with substantially lower levels of pathogen prevalence (e.g., Hardyck, Petrinovich, & Goldman, 1976). And, of course, there are empirical literatures documenting the individual-level psychological phenomena that provide the raw materials for cultural evolution—including perceptual hypervigilance to cues connoting the presence of threat, selective communication about threat, social learning of avoidant responses to threat, and many different forms of selective behavioral mimicry and conformity.

On the other hand, there is scant evidence that bears specifically on the implications of pathogens for cultural evolution. Among the many studies that document hypervigilance to threat (Öhman, Flykt, & Esteves, 2001; Schupp et al., 2004), there are only a few that suggest hypervigilance to disease-connoting cues in particular (e.g., Ackerman et al., 2009). And while there are some empirical results suggesting that people are especially likely to communicate about threat-connoting information (Schaller & Conway, 1999; Schaller, Faulkner, Park, Neuberg, & Kenrick, 2004), there are none that focus on disease-relevant information in particular. Similarly, while there is evidence showing that humans and other primates learn from other individuals' aversive emotional responses to threats (Cook & Mineka, 1990; Hornick, Risenhoover, & Gunnar, 1987), none of this evidence pertains specifically to pathogens. And while there is evidence that collective human behavior is sensitive to emotionally charged communications connoting the threat of disease (Sinaceur, Heath, & Cole, 2005), this evidence does not link the nature of these communications to the actual prevalence of disease in the natural ecology. Thus, as yet, there is virtually no empirical evidence that directly tests the hypothesis that cultural transmission processes might mediate any of the observed relationships between pathogen prevalence and cultural characteristics.

B. Neurocognitive Processes: Ecological Influence on Adaptively Flexible Cognition and Behavior

Human cognitive functioning is characterized by perceptual mechanisms that are highly sensitive to fitness-relevant information in the immediate environment. When this information is perceived, it triggers a cascade of neurochemical activity that ultimately influences how individuals respond affectively, cognitively, and behaviorally to their environment. In a relatively benign environment, these perceptual cues are likely to trigger approach-oriented cognitions and behaviors. In a more dangerous environment, however, these perceptual cues are likely to trigger more avoidant cognitions and risk-averse behaviors. Thus, for instance, under conditions in which threats are temporarily salient, people show less evidence of independent thinking and a greater tendency toward social conformity (Griskevicius et al., 2006).

Many of the cultural variables predicted by pathogen prevalence (including not only conformity but also basic personality traits and the endorsement of individualistic/collectivistic values) are, at an individual level of analysis, highly malleable in response to immediate contextual circumstances (e.g., Gardner, Gabriel, & Lee, 1999; Hong et al., 2000; Kunda & Santioso, 1989), and there is now abundant evidence that the perceived threat of pathogen transmission has an immediate causal influence on human cognition. For instance, under conditions in which the threat of pathogenic infection is either especially high or especially salient, people respond by being more likely to display more xenophobic and ethnocentric attitudes toward foreigners (Faulkner, Schaller, Park, & Duncan, 2004; Navarette et al., 2007). The salience of infectious diseases also leads to reduced levels of self-reported extraversion and to behavioral withdrawal from social stimuli (Mortensen et al., 2010).

Thus, it is entirely plausible that a causal relation between pathogen prevalence and cultural outcomes could be mediated, in part, by the operation of adaptively flexible neurocognitive mechanisms. Under ecological conditions characterized by high pathogen prevalence, these mechanisms may induce individuals to think and behave in an adaptively cautious manner (characterized by lower levels of extraversion, higher levels of xenophobia and ingroup conformity, etc.) In contrast, under ecological conditions characterized by low pathogen prevalence, these neurocognitive mechanisms are less likely to be triggered by disease-connoting perceptual cues, and so individuals are likely to be more open-minded and approach-oriented instead.

However, while there is empirical evidence documenting the causal influence of disease salience on ethnocentrism, xenophobia, and extraversion (e.g., Faulkner et al., 2004; Mortensen et al., 2010), these are just a few of the many variables that, at a cultural level of analysis, have been linked to pathogen prevalence. There is no published empirical evidence showing that the mere perception of disease threat might lead people to be more conforming, to endorse more collectivistic values, to be more sexually restricted, or to be more likely to put spices in one's food.

Even if such evidence is eventually found, additional empirical considerations suggest that neurocognitive mechanisms are unlikely to offer a complete explanation for the cultural consequences of pathogen prevalence. The cognitive and behavioral consequences of these neurocognitive mechanisms occur very quickly. (In the typical experiment documenting the causal consequences of a disease salience manipulation, the effects are observed in mere minutes.) Thus, if the cross-cultural differences of pathogen prevalence were due solely to the operation of neurocognitive mechanisms, one would expect contemporary measures of pathogen prevalence to predict cultural outcomes more strongly than historical measures. This is not the case. Moreover, one would expect immigrants to show a virtually instantaneous change in dispositions and values upon migrating to a novel ecological niche. Such instantaneous change is rarely observed. Thus, while there is a compelling conceptual case to be made for the mediating role of neurocognitive mechanisms, and this conceptual case is buttressed by some recent empirical results, it is also clear that other mechanisms, operating at different levels of analysis, must also be considered.

C. Epigenetic Processes: Ecological Influence on Developmental Expression of Genes

A third plausible process that might account for an effect of pathogen prevalence on cultural outcomes is a developmental process—not "developmental" in the sense that the word is employed by psychologists, but instead in the sense that it is employed by developmental biologists. This is the kind of process to which evolutionary psychologists typically refer when they talk of "evoked culture" (e.g., Gangestad et al., 2006; Tooby & Cosmides, 1992). The basic idea is as follows: Attitudes, traits, and other dispositional tendencies are influenced by genes. The phenotypic consequences of genes depend, however, on whether (and how) the genes are expressed during the course of development. Gene expression is profoundly influenced—typically in functionally adaptive ways—by the ecological circumstances within which an individual organism develops.

When this developmental reasoning is applied to pathogen prevalence, the logic is straightforward: Under ecological circumstances characterized by higher levels of pathogen prevalence, genes associated with cautious dispositional tendencies (e.g., introversion, sexual restrictedness, the endorsement of conformist values) are relatively more likely to be expressed during development, and to exert a greater influence on individuals' eventual dispositional tendencies. Conversely, under ecological circumstances characterized by relatively fewer pathogens, genes associated with more risk-tolerant and approach-oriented dispositional tendencies (e.g., extraversion, openness, nonconformity) are relatively more likely to be expressed. This context-contingent developmental process results, inevitably, in regional populations characterized by somewhat different attitudes, values, and personality traits.

The plausibility of this epigenetic explanation is supported by a considerable body of evidence documenting gene–environment interactions in the prediction of human cognition and behavior (e.g., Cole, 2009). Its plausibility is also supported by an extensive literature in the biological sciences bearing on the evolutionary advantages associated with phenotypic plasticity and the many ways in which phenotypic plasticity manifests in the natural world (Ridley, 2003). Among many mammal species, developing fetuses obtain information about postnatal environments via chemical cues obtained through the placenta; these cues influence gene expression in ways that promote the development of adaptive phenotypic responses (Gluckman & Hanson, 2005). Among meadow voles, for example, the placental transfer of melatonin (a chemical signal diagnostic of the length of the day) has the adaptive developmental consequence that, as winter (rather than summer) approaches, infants are born with thicker coats (Lee & Zucker, 1988).

Just as development is adaptively influenced by the placental transfer of melatonin, development may also be adaptively influenced by the placental transfer of chemical signals that are produced maternally when mothers are exposed to pathogens. These chemical signals include corticosteroids and other hormones associated with stress and immune response. In research with nonhuman mammals, prenatal exposure to maternal corticosteroids has been linked to dispositional tendencies later in life, including lower levels of sexual aggression, reduced social interaction, and less exploratory behaviors in novel environments (e.g., Takahashi, Haglin, & Kalin, 1992; see Edwards & Burnham, 2001, for a review). In one particularly notable study with mice, pregnant dams who were exposed to pathogen-infected conspecifics produced higher levels of corticosterone and produced offspring who, upon reaching adulthood, were meeker and less socially aggressive than controls (Curno, Behnke, McElligot, Reader, & Barnard, 2009). Analogously, among humans, pregnant mothers treated with a stress hormone (dexamethasone) gave birth to children who, compared to controls, were relatively more shy and less sociable (Trautman, Meyer-Bahlburg, Postelnek, & New, 1995).

These developmental results neatly parallel the cross-cultural findings reported by Schaller and Murray (2008), and so they give special credence to an explanation based upon the effects of pathogen prevalence on gene expression and development. Still, this evidence is indirect, at best. More compelling tests of this explanation must focus more specifically on human development and must consider a fuller range of the attitudes, traits, values, and behavioral tendencies that have been linked, cross-culturally, to pathogen prevalence.

D. Genetic Evolution: Ecological Influence on Population-Level Gene Frequencies

Finally, we must consider the possibility of a genetic evolutionary process, such that alleles that predispose individuals to specific kinds of traits and values are differentially likely to proliferate under different kinds of ecological circumstances. Thus, just as alleles promoting post-weaning production of lactase have been differentially selected for (and consequently have become relatively more common) within pastoral populations that domesticate milk-producing animals (Durham, 1991), alleles promoting extraversion, openness, and individualism may have been differentially selected for (and become relatively more common) within populations characterized by relatively low levels of pathogen prevalence.

Like the cultural evolution explanation, the genetic evolution explanation is consistent with findings showing that historical pathogen prevalence predicts cultural outcomes more strongly than contemporary pathogen prevalence. The plausibility of a genetic evolution process is supported by evidence of relatively rapid evolution of different gene frequencies within populations that differ in the prevalence of specific kinds of pathogens (Williamson et al., 2007). Its plausibility is supported also by evidence of a heritable basis for the kinds of attitudes, traits, and values that characterize worldwide cross-cultural differences. For example, the Big Five personality traits—including extraversion and openness to experience—all have substantial heritability coefficients (Henderson, 1982; Jang, Livesely, & Vemon, 1996), and there is also evidence of genetic influence on behavioral tendencies toward individualism and collectivism (Bouchard & McGue, 2003).

But in order to be truly compelling, the genetic evolution explanation must be tested directly against empirical data pertaining to specific genetic polymorphisms that (*a*) are statistically associated with specific kinds of dispositional tendencies, and (*b*) exist in at different frequencies within different cultural populations. Presumably, future genetics research will reveal many such genetic polymorphisms, but the extant literature has identified only a few promising candidates for consideration. One such candidate is a coding-sequence polymorphism on the DRD4 dopamine receptor gene. The long version of this polymorphism has been linked to novelty-seeking behaviors in humans and other primates (Bailey et al., 2007; Schinka et al., 2002), and there are widely different frequencies of this allele in different populations throughout the world (Chen et al., 1999). Another promising candidate is the 5-HTTLPR polymorphic region of the SLC6A4 serotonin transporter gene. The short allele version of this polymorphism has been associated with a variety of cautious and avoidant behavioral tendencies (e.g., Beevers, Gibb, McGeary, & Miller, 2007; Munafo, Clark, & Flint, 2005), and the relative frequencies of short versus long 5-HTTLPR alleles vary substantially across different populations (Gelernter, Kranzler, & Cubells, 1997). Although cultural psychologists have speculated that variability in these (or other) gene frequencies might covary with psychologically meaningful cross-cultural differences (e.g., Chiao & Ambady, 2007), there has been almost no rigorous research addressing this possibility, nor the possibility that these gene frequencies might help to account for the relationships between pathogen prevalence and cultural outcomes.

This state of affairs may be changing. Recently, Chiao and Blizinksy (2010) reported a provocative result showing that, across several dozen countries worldwide, the relative frequency of short 5-HTTLPR alleles is strongly positively associated with country-level values of collectivism. Moreover, the frequency of short 5-HTTLPR alleles is also positively associated with country-level values of pathogen prevalence, and it partially mediates the relationship between pathogen prevalence and collectivism. These results provide the first empirical evidence to directly test, and support, a gene-frequency explanation for the effects of pathogen prevalence on cultural outcomes.

Of course, regardless of evidence such as this, genetic evolution can provide, at best, only a partial explanation. Even though pathogen prevalence imposes the kind of powerful selection pressure that can result in relatively fast changes in gene frequencies, the pace of genetic evolution is still slow compared to the pace of the other causal processes that may contribute to cross-cultural differences. Genetic evolution certainly cannot account for changes in cultural values that often occur over the course of just one or two generations. For example, compared to populations in East Asia, left-handedness occurs more frequently among populations of East Asian immigrants to North America (Hardyck et al., 1976). This particular difference is consistent with the broader pattern of evidence pertaining to the effects of pathogen prevalence, but a genetic evolution process cannot logically account for it. An additional explanation is required.

E. Conclusion

So which of these four processes provides the best explanation for the relation between pathogen prevalence and cultural differences? All of them. Each process is conceptually compelling in its own right, and each is buttressed by either direct or indirect empirical evidence of one sort or another. Moreover, not a single one of these processes seems capable of accounting for all the different pieces of empirical evidence. And given that these processes are conceptually independent, there is no logically sensible reason to suppose that any one process operates to the exclusion of others. All things considered, the most plausible conclusion to draw at this point is that, if pathogen prevalence does indeed exert causal influences on cultural outcomes, these effects are likely to be the result of multiple processes operating at multiple levels of analysis.

It is possible that some of these processes account for some cultural outcomes, but not others. For instance, while epigenetic and neurocognitive processes might mediate the relationship between pathogen prevalence and extraversion, that does not mean they must also play a role in mediating the relationship between pathogen prevalence and conformity, or the relationship between pathogen prevalence and culinary spicing. And while the effect of pathogen prevalence on collectivism might be partially explained by a genetic evolutionary process, the effect on culinary spicing might not reflect any kind of genetic mechanism whatsoever; it might instead reflect a cultural evolutionary process.

Of course, it is also possible that two or more processes might contribute jointly to any particular cultural outcome. Because these processes operate at different levels of analysis, they might operate entirely in parallel. Or, in some cases, they might be causally connected. There is considerable theoretical basis to expect that cultural and genetic evolutionary processes may be entwined in a more complicated coevolutionary process (e.g., Durham, 1991). For instance, within the domain of food preparation, the threat of bacterial infections might lead, through cultural evolutionary processes, to the emergence of cultural norms prescribing the liberal use of spices. Once established, these cultural norms may impose selection pressures on genes associated with a tolerance or craving for spicy foods.

Future research must probe much more deeply into all these possible processes, and it must find ways of more directly testing the implications of each. For example, it would be illuminating to conduct longitudinal studies that document changes in pathogen prevalence within a cultural region (e.g., epidemic outbreaks of infectious disease) and track the cultural effects over time (e.g., consequent changes in social behavior and value systems). This kind of methodology would not only help to identify *which* cultural outcomes are influenced by pathogen prevalence, but it also could document *when* those changes occur. The time frame for those changes could reveal clues to the underlying processes. Any change in population-level norms that transpires within days or weeks of a disease outbreak would indicate the operation of neurocognitive mechanisms. Changes that are specific to a one-generation lag behind a disease outbreak are more likely to implicate an epigenetic process. And changes that accumulate across multiple generations would be more indicative of a cultural evolutionary process. If the selection pressure imposed by a disease outbreak is substantial enough, longitudinal studies might even be able to test genetic evolutionary processes as well, by assessing whether changes in population-level behavioral norms are accompanied by changes in gene frequencies as well.

This kind of study is ambitious, of course, and would require considerable resources and considerable patience as well, given that some of the most interesting results might take decades to emerge. But, as we noted earlier, it is no simple task to inquire empirically into the origins of cultural differences. For scientists who care about psychology and culture, it is important to ask big questions of this sort; however, we cannot expect the answers to arrive quickly, or easily.

ACKNOWLEDGMENTS

This research was supported by a Standard Research Grant (awarded to M.S.) and a Canada Graduate Scholarship (awarded to D.R.M.) funded by the Social Sciences and Humanities Research Council of Canada. Correspondence may be addressed to Mark Schaller, Department of Psychology, University of British Columbia, 2136 West Mall, Vancouver BC, Canada V6T1Z4. Email: schaller@psych.ubc.ca

REFERENCES

Acemoglu, D., Johnson, S., & Robinson, J. A. (2001). The colonial origins of comparative development: An empirical investigation. *American Economic Review, 91*, 1369–1401.

Ackerman, J. M., Becker, D. V., Mortensen, C. R., Sasaki, T., Neuberg, S. L., & Kenrick, D. T. (2009). A pox on the mind: Disjunction of attention and memory in the processing of physical disfigurement. *Journal of Experimental Social Psychology, 45*, 478–485.

Asch, S. E. (1956). Studies of independence and conformity: A minority of one against a unanimous majority. *Psychological Monographs, 70*(9, Whole No. 416).

Bailey, J. N., Breidenthal, S. E., Jorgensen, M. J., McCracken, J. T., & Fairbanks, L. A. (2007). The association of DRD4 and novelty seeking is found in a nonhuman primate model. *Psychiatric Genetics, 17*, 23–27.

Beevers, C. G., Gibb, B. E., McGeary, J. E., & Miller, I. W. (2007). Serotonin transporter genetic variation and biased attention for emotional word stimuli among psychiatric inpatients. *Journal of Abnormal Psychology, 116*, 208–212.

Berry, D. S., & Miller, K. M. (2001). When boy meets girl: Attractiveness and the Five-Factor Model in opposite-sex interactions. *Journal of Research in Personality, 35,* 62–77.

Berry, J. W. (1967). Independence and conformity in subsistence-level societies. *Journal of Personality and Social Psychology, 7,* 415–418.

Berry, J. W. (1979). A cultural ecology of social behavior. In L. Berkowitz (Ed.), *Advances in experimental social psychology,* (Vol. 12, pp. 177–206). New York: Academic Press.

Billing, J., & Sherman, P. W. (1998). Antimicrobial functions of spices: Why some like it hot. *Quarterly Review of Biology, 73,* 3–49.

Bond, R., & Smith, P. B. (1996). Culture and conformity: A meta-analysis of studies using Asch's line judgment task. *Psychological Bulletin, 119,* 111–137.

Brown, J. K. M. (2003). A cost of disease-resistance: Paradigm or peculiarity. *Trends in Genetics, 19,* 667–671.

Bouchard, T. J., Jr., & McGue, M. (2003). Genetic and environmental influences on human psychological differences. *Journal of Neurobiology, 54,* 4–45.

Buss, D. M. (1989). Sex differences in human mate preferences: Evolutionary hypotheses tested in 37 cultures. *Behavioral and Brain Sciences, 12,* 1–14.

Chiao, J. Y., & Ambady, N. (2007). Cultural neuroscience: Parsing universality and diversity across levels of analysis. In S. Kitayama & D. Cohen (Eds.), *Handbook of cultural psychology* (pp. 237–254). New York: Guilford.

Chiao, J. Y., & Blizinksy, K. D. (2010). Culture-gene coevolution of individualism-collectivism and the serotonin transporter gene. *Proceedings of the Royal Society B, 277,* 529–527.

Chen, C., Burton, M. Greenberger, E., & Dmitrieva, J. (1999). Population migration and the variation of dopamine D4 receptor (DRD4) allele frequencies around the globe. *Evolution and Human Behavior, 20,* 309–324.

Chen, J., Chiu, C-Y., & Chan, S. F. (2009). The cultural effects of job mobility and the belief in a fixed world: Evidence from performance forecast. *Journal of Personality and Social Psychology, 97,* 851–865.

Cohen, D. (2001). Cultural variation: Considerations and implications. *Psychological Bulletin, 127,* 451–471.

Cohen, D., Nisbett, R. E., Bowdle, B., & Schwarz, N. (1996). Insult, aggression, and the southern culture of honor: An "experimental ethnography." *Journal of Personality and Social Psychology, 70,* 945–960.

Cole, S. W. (2009). Social regulation of human gene expression. *Current Directions in Psychological Science, 18,* 132–137.

Conway, L. G., III, & Schaller, M. (2007). How communication shapes culture. In K. Fiedler (Ed.), *Social communication* (pp. 107–127). New York: Psychology Press.

Conway, L. G., III, Sexton, S. M., & Tweed, R. G. (2006). Collectivism and governmentally initiated restrictions: A cross-sectional and longitudinal analysis across nations and within a nation. *Journal of Cross-Cultural Psychology, 37,* 20–41.

Cook, M., & Mineka, S. (1990). Selective associations in the observational conditioning of fear in rhesus monkeys. *Journal of Experimental Psychology: Animal Behavior Processes, 16*, 372–389.

Costa, P. T., Jr., & McCrae, R. R. (1992). *Revised NEO Personality Inventory (NEO PI-R) and the NEO Five-Factor Inventory (NEO-FFI) professional manual.* Odessa, FL: Psychological Assessment Resources.

Cukur, C. S., De Gusman, M. R. T., & Carlo, G. (2004). Religiosity, values, and horizontal and vertical individual-collectivism: A study of Turkey, the United States, and the Phillipines. *Journal of Social Psychology, 144*, 613–634.

Curno, O., Behnke, J. M., McElligott, A. G., Reader, T., & Barnard, C. J. (2009). Mothers produce less aggressive sons with altered immunity when there is a threat of disease during pregnancy. *Proceedings of the Royal Society B, 276*, 1047–1054.

Daly, M., & Wilson, M. (2010). Cultural inertia, economic incentives, and the persistence of "southern violence." In M. Schaller, A. Norenzayan, S. J. Heine, T. Yamagishi, & T. Kameda (Eds.), *Evolution, culture, and the human mind* (pp. 229–241). New York: Psychology Press.

Dow, M. M. (2007). Galton's problem as multiple network autocorrelation effects. *Cross-Cultural Research, 41*, 336–363.

Durham, W. H. (1991). *Coevolution: Genes, culture and human diversity.* Stanford, CA: Stanford University Press.

Edwards, H. E., & Burnham, M. (2001). The developing nervous system: A series of review articles. *Pediatric Research, 50*, 433–440.

Eff, E. A. (2004). Does Mr. Galton still have a problem? Autocorrelation in the standard cross-cultural sample. *World Cultures, 15*, 153–170.

Epstein, P. R. (1999). Climate and health. *Science, 285*, 347–348.

Ewald, P. W. (1993). *Evolution of infectious disease.* New York: Oxford University Press.

Fagard, J., & Dahmen, R. (2004). Cultural influences on the development of lateral preferences: A comparison between French and Tunisian children. *Laterality, 9*, 67–78.

Faulkner, J., Schaller, M., Park, J. H., & Duncan, L. A. (2004). Evolved disease-avoidance mechanisms and contemporary xenophobic attitudes. *Group Processes and Intergroup Behavior, 7*, 333–353.

Fincher, C. L., & Thornhill, R. (2008a). A parasite-driven wedge: Infectious diseases may explain language and other biodiversity. *Oikos, 117*, 1289–1297.

Fincher, C. L., & Thornhill, R. (2008b). Assortive sociality, limited dispersal, infectious disease and the genesis of the global pattern of religious diversity. *Proceedings of the Royal Society B, 275*, 2587–2594.

Fincher, C. L., Thornhill, R., Murray, D. R., & Schaller, M. (2008). Pathogen prevalence predicts human cross-cultural variability in individualism/collectivism. *Proceedings of the Royal Society B, 275*, 1279–1285.

Fleeson, W., Malanos, A. B., & Achille, N. M. (2002). An individual process approach to the relationship between extraversion and positive affect: Is acting extraverted as "good" as being extraverted? *Journal of Personality and Social Psychology, 83*, 1409–1422.

Gangestad, S. W., & Buss, D. M. (1993). Pathogen prevalence and human mate preferences. *Ethology and Sociobiology, 14*, 89–96.

Gangestad, S. W., Haselton, M. G., & Buss, D. M. (2006). Evolutionary foundations of cultural variation: Evoked culture and mate preferences. *Psychological Inquiry, 17*, 75–95.

Gardner, W. L., Gabriel, S., & Lee, A. Y. (1999). "I" value freedom but "we" value relationships: Self-construal priming mirrors cultural differences in judgment. *Psychological Science, 10*, 321–326.

Gelernter, J., Kranzler, H., & Cubells, J. F. (1997). Serotonin transporter protein (SLC6A4) allele and haplotype frequencies and linage disequilibria in African- and European-American and Japanese populations and in alcohol-dependent subjects. *Human Genetics, 101*, 243–246.

Gelfand, M. J., Bhawuk, D. P. S., Nishii, L. H., & Bechtold, D. J. (2004). Individualism and collectivism. In R. J. House, P. J. Hanges, M. Javidan, P. W. Dorfman, & V. Gupta (Eds.), *Culture, leadership, and organizations: The GLOBE study of 62 societies* (pp. 437–512). Thousand Oaks, CA: Sage.

Gelfand, M. J., Nishii, L. H., & Raver, J. L. (2006). On the nature and importance of cultural tightness-looseness. *Journal of Applied Psychology, 91*, 1225–1244.

Gluckman, P. D., & Hanson, M. A. (2005). *The fetal matrix: Evolution, development, and disease*. Cambridge, England: Cambridge University Press.

Goodall, J. (1986). Social rejection, exclusion, and shunning among the Gombe chimpanzees. *Ethology and Sociobiology, 7*, 227–239.

Griskevicius, V., Goldstein, N., Mortensen, C., Cialdini, R. B., & Kenrick, D. T. (2006). Going along versus going alone: When fundamental motives facilitate strategic (non)conformity. *Journal of Personality and Social Psychology, 91*, 281–294.

Guernier, V., Hochberg, M. E., & Guégan, J-F. (2004). Ecology drives the worldwide distribution of human diseases. *PloS Biology, 2*, 740–746.

Gupta, V., & Hanges, P. J. (2004). Regional and climate clustering of societal cultures. In R. J. House, P. J. Hanges, M. Javidan, P. W. Dorfman, & V. Gupta (Eds.), *Culture, leadership, and organizations: The GLOBE study of 62 societies* (pp. 178–218). Thousand Oaks, CA: Sage.

Hamilton, W. D., & Zuk, M. (1982). Heritable true fitness and bright birds: A role for parasites? *Science, 218*, 384–387.

Hamrick, N., Cohen, S., & Rodriguez, M. S. (2002). Being popular can be healthy or unhealthy: Stress, social network diversity, and incidence of upper respiratory infection. *Health Psychology, 21*, 294–298.

Hardyck, C., Petrinovich, L., & Goldman, R. (1976). Left handedness and cognitive deficit. *Cortex, 12*, 266–278.

Heath, C., Bell, C., & Sternberg, E. (2001). Emotional selection in memes: The case of urban legends. *Journal of Personality and Social Psychology*, *81*, 1028–1041.

Heine, S. J. (2008). *Cultural psychology*. New York: Norton.

Heine, S. J., Buchtel, E., & Norenzayan, A. (2008). What do cross-national comparisons of self-reported personality traits tell us? The case of conscientiousness. *Psychological Science*, *19*, 309–313.

Heine, S. J., Lehman, D. R., Markus, H. R., & Kitayama, S. (1999). Is there a universal need for positive self-regard? *Psychological-Review*, *106*, 766–794.

Henderson, N. D. (1982). Human behavioral genetics. *Annual Review of Psychology*, *33*, 403–440.

Henrich, J., Boyd, R., Bowles, S., Camerer, C., Fehr, E., Gintis, H. et al. (2005). "Economic man" in cross-cultural perspective: Ethnography and experiments from 15 small-scale societies. *Behavioral and Brain Sciences*, *28*, 795–855.

Hofstede, G. (2001). *Culture's consequences. Comparing values, behaviors, institutions, and organizations across nations* (2nd ed.). Thousand Oaks, CA: Sage.

Hofstede, G., & McCrae, R. R. (2004). Personality and culture revisited: Linking traits and dimensions of culture. *Cross-Cultural Research*, *38*, 52–88.

Hong, Y-Y., Morris, M. W., Chiu, C-Y., & Benet-Martinez, V. (2000). Multicultural minds: A dynamic constructivist approach to culture and cognition. *American Psychologist*, *55*, 709–720.

Hornick, R., Risenhoover, N., & Gunnar, M. (1987). The effects of maternal positive, neutral, and negative affective communications on infant responses to new toys. *Child Development*, *58*, 937–944.

Jang, K. L., Livesley, W. J., & Vemon, P. A. (1996). Heritability of the Big Five personality dimensions and their facets: A twin study. *Journal of Personality*, *64*, 577–592.

John, O. P., & Srivastava, S. (1999). The Big Five trait taxonomy: History, measurement, and theoretical perspectives. In L. A. Pervin & O. P. John's (Eds.), *Handbook of personality: Theory and research*. New York: Guilford Press.

Kashima, E. S., & Kashima, Y. (1998). Culture and language: The case of cultural dimensions and personal pronoun use. *Journal of Cross-Cultural Psychology*, *29*, 461–486.

Kashima, Y., & Kashima, E. S. (2003). Individualism, GNP, climate, and pronoun drop: Is individualism determined by affluence and climate, or does language use play a role? *Journal of Cross-Cultural Psychology*, *34*, 125–134.

Kavaliers, M., & Colwell, D. D. (1995). Discrimination by female mice between the odours of parasitized and non-parasitized males. *Proceedings of the Royal Society B*, *261*, 31–35.

Kiesecker, J. M., Skelly, D. K., Beard, K. H., & Preisser, E. (1999). Behavioral reduction of infection risk. *Proceedings of the National Academy of Sciences*, *96*, 9165–9168.

Kitayama, S., & Bowman, N. A. (2010). Cultural consequences of voluntary settlement in the frontier: Evidence and implications. In M. Schaller,

A. Norenzayan, S. J. Heine, T. Yamagishi, & T. Kameda (Eds.), *Evolution, culture, and the human mind* (pp. 205–227). New York: Psychology Press.

Kitayama, S., Ishii, K., Imada, T., Takamura, K., & Ramaswamy, J. (2006). Voluntary settlement and the spirit of independence: Evidence from Japan's "northern frontier." *Journal of Personality and Social Psychology, 91,* 369–384.

Klein, S. L., & Nelson, R. J. (1999). Influence of social factors on immune function and reproduction. *Reviews of Reproduction, 4,* 168–178.

Kunda, Z., & Santioso, R. (1989). Motivated changes in the self-concept. *Journal of Experimental Social Psychology, 25,* 272–285.

Larsen, R. J., & Buss, D. M. (2005). *Personality psychology* (2nd ed.). New York: McGraw-Hill.

Latané, B. (1996). Dynamic social impact: The creation of culture by communication. *Journal of Communication, 46*(4), 13–25.

Lee, T. M., & Zucker, I. (1988). Vole infant development is influenced perinatally by maternal photoperiodic history. *American Journal of Physiology, 255,* 831–838.

Lehman, D. R., Chiu, C-Y., & Schaller, M. (2004). Psychology and culture. *Annual Review of Psychology, 55,* 689–714.

Lively, C. M. (1996). Host-parasite coevolution and sex. *BioScience, 46,* 107–114.

Low, B. S. (1990). Marriage systems and pathogen stress in human societies. *American Zoologist, 30,* 325–339.

Mace, R., & Holden, C. J. (2005). A phylogenetic approach to cultural evolution. *Trends in Ecology and Evolution, 20,* 116–121.

Masuda, T., & Nisbett, R. E. (2006). Culture and change blindness. *Cognitive Science, 30,* 381–399.

Mayer, G. (2006). "Immunology—chapter one: Innate (non-specific) immunity." *Microbiology and Immunology On-Line Textbook.* USC School of Medicine. Retrieved on March 8, 2009, from http://pathmicro.med.sc.edu/ghaffar/innate.htm

McCrae, R. R. (2002). NEO-PI-R data from 36 cultures: Further intercultural comparisons. In R. R. McCrae & J. Allik (Eds.), *The five-factor model of personality across cultures* (pp. 105–126). New York: Kluwer Academic/Plenum.

McCrae, R. R., & Terracciano, A. (2008). The five-factor model and its correlates in individuals and cultures. In F. J. R. van de Vijver, D. A. van Hemert, & Y. Poortinga (Eds.), *Individuals and cultures in multi-level analysis* (pp. 247–281). Mahwah, NJ: Erlbaum.

McCrae, R. R., Terracciano, A., & 79 Members of the Personality Profiles of Cultures Project. (2005). Personality profiles of cultures: Aggregate personality traits. *Journal of Personality and Social Psychology, 89,* 407–425.

McNeill, W. H. (1976). *Plagues and peoples.* New York: Anchor Press/Doubleday.

Møller, A. P. (1996). Parasitism and developmental instability of hosts: A review. *Oikos, 77,* 189–196.

Mortensen, C. R., Becker, D. V., Ackerman, J. M., Neuberg, S. L., & Kenrick, D. T. (2010). Infection breeds reticence: The effects of disease salience on self-perceptions of personality and behavioral tendencies. *Psychological Science, 21,* 440–447.

Munafo, M. R., Clark, T., & Flint, J. (2005). Does measurement instrument moderate the association between the sorotonin transporter gene and anxiety-related personality traits? A meta-analysis. *Molecular Psychiatry, 10,* 415–419.

Murdock, G. P. (1949). *Social structure.* New York: MacMillan.

Murdock, G. P., & White, D. R. (1969). Standard cross-cultural sample. *Ethnology, 8,* 329–360.

Murdock, G. P., & White, D. R. (2006). Standard cross-cultural sample: On-line edition. *Social Dynamics and Complexity. Working Papers Series.* Retrieved June 1, 2010, from http://repositories.cdlib.org/imbs/socdyn/wp/Standard_Cross-Cultural_Sample/

Murray, D. R., & Schaller, M. (2010). Historical prevalence of disease within 230 geopolitical regions: A tool for investigating origins of culture. *Journal of Cross-Cultural Psychology, 41,* 99–108.

Murray, D. R., Trudeau, R., & Schaller, M. (in press). On the origins of cultural differences in conformity: Four tests of the pathogen prevalence hypothesis.

Navarrete, C. D., Fessler, D. M. T., & Eng, S. J. (2007). Elevated ethnocentrism in the first trimester of pregnancy. *Evolution and Human Behavior, 28,* 60–65.

Nettle, D. (1996). Language diversity in West Africa: An ecological approach. *Journal of Anthropological Archaeology, 15,* 403–438.

Nettle, D. (1998). Explaining global patterns of language diversity. *Journal of Anthropological Archaeology, 17,* 354–374.

Nettle, D. (2005). An evolutionary approach to the extraversion continuum. *Evolution and Human Behavior, 26,* 363–373.

Nettle, D. (2009). Ecological influences on human behavioral diversity: A review of recent findings. *Trends in Ecology and Evolution, 24,* 618–624.

Nisbett, R. E., & Cohen, D. (1996). *Culture of honor: The psychology of violence in the South.* Boulder, CO: Westview Press.

Nisbett, R. E., Peng, K., Choi, I., & Norenzayan, A. (2001). Culture and systems of thought: Holistic versus analytic cognition. *Psychological Review, 108,* 291–310.

Norenzayan, A., Choi, I., & Peng, K. (2007). Cognition and perception. In S. Kitayama & D. Cohen (Eds.), *Handbook of cultural psychology* (pp. 569–594). New York: Guilford.

Oaten, M., Stevenson, R. J., & Case, T. I. (2009). Disgust as a disease-avoidance mechanism. *Psychological Bulletin, 135,* 303–321.

Öhman, A, Flykt, A., & Esteves, F. (2001). Emotion drives attention: Detecting the snake in the grass. *Journal of Experimental Psychology: General, 130,* 466–478.

Oishi, S., Lun, J., & Sherman, G. D. (2007). Residential mobility, self-concept, and positive affect in social interactions. *Journal of Personality and Social Psychology, 93,* 131–141.

Oishi, S., Schimmack, U., Diener, E., & Suh, E. M. (1998). The measurement of values and individualism-collectivism. *Personality and Social Psychology Bulletin*, *24*, 1177–1189.

Park, J. H., Faulkner, J., & Schaller, M. (2003). Evolved disease-avoidance processes and contemporary anti-social behavior: Prejudicial attitudes and avoidance of people with physical disabilities. *Journal of Nonverbal Behavior*, *27*, 65–87.

Park, J. H., Schaller, M., & Crandall, C. S. (2007). Pathogen-avoidance mechanisms and the stigmatization of obese people. *Evolution and Human Behavior*, *28*, 410–414.

Porac, C., & Martin, W. L. B. (2007). A cross-cultural comparison of pressures to switch left-handed writing: Brazil versus Canada. *Laterality*, *12*, 273–291.

Quinlan, R. J. (2007). Human parental effort and environmental risk. *Proceedings of the Royal Society B*, *274*, 121–125.

Rhodes, G. (2006). The evolutionary psychology of facial beauty. *Annual Review of Psychology*, *57*, 199–226.

Ridley, M. (1993). *The red queen: Sex and the evolution of human nature*. New York: Penguin Books.

Ridley, M. (2003). *The agile gene*. New York: HarperCollins.

Ross, M. H., & Homer, E. (1976). Galton's problem in cross-national research. *World Politics*, *29*(1), 1–28.

Sachs, J., & Malaney, P. (2002). The economic and social burden of malaria. *Nature*, *415*, 680–685.

Sagiv, L., & Schwartz, S. H. (1995). Value priorities and readiness for out-group contact. *Journal of Personality and Social Psychology*, *69*, 437–448.

Schaller, M. (2006). Parasites, behavioral defenses, and the social psychological mechanisms through which cultures are evoked. *Psychological Inquiry*, *17*, 96–101.

Schaller, M., & Conway, L. G., III (1999). Influence of impression-management goals on the emerging contents of group stereotypes: Support for a social-evolutionary process. *Personality and Social Psychology Bulletin*, *25*, 819–833.

Schaller, M., & Crandall, C. S. (2004). *The psychological foundations of culture*. Mahwah, NJ: Erlbaum.

Schaller, M., & Duncan, L. A. (2007). The behavioral immune system: Its evolution and social psychological implications. In J. P. Forgas, M. G. Haselton, & W. von Hippel (Eds.), *Evolution and the social mind: Evolutionary psychology and social cognition* (pp. 293–307). New York: Psychology Press.

Schaller, M., Faulkner, J., Park, J. H., Neuberg, S. L., & Kenrick, D. (2004). Impressions of danger influence impressions of people: An evolutionary perspective on individual and collective cognition. *Journal of Cultural and Evolutionary Psychology*, *2*, 231–247.

Schaller, M., & Murray, D. M. (2008). Pathogens, personality, and culture: Disease prevalence predicts worldwide variability in sociosexuality, extraversion, and openness to experience. *Journal of Personality and Social Psychology*, *93*, 212–221.

Schaller, M., & Murray, D. M. (2010). Infectious diseases and the evolution of cross-cultural differences. In M. Schaller, A. Norenzayan, S. J. Heine, T. Yamagishi, & T. Kameda (Eds.), *Evolution, culture, and the human mind* (pp. 243–256). New York: Psychology Press.

Schinka, J. A., Letsch, E. A., & Crawford, F. C. (2002). DRD4 and novelty seeking: Results of meta-analyses. *American Journal of Medical Genetics Part B: Neuropsychiatric Genetics*, *114*, 643–648.

Schmitt, D. P. (2005). Sociosexuality from Argentina to Zimbabwe: A 48-nation study of sex, culture, and strategies of human mating. *Behavioral and Brain Sciences*, *28*, 247–311.

Schmitt, D. P., Alcalay, L., Allensworth, M., Allik, J., Ault, L., Austers, I. et al. (2004). Patterns and universals of adult romantic attachment across 62 cultural regions. *Journal of Cross-Cultural Psychology*, *35*, 367–402.

Schmitt, D. P., Allik, J., McCrae, R. R., Benet-Martinez, V., et al. (2007). The geographic distribution of Big Five personality traits: Patterns and profiles of human self-description across 56 nations. *Journal of Cross-Cultural Psychology*, *38*, 173–212.

Schupp, H. T., Öhman, A., Junghofer, M., Weike, A. I., Stockburger, J., & Hamm, A. O. (2004). The facilitated processing of threatening faces: An ERP analysis. *Emotion*, *4*, 189–200.

Schwartz, S. H. (2004). Mapping and interpreting cultural differences around the world. In H. Vinkin, J. Soeters, & P. Ester (Eds.), *Comparing cultures: Dimensions of culture in a comparative perspective* (pp. 43–73). Leiden, The Netherlands: Brill.

Sherman, P. W., & Billing, J. (1999). Darwinian gastronomy: Why we use spices. *Bioscience*, *49*, 453–463.

Segall, M. H., Campbell, D. T., & Herskovits, M. J. (1963). Cultural differences in the perception of geometric illusions. *Science*, *139*, 769–771.

Simpson, J. A., & Gangestad, S. W. (1991). Individual differences in sociosexuality: Evidence for convergent and discriminant validity. *Journal of Personality and Social Psychology*, *60*, 870–883.

Silverthorne, C. (2001). Leadership effectiveness and personality: A cross cultural evaluation. *Personality and Individual Differences*, *30*, 303–309.

Sinaceur, M., Heath, C., & Cole, S. (2005). Emotional and deliberative reactions to a public crisis: Mad cow disease in France. *Psychological Science*, *16*, 247–254.

Suh, E., Diener, E., Oishi, S., & Triandis, H. C. (1998). The shifting basis of life satisfaction judgments across cultures: Emotions versus norms. *Journal of Personality and Social Psychology*, *74*, 482–493.

Takahashi, L. K., Haglin, C., & Kalin, N. H. (1992). Prenatal stress potentiates stress-induced behavior and reduces the propensity to play in juvenile rats. *Physiology and Behavior*, *51*, 319–323.

Tavassoli, N. T. (2009). Climate, psychological homeostasis, and individual behaviors across cultures. In R. S. Wyer, C-Y. Chiu, & Y-Y. Hong (Eds.), *Understanding culture: Theory, research, and application* (pp. 211–221). New York: Psychology Press.

Thornhill, R., Fincher, C. L., & Aran, D. (2009). Parasites, democratization, and the liberalization of values across contemporary countries. *Biological Reviews*, *84*, 113–131.

Thornhill, R., Fincher, C. L., Murray, D. R., & Schaller, M. (2010). Zoonotic and non-zoonotic diseases in relation to human personality and societal values: Support for the parasite stress model. *Evolutionary Psychology*, *8*, 151–169.

Thornhill, R., & Gangestad, S. W. (1999). Facial attractiveness. *Trends in Cognitive Sciences*, *3*, 452–460.

Thornhill, R. & Møller, A. P. (1997). Developmental stability, disease and medicine. *Biological Reviews*, *72*, 497–548.

Tooby, J., & Cosmides, L. (1992). The psychological foundations of culture. In J. H. Barkow, L. Cosmides, & J. Tooby (Eds.), *The adapted mind* (pp. 19–136). New York: Oxford University Press.

Trautman, P. D., Meyer-Bahlburg, H. F. L., Postelnek, J., & New, M. I. (1995). Effects of early prenatal dexamethasone on the cognitive and behavioral development of young children: Results of a pilot study. *Psychoneuroendocrinology*, *20*, 439–449.

Triandis, H. C. (1995). *Individualism & collectivism*. Boulder, CO: Westview Press.

Uskul, A. K., Kitayama, S., & Nisbett, R. E. (2008). Ecocultural basis of cognition: Farmers and fishermen are more holistic than herders. *Proceedings of the National Academy of Sciences*, *105*, 8552–8556.

Van de Vliert, E. (2009). *Climate, affluence, and culture*. Cambridge, England: Cambridge University Press.

Vandello, J. A., & Cohen, D. (1999). Patterns of individualism and collectivism across the United States. *Journal of Personality and Social Psychology*, *77*, 279–292.

Wedekind, C. (2002). Induced hatching to avoid infectious egg disease in whitefish. *Current Biology*, *12*, 69–71.

Weeden, J., & Sabini, J. (2005). Physical attractiveness and health in Western societies: A review. *Psychological Bulletin*, *131*, 635–653.

Williamson, S. H., Hubisz, M. J., Clark, A. G., Payseur, B. A., Bustamante, C. D., & Nielsen, R. (2007). Localizing recent adaptive evolution in the human genome. *PloS Genetics*, *3*(6), e90. doi:10.1371/journal.pgen.0030090

Wolfe, N. D., Dunavan, C. P., & Diamond, J. (2007). Origins of major human infectious diseases. *Nature*, *447*, 279–283.

Zuk, M. (1992). The role of parasites in sexual selection: Current evidence and future directions. *Advances in the Study of Behavior*, *21*, 39–68.

Zuk, M. (2007). *Riddled with life: Friendly worms, ladybug sex, and the parasites that make us who we are*. Orlando, FL: Harcourt.

CHAPTER 4

Attachment, Learning, and Coping
The Interplay of Cultural Similarities and Differences

FRED ROTHBAUM
Tufts University

GILDA MORELLI
Boston College

NATALIE RUSK
Tufts University

Significantly, it was the West that explored the East, and not the other way around.

—Choi & Nisbett, 2000, p. 903

I. INTRODUCTION

A. Our Interest in Culture and Attachment

Attachment theory is concerned with children's closeness to their primary caregivers and with implications of closeness for learning and loss. Attachment theorists hypothesize that, across culture, there is a fundamental similarity in the nature of attachment, in the antecedents and consequences of security, and in the forms and incidence of insecurity (Ainsworth, Blehar, Waters, & Wahl, 1978; Bowlby, 1969/1982; Cassidy & Shaver, 2008). Decades of research have led attachment theorists to conclude that these hypotheses have been largely confirmed (van IJzendoorn & Sagi, 1999; van IJzendoorn & Sagi-Schwartz, 2008). So compelling are the findings that attachment theory has reshaped developmental psychologists' understanding of what constitutes healthy relationships for humans around the world.

Not all researchers have agreed with the universal position (Harwood, Miller, & Irizarry, 1995; Keller, 2008; LeVine & Norman, 2001). Ten years ago, we waded into the debate about universality (Rothbaum, Weisz, Pott, Miyake, & Morelli, 2000). We accepted that there are important similarities in attachment worldwide. Children everywhere develop close ties with the people who care for them and these ties are fundamental to their well-being. We questioned, however, the universality of core hypotheses of the theory, and we encouraged greater understanding of the interplay of cultural similarities and differences. For the most part, attachment theory has been informed by Western assumptions and by findings from Western samples and as such is itself culturally grounded. We asked how the theory might shift if it were informed by assumptions and findings from other communities.

Research studies derived from cultural approaches, which foreground the importance of context in mediating the ways in which children think, feel, and act, have helped to answer this question. The cultural research shows that attachment theory as described by Bowlby, Ainsworth, and colleagues has much to tell us about early relationships in many communities. At the same time, the research points to important cultural variation. The differences are not simply a veneer or overlay on the hypotheses of attachment theory—they lend color, texture, and shape to the theory (Morelli & Rothbaum, 2007; Rothbaum & Trommsdorff, 2007). Attachment theory grows as it considers the diverse ways in which people in different communities form, are influenced by, and make meaning of attachment relationships.

The context dependency of attachment has often been ignored by attachment theorists because they, and the people they studied, were not themselves highly context dependent. In Western communities, children are not socialized to develop a situation-centered view of reality (Hsu, 1981), to be "field dependent" (Cohen, Hoshino-Browne, & Leung, 2007; Norenzayan, Choi, & Peng, 2007), nor to learn a repertoire of context-dependent skills (Rogoff, 2003).

The evidence we review indicates that children everywhere develop attachment relationships with the people who care for them, and that attachments continue throughout the life span. Moreover, the security of children's attachment relationships relates to children's learning. But the expression and experience of attachment relationships, and how and why children engage in learning, varies across communities. For European Americans, attachment is often characterized by recurring separations from primary caregivers and reunions with them, and learning centers on autonomous exploration. As the opening quote suggests, the West has historically been more oriented to exploration. For East Asians, by contrast, attachment entails more continuous care and union, and learning centers more on ways of accommodating to others and to the context. Yet children in all communities experience separations, exploration, and accommodation, and so the dance of regularity and variation continues.

B. Organizing Constructs

To understand cultural similarities and differences in attachment, we rely on several well-researched cultural constructs. In particular, we focus on the distinction between the independent and interdependent self. The independent self values being unique, autonomous, asserting itself, expressing its inner attributes, and promoting its own goals. The interdependent self, by contrast, values belonging, fitting in, maintaining harmony, self restraint, and promoting others' goals (Kitayama, Duffy, & Uchida, 2007; Markus & Kitayama, 1991). While people develop aspects of these two selves in all communities, the circumstances of their lives make it likely that one pattern is privileged over another within a given culture (Kitayama, Markus, Matsumoto, & Norasakkunkit, 1997).

Closely related to different conceptions of self are different "phenomenologies"—ways of viewing the self and world (Cohen et al., 2007; Kitayama, Snibbe, Markus, & Suzuki, 2004). People with an independent self more often view the world from a first-person perspective, from the inside out, whereas those with an interdependent self more often view the world from a third-person perspective, from the outside in—as others see them. Cohen et al. (2007) demonstrated that Asian Americans as compared to European Americans are more likely to view their own experience from a third-person perspective and view their friends' experience from a first-person perspective. Asian Americans are also more likely to experience a variety of emotions as if others were looking back at them (e.g., when they felt ashamed, they saw faces of others looking at them with contempt), and to enter into others' internal experiences at an earlier age. European Americans are more likely to fall prey to egocentric errors, to project their internal experiences onto the outside world, to confuse what is in their own heads with what is objectively in the world or in other people's heads, and to empathize by projecting their own internal thoughts and feelings onto others.

Conceptions of self also relate to conceptions of control (Rothbaum, Weisz, & Snyder, 1982). Primary control, which is more common in the West, occurs when people view themselves as independent agents and seek to change the world to fit personal goals and standards. Secondary control, which is more common in East Asia, occurs when people see themselves as aligned with powerful forces, particularly other people, and seek to change themselves to fit the goals and standards of those forces. Weisz, Rothbaum, and Blackburn (1984a) reviewed evidence on child rearing, socialization, religion, philosophy, work, and psychotherapy, indicating that secondary control is more valued and anticipated by Japanese than Americans. Since then, hundreds of studies have supported the importance of the primary-secondary control distinction and have documented cultural differences predicted by the model (reviewed in Morling & Evered, 2006). The distinction between primary and secondary control gave rise to our distinction between change-based and acceptance-based coping, described later.

What is universal, we suggest, is the potential to become attached in particular ways in particular contexts. What is different, we suggest, are the particulars, their meanings, and the ways they are organized within situations and settings. This is true for attachment as well as for views of self, for perspective taking, and for control. We believe that when most situations in a culture afford opportunities for initiating exploration and asserting the self, attachment is likely to be linked with types of learning that build on these opportunities. By contrast, when most situations in a culture require adjustment of the self and accommodating to others and to the context, attachment is likely to be linked with different types of learning. Cultures differ in the number of situations of each type and in their default self, default perspective, and default control (Cohen et al., 2007; Kitayama et al., 2007). People construct situations and settings to fit their default orientations, and people are in turn constructed by their situations and settings (Kitayama & Markus, 1999; Shweder et al., 2006).

In this chapter, we expand on these ideas. We review support for a universalistic position regarding attachment relationships, and we provide evidence that questions this position. Our interest is in the relation between security and learning in different communities, and how security and learning relate to coping. First, we provide an overview of our thesis.

C. On Attachment Relationships, Learning, and Coping

Some investigators who study culture and attachment have focused on documenting the theory's universality (reviewed in Van IJzendoorn & Sagi-Schwartz, 2008). For them, the "linked behavioral systems" of attachment and exploration is assumed, and exploration is viewed as the springboard for learning. These researchers ascribe numerous meanings to exploration, such as pursuit of personal preferences and individual accomplishments; curiosity about novel objects and settings; self-confidence and self-initiative; and mastery of the environment. Attachment researchers with a univeralist perspective view exploration as typically occurring in relative isolation from peers, and at some distance from caregivers, but critically aided by their support (Grossmann, Grossmann, Kindler, & Zimmermann, 2008). Fundamental to this view is that exploration reflects and fosters the development of autonomy. When variation in attachment relationships is considered, it is limited to relatively superficial behavioral differences and is not considered relevant to the core hypotheses of the theory.

For us, and for colleagues such as Harwood, Miller, and Irzarry (1995), the question is not whether the theory applies everywhere, but ways in which the theory needs to be modified or changed to explain attachment relationships in specific contexts. We ask how basic assumptions of attachment theory, involving the nature of security, learning, and the link between them, should be adapted when applied elsewhere. In many communities, especially in East Asia, security has more to do with continuous union (than with separations and reunions), and goals of learning have more to do with accommodation (than with exploration). Accommodation refers to harmonious adjustment of self to others and the context, as seen in imitation, adherence to prescribed roles, self-criticism, self-perfection, group accomplishments, and self-control (Heine et al., 2001). People accommodate when they seek to change themselves so as to align with others' standards and expectations (Rothbaum et al., 1982). Accommodative forms of learning typically occur in close cooperation with others.

We suggest that differences in security relate to differences in learning. We focus on two goals for learning, exploration and accommodation, and two ways of thinking, analytic and holistic. In communities where people prioritize forms of attachment associated with exploration and frequent separations and reunions, ways of thinking are more analytic. Analytic thought involves dividing the perceptual field into parts whose inherent qualities can be understood (Nisbett, Peng, Choi, & Norenzayan, 2001). Separating parts from their context makes people better able and more motivated to explore them. In communities where attachment is associated with accommodation and more continuous union, ways of thinking are more holistic. People engaging in holistic thought treat the perceptual field as indivisible and as shaping the meaning of the parts constituting the field. Holistic ways of thinking facilitate fitting in with the environment and serve goals for accommodation. To our knowledge, the rich literatures on cultural differences in attachment and in learning have not been linked with one another.

Findings regarding cultural differences in attachment and learning have led us to consider cultural differences in children's coping. The link between attachment and coping is less central to core hypotheses of attachment theory, but it has contributed to the theory's popularity. We define constructive coping as learning in stressful situations. In communities where the attachment relationship is experienced as a base for exploring and analyzing the world, children who are secure develop constructive coping strategies involving learning how to change and master the environment (change-based coping). Different forms of constructive coping are likely in communities where children develop attachments that serve as a base for learning to accommodate to a world they see holistically. In those communities, secure children are likely to develop constructive coping strategies for accepting situations (acceptance-based coping).

II. ATTACHMENT THEORY

A. Overview of Attachment Theory

According to Bowlby (1969/1982, 1973), the attachment system consists of biologically based behaviors, such as clinging, crying, sucking, and following, that enable children to obtain and maintain contact with and proximity to their primary caregivers, and caregivers exhibit complementary behaviors. These behaviors are most common when children are distressed—frightened, fatigued, hungry, sick, or alone—and they are assuaged by sensitive and responsive caregiving. Repeated experiences in which a caregiver provides protection and care lead children to rely on the caregiver as a "safe haven" (Bowlby, 1969/1982).

Bowlby recognized that the function and set goal of the attachment system transcends infant survival and proximity. The attachment system also serves to support the infant's innate drive for exploration and mastery of the inanimate and social world through the provision of a "secure base" (Ainsworth & Bowlby, 1991). Infants rely on their mother as a secure base for venturing forth to explore the environment when they believe that they can safely return to her if external dangers dictate a need for protection.

The secure base reflects links between, and the balancing of, attachment and exploration. When children's needs have been met and the caregiver is seen as available as needed, the attachment system is deactivated and the exploration system is activated, as evidenced by the child's willingness to engage in autonomous exploration. When the child discerns a threat, the security system is activated, leading children to regain proximity with the attachment figure, and the exploration system is deactivated. This moment-to-moment incompatibility in activation of the two systems is part of a larger system of mutuality. In the long run, attachment security and exploration, which is the prototype of autonomous functioning, are highly related to one another. In the preschool years and at older ages, children who are the most secure are most likely to explore and to engage in other forms of autonomous behavior (Grossmann et al., 2008).

As they get older, children are increasingly able to respond to stressors by relying on "internal working models" when attachment figures are not present. These models are mental representations of the self (e.g., as worthy of care, or not), of others (e.g., as reliably providing care, or not) and of the attachment relationship (Weinfield, Sroufe, Egeland, & Carlson, 2008). Attachment theory claims that positive conceptions of self provide the psychological fuel for autonomy (Sroufe, Fox, & Pancake, 1983).[1] In adolescence and adulthood the set goal of attachment relationships still involves the provision of care and protection to support autonomous exploration (Allen, 2008; Feeney, 2008; Kerns, 2008).

Security of attachment in infancy is assessed most commonly by using a laboratory-based procedure developed by Ainsworth, based on her observations in Uganda and later in the United States (Ainsworth et al., 1978). The Strange Situation, as the procedure is called, examines how well infants organize their attachment and exploration behaviors following repeated separations from, and reunions with, their caregiver. Securely attached infants are able to derive comfort from reunion with their caregiver and to use the caregiver as a

---

[1] Later we argue that attachment theory assumes an independent self. People with an independent self seek positive self-evaluations in part because those evaluations support autonomous behavior (Kitayama et al., 2007).

base from which to explore the environment. Secure attachment is the pre-dominate pattern of attachment worldwide. Insecurely attached infants, who either avoid their caregivers at reunion or seek but also resist closeness, and infants whose attachment behavior is "disorganized," together constitute about 40% of children in middle-class, nonclinical, North American samples (van IJzendoorn, Schuengel, & Bakermans-Kranenburg, 1999).

Sensitive responsiveness to infants' positive and negative signals is the primary antecedent of secure attachment (Belsky & Fearon, 2008; Weinfield et al., 2008). Ainsworth's (1976) assumption that sensitive responsiveness fosters autonomy is evident in her description of high-level caregiving: "This mother views her baby as a separate, active, autonomous person, whose wishes and activities have validity of their own. Since she [the mother] respects his autonomy, she avoids situations in which she might have to impose her will on his" (p. 4; see Rothbaum, Weisz, et al., 2000, for other examples). Insensitive care that thwarts children's exploration and sense of autonomy can take the form of intrusive, hostile, controlling caregiving, which predicts avoidant attachment, or unresponsive, underinvolved caregiving, which predicts anxious-resistant attachment (Belsky & Fearon, 2008).

A secure attachment relationship plays a key role in fostering children's autonomy and other manifestations of social competence (Sroufe, 1990; Weinfield et al., 2008). Secure children, as compared to their insecure age mates, are more confident and higher in self-esteem, are less dependent, exhibit more mature forms of exploration, exhibit fewer problem behaviors of both an internalizing and externalizing type, have closer friendships, are more prosocial, and take more social initiative (Kerns, 2008; Weinfield et al., 2008). In adults, security is referred to as autonomous attachment; people with that classification value attachment relationships and objectively evaluate rather than idealize their caregivers (Hesse, 2008; Main, 1996).

B. Support for the Universality of Attachment

Bowlby (1969/1982) claimed that the dynamics he was describing were universal. He theorized that children's needs for proximity and care, as well as caregivers' willingness to provide such care, were deeply rooted in human evolutionary history. Contributing to the belief that attachment theory applies universally was Ainsworth's (1967) systematic observations of Ugandan infants and their mothers. Most important were the similarities she noted between U.S. and Ugandan infants' wariness of unfamiliar adults; the way mothers served as a secure base for exploration; and the importance of sensitive care. Ainsworth's focus on similarities led her to downplay cultural variation. She cited only "specific" differences in "particular conditions" and emphasized "similarities across cultures" (Ainsworth & Marvin, 1995, pp. 8–9).

Because universals were widely assumed, there were few studies of attachment in non-Western communities before the turn of the twenty-first century. A seminal 1999 review of culture and attachment by van IJzendoorn and Sagi included only 14 studies. That review focused on four core hypotheses, involving the universality of attachment dynamics, the prevalence of security, and the antecedents and consequences of security. The authors concluded: "Taken as a whole, the [cross-cultural] studies are remarkably consistent with the theory. Attachment theory may therefore claim cross-cultural validity" (p. 731). In a later review, with more studies and more cultures represented, the authors reached similar conclusions (vanIJzendoorn & Sagi-Schwartz, 2008).

According to van IJzendoorn and Sagi (1999, 2008), the studies investigating the universality of attachment, including the safe haven and secure base dynamics, have supported it, and the vast majority of studies have found that security is the normative pattern. Although there are fewer studies examining the hypotheses that maternal sensitivity leads to secure attachment and that security leads to later competence, most of the studies support these hypotheses as well. The cultural studies are thus largely consistent with the hundreds of studies on attachment that did not focus on culture (Cassidy & Shaver, 2008; Mikulincer & Shaver, 2007a). However, the vast majority of those studies were conducted with predominantly middle-class European American samples, particularly U.S. samples. Few studies of attachment have focused on minority group members, people living in extreme poverty, or people from countries outside North America and Europe. The question thus remains whether there is sufficient support for the claim that the theory applies universally.

III. RESEARCH HIGHLIGHTING CULTURAL DIFFERENCES IN ATTACHMENT

Research informed by attachment theory, *including research conducted in non-Western communities*, regularly employs methods that are developed by Westerners, relies on measures that were tested for validity with Western samples, and interprets findings from a Western perspective (Rothbaum, Weisz, et al., 2000). Chief among the Western assumptions is the notion that autonomy and related constructs, such as exploration and independence, are central goals for development of children in all communities. However, most cultural studies of children's close relationships present a different picture of attachment. This research, including our own, suggests that close relationships are more linked to the valuing of harmony than autonomy in East Asia, whereas the opposite is true in the West (Keller, 2008; Miller, 2003; Rothbaum, Pott, Azuma, Miyake, & Weisz, 2000). While cultural differences in values have been documented by many other investigators (Hsu, 1981; Schwartz, 1999; Triandis, 1995), prior to the 1990s the differences were rarely applied to close relationships.

To address this gap in the literature, Rothbaum and colleagues examined lyrics of songs about close relationships in China and the United States. One study examined songs about parent–child relations, focusing on how giving back to parents was expressed (Rothbaum & Xu, 1995). The authors hypothesized that the emphasis on harmony in Chinese relationships would give rise to positive giving back, evident in positive feelings, and that the tension between closeness and autonomy in U.S. relationships would give rise to negative giving back, manifested in feelings of resentment about unmet needs. As expected, almost all of the Chinese songs expressed appreciation, love, and devotion toward parents and almost none expressed dissatisfaction, anger, or blame. U.S. songs, by contrast, expressed more negative than positive feelings. Suppression of negative feelings toward others in China and open expression of negative feelings in the United States may also reflect cultural differences in harmony versus autonomy.

In a second study, involving songs about romantic love (Rothbaum & Tsang, 1998), Chinese as compared to U.S. lyrics were expected and found to more often depict love as embedded within a larger context involving nature or feelings of devotion. When love is embedded, it is more likely to promote harmony with, as opposed to disruption of, the surrounding context. U.S. lyrics emphasis on autonomy was evident in the focus on individuals' feelings rather than the surrounding context.

In a third study, European American and immigrant Chinese parents were interviewed about their physical closeness with young children (Rothbaum, Morelli, Pott, & Liu-Constant, 2000). The Chinese respondents were invested in harmony. They described themselves as sleeping in closer proximity with their children; they focused on the family unit; they valued inhibition of expression, adherence to correct values, and hierarchy of relations; and they viewed independence as children growing with the family. European Americans, by contrast, were invested in autonomy and self-expression as evident in accepting nudity, focusing on the child's expression of desires, and valuing individual pleasure. In addition, they viewed independence as a celebration of the child's distinctiveness and as growing away from the family.

This research pointed to the relevance of the harmony-autonomy distinction for understanding Chinese-U.S. differences in close relationships. Later, Rothbaum and colleagues shifted their attention to Japanese-U.S. differences, allowing them to build on the substantial research comparing these communities in close relationships and attachment in particular (Rothbaum, Pott, et al., 2000; Rothbaum, Weisz, et al., 2000). These cultures are interesting to compare because, despite economic similarities, they have profoundly different histories, demographics, and philosophies.

Rothbaum, Weisz, et al.'s (2000) review of Japanese-U.S. differences centered on several attachment theory hypotheses addressed in van IJzendoorn's and Sagi's (1999) review: (*a*) maternal responsive sensitivity increases children's security (sensitivity hypothesis); (*b*) secure children become more socially and emotionally competent than do insecure children (competence hypothesis); (*c*) the attachment system and the exploration system are inexorably linked (secure base hypothesis); and (*d*) the distribution of attachment types is consistent across cultures. We regarded the cultural differences in attachment as a subset of broader differences in close relationships: In the United States, close relationships involve relatively more generative tension, which centers on autonomy, whereas in Japan they involve relatively more symbiotic harmony (Rothbaum, Pott, et al., 2000).

In contrast to cultural theorists who have tended to depict Americans as less invested in relationships than Japanese because Americans are focused on the individuated self, Rothbaum, Pott, et al. (2000) highlighted evidence that the desire for close relationships is strong in the United States as well as Japan. They sought to shift the focus from cultural differences in the importance and strength of relationships to cultural differences in the meanings and dynamics of relationships. They argued that key aspects of attachment, such as proximity seeking, contact maintaining, separation protest, and safe haven, are rooted in biological predispositions and are manifest in all cultures. These biological predispositions for relatedness can be seen as passing through cultural lenses (i.e., values, practices, and institutions)—one lens emphasizing accommodation (in Japan) and one lens emphasizing individuation (in the United States)—leading to distinctive paths of development. The path of symbiotic harmony, which reflects the link between relatedness and accommodation, is characterized by a continual pull toward adapting the self to fit the needs of others. The path of generative tension, which reflects the link between relatedness and individuation, is characterized by a continual tug between the desire for closeness and individuation.

While Rothbaum, Pott, et al. (2000) examined Japanese–U.S. differences in close relationships from infancy to adulthood, they regarded differences in early attachment as key: "A prototype of generative tension is the securely attached U.S. infant's competing desires for proximity and contact with the caregiver on one hand and separation from the caregiver and exploration of the environment on the other. These desires are complementary in that separation fosters and is fostered by closeness, but they are also 'antithetical' in that they cannot operate simultaneously" (p. 1123). By contrast, Japanese attachment is grounded in a more harmonious union.

Subsequent reviews of culture and attachment (Morelli & Rothbaum, 2007; Rothbaum & Morelli, 2005) were not limited to Japanese-U.S. differences. Also included was attachment research in the Congo, Kenya, Puerto Rico, and other countries. In each of the next four sections, which correspond to the four attachment theory hypotheses regarding universality, we begin by considering the evidence on Japan and then consider evidence from other communities.

Our reviews of the attachment literature, summarized next, suggest that differences in cultural goals contribute to differences in attachment, as seen in expressions of sensitivity, in the social competence that attachment fosters, in the nature of security, and the frequency of different types of insecurity. As noted earlier, goals in the United States center on autonomy, exploration, independence, and individuation; goals in Japan and in many other communities center more on harmony, accommodation, interdependence, and situation-centeredness. Most attachment theorists make almost no mention of these different goals, or of the settings, practices, and beliefs that accompany them.

A. Sensitivity Hypothesis

1. Evidence from Japan

Ainsworth's (1976) scales of sensitive, responsive caregiving reflect the value she placed on children's autonomy and related constructs (Rothbaum, Weisz, et al., 2000). Three of her four caregiving scales explicitly highlighted the importance of autonomy. For example, the sensitive mother is described as one who "values the fact that the baby has a will of its own, even when it opposes hers . . ." (Ainsworth, 1976, p. 4). Ainsworth's measure of sensitive, responsive caregiving served as the prototype for subsequent measures and is regarded as the gold standard in the field (Sroufe & Waters, 1997).

The first author's awareness of the autonomy-laden nature of extant measures of sensitive responsiveness stemmed from almost a decade of research seeking to develop new measures of caregiving (Rothbaum, 1986, 1988; Rothbaum & Weisz, 1994). His work focused on parental acceptance, a construct core to attachment theorists' notion of sensitive responsiveness (Ainsworth, 1976) as well as to many other Western notions of positive caregiving (Baldwin, 1955). Rothbaum's research led him to conclude that measures of acceptance and measures of sensitive responsiveness were infused with notions of autonomy and allied concepts like individuation, self-initiative, and self-expression. Rothbaum and colleagues' earlier work contrasting Japanese and U.S. caregiving (Weisz et al., 1984a) also highlighted ways in which European American constructs of caregiving were biased toward Western meanings.

Stated simply, sensitive, responsive caregiving reflects indigenous values and goals. In contrast to U.S. parents, who seek to promote their children's autonomy and assertion of personal desires by encouraging self-expression and by responding promptly to infants' explicit signals, Japanese parents prefer to respond to extremely subtle, often nonverbal cues, or to anticipate their infants' needs by relying on situational cues so as to foster emotional closeness. Other ways in which Japanese maternal sensitivity promotes infants' harmonious accommodation to their parents' expectations, rather than infants' autonomous exploration of their environment, include maintaining prolonged physical contact rather than distal eye contact, and orienting their children's attention to social objects, particularly themselves, rather than to physical objects. Japanese sensitivity is seen as relatively more responsive to infants' need for social engagement and shared experiences, and U.S. sensitivity is seen as more responsive to infants' need for individuation and personal accomplishment (Dennis, Cole, Zahn-Waxler, & Mizuta, 2002; Rothbaum, Weisz, et al., 2000).

Perhaps most telling of cultural differences are findings regarding insensitive U.S. mothers of insecurely attached (i.e., anxious-resistant) babies. These mothers "described strategies to keep their children close . . . promoted dependency . . . tend[ed] to . . . overinterpret their children's attachment cues [and] emphasized their children over themselves . . ." (George & Solomon, 1999, pp. 661–662). Japanese mothers view these very behaviors—skin-to-skin contact ("skinship"), indulgence of dependency, and self-sacrifice—as key ingredients of sensitive caregiving (see Rothbaum, Pott, et al., 2000, for a review of these findings).

2. Evidence from Other Cultures

Later reviews highlighted other evidence of cultural differences in sensitivity, and especially differences in whether sensitivity entails autonomy fostering (Morelli & Rothbaum, 2007; Rothbaum & Morelli, 2005). Carlson and Harwood (2003) found support for the attachment theory claim that parental control is insensitive and undermines security within their European American sample. Consistent with the theory, mothers' physical control of their children related to insecure attachment. Children granted limited freedom are restricted in their ability to explore and to develop a sense of self as inner directed, willful, and autonomous. Yet just the opposite pattern emerged in Puerto Rican families: Parents scoring highest in physical control had children who were securely attached. Carlson and Harwood note, "This apparently paradoxical finding highlights the need for culturally specific definitions of sensitive caregiving" (p. 17). Similar findings were obtained by Posada et al. (2002): Parental interference was related (inversely) to security in a U.S. sample but not in a Bogata, Colombia sample.

The findings involving Puerto Rican and Bogota mothers are more representative of worldwide patterns than are the findings involving European American mothers. Parental control and strictness are more common and valued in such diverse groups as African Americans, Koreans, Chinese, and Iranians than they are among European Americans (Carlson & Harwood, 2003). Members of these groups are relatively more likely to value accommodation of self to others' expectations and to situational demands, to adhere to ethics of duty and obligation, and to seek cooperative, harmonious relations (Morelli & Rothbaum, 2007). To encourage children to live up to these values, caregivers must exercise high levels of control as well as provide love and care—control and sensitivity to children's needs are seen as working in tandem rather than in opposition to one another (Rothbaum & Trommsdorff, 2007). A positive correlation between measures of parental control and parental warmth or sensitivity has been found in many communities worldwide; it is largely in European American communities that the two are negatively correlated (Kim & Rohner, 2002; Rohner & Pettengill, 1985).

Attachment investigators who conduct research in European American communities, where caregivers focus on fostering a strong ego and an independent self, have found that efforts to physically control or interfere with

infants' activity are associated with insensitivity, insecurity, and lack of autonomy (Belsky & Fearon, 2008; Belsky, Rosenberger, & Crnic, 1995). From our
perspective, sensitivity is universally valued, but what it means to be sensitive
among people who prioritize an interdependent self is very different from
what it means to those prioritizing an independent self (Dennis et al., 2002;
Rothbaum, Kakinuma, Nagaoka, & Azuma, 2007).

It is not just the element of control that distinguishes between types of
sensitivity. Cultural studies suggest as well that the timing of caregivers'
response to babies' signals may not be the same across cultures. Contingent
responsiveness—responding to infants soon after they signal their need—is
of primary importance to Western investigators and Western parents. By contrast, studies in other cultures emphasize the ways caregivers anticipate the
needs of their children based on situational cues and prior knowledge, or
respond to extremely subtle, often nonverbal signals. Whereas many European
American caregivers prefer responsive forms of sensitivity, a preference for
anticipatory sensitivity is reported among the Japanese (Rothbaum, Nagaoka,
& Ponte, 2006) and among Puerto Ricans and Central American immigrants
in the United States (Harwood, 1992).[2]

Yet another difference in sensitivity has to do with responsiveness to positive versus negative signals. Cameroonian mothers are more likely to respond
to infants' signs of distress, whereas German mothers are more likely to
respond to infants' positive signals (Keller et al., 2006). Friedlmeier and
Trommsdorff (1999) and LeVine (2004) report similar differences between
non-Western (Japanese and Gusii, respectively) and European American
mothers. The differences may have to do with goals and emotions associated
with the interdependent versus independent self. Interdependent selves are
more oriented to "prevention goals," avoiding losses, fulfillment of obligations,
maintaining harmony, and alleviating distress; independent selves are more
oriented to "promotion goals," maximizing gains, achieving ideals, exploring
new frontiers, and fostering positive emotions (Elliot, Chirkov, Kim, & Sheldon
2001; Hamamura, Meijer, Heine, Kayama, & Hori, 2009; Higgins, Pierro, &
Kruglanski, 2007; Lee, Aaker & Gardner, 2000; Lockwood, Marshall, & Sadler,
2005). Whereas Gusii mothers are shocked to see videos of American mothers
allowing infants to cry without soothing them, they are much less likely than

---

[2]Interestingly, both Japanese and U.S. caregivers maintain that adults' anticipation is more
likely to foster children's interdependence (empathy, propriety, and compliance) than independence (exploration, autonomy, and self-assertion), and that adults' responsiveness is
more likely to foster independence than interdependence (Rothbaum et al., 2007).

their American counterparts to amplify their children's positive signals, including children's excitement about new discoveries gained through exploration (LeVine, 2004).

B. Competence hypothesis

1. Evidence from Japan

Attachment theorists have typically equated competence with qualities associated with autonomy and independence, such as exploration, self-efficacy, individuation, and self-initiative (Allen, 2008; Grossmann et al., 2008; Levy, Blatt, & Shaver, 1998). In Japan, competence is more often equated with harmony and interdependence, as manifested in accommodation, reading others' minds, conformity, and coordinating one's needs with the needs of others (Azuma, Kashiwagi, & Hess, 1981; Kitayama et al., 1997; Lebra, 1994; Morling, Kitayama, & Miyamoto, 2002; Roland, 1988; Rothbaum et al., 2007; Weisz et al., 1984a, 1984b). These Japanese behaviors are devalued and often associated with insecurity in the West (Rothbaum, Weisz, et al., 2000).

Security may relate to other differences in competence as well. In the United States, secure children are more sociable, communicate their emotions more openly, and maintain eye contact when losing to a competitor—all features of social competence. Japanese mothers, by contrast, often warn children that expressive behavior will elicit negative reactions from others, thereby instilling wariness of outsiders rather than sociability (Lebra, 1994; Trommsdorff & Friedlmeier, 1993). In the United States, secure adults are autonomous, have a positive view of self, emphasize verbal communication even about strong emotions, and do not equate love with union. Japanese adults view an autonomous, assertive adult as immature rather than as competent; they value self-criticism more than self-enhancement; they restrain verbal expression of strong emotions that can disrupt social harmony; and they have a stronger desire for union (Fiske, Kitayama, Markus, & Nisbett, 1998). The limited cultural evidence in support of the competence hypothesis may be due to the failure to recognize that competence takes different forms in different communities.

2. Evidence from Other Cultures

Investigators who study other cultures identify differences in competence that map onto the distinction between independent and interdependent selves. Keller's (2003) research is of particular interest because the qualities on which she focuses pertain to learning, and thus are especially relevant to attachment. She claims that qualities of learning emphasized by Westerners, such as exploration, discovery, individual ability, and personal achievement, are fundamentally different than those emphasized by people in many other societies, including the Baolue of the Ivory Coast, A-Chew of Zambia, Nso of Cameroon, Cree of Alaska, Hindu of India, and Chinese of mainland China and Taiwan. In these majority world societies, competence and learning are more often seen as "moral self-cultivation, a social contribution, discouraging individual celebration of achievement . . . [and] communal achievements, including the ability to maintain social harmony implying social respect and acceptance of social roles" (Keller, 2003, p. 289).

Other cultural studies support Keller's view. Puerto Rican, as compared to European American, mothers' views of competence center on proper demeanor and interdependence, as seen in their frequent mention of respect, obedience, calmness, and politeness. European American views, by contrast, center relatively more on self-maximization and independence, as seen in frequent mention of autonomy, happiness, confidence, and exploration. Proper demeanor refers to the capacity and willingness to learn in accommodative ways. It involves being "teachable," receptive, especially to elders, and developing interpersonal competencies (Harwood et al., 1995). Notions like proper demeanor and the Japanese notion of *sunao*, which refers to open-mindedness, nonresistance, and obedience (White & LeVine, 1986), suggest a different orientation to learning—and thus to competence—than the more exploratory and self-determined process emphasized by people with independent selves (Rothbaum et al., 2007).

If attachment research had its origins in cultures that prioritize interdependent selves, and if those cultures enjoyed the scientific dominance that the West currently enjoys, it is possible that current theories would hypothesize that qualities like proper demeanor and accommodation, rather than autonomy and exploration, are universal consequences of security.

C. Secure Base Hypothesis

1. Evidence from Japan

If the antecedents (caregiver sensitivity) and consequences (competence) of attachment security are conceptualized and expressed differently in different cultures, then the conception and expression of the secure base may also depend on the culture examined. Attachment theorists' conceptualization of the secure base reflects the Western emphasis on exploration and the belief that exploration leads to individuation, which is viewed as a healthy, positive outcome. As noted by Seifer and Schiller (1995), "Secure base behavior provides a context in which differentiation of self and other can take place" (p. 149). Japanese experts are less likely to emphasize a dynamic that is so centered on individuation. Takahashi's (1990) research led her to conclude that the secure base was less relevant in Japan because Japanese attachment has less to do with independence and self-reliance. In the Strange Situation, Japanese as compared to U.S. mothers are less willing to separate from young children, even briefly (Rothbaum et al., 2007).

There are Japanese-U.S. differences in the amount of exploration, including in the Strange Situation (Rothbaum, Weisz, et al., 2000; Rothbaum et al., 2007). In Japan, the link between attachment and accommodation is more heavily weighted (Rothbaum et al., 2007). Accommodation is a foundation for many valued behaviors in Japan, such as empathy, propriety (adhering to norms and fulfilling roles), and other expressions of harmony—just as exploration is a foundation for self-initiative, independence, assertion of personal preferences, and other expressions of autonomy. For children in all communities, the secure base is a springboard for learning about the outside world, but what varies is the extent to which children rely on exploration versus accommodation when engaged in learning (Rothbaum, Weisz, et al., 2000; Rothbaum et al., 2007).

2. Evidence from Other Cultures

Evidence from diverse cultures strongly suggests that the link between attachment and exploration has a biological basis to it because of the importance of exploration for learning. The evidence also suggests that a balance of the two systems is likely to have adaptive value worldwide (Grossmann, Grossmann, & Keppler, 2005). We claim that there is also a biologically based link between attachment and accommodation, another foundation for learning, and that cultures influence which link is prioritized. European American children generally engage in more exploration than Chinese and Korean children (Chen et al., 1998; Farver, Kim, & Lee, 1995; Liu et al., 2005; Rubin et al., 2006). Differences in the prevalence and experience of exploration likely translate into differences in the strength of the security-exploration link. Since East Asians are higher on accommodation than are European Americans, the strength of the security-accommodation link may be correspondingly greater for them.

This view, that the link between attachment and autonomy or accommodation is differentially prioritized depending on context, is supported by one of the few studies of attachment that relied on culturally sensitive methods. Harwood et al. (1995) used open-ended interviews to assess indigenous concepts pertaining to the nature of the secure base (see also Rothbaum et al., 2007). Building on the attachment theory notion that optimal balance involves tradeoffs between exploration-autonomy on one hand and attachment-relatedness on the other, Harwood et al. (1995) asked the question: What do mothers in different cultures see as the optimal balance for their children? They found that, for Puerto Rican mothers, what is seen as optimal is "a contextually appropriate balancing of calm respectful attentiveness with positive engagement in interpersonal relationships. . . [rather than a balancing] of autonomy and relatedness" (p. 112). As expected, the balance of autonomy and relatedness *was* the dominant theme emerging from the interviews with the European American mothers.

Harwood et al. (1995) comment in their discussion: "The construct of security versus insecurity has become equated in U.S. psychology with a host of culturally valued qualities that are specific to the socialization goals of our highly individualistic society, thus limiting their cross-cultural meaningfulness" (p. 114). In Puerto Rico, people more often experience themselves as interdependent beings, and accordingly are more oriented to accommodative matters like respect, duty, and obligation. They are more concerned with awareness of and alignment with important other people and situation-based expectations.

Reviews of culture and attachment often give short shrift to Harwood's research. Yet her findings indicate the kinds of cultural differences in the meaning of security to which we should be paying more attention. Cultural differences in the meaning of attachment do not diminish the universal importance of attachment. Rather, they reflect the fact that attachment is a cultural as well as biologically based phenomenon and that the form and meaning of attachment are only fully understood within particular contexts.

D. Differences in Subtypes of Insecure Attachment

There are many studies of culture and attachment indicating support for the normativity hypothesis—in almost all cultures examined, the majority of children are classified as secure. The consistency of this finding is impressive (van IJzendoorn & Sagi-Schwartz, 2008). Despite concerns raised earlier about differences in the meaning of security, the evidence regarding normativity as well as studies indicating cross-cultural similarities in the definition of the secure base (Posada et al., 1995) point to ways in which the secure base is similar across diverse cultures: a protective and sensitive caregiver provides a foundation for children to explore *and in other ways learn* about their environment.

What distinguishes communities is the prevalence of avoidant and anxious-resistant attachments. Children are avoidant of caregivers in stressful situations when they anticipate rejection; children anxiously resist their caregivers, even after seeking them out, when they are uncertain of the responses they will receive (Kobak & Madsen, 2008). Next we review evidence regarding cultural differences in the incidence of these two forms of insecurity.

1. Evidence from Japan

A few studies have examined the percentage of Japanese children classified into the two major insecure categories: avoidant and anxious-resistant. Three studies found more anxious-resistant than avoidant children; in two of those studies no Japanese children were classified as avoidant (reviewed in Rothbaum, Weisz, et al., 2000). Studies of European American samples, by contrast, typically report more children with an avoidant compared to a anxious-resistant pattern of insecure attachment (van IJzendoorn & Sagi-Schwartz, 2008).

As noted by van IJzendoorn and Sagi-Schwartz (2008), these findings regarding the distribution of insecure attachment types pose a challenge to a universalist theory of attachment. However, van IJzendoorn and Sagi highlight a fourth study, by Behrens, Hesse, and Main (2007), which found that the three-way distribution of attachment classifications in their Sapporo[3] (Japan) sample was similar to that found in most Western samples. Behrens et al. also found that the Japanese mothers' attachment classifications were similar to the global norm, with most scoring as secure-autonomous. Based largely on Behrens et al.'s findings, van IJzendoorn and Sagi-Schwartz (2008) concluded that the classification of insecure attachment styles in Japan is similar to that found worldwide.

---

[3] Japanese-U.S. differences in subtypes of attachment based on a sample from Sapporo are likely to be less pronounced than differences based on a mainstream Japanese sample. Sapporo, compared to other cities in Japan, is more similar to the United States in that it is situated on the island of Hokkaido, a frontier region. People from that island have relatively independent conceptions of self, which relates to high levels of autonomous exploration (Kitayama, Ishii, Imada, Takemura, & Ramaswamy, 2006).

We have doubts about this conclusion. The Behrens et al. (2007) findings that resembled the U.S. findings were based on a forced three-category (avoidant, secure, anxious-resistant) *reclassification* of participants who were initially classified as disorganized and who constituted almost half of the sample. Most of the children later classified as avoidant were originally classified as disorganized. The forced reclassification ignores the possibility that children classified as disorganized in other communities may exhibit forms of behavior which might be more organized and meaningful, and not viewed as insecure, by local standards (Keller, 2008). The large group of children in this sample categorized as disorganized may be telling us something important about the meaning of attachment behavior in cultural context.[4]

The tendency of European American children to more clearly fall into the avoidant than anxious-resistant pattern of insecurity may reflect the relatively greater emphasis on autonomy and independence in the West. When expectations for autonomy are not balanced by sufficient responsiveness to children's needs, avoidance is a likely outcome. European American children who receive avoidant classifications often continue to explore; indeed, they may turn to the physical environment as a defensive strategy for coping with an unavailable and rejecting caregiver (Ainsworth et al., 1978; Cassidy & Kobak, 1988; McElwain, Cox, Burchinal, & Macfie, 2003). The low levels of empathy and high levels of aggression associated with avoidant insecurity (McElwain et al., 2003) may contribute to the infrequency of that type of insecurity in Japan.

Children classified as anxious-resistant, by contrast, have difficulty sustaining attention to the nonsocial environment in a self-initiated manner. They also show less assertion and control among friends and more dependency (McElwain et al., 2003). These behaviors characterize many Japanese children (Rothbaum, Pott, et al., 2000; Rothbaum, Weisz, et al., 2000). When Japanese children are insecure, it makes sense that they are more likely to be the anxious-resistant type.

---

[4]Disorganized attachment is associated with highly maladaptive strategies, but culture is likely to play a key role in determining what is deemed maladaptive. In a study comparing European (Icelandic) disorganized and secure children, the biggest difference between the groups was that secure children had more logical, syllogistic reasoning skills (Jacobsen, Edelstein, & Hofmann, 1994)—skills essential for analytic reasoning (Nisbett et al., 2001). Disorganized children's deficits in analytic reasoning were evident in their contradictory responses, which are more consistent with holistic, and specifically dialectic, reasoning than with analytic reasoning (Norenzayan et al., 2007). Children in East Asian cultures who manifest this profile may be seen as less disorganized because of the relatively greater value placed on holistic reasoning and the lesser value on analytic reasoning.

One of the greatest challenges to a universalist position comes from the Japanese indigenous concept of *amae*. *Amae* is defined as depending and pre-suming upon another's love and indulgence (Doi, 1992). It closely resembles the Western notion of attachment but also differs from that notion. In *amae* there is a link between attachment and dependence (or interdependence) rather than between attachment and independence or autonomy (Rothbaum & Kakinuma, 2004). Van IJzendoorn and Sagi-Schwartz (2008) discount the similarity between the two constructs on the basis of evidence that *amae* is a less desirable phenomenon than attachment security, even among Japanese (Vereijken, Riksen-Walraven, & Van Lieshout, 1997). However, comparing security with *amae* is like comparing apples with fruit; the appropriate com-parison is between security and *positive amae* (Maruta, 1992; Niiya, Yamaguchi, Murakami, & Harihara, 2001; see also Kitayama, Markus, & Kurokawa, 2000; Niiya, Ellsworth, & Yamaguchi, 2006).

Amae behavior combines elements of both secure and anxious-resistant behavior. Like attachment, which is divided into secure and insecure subtypes, *amae* has both positive and negative forms. What distinguishes positive from negative *amae* is less the amount of anxious-resistant behavior than the con-texts and ways in which *amae* is exhibited. Because people in Japan are highly sensitive to contextual cues, *amae* is seen as positive when it is interpersonally and situationally appropriate.[5] It is not the dependency (the anxious-resistant behavior) per se that is seen as negative; rather, *amae* is negative when the child fails to attend to others' needs and expectations and to the social situa-tion (Rothbaum & Kakinuma, 2004; Yamaguchi, 2004).

2. Evidence from Other Cultures

In contrast to the frequent finding of more avoidant than anxious-resistant children among European Americans, anxious-resistant classifications are at least as common, and often more common, in several other communities, including Israel (findings in the kibbutz and city), Indonesia, and the Dogon of Africa (but not among the Khayelitsha of Africa) (van IJzendoorn & Sagi-Schwartz, 2008). In a sample of 19 Efe hunters and gatherers of the Democratic Republic of Congo, Morelli, Tronick, and Beeghley (1999) identified two

---

[5] Ironically, part of the definition of *amae* is that it is "inappropriate"—in the sense that the child does not need what she or he is requesting from the caregiver (Yamaguchi, 2004). *Amae* is positive when the child knows when and with whom to express this "inappropri-ate" behavior.

children who were anxious-resistant (11%) and none who were avoidant. Moreover, a multicountry study of adults' romantic relationships found more anxious-resistant ("preoccupied") participants from Asian countries than elsewhere, including European American countries. That study did not find cultural differences in avoidant-type classifications (Schmitt, 2004).

Our interest in these differences has to do with what they tell us about the meaning of attachment—among both secure and insecure individuals. We suspect that the findings relate to the findings mentioned earlier—people with a more interdependent self are more prone to anxious-resistant behaviors such as dependency, blurring of the boundaries between self and other, failure to engage in exploration, and low self-esteem (high self-criticism) (Fiske et al., 1998; Rothbaum, Weisz, et al., 2000).

E. The Interplay of Differences and Similarities

Evidence of cultural variation does not call into question the enormous contributions of attachment theory. Rather, it challenges attachment researchers to look more deeply into the interplay of similarity and difference. Too often researchers focus on superficial cultural variation, such as whether children expect their caregivers to greet them with a simple handshake or more intimate physical contact (van IJzendoorn & Sagi-Schwartz, 2008). Cultural differences lie nearer to the heart of the theory. Next we look more closely at the differences *and* the similarities, summarized in Table 4.1.

TABLE 4.1: **Summary of Similarities and Differences in Attachment When Comparing European American and Other Communities**

	Observed Similarities	Observed Differences
Sensitivity	Sensitive, responsive care predicts security	Nature of sensitive, responsive care (e.g., responding to overt signals versus anticipating signals)
Competence	Security predicts later competence	Nature of competence (e.g., prioritizing autonomy versus harmony)
Secure base	Secure base fosters learning	Nature of learning (e.g., emphasis on learning through exploration versus learning through accommodation)
Attachment styles	Secure attachment is the most common style	Distribution of insecure attachment styles (e.g., greater proportion of avoidant versus anxious-resistant styles)

Despite cultural differences in sensitivity, there is impressive evidence of the sensitivity-security association. Studies in Bogota, Colombia (Posada et al., 1999), in Mali (True, Pisani, & Oumar, 2001), and in Chile (Valenzuela, 1997) show that sensitivity predicts attachment security even when sensitivity and security are assessed at different times and in different situations and when coded by different observers (Rothbaum & Morelli, 2005).

In these studies, measures of caregiving were defined in ways consistent with attachment theory, and specifically with Ainsworth's (1976) measures. Her broad constructs, which include maternal accessibility, cooperation with the child's ongoing behavior, acceptance of the child, and sensitivity to signals, seemingly tap important qualities of human caregiving worldwide. If, as we claim, Ainsworth's detailed descriptions of these constructs are grounded in Western values, how is it possible that they predict security in communities with very different values?

We speculate that when Ainsworth's scales are applied in other communities, coders adapt their meaning to make them relevant to local values and practices. One way to tap into issues of meaning would be to study the perspective of coders from different communities. There is evidence that coders with different backgrounds make different interpretations, and assign different codes, when given the same categories (Wang, Wiley, & Zhou, 2007). Yet, even if we are correct about coder effects, the fact that Ainsworth's scales lend themselves to such adaptation is a tribute to the widespread relevance of her broader caregiving constructs.

While there is only limited support for the hypothesis that security predicts later competence, when competence is defined as physical health, security relates rather consistently to competence across a range of communities (van IJzendoorn & Sagi-Schwartz, 2008). Health has rarely been considered a universal outcome of attachment, because relatively good health (low child mortality) is more taken for granted in middle-class Western communities. In poor communities, which are more common in the non-Western world, there is far greater variability in illness and physical well-being than in the West. Parents in those communities engage in forms of sensitivity and foster forms of secure attachment that relate to their children's future physical health and well-being. Those parents are more likely to organize their care to ameliorate health risks, even though the way they do this is culturally situated. As noted by LeVine (1974, 1988), parents are first and foremost concerned with the physical health and survival of their children. Practices intended to foster other cultural values are relatively less emphasized until there are clear signs that this first goal is met.

All children, despite differences in the nature of their security, seek proximity and contact in situations that are stressful to them. They are afraid of strangers, look to caregivers for ways to act in ambiguous situations, and rely on them for safety and comfort. Even though cultures vary in how these attachment-related behaviors are expressed and how they are made sense of by the infant and others, their survival value is evident and a testament to the universal nature of core aspects of attachment (Grossmann et al., 2008; van IJzendoorn & Sagi-Schwartz, 2008).

There is also evidence that the secure base phenomenon is widespread. The work by Posada et al. (1995) in seven cultures points to commonalities in informants' secure base beliefs. The work by Grossmann et al. (2005) points to predictable variation in exploration behavior across the strange situation episodes in different cultures. If investigators examined ways of learning besides exploration, such as accommodation, or even if they examined indigenous ways of exploring, it would lead to a richer understanding of the ways in which the secure base functions (Keller, 2008; Rothbaum et al., 2007). Exploration is one of several systems of behavior which enable children to learn about the wider world. The balance between attachment on one hand and learning about the environment on the other is widespread if not universal, and exploration is an essential and widespread, but not the only, form of learning.

Perhaps the best evidence of the interplay of cultural similarities and differences in attachment comes from research on *amae* (Behrens, 2004; Rothbaum & Kakinuma, 2004; Rothbaum et al., 2007; Yamaguchi, 2004), the indigenous Japanese concept described earlier. *Amae* and attachment are similar in that both are first manifested at around 9 months; are linked to desires for closeness and security; are especially evident when children are distressed; are manifested as proximity seeking and contact maintaining; and are divided into positive and negative forms.

Amae also differs from attachment in several respects. *Amae* is more closely linked to (inter)dependence and accommodation than to independence and exploration. *Amae* is more associated with mild stress, needs for merging, unity or symbiosis, and feelings of loneliness or sadness; attachment is more associated with major stressors, needs for protection or basic care, and feelings of fear. *Amae* is positive when it is context appropriate—for example, when children's requests are infrequent and occur in circumstances where caregivers are able to indulge them. Attachment is positive (secure) when the child is able to use the caregiver as a base for exploration and to reunite with the caregiver following separations (Rothbaum & Kakinuma, 2004; see also Behrens, 2004; Mizuta, Zahn-Waxler, Cole, & Hiruma, 1996).

F. Summary

Much of our work has been intended to show how attachment relationships are grounded in goals for autonomy, common in the United States, and goals for harmony, common in Japan. Our reason for comparing cultures is not to question the biological or evolutionary underpinnings of attachment relationships. Rather, we seek to understand how biological and cultural processes interrelate to foster different experiences of attachment. Cultural research can illuminate ways in which attachment processes are shaped by and derive meaning from the contexts in which they are embedded. Such research cannot rely only on theories developed in the West; indigenous theories of attachment, such as the theory of *amae* in Japan, must be considered. Like us, Bruner (1990) highlights the merits of approaches which view biology and culture as inseparable, in contrast to approaches that view culture as an overlay on biologically determined human nature.

Because Ainsworth's work in Uganda constituted the first cultural research on attachment, it is noteworthy that she emphasized the role of context. In her conclusion she wrote, "Attachment does not develop willy nilly according to some inner genetic regulating mechanism, but rather is influenced by conditions in the baby's environment" (Ainsworth, 1967, p. 387).

IV. RESEARCH ON CULTURAL DIFFERENCES IN LEARNING

A. Overview

The secure base, the crowning achievement in the development of attachment, provides children the psychic fuel they need to explore and learn about their environment. Unfortunately, attachment investigators have not devoted a great deal of attention to cultural differences in exploration and learning (see Grossmann et al., 2005, 2008 for reviews of the literature on attachment and exploration), even though there has been a recent explosion of research on culture and learning (Greenfield, Keller, Fuligni, & Maynard, 2003; Keller, 2008; Nisbett et al., 2001; Norenzayan et al., 2007). As indicated in the following discussion, this recent scholarship informs our understanding of how attachment and learning relate. Here we use the term *learning* to refer both to goals of learning (exploration and accommodation) and ways of thinking (analytic and holistic). We focus our attention on the association between attachment, conceptions of self, and learning.

1. Attachment, Conceptions of Self, and Ways of Thinking

Research on cultural differences in conceptions of self helps clarify cultural differences in attachment and learning. Children are more likely to develop an independent self that is separate and distinct from others, and that functions autonomously, when their early attachment relationships are distinguished by frequent separations and reunions and when they have a secure base from which to explore their environment. Children are more likely to develop an interdependent self when their attachments are characterized by more con-tinuous unions and when they have a secure base for accommodating others (Morelli & Rothbaum, 2007). These differences in attachment correspond to differences in social relations identified by self-theorists. For people with an independent self, social relations are "governed by instrumental goals of sepa-rated selves" (Kitayama et al., 2007, p. 140). For people with an interdepen-dent self, social relations provide "the context for the definitions of connected selves" and the focus is on "responsiveness to social contingencies" (Kitayama et al., 2007, p. 140).

Conceptions of self also relate to ways of thinking. Those prioritizing an independent self view themselves and others as distinct and separate, and their world as divisible into distinct and separate parts. These individuals are likely to analyze specific parts of the environment and to explore the parts, as shown in dozens of studies on adult memory, perception, and reasoning (for reviews, see Nisbett et al., 2001; Norenzayan et al., 2007). Analytic thinking, which is more common among European Americans as compared to East Asians, involves a tendency to detach objects from the surrounding field, to focus on goal-relevant attributes of objects, to rely on logical rules, and to avoid contradictions.

By contrast, people prioritizing an interdependent self view themselves as "embedded in interdependent contexts," and they typically attend to and per-ceive contextual information and relationships between parts, including between people (Kitayama et al., 2007, p. 163; see also Masuda & Nisbett, 2001). Their wider awareness leads them to adjust or accommodate them-selves to others' expectations and to demands from the environment. Consistent with this way of conceptualizing self and engaging the world is an orientation to learning that is more holistic. Holistic thought, which is more common among East Asians as compared to European Americans, involves attention to the field as a whole, especially to relationships, contradictions, and multiple perspectives. For example, when shown different scenes, Japanese make far more statements about the background and relationships between objects, whereas Americans comment more on focal objects (Masuda & Nisbett, 2001). Similar findings are obtained when eye movements are used to assess attention and when Americans are compared to Chinese (Chua, Boland, & Nisbett, 2005).

It is possible to momentarily prioritize holistic ways of thinking among people with chronically independent selves by priming their interdependent selves—for example, asking them what they have in common with family and friends (Kuhnen, Hannover, & Schubert, 2001). A meta-analysis of studies priming individualism versus collectivism, a distinction paralleling independent versus interdependent conceptions of self, indicated moderate effects on analytic (contrasting and separating) versus holistic (integrating and connecting) ways of thinking, respectively (Oyserman & Lee, 2008; see also Oyserman, Sorensen, Reber, Chen, & Sannum, 2009). Cultural differences also emerge in the absence of primes or of situations that pull for a particular conception of self, indicating that people differ in their default ways of thinking.

2. How Ways of Thinking Relate to Perspective-Taking and Learning Goals

People who experience themselves as independent, and who adopt analytic ways of thinking, tend to adopt a first-person, relatively egocentric, perspective (Cohen et al., 2007; Kitayama et al., 2004; Masuda et al., 2008). Interdependent selves, and people with a holistic approach to thinking, are more likely to adopt a third-person, outsider perspective and to adopt multiple viewpoints (Masuda et al., 2008). When viewing the world from the eyes of others, it is more apparent that self, other people, and aspects of the environment are interrelated and constitute a larger whole. Asian American, as compared to European American, children show an earlier developmental trend away from describing scenes by observable behaviors that they can see with their own eyes, toward entering into another's perspective and attempting to describe the other's unobservable thoughts and feelings (Cohen et al., 2007).

As people with a first-person perspective explore the world, there is a sense of excitement about learning. They view themselves as discovering reality on their own and, in a sense, for the first time. Their adoption of a single standpoint allows for limited contextual information but fosters analysis of focal objects—their properties, categorization, and the discovery of universal rules (Masuda et al., 2008). An insider perspective leads parents and, eventually, children to believe that what is true for them is true for others, and to set about discovering the truth—piece by piece (Cohen et al., 2007). By contrast, when the individual adopts a third-person perspective, he "learns the truth about himself through the intermediary of others" (Bourdieu, 1965, p. 212, cited in Cohen et al., 2007). From this third-person perspective, exploration is less necessary—what one really needs to learn is what others see and know to be true.

Analytic and holistic thinking go hand in hand with goals for exploration and accommodation, respectively. The first meaning of the word *explore* is "to investigate, study, or analyze" and "to become familiar with by testing or experimenting" (Merriam-Webster, 2003). It is also the meaning intended by attachment theorists who define exploration as investigating, manipulating, and mastering the environment (Bowlby, 1969/1982; Mikulincer & Shaver, 2007a). Children's autonomous exploration of easily manipulable objects fosters concentrated attention to a limited set of characteristics (parts) of objects, and to later analytic abilities. Other features of exploration described by attachment theorists that pave the way for analytic thinking include making new discoveries, curiosity, freedom, and pursuit of self's interests. People break things down into parts, categorize the parts, and apply logical rules to them when they have an "epistemic curiosity" (Choi & Nisbett, 2000, p. 901) about contradictions and a desire to explore and resolve those contradictions.

Holistic thought is more likely driven by accommodative goals of fitting in with a larger context than with goals of exploration. In order to accommodate effectively, people must be mindful of relationships between people and between people and their situations. When people's posture and behavior are unobtrusively mimicked, a manipulation that is likely to prime goals of accommodation, they subsequently process information in a more holistic (field-dependent) manner than do nonmimicked participants (van Baaren, Maddux, Chartrand, de Bouter, & van Knippenberg, 2003).

The influence of learning goals and ways of thinking may be bidirectional. When people see themselves as separate and their context as divisible into parts, they are motivated to explore the properties of those parts. When attention is directed to the wider field, especially the social field, and to a large number of *interrelated* factors, there is little room for the process of discovery, for novelty, or for the experience of surprise at outcomes (the "aha" experience) that is so central to exploration (Choi & Nisbett, 2000), and there is more felt necessity to align the self with others and the wider context (Kitayama et al., 2007).

While there is no research linking differences in early attachment to differences in ways of thinking, there is evidence that fear of isolation, even in Western samples, leads to increases in holistic thinking (Kim & Markman, 2006). Since East Asian children's early experiences of continuous union leaves them poorly prepared for coping with separations, and since East Asian adults are more concerned about loneliness and loss of social approval (Kim & Markman, 2006), East Asians' holistic thought may be partly due to lack of familiarity with, and fear of, isolation.

3. Summary

Though indirect, the evidence suggests that differences in attachment relate to differences in learning goals and ways of thinking. People who prioritize the interdependent self, and whose attachments entail continuous union, may be more motivated to accommodate—to fit in with others and the context. We hypothesize that goals of accommodation are associated with holistic ways of thinking—focusing on the context in which self is embedded. People who prioritize an independent self, and whose attachments entail frequent separations and reunions, may be more motivated to explore—to manipulate objects and make new discoveries, largely on their own. We hypothesize that goals of exploration are associated with analytic ways of thinking—breaking objects down into parts, categorizing the objects, and identifying rules that explain them.

B. Socialization Experiences and Learning

In this section we spotlight aspects of cultural practices and traditions that promote different ways of relating and learning. We review research indicating that children who experience caregiving that supports an independent self and attachments that are closely linked with exploration are oriented to analyzing specific objects in their environment. Children who experience caregiving that supports an interdependent self and attachments closely linked with accommodation, by contrast, are oriented to thinking holistically about their contexts. Even though we distinguish between goals of exploration and accommodation, and between analytic and holistic thought, we believe that attachment is linked with both goals and both ways of thinking in all children. Cultures differ in how much they prioritize those different goals and ways of thinking, and in the number of situations that call for each.

1. *Differences in Early Closeness and Learning*

Children's learning relates to their early experiences of closeness. Holistic thinking relates to forms of attachment that are characterized by continuous union and that have been influenced by prolonged physical contact with caregivers. "Skinship," as manifest in practices like co-sleeping, co-bathing, and prolonged breastfeeding, as well as lack of separation from caregivers, foster in children a sharing of selves and of perspectives (Morelli & Rothbaum, 2007; Rothbaum & Trommsdorff, 2007). Caregivers' empathy with the child is tied to their children's development of empathy with them, and in fact the latter is an explicit socialization goal, at least in Japan (Clancy, 1986). These experiences of physical and psychological closeness put the child in the position of the caregiver—the child and caregiver literally experience the same reality. The mutuality that develops as part of the taking-and-sharing of perspectives maintains the caregiver–child union and is the first step in the process of taking the perspective of the generalized other.

Because East Asian children experience relatively continuous proximity and prolonged physical contact, they are not accustomed to venturing far from attachment figures for purposes of exploration and are instead accustomed to accommodating to others' expectations (Morelli & Rothbaum, 2007; Rothbaum, Pott, et al., 2000). Social expectations are greatest in interactions outside the home and when nonintimate others are present in the home (Hendry, 1993; Rothbaum, Pott, et al., 2000). Anxiety about accurately attending to cues and about behaving appropriately encourages children to adopt their caregivers' perspective and, later, a third-person perspective (Clancy, 1986; Lebra, 1994; Vogel, 1996). Adopting a third-party perspective, in turn, fosters children's ability to see themselves as embedded within a wider field—a critical ingredient of holistic thought (Cohen et al., 2007). East Asians' efforts to accommodate to the wider reality, by joining the perspective of others, and to return to the caregiver in times of anxiety renders the secure base they experience different from the secure base experienced by European Americans.

By contrast, European American parents' and children's focus on the importance of physically separating from caregivers, and returning to them in times of danger, presumes that the process of individuation and development of an independent self is already well underway. Instead of adopting the perspective of the other, these children assume that what is in their head is also in the head of others; European American children aged 5 to 12 years are considerably less able to take a third-person perspective than their East Asian counterparts (Cohen et al., 2007). Children who are accustomed to separations and to honing their first-person perspective have "no reason to be reticent, to doubt [their] perceptions . . . These experiences create the person with the self-assurance, the confidence, the certitude in one's convictions, and the action orientation that is one of the ideal American types" (Cohen et al., 2007, p. 47). That confidence is especially evident when European Americans are engaging in analytic skills and seeking to control the environment (Ji, Peng, & Nisbett, 2000).

2. Later Differences in Closeness and Learning

As children in all communities mature, there are increasing opportunities for them to take part in the social rhythms of everyday life that foster different ways of relating and learning. In settings where the interdependent self is prioritized, keen observational skills, attentiveness to the environment, and empathic listening are ways in which young children learn. In these settings, apprenticeships involving cooperation and intergenerational modeling are common. Here, it is the responsibility of the child to participate in (by watching and doing) and integrate into ongoing activities, rather than being singled out and instructed in them (Morelli, Rogoff, & Angelillo, 2003; Rogoff, 1990; Romero, 1994). Elsewhere, in communities prioritizing the independent self, caregivers are relatively more likely to serve as interactional partners and relatively less likely to serve as authority figures (Farver et al., 1995). Caregivers in these settings encourage the child's questioning, skepticism, and curiosity. Independent selves learn for their own benefit more than the benefit of the group (Greenfield et al., 2003; Suina & Smolkin, 1994). These cultural differences foster the relatively greater accommodation and holistic thought of interdependent selves, as well as the relatively greater exploration and analytic thought of independent selves.

What caregivers talk about with children reflects differences in cultural emphasis on ways of relating and learning. European American parents ask children to share detailed, specific memories of self's feelings, wants, and thoughts. These parents talk with their children about the causes and consequences of feelings and provide elaborate explanations as to how and why an emotion is experienced (Wang & Ross, 2007). Their ways of exploring and analyzing children's memories contrast starkly with the approach of East Asian mothers who use talk of memories to teach moral lessons, to resolve conflicts between the child and significant others, and to establish the child's proper place in his or her social world (Wang, 2004).

While East Asian mother–child discussion of memories focuses more on moral and social matters, and less on personal ones, there are ways in which European American mothers use memories in more social ways. They are more likely to use shared memories to elicit emotional responses and to deepen intimacy with their young children (Fivush, 1994; Wang & Ross, 2007). East Asians' more assured and guaranteed role relationships and their sustained attention to group action and interdependent connections enable them to assume intimacy rather than to periodically strive to attain it (Rothbaum, Pott, et al., 2000). East Asians' more continuous unions render reunions less valued and less meaningful.

Play is another context in which children learn about themselves and their relationship with others. European American children are more willing to initiate play, especially in novel situations, than are East Asian children (Chen et al., 1998; Rubin et al., 2006; also see Edwards, 2000). This may be because, when children confront unfamiliar and challenging tasks, European American mothers are more likely than East Asian mothers to encourage initiation and autonomy, and less likely to elicit bids for affiliation and connection (Liu et al., 2005). European American mothers are likely to encourage play involving self-expression and personal choice—other qualities associated with exploration (Farver et al., 1995; Greenfield et al., 2003).

However, European American mothers, as compared to Korean American, Indonesian, and Mexican mothers, are *less* likely to recognize children's play as imitation of, and accommodation to, adult models (Farver & Wimbarti, 1995). European American children engage in less cooperative play with peers, which also requires accommodation, than do children in many other communities (Farver et al., 1995; Fromberg & Bergen 2006; Martini, 1994). On academic tasks, European American as compared to East Asian parents are less likely to expect children to attend to failures, redress mistakes, and increase effort (evidence reviewed in Pomerantz, Ng, & Wang, 2008). Thus, their children are less likely to accommodate to the demands of the situation.

East Asian and Western educational systems also foster differences in learning. Peak (1993) provides a compelling example of the differences. When Peak began her field study of preschools in Japan, she drew mostly blank stares from teachers in response to questions about their teaching curriculum. Only later did she resolve the misunderstanding. She had assumed that the purpose of preschool was for children to learn individual skills, whereas Japanese teachers assumed that the purpose of preschool was for children to learn that they are embedded within the group and that the group is part of them. In East Asia, and in other communities with relatively interdependent selves, learning is closely related to the social context and social goals. The fact that teachers had a single word for this type of learning, which involves concepts (the group is part of you) that are difficult for Westerners to grasp, speaks volumes about differences in conceptions of learning (see also Watkins, 2000).

Differences in educational priorities and practices contribute to later differences in learning. Educational systems grounded in Confucian ideology promote relatively greater social conformity, attention to the expectations of authority figures, and acquisition of basic knowledge and skill, whereas systems based in democratic ideology promote greater originality and inspire students to question and challenge conventional wisdom and extant curricula (Dineen & Niu, 2008; Purdie, Hattie, & Douglas, 1996; Tweed & Lehman, 2002). The differences are partly due to timing—East Asian educators foster questioning *after* knowledge is gained (Watkins, 2000). Yet, even in high school, Japanese as compared to Australian students engage in more memorization, repetition, and related strategies (Purdie et al., 1996), which can be seen as fostering accommodation. East Asian educators view these strategies not as an end in their own right, but as a route to understanding (Dahlin & Watkins, 2000; Hess & Azuma, 1991; Purdie et al., 1996).

Li (1997) describes cultural differences in the education of artists. In China, artists are encouraged to create within the boundaries set by the painting community. There are limited ways of representing objects, the materials and tools are prescribed, and the focus is on perfecting one's skills through repeated practice. Students are proud to imitate masters, and doing so does not reflect a lack of creativity. By contrast, Western artists are free to focus on an unlimited number of forms. They are allowed to deviate markedly from precedent, to be unpredictable, and to "explore" new ways of going about their craft. For them, imitation is often viewed as a lack of creativity. Similar differences are reported in other domains: Chinese magicians seek to reproduce tricks exactly as shown to them by their masters; North American magicians prefer improvising tricks (Bienstock, Goran, & Smith, 2003). Chinese educators typically support exploration and creativity only after students gain basic knowledge and skills; Western educators support those behaviors early in the learning process (Jin & Cortazzi, 1998; Wong, 2002, 2006).

Conceptions of knowledge align with the distinctions already noted. Knowing in Latino, Mayan, and East Asian communities is closely tied to character and social behavior, reflecting the interrelatedness of intellectual and social-moral pursuits (Greenfield et al., 2003: Watkins, 2000). Intelligence as a means to a social end is valued in African and Asian communities compared to a more impersonal (scientific) concept of intelligence that is the predominant ideal in the United States (e.g., Grigorenko, Geissler, Prince, Okatcha, & Nokes, 2001; Serpell, 1993; Super, 1983). Grossmann et al.'s (2008) review of findings on exploration, which is based largely on Western studies, makes much more mention of autonomous learning about objects, tasks, and activities of personal interest than about moral self-perfection, obligations, role responsibilities, imitation of and cooperation with others, learning about social relationships and the social context, and other goals of accommodation.

3. *Summary of Differences in Socialization and Learning*

Viewing things as others see them and adjusting to them, rather than viewing them from a first-person perspective and imposing one's will on them, lies at the heart of the distinction between holistic thought and accommodation on one hand and analytic thought and exploration on the other. For people prioritizing an interdependent self, learning is social in multiple ways. It entails a shared third-party perspective; it emanates from experiences of physical closeness and from opportunities for cooperative exchange requiring adherence to others' expectations; it is concerned with relationships between people and with the fit between behavior and context; and it is for purposes of social ends. For people prioritizing an independent self, learning entails a more ego-centric perspective. It emanates from experiences of separation and opportunities for autonomy which allow for creative self-expression; it is more focused on impersonal objects and activities; and it serves relatively individual and instrumental ends.

In depicting holistic thinking and accommodation-based learning as social, we do not mean that it always occurs in the company of others or with support from others. Learning in East Asia is seen as entailing substantial self-control and self-perfection which, when necessary, occur in the absence of others. It is also seen as entailing self-sacrifice, endurance of hardship, and steadfast perseverance. Thus, learning based in accommodation and holistic thought is distinguished by self-discipline as well as by social concerns—responsibilities to and reliance on others (Li, 2002; Purdie et al., 1996). Conversely, learning based in exploration and analytic thought is not asocial, but differently social. Young children engaged in this type of learning require a secure base and caregivers who are responsive to overt signals (Grossmann et al., 2008). Perhaps because of the risks involved in independent exploration, Westerners are more likely than East Asians to *explicitly* seek support from teachers and caregivers (Liang & Bogat, 1994; Purdie et al., 1996; Taylor et al., 2004).

V. ATTACHMENT AND COPING

A. Secure Attachment and Constructive Coping

Children's strategies for coping in situations where they confront failure, loss, rejection, and other stressors are related to attachment, conceptions of self, and learning. We see children's coping as constructive when they are able to learn in stressful situations. For individuals with secure attachments, coping is often constructive. They remain open, maintain effort, engage in deep processing, and draw from their full capacity for learning even when stressed. For individuals with insecure attachments, by contrast, coping is often compromised and learning is restricted (Mikulincer & Shaver, 2007a, 2008; Rusk & Rothbaum, 2010). In this section we examine how children with different conceptions of self engage in different forms of constructive coping as well as how coping relates to attachment and learning.

What is common across cultures is that secure children are likely to constructively cope because of the validation they receive from attachment figures. What differs is the nature of validation. As discussed next, independent selves more often seek to enhance self-esteem; interdependent selves more often seek to maintain face (Heine, 2005, 2007). When children are validated, they are more likely to engage in learning, which also varies across cultures. Independent selves seek to explore and engage in analytic thought; interdependent selves seek to accommodate and engage in holistic thought. As shown in the following discussion, these ways of learning are reflected in different coping strategies. Thus, coping strategies reflect cultural differences in types of validation and in ways of learning about the world.

Our understanding of culture and coping borrows from the scholarship on attachment, views of self, and learning reviewed earlier. Stated simply, how children think and how they respond to stressors when they have secure attachment relationships differs across cultures. For European American children, a secure attachment relationship reminds children that they are loveable, competent, and worthy, and that they possess the wherewithal to overcome stressors. Reconnecting with a sensitive and responsive attachment figure, or an internalized representation of such a figure, affirms children's esteem and efficacy, and provides them with the "emotional fuel"—the felt security and alleviation of distress—they need to continue to explore the environment. Exploration, in turn, leads to solutions to problems and mastery of stressors (Grossmann et al., 2008; Mikulincer & Shaver, 2008). When necessary, children are willing to confront people and obstacles that stand in their way (Mesquita & Leu, 2007; Tweed, White, & Lehman, 2004). Their conviction in the correctness of their own perspective (Cohen et al., 2007) and their analytic approach to emotions (Wang & Ross, 2007) enable them to change stressful situations in ways they desire.

Attachment and coping are experienced very differently in East Asian settings. Because East Asians focus more on avoiding loss of face and less on enhancing self-esteem, they are more likely to rely on attachment figures to reassure them that face can be maintained, or regained, by correcting behavior. East Asian attachment figures believe that when they celebrate children's worthiness (e.g., capability, competence, likeability) and autonomy they undermine children's willingness to correct their behavior (Miller, Fung, & Koven, 2007; Miller, Wiley, Fung, & Liang, 1997). Differences in learning as well as attachment contribute to differences in coping. Learning that prioritizes accommodation and holistic thought is reflected in coping that is accepting of external constraints, considerate of others' emotions, and seeking to improve self. In marked contrast is learning that prioritizes autonomous exploration of the environment and analytic thought. Those goals and ways of learning foster children's confident and assertive attempts to gain mastery over stressors (Mesquita & Leu, 2007; Rothbaum & Rusk, in press).

These claims fit well with research on culture and coping. Children and adults cope by changing the world to fit themselves or by changing themselves to fit in with their world (Kitayama et al., 2007; Olah, 1995; Tweed et al., 2004; Weisz et al., 1984a; see Morling & Evered, 2006, for a review). Changing the world to fit self, or primary control, is linked to change-based coping, and it is more common among people with independent than interdependent selves. Changing self to fit the world, or secondary control, is linked to acceptance-based coping, and it is characteristic of coping among people with interdependent selves. Differences between primary and secondary control are summarized in Table 4.2, reproduced from Weisz et al. (1984a).

TABLE 4.2: **Primary and Secondary Control: An Overview**

Type of Control	General Strategy	Typical Targets for Causal Influence	Overall Intent
Primary	Influence existing realities	Other objects, people, environmental circumstances, status or standing relative to others, behavior problems	Enhance reward (or reduce punishment) by influencing realities to fit self
Secondary	Accommodate to existing realities	Self's expectations, wishes, goals, perceptions, attitudes, interpretations, attributions	Enhance reward (or reduce punishment) by influencing psychological impact of realities on self

NOTE. This table is reproduced from Weisz et al. (1984a). It represents an extension and refinement of ideas first presented in "Changing the World and Changing Self: A Two-Process Model of Perceived Control," by F. M. Rothbaum, J. R. Weisz, and S. S. Snyder, 1982, *Journal of Personality and Social Psychology, 42*, pp. 5–37.
Source. From Weisz, J. R., Rothbaum, F., & Blackburn, T. C. (1984). Standing out and standing in: The psychology of control in the U.S. and Japan. *American Psychologist, 39*, 955–969. The use of APA information does not imply endorsement by the APA. Copyright © 1984 by the American Psychological Association. Reproduced with permission.

Rothbaum et al. (1982) described four types of secondary control, in each of which the self is aligned with a more powerful force: external circumstances (predictive control), chance (illusory control), other people (vicarious control), or meanings and values (interpretive control). People seeking secondary control change themselves (exercise self-control) so as to seek goals and standards mandated by the external forces. There are corresponding forms of primary control, but in primary control the self acts independently and seeks to change the world to satisfy goals and standards desired by the self. Primary control is linked to efforts to influence outcomes, master events, and other change-based strategies, and secondary control is linked to efforts to comply with fate, reappraise negative events, and other acceptance-based strategies.

The form of change-based coping that is probably the most commonly investigated by researchers in the United States is problem solving (Chang et al., 2007; D'Zurilla & Nezu, 2007; Haley, 1987; Malouff, Thorsteinsson, & Schutte, 2007; Stark, Reynolds, & Kaslow, 1987; Weisz, Jensen-Doss, & Hawley, 2006). Coping researchers divide problem solving into discrete steps, each of which entails exploration and analytic reasoning. The first step is to identify one aspect of the stressor that is of particular concern to the self. Selecting a part of the larger context—a part that the individual can confidently tackle—is consistent with analytic thought and mastery of the environment. Subsequent steps involve the following: *(a)* brainstorming possible solutions—a creative process often requiring exploration of novel ideas and new techniques; *(b)* choosing a solution—an expression of personal autonomy based in part on self's preferences; and *(c)* testing whether it works, relying on logical rules that are core to analytic reasoning. These steps are aided by supportive others, but they are initiated and executed largely on one's own. When the stressor entails conflict with others, problem solving typically requires open sharing of negative emotions. Security in the United States relates to this kind of openness (Mikulincer & Shaver, 2008; Simpson, Rholes, & Phillips, 1996; Thompson, 2008).

Change-based coping is less often relied upon by people with interdependent selves. Analytic problem solving requires open sharing of problems and breaking problems into parts—activities in which interdependent selves less often engage. They are more likely to suppress than express negative feelings (Matsumoto, Yoo, & Nakagawa, 2008) and to view problems holistically, especially in conflict situations (Nisbett et al., 2001). When they do engage in change-based coping, people with interdependent selves are more likely to consider the larger context, including others' feelings (Kitayama et al., 2000, 2006; Matsumoto et al., 2008). They are also more likely to seek change indirectly, by waiting, showing indifference, or refusing to speak (Mesquita & Leu, 2007). Alternately, they seek change by relying on "proxy" agents—a form of indirect coping involving reliance on others (Yamaguchi, 2001). A common denominator of all of these strategies is that people with interdependent selves seek to cope by fitting in with the larger context rather than by standing out (Heine, 2001; Weisz et al., 1984a, 1984b).

Interdependent selves prefer acceptance-based strategies because they are more aware of limitations in individual ways of approaching stressors and they have more confidence in collective forms of efficacy (Bandura, 1997; Chang, 1998; Yamaguchi, Gelfand, Ohashi, & Zemba, 2005). They view effective coping as accepting and aligning with others' perspectives and with more powerful forces, such as the group, social norms, fate, and circumstances (Tsai, 2007; Weisz et al., 1984a). Instead of discovering what makes them feel best about themselves, and maximizing positive and minimizing negative feelings, they seek emotional calm—experiencing both good and bad feelings and moderating both (see Mesquita & Leu, 2007, for several references). Tolerance of conflicting elements is a central aspect of holistic thinking (Nisbett et al., 2001; Norenzayan et al., 2007). Another element of acceptance is compassion—nonjudgment of, and empathy for, others. Compassion relates to perspective taking—gaining distance from one's immediate experience by adopting a more removed or an alternative vantage point from which to view events. Perspective taking is also a feature of holistic thinking (Cohen et al., 2007; Masuda et al., 2008; Nisbett et al., 2001).

Acceptance is a less common coping strategy for people with independent selves, and they have a different understanding of acceptance. Independent selves often link acceptance with self-acceptance and self-esteem, and they value self-esteem because it is a springboard for change-based strategies (Rothbaum & Wang, in press). At other times people with independent selves link acceptance with resignation (Nakamura & Orth, 2005; Scheier, Weintraub, & Carver, 1986), which can be an effective form of coping if it fosters letting go of disturbing emotions and "moving on" to consider new possibilities. Acceptance is linked with self-esteem and new possibilities for people who prioritize exploration and analytic thinking more than for people who prioritize accommodation and holistic thinking.

Emotion-focused coping, which subsumes acceptance, is sometimes regarded as more common among people with interdependent selves, particularly East Asians (Tweed et al., 2004). Yet there are forms of emotion-focused coping that are likely to be more common among people with independent selves. Many forms of distraction and reappraisal by European Americans are attempts to feel better, in particular to feel better about the self. Meta-analyses indicate that the latter forms of coping are more common among people with an independent self (Heine & Hamamura, 2007). People with an independent self are also more likely to cope by analyzing their emotions (Mesquita & Leu, 2007; Wang & Ross, 2007). Emotion-focused coping is more common among people with an interdependent self when it entails attending to and accepting others' emotions, and when others' emotions are seen as closely linked to one's own emotions.

Table 4.3 summarizes our ideas regarding cultural differences in constructive coping. While we have emphasized the coping of people with independent and interdependent selves, the table clarifies that it is the situation that calls for a particular type of coping. People with independent selves, particularly European Americans, more often find themselves in situations that call for exploration and analytic thinking. People with interdependent selves, particularly East Asians, more often find themselves in situations that call for accommodation and holistic thinking. Cultures differ in the prevalence of these situations, and thus in the type of coping that is most common. Yet, even

TABLE 4.3: **How Acceptance-Based and Change-Based Strategies Are Manifested in Different Types of Situations**

Type of Constructive Coping Strategy		
Type of Situation	**Acceptance-Based**	**Change-Based**
Situations that call for accommodation and holistic ways of thinking	*Openness, letting in and letting go, compassion, perspective taking (secondary control coping strategies)*	Indirect problem solving; changing the problem by changing the self or by relying on others
Situations that call for exploration and analytic ways of thinking	Self-acceptance; resigned acceptance of what one cannot change so as to open up new possibilities	*Identify the problem, brainstorm solutions, choose possibilities, and test them (primary control coping strategies)*

Note: Italics indicate strategies that are most common.

when controlling for situation, people with different conceptions of self are likely to differ in their preferred, or default, forms of coping (Kitayama et al., 1997; Morling et al., 2002).

B. Insecure Attachment and Defensive Coping

Compared to people with secure attachments, people who are insecure experience greater threat in stressful situations because they have fewer representations of sensitive and supportive caregivers, and they do not feel worthy of care and protection (Dweck, 1999; Kaplan & Maehr, 2007; Mikulincer & Shaver, 2007a, 2008; Rusk & Rothbaum, 2010). For insecure individuals, stress is associated with a hyperactivation of and preoccupation with attachment needs, including the need for validation (for people classified as anxious-resistant), or with a deactivation of and denial of those needs (for people classified as avoidant). In both cases, insecure individuals' pursuit of validation goals leaves them with fewer resources to pursue learning goals (Mikulincer & Shaver, 2007a, 2007b). In this section we examine how validation goals and the defensive strategies for fulfilling them differ across cultures.

1. Differences in Validation Goals

As indicated in the last section, there are differences in the kinds of validation that caregivers provide their children—maintaining face and enhancing self-esteem (Heine, 2007). Both kinds of validation contribute to feelings of being competent, likeable, and worthy, but they differ in how they are achieved. Ho (1976) defines face as respectability and/or deference, which is derived from one's relative standing. Face is maintained by fulfilling one's role obligations. It is concerned with reputation and thus with how one appears to others. Face is valued, elaborated, and pursued by interdependent selves more than independent selves (Heine, 2005, 2007). By contrast, self-esteem is apprehended from a first-person perspective and is concerned with individuals' liking and positive evaluation of themselves. Self-esteem is pursued more often by independent than interdependent selves. While there are several key differences involved, we focus on the fact that face is heavily dependent on others; people cannot claim face for themselves in the same sense that they enhance themselves and claim esteem (Heine, 2005, 2007).[6] As noted by Cohen et al. (2007):

> The metaphor of "face" is one of the central concepts in East Asian societies, and this metaphor fits in quite nicely with the phenomenological third-person experiencing of self . . . Literally, one can never see one's own face, *except by taking the perspective of other people and looking at oneself the way others would*. The face is something that can *only* be seen from the outside. The West, too, uses the metaphor of "face," but it is probably not a coincidence that the metaphor was imported from the East. "Saving face" is an idiom derived from Chinese expressions and developed by English expatriates in China. (pp. 45–46)

2. Validation Goals and Defensive Strategies

When insecure children are stressed, caregivers cannot be counted on to meet their need for validation—for face or esteem. In those situations, they adopt validation goals. There are two basic kinds of strategies that insecure children adopt to fulfill validation goals: defensive self-enhancement and defensive intensification of needs.

---

[6]The distinction between face maintenance and self-enhancement parallels differences other investigators have drawn within the self-esteem construct, between the self as social object and the instrumental self (Baranik et al., 2008; Tafarodi & Milne 2002). The self as social object (i.e., the self as seen from a third-person perspective), which is more accentuated by East Asians than European Americans, refers to a focus on role-prescribed behavior and on factors contributing to group harmony. The instrumental self, which is more accentuated by European Americans, refers to the sense of self as a confident, capable, and efficacious causal agent.

Mikulincer and Shaver, (2007a) review evidence that people with the avoidant pattern engage in "defensive self-enhancement" (p. 468) to deal with distress—they seek to convince themselves and others of their self-sufficiency and superior abilities. Toward that end, they deny negative information about the self, and they suppress their anxiety that their needs for care and protection will not be met. Their reluctance to rely on others can take the form of compulsive self-reliance. While people with avoidant attachment do not enjoy as high a level of self-esteem as people who are secure, their esteem and efficacy are higher than those with other forms of insecurity (Mikulincer & Shaver, 2007a; Schmitt & Allik, 2005). Moreover, their esteem is not low with regard to impersonal domains, and their low esteem in social domains is not weighed heavily when they assess their overall worth (Mikulincer & Shaver, 2007a). Yet their self-esteem is defensive, fragile, and likely to break down under high levels of stress (Mikulincer & Shaver, 2007a).

People are most likely to engage in defensive self-enhancement when they equate validation with self-esteem. Since self-esteem is something one confers on the self, it can be validated through compulsive self-reliance—by proving one's worthiness to oneself. Denial and suppression of negative evaluations by others, and of self's needs for care and protection, are made easier if one enhances one's opinion about the self and focuses on the ability to meet one's own needs. Importantly, the self-definition of people in America as compared to Hong Kong is less influenced by what others think of self, and more influenced by private self-evaluations; Americans seek to protect their sovereignty to define themselves (Kim & Cohen, 2010; Kim, Cohen, & Au, 2010). Since people with independent as compared to interdependent selves are more invested in self-esteem (Heine & Hamamura, 2007; Kitayama et al., 1997), they are more prone to defensive self-enhancement, a strategy which is characteristic of avoidant attachment (Mikulincer & Shaver, 2007a).

People with the anxious-resistant pattern seek others' approval to defend against the sense that one's self is not worthy of anyone's care. They intensify and openly express their distress and needs for care, in part because those strategies sometimes lead to others' sympathy, approval, and support. There is consistent cross-cultural evidence that anxious-resistant insecurity relates to low self-esteem, low self-efficacy, and high self-criticism (Mikulincer & Shaver, 2007a; Schmitt & Allik, 2005). These individuals' negative self-evaluations and their accentuation of distress are attempts to gain validation and support from others (Mikulincer & Shaver, 2007a, 2007b).

Since face can only be gained from others, people concerned with face understandably rely on others to meet their validation needs. "What everyone knows that everyone knows" is crucial to their self-definition (Kim & Cohen, 2010; Kim, Cohen, & Au, 2010). When self is dependent on others, and others are seen as insufficiently responsive, exaggeration of needs is a reasonable strategy. Since people with interdependent as compared to independent selves are more invested in face, they are more prone to this anxious-resistant strategy.

3. Defensive Strategies and Types of Insecurity

As noted earlier, in European American communities, insecure individuals are more often classified as avoidant than anxious-resistant. They seek to minimize attachment needs because of concerns that attachment figures will be unavailable or rejecting and because they have been successful at meeting their needs for self-esteem through autonomous pursuits. By contrast, the anxious-resistant type of insecurity is more common among people from communities in which interdependent selves are prioritized, especially East Asian communities. They exaggerate efforts to gain proximity with and support from attachment figures because they have to rely on attachment figures for reassurance about face concerns.

In keeping with our larger theme of an interplay between cultural similarity and difference, we note that no culture has a monopoly on needs for face or self-esteem. While independent selves prioritize self-esteem, needs for self-esteem have embedded within them needs for validation by others (i.e., face needs). And while interdependent selves are relatively more concerned with face than with self-esteem, they also have self-esteem needs (Sedikides, Gaertner, & Vevea, 2005). If we are correct that self-esteem concerns relate more to avoidant insecurity and that face concerns relate more to anxious-resistant insecurity, it follows that both forms of insecurity are likely in all cultures, albeit to different degrees.

Also in keeping with this larger theme, we contend that there are cultural differences in avoidant insecurity and there are cultural differences in anxious-resistant insecurity. On the relatively infrequent occasions when independent selves fall in the anxious-resistant category, their exaggerated appeals for support are likely to be expressed in autonomous forms. For example, they are likely to directly and openly express their needs. Interdependent selves who are anxious-resistant are more likely to rely on indirect—somatic and nonverbal—appeals for reassurance. This is in keeping with their reliance on others for validation.

Similarly, on the relatively infrequent occasions when interdependent selves fall in the avoidant category, they are likely to rely on forms of compulsive self-reliance that involve others. For example, they fulfill social role expectations and go out of their way to meet others' needs. These social behaviors should not be confused with securely attached behaviors; in fact, they are used to deny attachment needs. Independent selves who are avoidant are more likely to meet validation needs in impersonal ways. This is in keeping with their focus on *self*-validation.

In summary, insecure individuals seek to validate themselves by maintaining face or by enhancing self-esteem. Interdependent selves, who are focused on maintaining face, are prone to anxious-resistant strategies in which they intensify relationship needs to elicit proof of worth from others. Independent selves, who are focused on enhancing self-esteem, are prone to avoidant strategies in which they deny the importance of relationships by satisfying needs for worth on their own. Validation goals are problematic because they often lead to defensive, self-defeating strategies, and because the more that people pursue them the less they pursue learning goals. In the absence of learning goals, people lack the cognitive openness and deep processing they need to engage in constructive change-based and acceptance-based strategies (see Table 4.4).

VI. IMPLICATIONS AND CONCLUSION

As noted in the introduction, a focus on cultural differences can enhance understanding of what is similar across communities. It increases awareness

TABLE 4.4: **The Relationship between Defensive Coping Strategies and Types of Validation**

Type of Validation	Type of Defensive Coping Strategy	
	Anxious-Resistant Strategies: Intensify Efforts to Elicit Validation	**Avoidant Strategies: Minimize Anxiety about Need for Validation**
Maintaining face	*Intensify self's needs indirectly, without being explicit about requesting support; depend on others to affirm self's face*	Restore face without relying extensively on others, through fulfilling social roles, excessive self-sacrifice, and rigid adherence to obligations
Enhancing self-esteem	Seek others' reassurance about self's esteem by demonstrating helplessness and need for others' approval	*Seek self-esteem without depending on others; defensive independence*

Note: Italics indicate strategies that are most common.

of how children in all communities develop differences in conceptions of self (independent and interdependent), in perspectives (first and third person), in perceptions of control (primary and secondary), in attachment relationships (continuous contact with caregivers and separating so as to reunite with them), in goals for learning (exploration and accommodation), in ways of thinking (analytic and holistic), in strategies for constructive coping (change-based and acceptance-based) and in defensive coping (avoidant and anxious-resistant). People in all communities experience all of these ways of functioning, albeit to different degrees and in different ways. Understanding these cultural differences provides a deeper appreciation of our common humanity.

In our early work on attachment we criticized the theory for being culturally blind. Yet before then (Rosen & Rothbaum, 1993; Rothbaum, Rosen, Pott, & Beatty, 1995) and afterwards (Morelli & Rothbaum, 2007; Rothbaum & Morelli, 2005), we have been aware of what an extraordinarily rich theory it is. Our criticisms and admiration are not incompatible. Attachment theory grew up in the West and was greatly influenced by Western assumptions and findings. The early theorizing sufficed as long as the focus was on Western samples. The task now is to determine in what ways the theory applies generally and in what ways it is culturally specific.

We are more and more impressed by the difficulty of disentangling cultural similarities and differences. Attachment-related concepts like sensitivity, closeness, and openness demand elaboration, but clarifications and exemplars lead to biased concepts if they do not borrow from a range of communities. Sensitivity that is equated with responsiveness-as-needed is biased toward Western ways of thinking, as is closeness that is equated with distal contact, and openness that is equated with verbal emotional expression. To understand how attachment and culture pertain to learning and coping, we must devote as much attention to what is different across communities as to what is similar, and to view similarities and differences as intertwined rather than as offsetting or competing with one another.

A. Deeper into Attachment and Culture: Proposed Research

We believe that the key to better understanding attachment in other communities is to rely on investigators who are native to those communities, even if trained in the West, and to employ emic methods. While Ainsworth began her work in Uganda and relied on local informants, it is highly likely that her findings were influenced by her Western assumptions. A critical starting point is to discern investigators' and caregivers' indigenous theory of attachment, including their ideas about the nature of security, what contributes to and follows from it, and types of insecurity. Observations conducted through the lens of indigenous theories are likely to be most revealing, since researchers carefully attend to events relevant to their theories.

If, as we presume, East Asian caregivers espouse a theory that attachment is linked with accommodation, observations should focus on the nature of that link. Attachment and accommodation may balance one another in the same way as do attachment and exploration. We hypothesize that accommodative forms of learning (e.g., imitation, cooperative participation, willing submission) are suppressed during times of stress (e.g., physical danger, the absence of the caregiver), and that they increase in proportion to the child's felt security.

Another hypothesis warranting investigation is that, in all cultures, secure as compared to insecure children are more adaptive in their use of coping strategies. Secure as compared to insecure children may be more likely to rely on constructive change-based strategies (e.g., problem solving) and less likely to rely on defensive change-based strategies (e.g., aggression) in communities where security is linked with exploration; and secure children may be more likely to rely on constructive acceptance-based strategies (e.g., empathy) and less likely to rely on defensive acceptance-based strategies (e.g., withdrawal) in communities where security is linked with accommodation. That is, secure children may be more likely to rely on the constructive strategies and less likely to rely on the defensive strategies that are common in their community.

In addition, secure children in all cultures may be better able to flexibly shift between strategies as situations call for them. For example, secure children in East Asia, who generally rely on acceptance-based strategies, may be able to smoothly transition to change-based strategies as needed. While relying on the dominant strategy as the default is often adaptive, so too is knowing the situations in which the nondominant strategy is most appropriate.

A corollary of the aforementioned hypothesis is that secure individuals in different communities may be more similar to one another in coping strategies than are insecure individuals from different communities, or even than secure and insecure individuals from the same community. Security, and the learning goals associated with it, is likely to foster receptivity to different types of strategies as well as awareness of when each is needed (Mikuliner & Shaver, 2007a, 2007b, 2008; Rothbaum & Rusk, in press; Sroufe, Egeland,

Carlson, & Collins, 2005; Thompson, 2008). There is evidence that children and adults who are secure are more cognitively open and more willing to try new strategies (Cassidy & Kobak, 1988; Mikulincer & Shaver, 2007a, 2007b).

The cultural study of attachment and learning may have implications for fostering constructive coping. We hypothesize that insecure individuals in all communities are more likely to relinquish validation goals and defensive strategies, and to adopt learning goals and constructive strategies, if their values are affirmed. One way of affirming people's values is by asking them to identify what is most important to them. Values affirmation fosters people's sense of worth, and it has proven to be an effective way of reducing defensiveness (Arndt, Schimel, Greenberg, & Pyszczynski, 2002; Creswell et al., 2005; Rothbaum, Morling, & Rusk, 2009; Rudman, Dohn, & Fairchild, 2007). Because people differ in individual and cultural values, identifying values to which they are personally committed and that are endorsed by their communities should be a major focus of research on affirmation.

B. Concluding Comments

We end with two thoughts. The first builds on the aphorism that the fish are the last to discover the ocean. Cultural study is profoundly interesting and important because it helps us discern things that are all around us and, for that very reason, we have difficulty seeing. With our cultural blinders removed, we—the authors—are more aware of the extent to which our society emphasizes exploration and change-based strategies, and the extent to which we downplay accommodation and acceptance-based strategies. Cultural study not only makes people more aware of what they prioritize but also what is essential to their humanity that they do not prioritize. It helps them take a closer look at the integration of biological and cultural processes—how setting and situation are critical to the expression of biological processes and the reverse. Knowing in what situations and settings different forms of attachment, different forms of learning, and different coping strategies are optimal will make people more adaptive human beings.

The second concluding thought echoes a point raised by Nisbett when he was summarizing his groundbreaking research on culture and learning (Nisbett et al., 2001). He acknowledged that, 20 years earlier, he was "shocked and dismayed" when the anthropologist Roy D'Andrade commented that Nisbett's work on human inference was "a good ethnography" (p. 307). Nisbett was dismayed because he assumed that his work applied universally even though he relied on Western theories, Western measures, and Western samples.

Subsequently Nisbett embraced cultural study, leading to his important work on analytic and holistic thought. We believe similar transformative change in attachment theory is possible if attachment theorists remain open to considering the various ways of becoming attached that people in different cultures experience, and if they are willing to accommodate attachment theory based on what they learn. What Nisbett and his colleagues have done for culture and learning, attachment investigators could do for culture and close relationships.

ACKNOWLEDGMENT

We are grateful to Mehelli Ghiara, who made valuable contributions to this chapter.

REFERENCES

Ainsworth, M. D. S. (1967). *Infancy in Uganda: Infant care and the growth of love*. Baltimore: John Hopkins Press.

Ainsworth, M. D. S. (1976). *System for rating maternal care behavior*. Princeton, NJ: ETS Test Collection.

Ainsworth, M. D. S., Blehar, M. C., Waters, E., & Wall, S. (1978). *Patterns of attachment: A psychological study of the Strange Situation*. Hillsdale, NJ: Erlbaum.

Ainsworth, M. D. S., & Bowlby, J. (1991). An ethological approach to personality development. *American Psychologist*, *46*, 333–341.

Ainsworth, M. D. S., & Marvin, R. S. (1995). On the shaping of attachment theory and research: An interview with Mary D. S. Ainsworth (Fall 1994). *Monographs of the Society for Research in Child Development*, *60*, 3–21.

Allen, J. P. (2008). The attachment system in adolescence. In J. Cassidy & P. R. Shaver (Eds.), *Handbook of attachment: Theory, research, and clinical applications* (2nd ed., pp. 419–435). New York: Guilford Press.

Arndt, J., Schimel, J., Greenberg, J., & Pyszczynski, T. (2002). The intrinsic self and defensiveness: Evidence that activating the intrinsic self reduces self-handicapping and conformity. *Personality and Social Psychology Bulletin*, *28*, 671–683.

Azuma, H., Kashiwagi, K., & Hess, R. (1981). *The influence of attitude and behavior upon the child's intellectual development*. Tokyo: University of Tokyo Press.

Baldwin, A. (1955). *Behavior and development in childhood*. New York: Dryden Press.

Bandura, A. (1997). *Self-efficacy: The exercise of control*. New York: Freeman.

Baranik, L., Meade, A. W., Lakey, C. E., Lance, C. E., Hu, C., Hua, W., & Michalos, A. (2008). Examining the differential item functioning of the Rosenberg Self-Esteem Scale across eight countries. *Journal of Applied Social Psychology*, *38*, 1867–1904.

Behrens, K. (2004). A multifaceted view of the concept of amae: Reconsidering the indigenous Japanese concept of relatedness. *Human Development*, 47, 1–27.

Behrens, K. Y., Hesse, E., & Main, M. (2007). Mothers' attachment status as determined by the Adult Attachment Interview predicts their 6-year-olds' reunion responses: A study conducted in Japan. *Developmental Psychology*, 43, 1553–1567.

Belsky, J., & Fearon, R. M. P. (2008). Precursors of attachment security. In J. Cassidy & P. R. Shaver (Eds.), *Handbook of attachment: Theory, research, and clinical applications* (2nd ed., pp. 295–316). New York: Guilford Press.

Belsky, J., Rosenberger, K., & Crnic, K. (1995). The origins of attachment security: "Classical" and contextual determinants. In S. Goldberg, R. Muir, & J. Kerr (Eds.), *Attachment theory: Social, developmental, and clinical perspectives* (pp. 153–183). Hillsdale, NJ: The Analytic Press.

Bienstock, R. E., Goran, M., & Smith, H. (Producers). (2003, September). *Penn and Teller's magic and mystery tour* [Television documentary special]. Toronto, ON: Canadian Broadcasting Centre.

Bourdieu, P. (1965). The sentiment of honour in Kabyle society. In J. Peristiany (Ed.), *Honour and shame* (pp. 191–242). London: Weidenfeld and Nicholson.

Bowlby, J. (1973). *Attachment and loss: Vol. 2. Separation: Anxiety and anger*. New York: Basic Books.

Bowlby, J. (1982). *Attachment and loss: Vol. 1. Attachment* (2nd ed.). New York: Basic Books. (Original work published 1969).

Bruner, J. (1990). *Acts of meaning*. Cambridge, MA: Harvard University Press.

Carlson, V. J., & Harwood, R. L. (2003). Attachment, culture, and the caregiving system: The cultural patterning of everyday experiences among Anglo and Puerto Rican mother-infant pairs. *Infant Mental Health Journal*, 24, 53–73.

Cassidy, J., & Kobak, R. R. (1988). Avoidance and its relation to other defensive processes. In J. Belsky & T. Nezworski (Eds.), *Clinical implications of attachment* (pp. 300–323). Hillsdale, NJ: Erlbaum.

Cassidy, J., & Shaver, P. R. (Eds.). (2008). *Handbook of attachment: Theory, research, and clinical applications* (2nd ed.). New York: Guilford Press.

Chang, E. C. (1998). Cultural differences, perfectionism, and suicidal risk: Does social problem solving still matter. *Cognitive Therapy and Research*, 22, 237–254.

Chang, E. C., Sanna, L., Riley, A. M., Thornburg, A. M., Zumberg, K. M., & Edwards, M. C. (2007). Relations between problem-solving styles and psychological adjustment in young adults: Is stress a mediating variable? *Personality and Individual Differences*, 42, 135–144.

Chen, X., Hastings, P., Rubin, K. H., Chen, H., Cen, G., & Stewart, S. L. (1998). Childrearing attitudes and behavioral inhibition in Chinese and Canadian toddlers: A cross-cultural study. *Developmental Psychology*, 34, 677–686.

Choi, I., & Nisbett, R. E. (2000). Cultural psychology of surprise: Holistic theories and recognition of contradiction. *Journal of Personality and Social Psychology*, 79, 890–905.

Chua, H. F., Boland, J. E., & Nisbett, R. E. (2005). Cultural variation in eye movements during scene perception. *Proceedings of the National Academy of Sciences USA, 102*, 12629–12633.

Clancy, P. M. (1986). The acquisition of communicative style in Japanese. In G. Schieffelin & E. Ochs (Eds.), *Language socialization across cultures* (pp. 213–250). New York: Cambridge University Press.

Cohen, D., Hoshino-Browne, E., & Leung, A. (2007). Culture and the structure of personal experience: Insider and outsider phenomonologies of the self and social world. In M. Zanna (Ed.), *Advances in experimental social psychology, 39* (pp. 1–67). San Diego: Academic Press.

Creswell, J. D., Welch, W. T., Taylor, S. E., Sherman, D. K., Gruenewald, T. L., & Mann, T. (2005). Affirmation of personal values buffers neuroendocrine and psychological stress responses. *Psychological Science, 16*, 846–851.

Dahlin, B., & Watkins, D. (2000). The role of repetition in the processes of memorising and understanding: A comparison of the views of Western and Chinese secondary school students in Hong Kong. *British Journal of Educational Psychology, 70*, 65–84.

Dennis, T. A., Cole, P. M., Zahn-Waxler, C., & Mizuta, I. (2002). Self in context: Autonomy and relatedness in Japanese and U.S. mother-preschooler dyads. *Child Development, 73*, 1803–1817.

Dineen, R., & Niu, W. (2008). The effectiveness of Western creative teaching methods in China: An action research project. *Psychology of Aesthetics, Creativity, and the Arts, 2*, 42–52.

Doi, T. (1992). On the concept of amae. *Infant Mental Health Journal, 13*, 7–11.

Dweck, C. S. (1999). *Self-theories: Their role in motivation, personality and development*. Philadelphia: Taylor and Francis/Psychology Press.

D'Zurilla, T. J., & Nezu, A. M. (2007). *Problem-solving therapy: A positive approach to clinical intervention* (3rd ed.). New York: Springer.

Edwards, C. P. (2000). Children's play in cross-cultural perspective: A new look at the Six Cultures Study. *Cross-Cultural Research, 34*, 318–338.

Elliot, A. J., Chirkov, V. I., Kim, Y., & Sheldon, K. M. (2001). A cross-cultural analysis of avoidance (relative to approach) personal goals. *Psychological Science, 12*, 505–510.

Farver, J. M., Kim, Y. K., & Lee, Y. (1995). Cultural differences in Korean- and Anglo-American preschoolers' social interaction and play behaviors. *Child Development, 66*, 1088–1099.

Farver, J. M., & Wimbarti, S. (1995). Indonesian children's play with their mothers and older siblings. *Child Development, 66*, 1493–1503.

Feeney, J. A. (2008). Adult romantic attachment: Developments in the study of couple relationships. In J. Cassidy & P. R. Shaver (Eds.), *Handbook of attachment: Theory, research, and clinical applications* (2nd ed., pp. 456–481). New York: Guilford Press.

Fiske, A., Kitayama, S., Markus, H., & Nisbett, R. (1998). The cultural matrix of social psychology. In D. Gilbert, S. Fiske, & G. Lindzey (Eds.), *The handbook of social psychology* (4th ed., Vol. 2, pp. 915–981). Boston: McGraw-Hill.

Fivush, R. (1994). Constructing narrative, emotion, and self in parent-child conversations about the past. In U. Neisser & R. Fivush (Eds.), *The remembering self: Construction and accuracy in the self-narrative* (pp. 136–157). Cambridge, England: Cambridge University Press.

Friedlmeier, W., & Trommsdorff, G. (1999). Emotion regulation in early childhood: A cross-cultural comparison between German and Japanese toddlers. *Journal of Cross-Cultural Psychology, 30,* 684–711.

Fromberg, D. P., & Bergen, D. (2006). *Play from birth to twelve: Contexts, perspectives and meanings* (2nd ed.). New York: Routledge.

George, C., & Solomon, J. (1999). Attachment and caregiving: The caregiving behavioral system. In J. Cassidy & P. R. Shaver (Eds.), *Handbook of attachment: Theory, research, and clinical applications* (pp. 649–670). New York: Guilford Press.

Greenfield, P. M., Keller, H., Fuligni, A., & Maynard, A. (2003). Cultural pathways through universal development. *Annual Review of Psychology, 54,* 461–490.

Grigorenko, E. L., Geissler, P. W., Prince, R., Okatcha, F., & Nokes, C. (2001). The organisation of Luo conceptions of intelligence: A study of implicit theories in a Kenyan village. *International Journal of Behavioral Development, 25,* 367–378.

Grossmann, K., Grossmann, K. E., Kindler, H., & Zimmermann, P. (2008). A wider view of attachment and exploration: The influence of mothers and fathers on the development of psychological security from infancy to young adulthood. In J. Cassidy & P. R. Shaver (Eds.), *Handbook of attachment: Theory, research, and clinical applications* (2nd ed., pp. 857–879). New York: Guilford Press.

Grossmann, K. E., Grossmann, K., & Keppler, A. (2005). Universal and culturally specific aspects of human behavior: the case of attachment. In P. Chakkarath, W. Friedlmeier, & B. Schwarz (Eds.), *Culture and human development: The importance of cross-cultural research to the social sciences* (pp. 75–98). New York: Psychology Press.

Haley, J. (1987). *Problem solving therapy.* San Francisco: Jossey-Bass.

Hamamura, T., Meijer, Z., Heine, S. J., Kayama, K., & Hori, I. (2009). Approach-avoidance motivation and information processing: A cross-cultural analysis. *Personality and Social Psychology Bulletin, 35,* 454–462.

Harwood, R. L. (1992). The influence of culturally derived values on Anglo and Puerto Rican mothers' perceptions of attachment behavior. *Child Development, 63,* 822–839.

Harwood, R. L., Miller, J. G., & Irizarry, N. L. (1995). *Culture and attachment: Perceptions of the child in context.* New York: Guilford Press.

Heine, S. J. (2001). Self as cultural product: An examination of East Asian and North American selves. *Journal of Personality, 69,* 881–906.

Heine, S. J. (2005). Constructing good selves in Japan and North America. In R. M. Sorrentino, D. Cohen, J. M. Olson, & M. P. Zanna (Eds.), *Culture and social behavior: The Tenth Ontario Symposium* (pp. 115–143). Mahwah, NJ: Erlbaum.

Heine, S. J. (2007). Culture and motivation: What motivates people to act in the ways that they do? In S. Kitayama, & D. Cohen (Eds.), *Handbook of cultural psychology* (pp. 714–733). New York: Guilford Press.

Heine, S. J., & Hamamura, T. (2007). In search of East Asian self-enhancement. *Personality and Social Psychology Review, 11*, 1–24.

Heine, S. J., Kitayama, S., Lehman, D. R., Takata, T., Ide, E., Leung, C., & Matsumoto, H. (2001). Divergent consequences of success and failure in Japan and North America: An investigation of self-improving motivations and malleable selves. *Journal of Personality and Social Psychology, 81*, 599–615.

Hendry, J. (1993). *Understanding Japanese society*. London: Routledge.

Hess, R. D., & Azuma, H. (1991). Cultural support for schooling: Contrasts between Japan and the United States. *Educational Researcher, 20*, 2–8.

Hesse, E. (2008). The Adult Attachment Interview: Protocol, method of analysis, and empirical studies. In J. Cassidy & P. R. Shaver (Eds.), *Handbook of attachment: Theory, research, and clinical applications* (2nd ed., pp. 552–598). New York: Guilford Press.

Higgins, E. T., Pierro, A., & Kruglanski, A. W. (2007). Re-thinking culture and personality: How self-regulatory universals create cross-cultural differences. In R. M. Sorrentino (Ed.), *Handbook of motivation and cognition within and across cultures* (pp. 161–190). New York: Guilford Press.

Ho, D. Y. (1976). On the concept of face. *The American Journal of Sociology, 81*, 867–884.

Hsu, F. L. K. (1981). *Americans and Chinese: Passage to differences* (3rd ed.). Honolulu: University of Hawaii Press.

Jacobsen, T., Edelstein, W., & Hofmann, V. (1994). A longitudinal study of the relation between representations of attachment in childhood and cognitive functioning in childhood and adolescence. *Developmental Psychology, 30*, 112–124.

Ji, L., Peng, K., & Nisbett, R. E. (2000). Culture, control, and perception of relationships in the environment. *Journal of Personality and Social Psychology, 78*, 943–955.

Jin, L., & Cortazzi, M. (1998). Dimensions of dialogue: Large classes in China. *International Journal of Educational Research, 29*, 739–761.

Kaplan, A., & Maehr, M.L. (2007). The contributions and prospects of goal orientation theory. *Educational Psychology Review, 19*, 141–184.

Keller, H. (2003). Socialization for competence: Cultural models of infancy. *Human Development, 46*, 288–311.

Keller, H. (2008). Attachment—past and present. But what about the future? *Integrative Psychological and Behavioral Science, 42*, 406–415.

Keller, H., Lamm, B., Abels, M., Yovsi, R., Borke, J., Jensen, H., et al. (2006). Cultural models, socialization goals, and parenting ethnotheories: A multicultural analysis. *Journal of Cross Cultural Psychology, 37*, 155–172.

Kerns, K. A. (2008). Attachment in middle childhood. In J. Cassidy & P. R. Shaver (Eds.), *Handbook of attachment: Theory, research, and clinical applications* (2nd ed., pp. 366–381). New York: Guilford Press.

Kim, K., & Markman, A. B. (2006). Differences in fear of isolation as an explanation of cultural differences: Evidence from memory and reasoning. *Journal of Experimental Social Psychology, 42*, 350–364.

Kim, S., & Rohner, R. P. (2002). Perceived parental acceptance and emotional empathy among university students in Korea. *Journal of Cross Cultural Psychology, 34*, 723–735.

Kim, Y-H., & Cohen, D. (2010). Information, perspective, and judgments about the self in face and dignity cultures. *Personality and Social Psychology Bulletin, 36*, 537–550.

Kim, Y-H., Cohen, D., & Au, W-T. (2010). The jury and abjury of my peers: The self in face and dignity cultures. *Journal of Personality and Social Psychology, 98*, 904–916.

Kitayama, S., Duffy, S., & Uchida, Y. (2007). Self as cultural mode of being. In S. Kitayama & D. Cohen (Eds.), *Handbook of cultural psychology* (pp. 136–174). New York: Guilford.

Kitayama, S., Ishii, K., Imada, T., Takemura, K., & Ramaswamy, J. (2006). Voluntary settlement and the spirit of independence: Evidence from Japan's "northern frontier." *Journal of Personality and Social Psychology, 91*, 369–384.

Kitayama, S., & Markus, H. (1999). Yin and yang of the Japanese self. In D. Cervone & Y. Shoda (Eds.), *The coherence of personality* (pp. 242–302). New York: Guilford.

Kitayama, S., Markus, H. R., & Kurokawa, M. (2000). Culture, emotion, and well-being: Good feelings in Japan and the United States. *Cognition and Emotion, 14*, 93–124.

Kitayama, S., Markus, H. R., Matsumoto, H., & Norasakkunkit, V. (1997). Individual and collective processes in the construction of the self: Self-enhancement in the United States and self-criticism in Japan. *Journal of Personality and Social Psychology, 72*, 1245–1267.

Kitayama, S., Snibbe, A. C., Markus, H. R., & Suzuki, T. (2004). Is there any "free" choice? Self and dissonance in two cultures. *Psychological Science, 15*, 527–533.

Kitayama, S., Mesquita, B., & Karasawa, M. (2006). Cultural affordances and emotional experience: Socially engaging and disengaging emotions in Japan and the United States. *Journal of Personality and Social Psychology, 91*, 890–903.

Kobak, R., & Madsen, S. (2008). Disruptions in attachment bonds: Implications for theory, research, and clinical intervention. In J. Cassidy & P. R. Shaver (Eds.), *Handbook of attachment: Theory, research, and clinical applications* (2nd ed., pp. 23–47). New York: Guilford Press.

Kuhnen, U., Hannover, B., & Schubert, B. (2001). The semantic-procedural interface model of the self: The role of self-knowledge for context-dependent versus context-independent modes of thinking. *Journal of Personality and Social Psychology*, *80*, 397–409.

Lebra, T. S. (1994). Mother and child in Japanese socialization: A Japan-U.S. comparison. In P. M. Greenfield & R. R. Cocking (Eds.), *Cross-cultural roots of minority child development* (pp. 259–274). Hillsdale, NJ: Guildford.

Lee, A. Y., Aaker, J. L., & Gardner, W. L. (2000). The pleasures and pains of distinct self-construals: The role of interdependence in regulatory focus. *Journal of Personality and Social Psychology*, *78*, 1122–1134.

LeVine, R. A. (1974). Parental goals: A cross-cultural review. *Teachers College Record*, *76*, 226–239.

LeVine, R. A. (1988). Human parental care: Universal goals, cultural strategies, individual behavior. *New Directions for Child Development*, *40*, 3–12.

LeVine, R. A. (2004). Challenging expert knowledge: Findings from an African study of infant care and development. In U. P. Gielen & J. L. Roopnarine (Eds.), *Childhood and adolescence in cross-cultural perspectives* (pp. 149–165). Westport, CT: Greenwood Publishing.

LeVine, R. A., & Norman, K. (2001). The infant's acquisition of culture: Early attachment reexamined in anthropological perspective. In C. C. Moore & H. F. Mathews (Eds.), *The psychology of cultural experience* (pp. 83–104). Cambridge, England: Cambridge University Press.

Levy, K. N., Blatt, S. J., & Shaver, P. R. (1998). Attachment styles and parental representations. *Journal of Personality and Social Psychology*, *74*, 407–419.

Li, J. (1997). Creativity in horizontal and vertical domains. *Creativity Research Journal*, *10*, 107–132.

Li, J. (2002). A cultural model of learning: Chinese "heart and mind for wanting to learn." *Journal of Cross-Cultural Psychology*, *33*, 248–269.

Liang, B., & Bogat, G. A. (1994). Culture, control and coping: New perspectives on social support. *American Journal of Community Psychology*, *22*, 123–147.

Liu, M. M., Chen, X. Y., Rubin, K. H., Zheng, S. J., Cui, L. Y., & Li, D. (2005). Autonomy vs. connectedness-oriented parenting behaviours in Chinese and Canadian mothers. *International Journal of Behavioral Development*, *29*, 489–495.

Lockwood, P., Marshall, T. C., & Sadler, P. (2005). Promoting success or preventing failure: Cultural differences in motivation by positive and negative role models. *Personality and Social Psychology Bulletin*, *31*, 379–392.

Main, M. (1996). Introduction to the special section on attachment and psychopathology: Overview of the field of attachment. *Journal of Consulting and Clinical Psychology*, *64*, 237–243.

Malouff, J. M., Thorsteinsson, E. B., & Schutte, N. S. (2007). The efficacy of problem solving therapy in reducing mental and physical health problems: A meta-analysis. *Clinical Psychology Review*, *27*, 46–57.

Markus, H. R., & Kitayama, S. (1991). Culture and the self: Implications for cognition, emotion, and motivation. *Psychological Review, 98*, 224–253.

Martini, M. (1994). Peer interactions in Polynesia: A view from the Marquesas. In J. P. Roopnarine, J. E. Johnson, & F. H. Hooper (Eds.), *Children's play in diverse cultures* (pp. 73–103). Albany: State University of New York Press.

Maruta, T. (1992). Does an American puppy amaeru? A comment on Dr. Doi's paper. *Infant Mental Health Journal, 13*, 12–17.

Masuda, T., Ellsworth, P., Mesquita, B., Leu, J. X., Tanida, S., & van de Veerdon, E. (2008). Placing the face in context: Cultural differences in the perception of facial emotion. *Journal of Personality and Social Psychology, 94*, 365–381.

Masuda, T., & Nisbett, R. E. (2001). Attending holistically versus analytically: Comparing the context sensitivity of Japanese and Americans. *Journal of Personality and Social Psychology, 81*, 922–934.

Matsumoto, D., Yoo, S. H., & Nakagawa, S. (2008). Culture, emotion regulation, and adjustment. *Journal of Personality and Social Psychology, 94*, 925–937.

McElwain, N. L., Cox, M. J., Burchinal, M. R., & Macfie, J. (2003). Differentiating among insecure mother-infant attachment classifications: A focus on child-friend interaction and exploration during solitary play at 36 months. *Attachment and Human Development, 5*, 136–164.

Merriam-Webster's Collegiate Dictionary (11th ed.). (2003). Springfield, MA: Merriam Webster.

Mesquita, B., & Leu, J. (2007). The cultural psychology of emotion. In S. Kitayama & D. Cohen (Eds.), *Handbook of cultural psychology* (pp. 734–759). New York: Guilford Press.

Mikuliner, M., & Shaver, P. R. (2007a). *Attachment in adulthood: Structure, dynamics and change.* New York: Guilford Press.

Mikuliner, M., & Shaver, P. R. (2007b). Adult attachment strategies and the regulation of emotion. In J. J. Gross (Ed.), *Handbook of emotion regulation* (pp. 446–465). New York: Guilford Press.

Mikulincer, M., & Shaver, P. R. (2008). Adult attachment and affect regulation. In J. Cassidy & P. R. Shaver (Eds.), *Handbook of attachment: Theory, research and clinical applications.* (2nd ed., pp. 503–531). New York: Guilford Press.

Miller, J. G. (2003). Culture and agency: Implications for psychological theories of motivation and social development. In V. Murphy-Berman & J. Berman (Eds.), *Nebraska Symposium on Motivation: Cross-cultural differences in perspectives on the self* (Vol. 49, pp. 59–99). Lincoln: University of Nebraska Press.

Miller, P. J., Fung, H., & Koven, M. (2007). Narrative reverberations: How participation in narrative practices co-creates persons and cultures. In S. Kitayama & D. Cohen (Eds.), *Handbook of cultural psychology* (pp. 595–614). New York: Guilford Press.

Miller, P. J., Wiley, A. R., Fung, H., & Liang, C. H. (1997). Personal storytelling as a medium of socialization in Chinese and American families. *Child Development, 68*, 557–568.

Mizuta, I., Zahn-Waxler, C., Cole, P. M., & Hiruma, N. (1996). A cross-cultural study of preschoolers' attachment: Security and sensitivity in Japanese and U.S. dyads. *International Journal of Behavioral Development*, *19*, 141–159.

Morelli, G., Rogoff, B., & Angelillo, C. (2003). Cultural variation in children's access to work or involvement in specialized child-focused activities. *International Journal of Behavioral Development*, *27*, 264–274.

Morelli, G. A., & Rothbaum, F. (2007). Situating the person in relationships: Attachment relationships and self-regulation in young children. In S. Kitayama & D. Cohen (Eds.), *Handbook of cultural psychology* (pp. 500–527). New York: Guilford Press.

Morelli, G. A., Tronick, E., & Beeghley, M. (1999, April). *Is there security in numbers? Child care in a hunting and gathering community and infants' attachment relationships*. Poster presented at the Society for Research on Child Development, Albuquerque, New Mexico.

Morling, B., & Evered, S. (2006). Secondary control reviewed and defined. *Psychological Bulletin*, *132*, 269–296.

Morling, B., Kitayama, S., & Miyamoto, Y. (2002). Cultural practices emphasize influence in the United States and adjustment in Japan. *Personality and Social Psychology Bulletin*, *28*, 311–323.

Nakamura, Y., & Orth, U. (2005). Acceptance as a coping reaction: Adaptive or not? *Swiss Journal of Psychology*, *64*, 281–292.

Niiya, Y., Ellsworth, P., & Yamaguchi, S. (2006). Amae in Japan and the United States: An exploration of a "culturally unique" emotion. *Emotion*, *6*, 279–295.

Niiya, Y., Yamaguchi, S., Murakami, F., & Harihara, M. (2001, July). *When being inappropriate is appropriate: The acceptability of Amae in the Japanese context*. Paper presented at the 4th Conference of Asian Association of Social Psychology, Melbourne, Australia.

Nisbett, R., Peng, K., Choi, I., & Norenzayan, A. (2001). Culture and systems of thought: Holistic vs. analytic cognition. *Psychological Review*, *108*, 291–310.

Norenzayan, A., Choi, I., & Peng, K. (2007). Perception and cognition. In S. Kitayama & D. Cohen (Eds.), *Handbook of cultural psychology* (pp. 569–594). New York: Guilford.

Olah, A. (1995). Coping strategies among adolescents: A cross-cultural study. *Journal of Adolescence*, *18*, 491–512.

Oyserman, D., & Lee, S. W. S. (2008). Does culture influence what and how we think? Effects of priming individualism and collectivism. *Psychological Bulletin*, *134*, 311–342.

Oyserman, D., Sorensen, N., Reber, R., Chen, S. X., & Sannum, P. (2009). Connecting and separating mindsets: Culture as situated cognition. *Journal of Personality and Social Psychology*, *97*, 217–235.

Peak, L. (1993). *Learning to go to school in Japan: The transition from home to preschool life*. Berkeley: University of California Press.

Pomerantz, E. M., Ng, F. F., & Wang, Q. (2008). Culture, parenting and motivation: The case of East Asia and the United States. In M. L. Maehr, S. A. Karabenick, & T. C. Urdan (Eds.), *Advances in motivation and achievement: Social psychological perspectives. Vol. 15* (pp. 209–240). Bingley, England: Emerald Group.

Posada, G., Gao, Y., Fang, W., Posada, R., Tascon, M., & Schoelmerich, A. (1995). The secure-base phenomenon across cultures: Children's behavior, mothers' preferences, and experts' concepts. In E. Waters, B. E. Vaughn, G. Posada, & K. Kondo-Ikemura (Eds.), Caregiving, cultural, and cognitive perspectives on secure-base behavior and working models. *Monographs of the Society for Research in Child Development, 60,* 27–48.

Posada, G., Jacobs, A., Carbonell, O.A., Alzate, G., Bustamante, M., & Arenas, A. (1999). Maternal care and attachment security in ordinary and emergency contexts. *Developmental Psychology, 35,* 1379–1388.

Posada, G., Jacobs, A., Richmond, M. K., Carbonell, O. A., Alzate, G., Bustamante, M. R., & Quiceno, J. (2002). Maternal caregiving and infant security in two cultures. *Developmental Psychology, 38,* 67–78.

Purdie, N., Hattie, J., & Douglas, G. (1996). Student conceptions of learning and their use of self-regulated learning strategies: A cross-cultural comparison. *Journal of Educational Psychology, 88,* 87–100.

Rogoff, B. (1990). *Apprenticeship in thinking.* New York: Oxford University Press.

Rogoff, B. (2003). *The cultural nature of human development.* New York: Oxford University Press.

Rohner, R., & Pettengill, S. M. (1985). Perceived parental acceptance-rejection and parental control among Korean adolescents. *Child Development, 56,* 524–528.

Roland, A. (1988). *In search of self in India and Japan: Toward a cross-cultural psychology.* Princeton, NJ: Princeton University Press.

Romero, M. E. (1994). Identifying giftedness among Keresan Pueblo Indians: the Keres study. *Journal of American Indian Education, 34,* 35–58.

Rosen, K. S., & Rothbaum, F. (1993). Quality of parental caregiving and security of attachment. *Developmental Psychology, 29,* 358–367.

Rothbaum, F. (1986). Patterns of parental acceptance. *Genetic Psychology Monographs, 112,* 435–458.

Rothbaum, F. (1988). Maternal acceptance and child functioning. *Merrill Palmer Quarterly, 34,* 163–184.

Rothbaum, F., & Kakinuma, M. (2004). Amae and attachment: Security in cultural context. *Human Development, 47,* 34–39.

Rothbaum, F., Kakinuma, M., Nagaoka, R., & Azuma, H. (2007). Attachment and amae: Parent-child closeness in the United States and Japan. *Journal of Cross-Cultural Psychology, 38,* 465–486.

Rothbaum, F., & Morelli, G. (2005). Attachment and culture: Bridging relativism and universalism. In W. Friedlmeier, P. Chakkararath, & B. Schwarz (Eds.), *Culture and human development: The importance of cross-cultural research to the social sciences* (pp. 99–124). New York: Psychology Press.

Rothbaum, F., Morelli, G., Pott, M., & Liu-Constant, Y. (2000). Immigrant-Chinese and Euro-American parents' physical closeness with young children: Themes of family relatedness. *Journal of Family Psychology*, 14, 334–348.

Rothbaum, F., Morling, B., & Rusk, N. (2009). How goals and beliefs lead people into and out of depression. *Review of General Psychology*, 13, 302–314.

Rothbaum, F., Nagoaka, R., & Ponte, I. (2006). Caregiver sensitivity in cultural context: Japanese and U.S. teachers' beliefs about anticipating and responding to children's needs. *Journal of Research in Childhood Education*, 21, 23–39.

Rothbaum, F., Pott, M., Azuma, H., Miyake, K., & Weisz, J. (2000). The development of close relationships in Japan and the United States: Paths of symbiotic harmony and generative tension. *Child Development*, 71, 1121–1142.

Rothbaum, F., Rosen, K. S., Pott, M., & Beatty, M. (1995). Early parent-child relationships and later problem behavior: A longitudinal study. *Merrill Palmer Quarterly*, 41, 133–151.

Rothbaum, F., & Rusk, N. (in press). Pathways to emotion regulation: Cultural differences in internalization . In X. Chen & K.H. Rubin (Eds.), *Socioemotional development in cultural context*. New York: Guilford Press.

Rothbaum, F., & Trommsdorff, G. (2007). Do roots and wings complement or oppose one another? The socialization of relatedness and autonomy in cultural context. In J. E. Grusec & P. Hastings (Eds.), *The handbook of socialization* (pp. 461–489). New York: Guilford Press.

Rothbaum, F., & Tsang, B. Y.-P. (1998). Love songs in the United States and China: On the nature of romantic love. *Journal of Cross-Cultural Psychology*, 29, 306–319.

Rothbaum, F., & Wang, Y. Z. (2010). Cultural differences in parental acceptance: Developmental pathways to self acceptance and acceptance of the world. In L. Jensen (Ed.), *Bridging developmental and cultural psychology: New syntheses in theory, research, and policy* (pp. 187–211). New York: Oxford University Press.

Rothbaum, F., & Weisz, J. R. (1994). Parental caregiving and child externalizing behavior in nonclinical samples: A meta-analysis. *Psychological Bulletin*, 116, 55–74.

Rothbaum, F., Weisz, J., Pott, M., Miyake, K., & Morelli, G. (2000). Attachment and culture: Security in the United States and Japan. *American Psychologist*, 55, 1093–1104.

Rothbaum, F., Weisz, J., & Snyder, S. (1982). Changing the world and changing the self: A two-process model of perceived control. *Journal of Personality and Social Psychology*, 42, 5–37.

Rothbaum, F., & Xu, X. (1995). The theme of giving back to parents in Chinese and American songs. *Journal of Cross-Cultural Psychology*, 26, 698–713.

Rubin, K. H., Hemphill, S. A., Chen, X., Hastings P., Sanson, A., Coco, A. L., Cui, L. Y. et al. (2006). A cross-cultural study of behavioral inhibition in toddlers: East-west-north-south. *International Journal of Behavioral Development*, 30, 219–226.

Rudman, L. A., Dohn, M. C., & Fairchild, K. (2007). Implicit self-esteem compensation: Automatic threat defense. *Journal of Personality and Social Psychology*, *93*, 798–813.

Rusk, N., & Rothbaum, F. (2010). From stress to learning: Attachment theory meets goal orientation theory. *Review of General Psychology*, *14*, 31–43.

Schmitt, D. P. (2004). Patterns and universals of adult romantic attachment across 62 cultural regions: Are models of self and of other pancultural constructs? *Journal of Cross-Cultural Psychology*, *35*, 367–402.

Schmitt, D. P., & Allik, J. (2005). Simultaneous administration of the Rosenberg Self-Esteem Scale in 53 nations: Exploring the universal and culture-specific features of global self-esteem. *Journal of Personality and Social Psychology*, *89*, 623–642.

Schwartz, S. H. (1999). A theory of cultural values and some implications for work. *Applied Psychology: An International Review*, *48*, 23–47.

Scheier, M. F., Weintraub, J. K., & Carver, C. S. (1986). Coping with stress: Divergent strategies of optimists and pessimists. *Journal of Personality and Social Psychology*, *51*, 1257–1264.

Sedikides, C., Gaertner, L., & Vevea, J. L. (2005). Pancultural self-enhancement reloaded: A meta-analytic reply to Heine (2005). *Journal of Personality and Social Psychology*, *89*, 539–551.

Seifer, R., & Schiller, M. (1995). The role of parenting sensitivity, infant temperament, and dyadic interaction in attachment theory and assessment. In E. Waters, B. Vaughn, G. Posada, & K. Kondo-Ikemura (Eds.), Caregiving, cultural, and cognitive perspectives on secure-base behavior and working models (pp. 146–174). *Monographs of the Society for Research in Child Development*, *60*, (2–3, Serial No. 244). Chicago: University of Chicago Press.

Serpell R. (1993). *The significance of schooling: Life journeys in an African society*. Cambridge, England: Cambridge University Press.

Shweder, R., Goodnow, J., Hatano, G., LeVine, R., Markus, H., & Miller, P. (2006). The cultural psychology of development: One mind, many mentalities. In W. Damon (Ed.), *Handbook of child psychology* (6th ed., Vol. 1, pp. 865–937). New York: Wiley.

Simpson, J. A., Rholes, W. S., & Phillips, D. (1996). Conflict in close relationships: An attachment perspective. *Journal of Personality and Social Psychology*, *71*, 899–914.

Sroufe, L. A. (1990). An organizational perspective on the self. In D. Cicchetti & M. Beeghly (Eds.), *The self in transition: Infancy to childhood* (pp. 281–307). Chicago: University of Chicago Press.

Sroufe, L. A., Egeland, B., Carlson, E. A., & Collins, W. A. (2005). *The development of the person: The Minnesota study of risk and adaptation from birth to adulthood*. New York: Guilford Press.

Sroufe, L. A., Fox, N. A., & Pancake, V. (1983). Attachment and dependency in developmental perspective. *Child Development*, *54*, 1615–1627.

Sroufe, L. A., & Waters, E. (1997). On the universality of the link between responsive care and secure base behavior. *Newsletter; International Society for the Study of Behavior and Development, 31*(1), 3–5.

Stark, K. D., Reynolds, W. M., & Kaslow, N. J. (1987). A comparison of the relative efficacy of self-control therapy and a behavioral problem-solving therapy for depression in children. *Journal of Abnormal Child Psychology, 15,* 91–113.

Suina, J., & Smolkin, L. B. (1994). From natal culture to school culture to dominant society culture: Supporting transitions for Pueblo Indian students. In P. M. Greenfield & R. R. Cocking (Eds.), *Cross-cultural roots of minority child development* (pp. 115–130). Hillsdale, NJ: Erlbaum.

Super, C. M. (1983). Cultural variation in the meaning and uses of children's "intelligence." In J. Deregowski, S. Dziurawiec, & R. Annis (Eds.), *Explorations in cross-cultural psychology* (pp. 199–212). Amsterdam: Swets & Zeitlinger.

Tafarodi, R. W., & Milne A. B. (2002). Decomposing global self-esteem. *Journal of Personality, 70,* 443–483.

Takahashi, K. (1990). Are the key assumptions of the "Strange Situation" procedure universal? A view from Japanese research. *Human Development, 33,* 23–30.

Taylor, S. E., Sherman, D. K., Kim, H. S., Jarcho, J., Takagi, K., & Dunagan, M. S. (2004). Culture and social support: Who seeks it and why? *Journal of Personality and Social Psychology, 87,* 354–362.

Thompson, R. A. (2008). Early attachment and later development: Familiar questions, new answers. In J. Cassidy & P. R. Shaver (Eds.), *Handbook of attachment: Theory, research, and clinical applications* (2nd ed., pp. 348–365). New York: Guilford Press.

Triandis, H. (1995). *Individualism and collectivism.* Boulder, CO: Westview.

Trommsdorff, G., & Friedlmeier, W. (1993). Control and responsiveness in Japanese and German mother-child interactions. *Early Development and Parenting, 2,* 65–78.

True, M. M., Pisani, L., & Oumar, F. (2001). Infant-mother attachment among the Dogon of Mali. *Child Development, 72,* 1451–1466.

Tsai, J. L. (2007). Ideal affect: Cultural causes and behavioral consequences. *Perspectives on Psychological Science, 2,* 242–259.

Tweed, R. G., & Lehman, D. R. (2002). Learning considered within a cultural context: Confucian and Socratic approaches. *American Psychologist, 57,* 89–99.

Tweed, R. G., White, K., & Lehman, D. R. (2004). Culture, stress, and coping: Internally- and externally-targeted control strategies of European-Canadians, East Asian-Canadians, and Japanese. *Journal of Cross-Cultural Psychology, 35,* 652–658.

Valenzuela, M. (1997). Maternal sensitivity in a developing society: The context of urban poverty and infant chronic undernutrition. *Developmental Psychology, 33,* 845–855.

van Baaren, R. B., Maddux, W. W., Chartrand, T. L., de Bouter, C., & van Knippenberg, A. (2003). It takes two to mimic: Behavioral consequences of self-construals. *Journal of Personality and Social Psychology*, *84*, 1093–1102.

van IJzendoorn, M. H., & Sagi, A. (1999). Cross-cultural patterns of attachment: Universal and contextual dimensions. In J. Cassidy & P. R. Shaver (Eds.), *Handbook of attachment: Theory, research, and clinical applications* (pp. 713–734). New York: Guilford Press.

van IJzendoorn, M. H., & Sagi-Schwartz, A. (2008). Cross-cultural patterns of attachment: Universal and contextual dimensions. In J. Cassidy & P. R. Shaver (Eds.), *Handbook of attachment: Theory, research, and clinical applications* (2nd ed., pp. 880–905). New York: Guilford Press.

van IJzendoorn, M. H., Schuengel, C., & Bakermans-Kranenburg, M. J. (1999). Disorganized attachment in early childhood: Meta-analysis of precursors, concomitants, and sequelae. *Development and Psychopathology*, *11*, 225–249.

Vereijken, C. J. J. L., Riksen-Walraven, J. M., & Van Lieshout, C. F. M. (1997). Mother-infant relationships in Japan: Attachment, dependency, and amae. *Journal of Cross-Cultural Psychology*, *28*, 442–462.

Vogel, S. (1996). Urban middle-class Japanese family life, 1958–1996: A personal and evolving perspective. In D. Schwalb & B. Schwalb (Eds.), *Japanese childrearing: Two generations of scholarship* (pp. 177–200). New York: Guilford Press.

Wang, Q. (2004). The cultural context of parent-child reminiscing: A functional analysis. In M. W. Pratt & B. Fiese (Eds.), *Family stories and the life course: Across time and generations* (pp. 279–301). Mahwah, NJ: Erlbaum.

Wang, Q., & Ross, M. (2007). Culture and memory. In S. Kitayama & D. Cohen (Eds.), *Handbook of cultural psychology* (pp. 645–667). New York: Guilford Press.

Wang, Y. Z., Wiley, A. R., & Zhou, X. (2007). The effect of different cultural lenses on reliability and validity in observational data: The example of Chinese immigrant parent-toddler dinner interactions. *Social Development*, *16*, 777–799.

Watkins, D. (2000). Learning and teaching: A cross-cultural perspective. *School Leadership and Management*, *20*, 161–173.

Weinfield, N. S., Sroufe, L. A., Egeland, B., & Carlson, E. (2008). Individual differences in infant-caregiver attachment. In J. Cassidy & P. Shaver (Eds.), *Handbook of attachment: Theory, research and clinical applications* (2nd ed., pp. 78–101). New York: Guilford Press.

Weisz, J. R., Rothbaum, F., & Blackburn, T. C. (1984a). Standing out and standing in: The psychology of control in the U.S. and Japan. *American Psychologist*, *39*, 955–969.

Weisz, J. R., Rothbaum, F., & Blackburn, T. F. (1984b). Swapping recipes for control. *American Psychologist*, *39*, 974–975.

Weisz, J. R., Jensen-Doss, A., & Hawley, K. M. (2006). Evidence-based chotherapies versus usual clinical care. *American Psychologist, 61,*

White, M. I., & LeVine, R. A. (1986). What is an ii ko (good child)? In H. Stc. H. Azuma, & K. Hakuta (Eds.), *Child development and education in Japan* (pp. 55–62). New York: Freeman.

Wong, N. Y. (2002). Conceptions of doing and learning mathematics among Chinese. *Journal of Intercultural Studies, 23,* 211–229.

Wong, N. Y. (2006). From "entering the way" to "exiting the way": In search of a bridge to span "basic skills" and "process abilities." In F. K. S. Leung, K-D. Graf, & F. J. Lopez-Real (Eds.), *Mathematics education in different cultural traditions: The 13th ICMI Study* (pp. 111–128). New York: Springer.

Yamaguchi, S. (2001). Culture and control orientations. In D. Matsumoto (Ed.), *The handbook of culture and psychology* (pp. 223–243). New York: Oxford University Press.

Yamaguchi, S. (2004). Further clarifications of the concept of amae in relation to dependence and attachment. *Human Development, 47,* 28–33.

Yamaguchi, S., Gelfand, M., Ohashi, M. M., & Zemba, Y. (2005). The cultural psychology of control: Illusions of personal versus collective control in the United States and Japan. *Journal of Cross-Cultural Psychology, 36,* 750–761.

CHAPTER 5

Culturally Situated Linguistic Ecologies and Language Use

Cultural Tools at the Service of Representing and Shaping Situated Realities

GÜN R. SEMIN

Faculty of Social and Behavioral Sciences, Utrecht University

I. INTRODUCTION

The words *culture*, *cognition*, *language*, and *communication* are indispensable in a number of intellectual traditions, some of which have long-standing research traditions and others less so. For instance, *language* and *culture* are associated with a classical puzzle that has dominated cultural research, namely the nature of the relationship between language and cognition. Recent developments in cultural social psychology use other combinations of *culture*, *cognition*, *language*, and *communication* with different emphases (e.g., Chiu & Hong, 2006, 2007; Lehman, Chiu, & Schaller, 2004). One of the issues arising from these new developments is that cultures constitute distinctive knowledge patterns and beliefs. The engaging questions arising from this perspective have—among other things—focused attention on communication processes (e.g., Fast, Heath, & Wu, 2009; Lehman et al., 2004; McIntyre, Lyons, Clark, & Kashima, 2004; Schaller, Conway, & Tanchuk, 2002) and the processes by which culturally relevant information is transmitted and how it contributes to the emergence of shared representations (e.g., Chiu & Hong, 2006; Sperber, 1996).

The purpose of this chapter is to bridge the language–cognition interface with a functional approach by changing the classic question from "What is language and cognition?" by simply adding a preposition to the question, namely, "What is language and cognition *for*?" This preposition inserts a functional lens on the language and cognition issue. Moreover, in reviewing the relevant research on the role of language as a tool at the service of adaptively successful interaction with other agents, the first section of this chapter treats language as an indispensable instrument of the social practices that contribute to the emergence of what I shall refer to as the "linguistic ecology of cultures." This is the subject of the second section of this chapter and introduces a complementary and novel perspective to our understanding of the processes by which shared knowledge and beliefs emerge as argued in current cultural social psychology. The distinctive twist of the second section is in introducing how culturally distinct linguistic ecologies emerge with the argument that such ecologies are the result of *unintended consequences* or by-products of communication not only at the face-to-face level of immediate communication but also at a much broader level. Communication in the broader sense is inclusive of not only the level of immediate dialogue but also as it is realized in a wide range of social practices as it is afforded by the mass media and its diverse instruments (radio, newspapers, TV, Internet, inter alia).

The kernel of the argument underlying the entire chapter is that language is a functional tool that is deployed to direct attention not only in dialogue but also in communication in society in general—in all types of social practices that rely on language for the adaptive regulation of social reality and interaction. Furthermore, one unintended consequence of these concurrent and continuous practices is the emergence of a regular language environment to which we are exposed continuously and which supersedes the immediacy of our ongoing reality by the production of a linguistic ecology of cultures. Take the simple sentence "The sun is rising," which is uttered between a married couple who are farmers. Simply put, dialogue, at whatever level, produces three things: *(a)* an intended message (i.e., "Get up and put the cows out so that they can graze"); *(b)* a set of nonsituated and generic regularities that carry the message (e.g., syntactical rules, etc.); and *(c)* specific timeless knowledge (e.g., the sun rises at a particular time at a particular location). The unnoticed products or unintended consequences of social practices (i.e., the dialogue) contain generic information (e.g., the sun sets at a particular time at a particular location). These features of a dialogue become even richer and more consequential in social practices that supersede the interindividual dialogue, as I shall argue in the second part of this chapter. Continuous and cumulative "general dialogues" that supersede the immediacy of inter-individual communication take place via the media, contain a diversity of information, and have broader unintended consequences. For instance, specific geographic locations may be mentioned with differing frequency over time. The specific content of the messages may be about particular incidents taking place such as a rally in Amsterdam, an exhibition in Rotterdam, a musical event in Paris, and so on. The sheer frequency with which the diverse towns have been mentioned over a period of time have a significant impact on human functioning that is very different from the standard view of the language–cognition interface. Thus, although the frequency with which the town names are mentioned in the news over a period of time is not intended, it is nevertheless likely to have an impact on how one represents the distances between the towns (see section C for details). This is a type of influence that language has and one that is distinctly different from, for example, different syntactical forms influencing cognition in different ways—one of the issues in the classic work on language and cognition. Dialogues superseding the interindividual level are the result of different forms of social practices that are omnipresent in our daily life (e.g., different forms of media as well as the mundane reality of dialogues with their immediate reality, inter alia) and that contain knowledge in terms of the regularities with which they occur across a broad range of linguistic manifestations.

Thus, the first part to follow introduces a functional approach to the language–cognition–culture interface, while the second part of this chapter addresses the novel issue of the linguistic ecology of a cultures and its impact on the shape of psychological realities.

II. A FUNCTIONAL APPROACH TO THE LANGUAGE–COGNITION–CULTURE INTERFACE ON THE SITUATED INTERACTION LEVEL

In addressing the language, culture, and psychological functioning puzzle, I shall first present briefly the traditional approach (but see Semin, 2009) by noting three problems of this approach, namely that it is *(1)* predominantly domain specific (e.g., color, time, space, gender); *(2)* focused on language and cognition as inner representational and amodal systems that are disembodied, timeless, and subjectless (for exceptions, see Boroditsky & Prinz, 2008; Glenberg, 2008; Slobin, 2003; Tomasello, 2003; also Chiu, Lee,

K-y, & Kwan, 2007); and has contained *(3)* methodological problems characteristic of comparative research in general.

I shall briefly spell these out to then focus on what I regard as a "functional"
approach that introduces a completely different complexion focusing on *the
situated interaction level of the language–cognition interface* and illustrate it with
some research. I shall then introduce the contrasting benefits that a functional
perspective provides. This will entail outlining a linguistic domain, namely
that of interpersonal predicates and their features to establish the implications of this domain for a functional view, which will constitute the next
section.

So, what are the problems inherent to the classical approach to the investigation of the language–cognition interface?

Domain specificity. Typically the examination of linguistic relativity entails
choosing a categorical domain (e.g., color) or syntactic feature that is linguisti-
cally represented in the two linguistic communities and comparing them. If
the comparison reveals a difference (e.g., color naming), then the question
becomes whether this difference affects nonlinguistic process (e.g., perception
of color, memory for color). One can thus visualize the typical research questions. Do cultural differences in color-coding influence the actual perception
of color (e.g., Özgen, 2004; Regier, Kay, & Cook, 2005), space (Majid,
Bowerman, Kita, Haun, & Levinson, 2004), and time (Boroditsky, 2001)? Do
differences between cultures in grammatical gender influence gender-related
memory (e.g., Boroditsky, Schmidt, & Phillips, 2003; Stahlberg, Sczesny, &
Braun, 2001)? Do differences in spatial metaphors influence the conception of
time (e.g., Boroditsky, 2001), and so on (see Gertner & Goldin Meadow, 2003;
Gumpertz & Levinson, 1996)? Oftentimes, the pattern of results obtained in
one specific domain is taken as a definitive answer to the language–cognition
puzzle: Language influences cognition, or language does not shape cognition.
Yet generalizability from findings in one domain to language as a whole is
questionable.

Language and cognition as representational and amodal systems. In the traditional approach, language and cognition are treated as inner representational
systems and therefore remain disembodied, timeless, and subjectless.
Consequently, a communicative or interpersonal context is ignored, thus
neglecting the chief function of language, which has shaped language in the
first place.

Methodological concerns. Studies comparing different linguistic communities
come with some serious methodological costs. One is the commensurability of

stimuli and instructions between the languages. It is impossible to ascertain—despite back-translation—that these are identical, even in the case of minimal verbal instructions (see Boroditsky, 2001; Gumpertz & Levinson, 1996; Ji, Zhang, & Nisbett, 2004; Stapel & Semin, 2007). Even minor variations in translations can lead the questions to be perceived as different (see, e.g., Brown, 1986). Examining speakers of different linguistic communities in their native languages has its own pitfalls. Differences in results can be ascribed to the effect of the particular language on thought. "These studies cannot tell us whether experience with a language affects language-independent thought such as thought for other languages or thought in nonlinguistic tasks" (Boroditsky, 2001, p. 3). An equally important problem is sample comparability across different linguistic communities. The question that is nearly impossible to answer is, What else covaries with linguistic differences? Obviously comparative research has yielded a wealth of insights. However, the problems that are listed simply underline the fact that the comparative approach poses a difficult task.

A. Toward a Functional View: Background

Here, I introduce a focus on language that is different and broader than the standard analysis of domain-specific categories or grammatical features. The focus is the entire domain of *interpersonal predicates* (transitive verbs and adjectives). The particular emphasis is on the function of these predicates. The function of language in general and interpersonal predicates in particular is to be found in *their use*. Their distinctive characteristic is that they draw attention to *different aspects of an event*. In other words, they embody different general attentional construals of the same events. Thus, the *very same event* can be construed concretely in *fine grain* with the use of *verbs of action* (e.g., John punched David, Mary confided in Ann, etc.), as well as in *coarse grain* and very abstractly by using adjectives (John is aggressive, Ann is trustworthy, etc). In the functional view, language is for use. And in more general terms, language use is a "design process" that extends (and is the result of) the cognitive and motivational processes with a view to affect and focus the attention of a listener on some aspect of the social, physical, or psychological reality. Thus, language is a tool to structure the cognitions of an addressee in the course of communication. Language functions as a tool to channel the direction of attention (Semin, 1998, 2000a; Tomasello, 2003).

There are three interdependent components to cognition in this context. On the speaker side, cognitive processes are involved in the production of utterances. These processes give shape to the utterance composition with the aim of directing the attention of the recipient. The utterances shape the cognitive processes of the recipient. Finally, the joint action of communication as an emergent product constitutes "cognition" in an interpsychological space, or "in the wild" (see Hutchins, 1996). Thus, communication itself constitutes an emergent reality steering the direction that the joint action takes, particularly in situations where the task demands supersede the abilities of an individual, such as navigating a large vessel, as Hutchins (1996) has documented.

This is an approach that is entirely different from the traditional view of language, which takes a symbolic representational perspective on language and thus examines it as a property of a linguistic community that can be conceived as abstract, "virtual and outside of time" (Riceour, 1955). The functional perspective introduces a novel way of looking at language, namely, its *attention-driving function*. In this view, language is a tool that is used to give public shape to people's goals, motives, or intentions and thereby directs attention to different aspects of reality. Accordingly, different linguistic devices serve different *perspectival* and *perceptual* functions. There are different versions of this view, one of which is expressed by Slobin (1987, 1996), who suggests that language may influence thought during "'thinking for speaking.'" In this view, we are forced to attend to specific aspects of our experiences and reality by making these aspects grammatically obligatory. Consequently, speakers of different languages are biased to attend to and encode different aspects of their experience while speaking. I argue here that these types of differences are prevalent not just *between,* but also *within,* linguistic communities. Thus, the very same linguistic community has different linguistic devices that permit attending to different aspects of the very same reality; these differences in turn give rise to distinctive differences in how the very same reality is perceived, as will be discussed next.

In the following I shall describe the domain of *interpersonal predicates* and then illustrate the significance of this approach for cultural psychology with some research examples.

B. The Domain of Interpersonal Predicates and their Features: The Linguistic Category Model

The Linguistic Category Model (LCM; Semin, 2000b; Semin & Fiedler, 1988, 1991) is a classificatory approach to the domain of interpersonal language, which consists of interpersonal (transitive) verbs that are used to describe *actions* (help, punch, cheat, surprise) or psychological *states* (love, hate, abhor), and *adjectives* and *nouns* that are employed to characterize persons (extroverted, helpful, religious). The LCM provides the framework to identify the nuances of how people use interpersonal terms and thus is informative about how verbal behavior is driven strategically by psychological processes and communication constraints. This is made possible by providing a systematic model of the meanings that are peculiar to the linguistic terms (verbs, adjectives, and nouns) that we use in communicating about social events and their actors.

In this model a distinction is made between five different categories of interpersonal terms, namely descriptive action verbs (DAVs), interpretative action verbs (IAVs), state action verbs (SAVs), state verbs (SVs), and adjectives (ADJs) (Semin & Fiedler, 1991). The distinction between the categories is obtained on the basis of a number of conventional grammatical tests and semantic contrasts (Bendix, 1966; Brown & Fish, 1983; Miller & Johnson-Laird, 1976; see Table 5.1).

TABLE 5.1: **The Classification of Linguistic Terms in the Interpersonal Domain and Their Classification Criteria**

Category	Examples	Characteristic Features
Descriptive action verbs (DAV)	Call Meet Kick Kiss	Reference to single behavioral event; reference to specific object and situation; context essential for sentence comprehension; objective description of observable events
Classification criteria: Refer to one particular activity and to a physically invariant feature of the action; action has clear beginning and end; in general do not have positive or negative semantic valence		
Interpretive action verbs (IAV)	Cheat Imitate Help Inhibit	Reference to single behavioral event; reference to specific object and situation; autonomous sentence comprehension; interpretation beyond description
Classification criteria: Refer to general class of behaviors; have defined action with a beginning and end; have positive and negative semantic valence		

(Cont'd)

TABLE 5.1: **The Classification of Linguistic Terms in the Interpersonal Domain and Their Classification Criteria** (*continued*)

Category	Examples	Characteristic Features
State action verbs (SAV)	Surprise Amaze Anger Excite	As IAV, no reference to concrete action frames but to states evoked in object of sentence by unspecified action
Classification criteria: As with IAV, except that the verb expresses emotional consequence of action rather than referring to action as such		
State verbs (SV)	Admire Hate Abhor Like	Enduring states, abstracted from single events; reference to social object, but not situation; no context reference preserved; interpretation beyond mere description
Classification criteria: Refer to mental and emotional states; no clear definition of beginning and end; do not readily take progressive forms; not freely used in imperatives		
Adjectives (ADJ)	Honest Impulsive Reliable Helpful	Highly abstract person disposition; no object or situation reference; no context reference; highly interpretive detached from specific behaviors

Source. From Semin & Fiedler, 1991. Reprinted with permission of Taylor & Francis Group, http://www.informaworld.com.

Descriptive action verbs are the most concrete terms and are used to convey the description of a single, observable event while preserving perceptual features of the event (e.g., "A punches B" whereby punching is always achieved by means of a fist). The second category (IAVs) also describes specific observable events. However, these verbs are more abstract in that they refer to a general class of behaviors and do not preserve the perceptual features of an action (e.g., "A hurts B"). Descriptive action verbs are distinct from IAVs in that they refer to an invariant physical feature of action as in the case of kick, kiss, inter alia. In contrast, IAVs serve as frames for a variety of actions that can be described by the same verb. Thus, the verb "to help" may refer to a wide variety of distinct and different actions, ranging from mouth-to-mouth resuscitation, to aiding an old lady to cross the street.

A third category (SAVs) refers to the affective consequences of actions that are not specified any further (to amaze, surprise, bore, thrill, etc.), but details and elaborations can be supplied when asked (e.g., "Why was she surprised?"). The distinction between DAVs and IAVs from the next two categories, namely SAVs and SVs is self-evident. State action verbs and SVs refer to psychological states, while DAVs and IAVs do not. State verbs typically describe an unobservable emotional state and not a specific event (e.g., "A hates B"). One can distinguish between SVs and the three action verbs (DAVs, IAVs, SAVs) on the basis of two separate criteria. It is difficult to use the imperative in the case of SVs (e.g., "Please admire me!" or "Need money!") Additionally, SVs resist taking the progressive form (e.g., "John is liking Mary"). Whereas both SVs and SAVs refer to psychological states in contrast to IAVs and DAVs, it is possible to distinguish between SAVs and SVs by means of the "but" test (Bendix, 1966; Johnson-Laird & Oatley, 1989, p. 98 ff.). State action verbs refer to states that are caused by the observable action of an agent and describe the emotional consequences of this action upon a recipient (surprise, bore, thrill). The latter, SVs, refer to unobservable states (love, hate, despise). Whereas one can say, "I like Mary, but I do not know why," it is awkward to say "Mary entertained me, but I do not know why." The reason is mainly because SAVs "signify a feeling that has a cause known to the individual experiencing it" (Johnson-Laird & Oatley, 1989, p. 99).

Finally, adjectives (e.g., "A is aggressive") constitute the last and most abstract category. Adjectives generalize across specific events and objects and describe only the subject. They show a low contextual dependence and a high conceptual interdependence in their use. In other words, the use of adjectives is governed by abstract, semantic relations rather than by the contingencies of contextual factors. The opposite is true for action verbs (e.g., Semin & Fiedler, 1988; Semin & Greenslade, 1985); these most concrete terms retain a reference to the contextual and situated features of an event. A sample of the predicates corresponding to the four categories can be found in Table 5.2.

This dimension of abstractness—concreteness of interpersonal predicates—has been operationalized in terms of a number of different inferential features or properties. These inferential properties include the following: *(1)* how enduring the characteristic is of the sentence subject; *(2)* the ease or difficulty of confirming and disconfirming statements constructed with these predicates; *(3)* the temporal duration of an interpersonal event depicted by

TABLE 5.2: **Sample Predicates of the Linguistic Category Model**

Linguistic Category			
DAV	**IAV**	**SV**	**ADJ**
Dance	Amuse	Detest	Aggressive
Dial	Betray	Dread	Anxious
Drive	Cheat	Envy	Charismatic
Hug	Deceive	Esteem	Impulsive
Kiss	Disobey	Like	Intelligent
Push	Flatter	Loath	Moody
Shout after	Harm	Notice	Outgoing
Touch	Help	Pity	Pessimistic
Wash	Save	Remember	Reliable
Wave	Warn	Trust	Reserved

ADJ, adjective; DAV, descriptive action verb; IAV, interpretive action verb; SV, state verb.

these terms; (4) how informative the sentence is about situational pressures or circumstances; and (5) the likelihood of an event reoccurring at a future point in time (Maass, Salvi, Arcuri, & Semin, 1989; Semin & Fiedler, 1988; Semin & Greenslade, 1985; Semin & Marsman, 1994). These variables have been shown to form a concrete–abstract dimension on which the categories of the LCM (Semin & Fiedler, 1988, 1991) are ordered systematically.

Descriptive action verbs (hit, kiss) constitute the most concrete category. Interpretative action verbs (help, cheat) are more abstract. State action verbs (surprise, bore) and SVs (like, abhor) follow next, and adjectives (friendly, helpful) are the most abstract predicates. Thus, one can determine how abstractly or concretely people represent an event in conversation. For example, the very same event can be described as somebody *hitting* a person, *hurting* a person (actions), *hating* a person (state), or simply as being *aggressive* (adjective).

The LCM affords the study of differential attention because the abstractness-concreteness characteristic is generic to the entire predicate class (e.g., Semin, 2000b; Semin & Fiedler, 1988, 1991). Thus, the difference between the LCM and the more conventional and domain-specific linguistic categories used to examine the relationship between language and cognition such as color is that the LCM is not domain specific. Moreover, the difference between conventional approaches to meaning (e.g., semantics) and the meaning of the concrete-abstract dimension is that the inferential properties identified by the LCM are not specific to particular semantic domains. That is, the LCM is *meta-semantic* (Semin, 2000b) in that the systematic inferences mediated by the different predicate categories as identified in the LCM apply across different semantic domains, thus rendering the LCM a useful model to investigate the attention-driving function of a generic linguistic category over and above the attention-driving functions of specific semantic domains. The latter are driven by specific, declarative meanings directly implicated in a domain (e.g., gender). Such semantic fields are concerned with how vocabulary is organized into domains or areas within which lexical items interrelate, with semantic or meaning relations addressing relationships such as synonymity (e.g., affable, amiable, friendly) and antonymity (e.g., friendly vs. unfriendly, good vs. bad).

Thus, there are two features to interpersonal language as examined by the LCM. The first one is independent of the lexical meanings that are subsumed in each of the different categories identified by the LCM. It is what is referred to here as the metasemantic feature. The second one is a "declarative" feature. Each of the LCM categories consists of a large number of words, which serve specific descriptive functions to represent the actions taking place in an event, the states people experience, and the characteristics of the actors to an event. This "declarative" feature of language is orthogonal to the metasemantic one.

The two distinctive characteristics of interpersonal predicates—declarative and metasemantic—have different implications. The declarative ability of a predicate directs attention to the *content or theme* of an act, while the orthogonal, metasemantic characteristic of the same predicate shapes how fine or coarse the attention should be. If it is the case that concrete terms such as verbs of action are used predominantly in situated contexts and refer to the specific details of a social event (i.e., a fine-grain representation of the event), then their obvious function, aside from providing a semantic representation of the event, is to draw attention to the situated, local features of the event. For instance, "Jack pushed David" or "Jack helped David" draws attention to the specifics of the act—the detail—aside from drawing attention to the positive or negative act itself. In contrast, adjectives draw attention to global features that are extracted from the very same event, namely "Jack is aggressive" or "Jack is helpful"—again, aside from drawing attention to the negative or positive properties of the person.

Thus, language can drive function in two ways. First, language can draw attention to a specific subject or theme (e.g., John *helped* David; John is a *kind* person) through a semantic route. Language can also drive attention in a subtler manner through the use of specific predicate classes. Whereas concrete predicates attract attention to contextual detail, abstract predicates draw attention to the global features of an event and thus drive basic perceptual processes in different ways. It is this latter function of language that I refer to as the "secret power" of language.

While the former semantic function is self-evident, the latter is a novel perspective that has received substantial empirical support (Semin, 1998; Stapel & Semin, 2007).

C. Language and Cognition From a Functional Perspective: Research Evidence

Why does the LCM introduce a relevant perspective toward understanding the functions of language in use and its interface with cognition and action? The LCM is an analytic tool, namely a classificatory system because the categories it distinguishes display universality across cultural boundaries in contrast to the domain-specific categories such as time or space. The language–cognition interface question then becomes the following: Which category instances are used prominently in describing or communication about an event, and how does category usage for the same event differ across cultures? These questions relate to the aspects of the event that people in different cultures draw attention to when they are representing the event in language.

Thus, I first turn to research evidence about the perceptual consequences of predicate categories (e.g., interpersonal verbs versus adjectives). Do generic predicate categories lead people to perceive the same physical reality differently? In a series of experiments, we (Stapel & Semin, 2007) showed that concrete predicate classes, namely action verbs, are more likely to direct attention to specific details of an object (i.e., its local properties). In contrast, abstract predicate categories such as adjectives are more likely to draw attention to the entirety of the object (i.e., its global properties). For example, participants were exposed to a simple film animation (Exp. 1). The film was a modern version of the famous Heider-Simmel film (Heider & Simmel, 1944), which was designed to study the activation of dispositional inferences when watching moving geometric figures, and involved chess pieces moving in ways that invite anthropomorphic interpretations. They were then asked to describe the events they saw in this short film clip either in terms of the behaviors they noted (concrete) or the dispositional makeup of the actors (abstract condition). In a second task that was ostensibly unrelated, we assessed differences in global versus specific focus (Kimchi & Palmer, 1982). The participants' task on each trial was to indicate which of two figures was more similar to a target figure. These two figures could be seen from either a global or a specific, local perspective. Participants who were induced to use abstract language by describing the *personality* of the chess pieces were more likely to identify the global figure as more similar to the target, as compared to those participants induced to use concrete language by describing the *behavior* of the chess pieces.

In a second experiment, participants were primed supraliminally with a scrambled sentence task (see Srull & Wyer, 1979) with either *action verbs* or *adjectives*. In an ostensibly unrelated experiment, they were asked to complete a categorization task, modeled after Isen and Daubman (1984). They were told to rate 10 items on a scale ranging from 1 (definitely does not belong to the category) to 9 (definitely does belong to the category). For each item, participants saw the general category (e.g., vehicle), the specific item (e.g., camel), and the rating scale. They were less inclusive in subsequent category inclusiveness task (Isen & Daubman, 1984) when they were primed with action verbs relative to when they were primed with adjectives (Fig. 5.1). These results were congruent with earlier findings indicating more global (local) processing following an adjective (verb) prime.

In a third experiment, using the same priming method and with the addition of a control condition, participants performed the Framed Line Test (Kitayama, Duffy, Kawamura, & Larsen, 2003). This is a test that can examine the ability to attend to or ignore global, context-insensitive versus specific, context-sensitive information on a basic, perceptual level. The version of the test that was used consisted of a square frame, within which a vertical line was

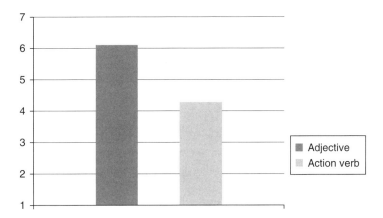

FIGURE 5.1: Category inclusiveness as a function of prime abstraction.

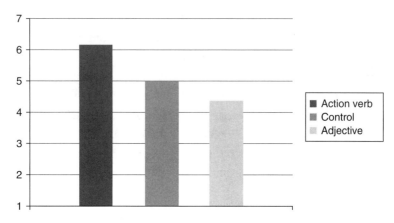

FIGURE 5.2: Framed Line Test error in mm's as a function of condition (prime: adjective vs. control vs. action verb).

extended down from the top of the square. Participants then received another (smaller or larger) square frame. Their task consisted of drawing a line that is *identical* to the first line in absolute length. To perform well, participants have to ignore both the first frame (when assessing the length of the line) and the second frame (when reproducing the line). As predicted (see Fig. 5.2), participants who were primed with the abstract predicate category (adjectives) performed better, that is, made smaller errors, than those primed with concrete predicates (verb) since they were independent, noncontextual, less situational, and tuned to be attentionally less localized. The errors of participants in the control condition were in between these two extremes.

In the final experiment, participants were subliminally primed with a parafoveal priming task, which has been used reliably to prime information without awareness (see Bargh & Chartrand, 2000). The participants' task consisted of pressing the left key, labeled "L," if a flash appeared on the left side of the screen, and the right key, labeled "R," if a flash appeared on the right side of the screen. A fixation point consisting of one X was presented continually in the center of the screen. After a practice trial, participants received 40 experimental trials, either with an adjective or an action verb. Twenty of the experimental trials were neutral object words (e.g., table, chair). Words were presented for 80 ms and immediately followed by a 120-ms mask. The control condition had only neutral words.

Subsequently, and in an ostensibly unrelated task, subjects performed the global-specific focus task (Kimchi & Palmer, 1982). As can be seen from Figure 5.3, participants in the adjective condition were more likely to use the

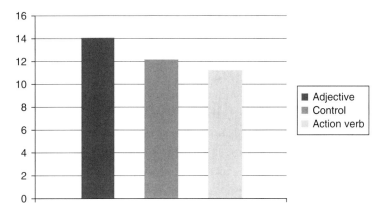

FIGURE 5.3: Global responses as a function of condition (prime: adjective vs. control vs. action verb).

global form as a basis for matching objects than participants in the action verb condition, with the scores of control participants located between these two extremes.

Consistent with earlier findings, participants had a more global focus on reality when they were subliminally primed with adjectives than when they were subliminally primed with action verbs.

What is the relevance of these findings for the classic question, Does language shape cognition?

D. And Back to the Intersection: Language, Cognition, and Culture

The findings reported by Stapel and Semin show clearly that generic predicate categories shape perception and provide evidence for the classic question that Whorf (1956) raised. The research demonstrates that different linguistic categories point people to different types of observations and underscores the functional argument that language is a tool that directs people's attention to different aspects of reality. Such an approach has the advantage of circumventing a variety of methodological problems noted earlier. In particular, the approach ascertains commensurability of instructions and comparability of samples across conditions, and it provides causal experimental evidence instead of correlational evidence. But the question remains: What is the relevance of these types of findings for the cultural dimension of the intersection that is the focus of this chapter?

The relevance is highlighted by the fact that although cultures may differ along the dimension of individualism–collectivism, all cultures have languages that include both predicate types (verbs of action and adjectives). More importantly, different cultures seem to vary in the relative accessibility of these terms in their everyday use. Our linguistic habits are shaped by recurrent cultural patterns of representing, acting, feeling, interpreting, and experiencing social events. Differences in cultural practices are therefore likely to give rise to variations in recurrent features of talk. For instance, variations in how the person is culturally oriented are likely to imply different constructions of social events reflecting the types of relationships between a person and his or her social world (Markus & Kitayama, 1991, 1994). Accordingly, the cultural formation of the person can be regarded to play an important role in the linguistic shaping of the interpretation and representation of events across cultures (Hofstede, 1980; Markus & Kitayama, 1991; Mauss, 1985/1938; Semin & Rubini, 1990; Shweder & Bourne, 1982; Triandis, 1989, 1994a, 1994b, 1995). One would therefore expect differences in the accessibility of concrete and abstract predicate categories as a function of the preferential focus to a situation or a person. While the former is a focus on the interdependencies in social events, the latter entails a focus that is directed toward the dynamics of a situation that emanate from the makeup of an individual. These differences in focus across cultures should be reflected in people's relative use of concrete and abstract predicates when describing social experiences and events, as well as when describing the persons involved in such events.

In an earlier study, we (Semin, Görts, Nandram, & Semin-Goossens, 2002) showed that concrete emotion categories implicating situated relationships are more accessible among those in a collectivist culture, namely Hindustani Surinamese. Further, emotion events are described using more concrete predicates among those in interdependent cultural contexts (Hindustani Surinamese) relative to independent cultural contexts (Dutch). The latter are more likely to access abstract emotion terms. As can be seen in Figure 5.4, Hindustani Surinamese participants are more likely to use state verbs when they spontaneously mention the emotion terms that come to their mind relative to the Dutch participants. In contrast, the Dutch participants are more likely to generate emotion words, which are nouns or adjectives compared to the Hindustani Surinamese.

The finding that there is more reliance on concrete linguistic categories among the Hindustani Surinamese relative to the Dutch is consistent with research suggesting that contextualizing predicates are more prominently

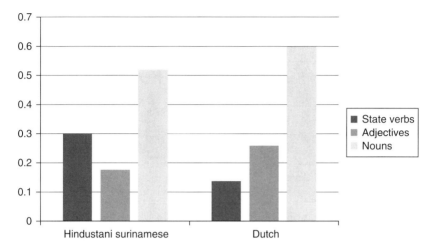

FIGURE 5.4: Relative proportion of grammatical categories mentioned in the emotion generation task as a function of culture.

used in attributional explanations in cultures where interdependence is more prominent (e.g., Miller, 1984; Miller & Bersoff, 1992; Morris & Peng, 1994). They also converge with the notion that the self itself is contextualized in such cultural contexts (e.g., Cousins, 1989; Markus & Kitayama, 1991). It is important to note that LCM analyses have been conducted in many different languages (English, German, French, Italian, Dutch, Spanish, and Greek), including Japanese (Suga & Karasawa, in press; Tanabe & Oka, 2001).

More recently, Maass, Karasawa, Politi, and Suga (2006) have presented a set of results complementing the Semin et al. (2002) pattern of outcomes in a series of experiments comparing Italian and Japanese participants. In their first study, they investigated whether Japanese participants would use less abstract categories relative to Italians in terms of the LCM when they are describing individual target persons and groups. As can be seen in Figure 5.5, Japanese participants used DAVs about four times as often as Italian participants. The largest difference was found for SVs. In Japanese participants' descriptions, SVs appeared approximately 12 times more frequently than in Italian descriptions. In contrast, Italians used adjectives more frequently than the Japanese.

In a second study, Maass et al. (2006) asked participants to describe a single individual (or a category) in general terms and in two specific situations, namely at home and at school or work. The pattern of language use in terms of the LCM categories mirrors the findings summarized in Figure 5.5,

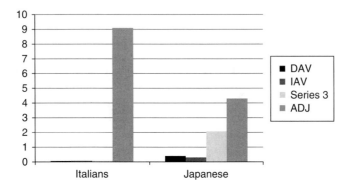

FIGURE 5.5: Number of descriptive action verbs (DAV), interpretive action verbs (IAV), state verbs (SV), and adjectives (ADJ) used by Italian and Japanese participants. (Adapted from Maass, A. Karasawa, M., Politi, F., & Suga, S. [2006]. Copyright 2006. Reprinted with permission of the American Psychological Association.)

suggesting a stable difference in the use of abstract versus concrete language by Italian versus Japanese participants.

Thus, an interesting question is whether cultures differing in the relative accessibility of predicate classes also differ in the way they perceive stimulus objects? In one of the studies described earlier (Stapel & Semin, 2007; Exp. 3) participants primed with abstract predicates were less sensitive to contextual information relative to participants primed with concrete predicates. Thus, if one were to generalize from these findings in conjunction with the research reported by Maass et al. (2006), then one would predict that a Japanese sample would outperform an American sample on the Framed Line Task should they be asked to reproduce a line that retains the same proportion relative to the square. In contrast, American participants would perform much better than their Japanese counterparts should they be asked to produce a line of equal length as the original line. Indeed, these were precisely the findings reported by Kitayama et al. (2003) who were the first to use this task to illustrate the difference between interdependents (Japanese) and independents (Americans) in that interdependents are more sensitive to contextual information compared to independents.

Taken together, these findings regarding the attentional functions of abstract and concrete predicate classes (Stapel & Semin 2007), the selective use of distinct linguistic categories by different cultures (Maass et al., 2006), and the cultural difference in attending to contextual information (Kitayama et al., 2003) suggest a fruitful window in our understanding of how language shapes cognition. The lessons I would like to advance and derive from these findings are as follows. First, generic features of language can drive attention to different features of a stimulus environment. Second, cultures differ in the habitual use of these same generic properties of language, which in turn gives rise to differences in the way the stimulus environment is perceived. These observations provide a first, if speculative, step in understanding the rather complex relationship between language, the cultural differences in habitual use of language, and perception.

Approaching this complex puzzle with the specific strategy adopted here holds the promise of avoiding the potential shortcomings that are always present in comparative research. It would appear to me that such a research strategy as the one outlined here may have an impact on the field by furnishing possibilities of investigating the language–cognition puzzle at a much broader level than has been done hitherto. We think that this research strategy issues an invitation to engage in a multilevel approach with the possible promise of integrative theory construction.

III. INTERLUDE: FROM LANGUAGE IN DIALOGUE TO OMNIPRESENT LANGUAGE

The preceding section focused on the specifics of language use from a functional perspective, arguing that the chief function of language is an attention-directing one. From a producer's perspective the role of cognition (as well as motivation) is about the processes involved in the selection of the linguistic devices or tools best suited in directing the attention of the listener to the intended themes, subject, or aspects of an event. From a perception–reception point of view, cognition in the listener is how the linguistic devices in use direct attention. Both production and reception are, however, located in a cultural context that has habitualized collective preferences of directing attention to specific facets of an event. Obviously, preferences do not mean a rigid adherence to invariably directing attention to the same features of an event. Cognition, and thus language use, is situated (Smith & Semin, 2004) and strategic (e.g., Maass et al., 1989). These strategic choices of language use are not only prevalent in interpersonal dialogue or immediate interpersonal communication but also communication at a broader, more inclusive level, as I mentioned in the introduction. Strategic choices drive the mass media and its diverse instruments, as well as sources of knowledge (such as school books and other educational devices) that are used to educate us by directing our attention to the geography, history, literature, and culture of our communities. Obviously, attention-directing devices are extensively used in novels, thrillers, science fiction, films, TV, and the Internet. All these "social practices" at all levels of possible discourse, irrespective of whether they are in written, visual, or auditory form, have a fundamental unintended consequence. They contain in their recursively reproductive regularities knowledge and information that we are not aware of at the individual level. If you are living in a specific area, if your newspaper and TV station are in the same area, then they are likely to direct your attention to a diverse set of events that happen in the more immediate proximity of your residence. This means that locations that are more distant will be less likely to be mentioned in the media. A number of things are happening in such social practices: *(1)* your attention is directed to events in your proximity; *(2)* the salience of the events determines how inclusive the reporting will be geographically. A less salient event (e.g., cyclist without helmet cracks his jaw while driving in Amsterdam) in your immediate proximity is equally likely to be drawn attention to as a very salient event in a distant location (e.g., car drives into local McDonald's in Paris; driver was protesting against junk food!). While the themes of these communicative acts will be of interest, they also mediate other types of information to which we do not have conscious access. Cumulatively, the frequency with which town names co-occur is likely to convey information about the relative distance of these towns from each other. This is just a very simple example of the unintended consequences of communication that are contained in the linguistic ecology of a community. These co-occurrences of town names, as well as a variety of other features in the language that are produced, instill implicit knowledge that we actually access and infer, as I shall argue in the next section.

And, thus, these concurrent and continuous practices constitute in their totality an emergent and continuously present linguistic environment to which we are exposed and with regularities that supersede the immediacy of our ongoing reality. I refer to this omnipresent by-product of our social practices as the linguistic ecology of cultures. The next section constitutes an analysis of the influence of language as in the linguistic ecologies of cultures upon human functioning and the shaping the psychological realities within cultures. The influence of this aspect of linguistic influence escapes conscious access because it is not a direct feature of language use in whatever context (dialogue, mass mediate, etc.) but rather the extraneous by-products of social practices involving language use, as will be clear in the next section.

IV. THE LINGUISTIC ECOLOGY OF CULTURES AND ITS IMPACT ON THE SHAPE OF PSYCHOLOGICAL REALITIES

What is a historically situated linguistic ecology, and how does it shape our psychological realities? To understand what is meant by these questions, we must examine the "unintended consequences" (e.g., Giddens, 1976) of language use in communication. The remarkable and underestimated aspect of any form of language use, every text, is that it achieves a multitude of goals at the same time, some intended and a number that are unintended. First of all, "every text (by virtue of constituting an utterance) represents something individual, unique, nonreiterative, and therein lies all its meaning (its intention, the reasons why it has been created) . . ." (Bakhtin, 1979, p. 283). Thus, any communicative act, may it be a dialogue, a radio show, a book, has a unique, specific, and situated message. At the very same time, each communicative act reproduces a critical institution, namely language. To the extent that language is a condition for speech, discourse, text, or communication, it is also *reproduced* in any speech event. As Giddens (1976) points out: "Language exists as a 'structure,' syntactical and semantic, only in so far as there are some kind of traceable consistencies in what people say, in the speech acts which they perform. From this aspect to refer to rules of syntax, for example, is to refer to the reproduction of 'like elements'; on the other hand, such rules *generate* the totality of speech acts which is the spoken language. It is this dual aspect of structure, as both inferred from observations of human doings, and yet as also operating as a medium whereby these doings are made possible, that has to be grasped through the notions of structuration and reproduction" (pp. 121–122, emphasis in the original, see also Bakhtin, 1979).

This means that when I utter a sentence in English, Dutch, or Turkish, this contributes to the reproduction of English, Dutch, or Turkish *as a language*. This is an unintended consequence (Giddens, 1979) of uttering that sentence. Thus, the use of language has at least two fundamental features (Bakthin, 1979; Giddens, 1976; Ricoeur, 1955). One is the communication of meaning, and the other is a structure that carries this meaning. Communication in whatever form has two interrelated fundamental and inseparable features. One is the reproduction of a structure. The second is conveying meaning, which would not be possible without the reproduction of language in communication. In short, any speech act presupposes a structured system of signs that is understood by everybody. These reiterative and reproducible properties of language constitute the *structural properties of language* (syntactical and semantic) that simultaneously carry unique and situated meanings. Language use then amounts to drawing on shared structures to convey a potentially novel and unique meaning.

This much applies to any linguistic community, and these considerations supersede cultural variations between human communities. However, there are differences in *what* is reiteratively reproduced and the *way in which they are institutionalized. These differences* distinguish between cultures. Obviously, the *structural properties of language* that are reproduced vary across linguistic communities. *But that is not all that is reproduced and varies across cultures.* The use of language also reproduces distinctive realities of the particular community. Let me illustrate with a recent example that has implications beyond its immediate message to cultural psychology, although it has not been conceptualized in this manner. Louwerse and Zwaan (2009) examined the degree to which it is possible to extract geographical information from a body of texts which in themselves do not provide spatial descriptions. They extracted a random sample text from three newspaper corpora for the analyses (i.e., *Wall Street Journal*, *New York Times*, and the *Los Angeles Times*, May 1994–August 1996) to examine the hypothesis that larger geographical entities (e.g., cities) will be mentioned more often than smaller ones and therefore the frequency with which Chicago is mentioned was expected to be higher than the frequency with which Memphis would be mentioned. More importantly, they examined the co-occurrence rates of geographical entities. The hypothesis driving this examination is that the names of geographical entities that are spatially closer were expected to show a higher co-occurrence rate than those entities that are distant. In other words, the names of cities that are close in space were expected to co-occur in text more frequently than the names of cities that are further apart in geographical distance. When the investigators transformed the co-occurrence frequencies of cities in their analysis transforming them into locations in two-dimensional space, they were able to show that this corresponded to the geographical relationships between the cities concerned. Moreover, the frequency with which cities were mentioned in the text corpora corresponded to their population sizes. This is an example of the unintended consequence of language use, which produces a linguistic ecology that is distinctive of a culture and is collectively authored. Obviously, such patterns of co-occurrence with respect to different domains will vary across cultures— and these types of cultural products that go beyond the individual are nevertheless likely to enter the representations of the cultures' members and exert an influence upon their psychological functioning. Indeed, more recently, Louwerse and Benesh (in press) performed a similar analysis examining the frequency with which the 30 cities in Actual Middle Earth are mentioned in the *Lord of the Rings* and report similarly high correlations with the map of Actual Middle Earth. Indeed, their research reveals that the ecological reality of language use does not only encode geographical information but also provides cues for people to reproduce topological information.

Obviously, this is not the only example or type of information that is contained in the historically situated linguistic ecology of a culture, an emergent ecology that is the unintended consequence of language-driven social practices. Another illustration can be found in an earlier study by Shepard and Cooper (1992), who investigated the color knowledge of the congenitally blind. They asked their participants to rate the similarity between different colors (e.g., how similar violet is to red, or orange to gold, or green to yellow, and so on). Given the same task, participants with normal color vision responses can be shown to reproduce a color circumplex with colors most similar positioned next to each other (e.g., yellow is next to gold), and dissimilar colors anchored on the opposite sides of the circle (e.g., green versus red). In contrast, for participants who have never perceptually experienced color, the two-dimensional shape that emerges from an analysis of their similarity judgments is different, but revealing. The solution preserves short-distance relationships (purple and violet; yellow and gold), but the overall shape is quite different. Obviously, these participants extract their similarity judgments from co-occurrence frequencies in language with no supportive perceptual information. Indeed, a further study like the one conducted by Louwerse and his colleagues (e.g., Louwerse & Zwaan, 2009) would throw light on the degree to which there is an overlap between co-occurrence frequencies of color terms in language and the solutions obtained by the congenitally blind with those with normal vision. Such a three-fold comparison would have furnished a perfect case of parceling out the different contributions of perception and language to the similarity judgments.

A further instance of how co-occurrences influence mental representations is found in the interrelations between words, namely the occurrence of masculine and feminine articles and nouns in languages that divide all nouns into feminine and masculine grammatical gender, such as French, German, or Spanish. Do the relations between the words have an influence on how people think about the properties of the category represented by the noun? Take the same word (e.g., sun). Do two languages that use different articles (masculine and feminine) for the same word think differently about it? Do the noun–article combinations have an influence on how users of that linguistic system conceive of the words' referents? Do German speakers think of the sun as being more like a biological female than do Spanish speakers? When an object's or entity's name is grammatically masculine in a language, speakers of that language are more likely to describe that object using more masculine adjectives, to judge it to be more similar to biological males, to represent it with more masculine properties, and so on (e.g., Boroditsky et al., 2003; Jacobson, 1959; Sera, Berge, & del Castillo, 1994).

Finally, I shall mention two further unintended consequences of collective practices that have to do with how text is deposited in written form. A variety of research findings have revealed that the unintended consequence of how written text is conventionalized has remarkable consequences upon our thinking and representation. For instance, the text format has undergone considerable changes before the familiar Western written text form that we have currently. This change was responsible, according to Saenger (1997), for the transition from ancient reading, which was oral, to the current silent reading. Specifically, he argues that the introduction of space between the words in writing during the period from late antiquity to the fifteenth century contributed to the development of silent reading. Thus, the emergence of separating the words in sentences, which until the tenth Century were written in continuous form in Europe, was critical in the emergence of silent reading. Silent reading versus reading aloud has considerable relevance in comparisons between cultures and invites novel research questions.

The second aspect of how text is deposited has been the subject of considerable research—namely how writing direction influences the way people organize events and abstract relationships. This spatial bias is shaped by writing direction, namely left-right (predominant in Western languages) or right-left (Arabic, Hebrew, or Urdu), and has been shown to influence the systematicity observed in a variety of psychological phenomena, such as the visual imaging of subject–verb–object sentences (e.g., Maass & Russo, 2003). Thus, in Western languages this visual imaging takes the following form: When participants are asked to draw a picture of specific sentences, such as "John gives the ball to Barak," they place the agent (John) to the left. The patient (Barak) is placed to the right.

The dependency of the spatial bias in visual imaging contrasts starkly with earlier noncomparative research that had only revealed a left-right bias as resulting from hemispheric biases in the processing of visual stimuli (e.g., Beaumont, 1985; Levy, 1976), including semantic representations of actions such as "pushing" and "giving" (see Chatterjee, 2001).

The influence of cultural differences in writing direction on spatial bias has now been extensively demonstrated for a variety of phenomena, such as inhibition of return (Spalek & Hammad, 2005); drawing, exploration of art, and aesthetic preferences (e.g., Chokron & De Agostini, 2000; Nachson, Argaman, & Luria, 1999; Tversky, Kugelmass, & Winter, 1991); representational momentum (McBeath, Morikawa, & Kaiser, 1992); imaginary number line (Dehaene, Bossini, & Giraux, 1993); and visual imaging of subject–verb–object sentences (Maass & Russo, 2003; e.g., Chokron & De Agostini, 2000; Nachshon, 1985; Nachshon et al., 1999; Tversky et al., 1991).

V. SUMMARY AND CONCLUSION

The historically situated linguistic ecology of cultures is a neglected gold mine of information about factors that give shape to human functioning. Systematic examination of this ecology is likely to be very informative, since such examination can reveal constraints that are driven by, for instance, the co-occurrence frequencies between words belonging to specific domains (e.g., color terms). The pattern of co-occurrence frequencies can in turn shape the types of relationships we produce in the color domain. Examples of others factors of this ecology are writing direction or indeed literacy (e.g., Luria, 1976).

These constraints upon psychological functioning supersede the immediate dynamics of communication and constitute a starkly neglected aspect of the interface between language, culture, and human functioning. This is evident in arguments suggesting that even when controlling for the "language of testing" categorization, bilingual Chinese display a more relational and less categorical way relative to European Americans, irrespective of the language in which they are tested (e.g., Ji et al., 2004). The finding that one group displays more categorically may be the result of the linguistic ecology in which participants partake, rather then the specific features of the language (e.g., syntax). What such research neglects is the influence of the linguistic ecology that displays differences in co-occurrence frequencies across cultures and, in all likelihood, exerts a strong influence upon the perception of reality and the categorization of objects inter alia. Thus, it is not only which language people speak or use but also the linguistic ecology within which they live that exerts an influence on cognitive processes such as categorization.

Recent developments in cultural social psychology (e.g., Chiu & Hong, 2006, 2007; Lehman et al., 2004) have introduced novel ways of thinking about cultures by conceptualizing culture in terms of distinctive patterns of knowledge and beliefs. Along with this, the significance of communication processes has acquired prominence (e.g., Fast et al., 2009; Lehman et al., 2004; McIntyre et al., 2004; Schaller et al., 2002) as well as the processes that contribute to the transmission of culturally relevant information and how these processes establish shared representations (e.g., Chiu & Hong, 2006; Sperber, 1996). The framework of the linguistic ecology of cultures presented here introduces a different level of analysis that locates shared knowledge and beliefs as the unintended consequence of situated communication process, whereby communication, the way I use it here, takes a multitude of forms, ranging from an informal conversation to a debate, to the language used in the news media, and so on. The information or knowledge that is contained in such social practices is not explicitly accessed, yet it exerts an influence on our representation of reality and the way we make inferences about features of reality that are actually not explicit in communication, but simply a by-product of the information contained in communication. The collection of these language-driven social practices, as I have argued, contributes to the emergence of an historically situated linguistic ecology which is a reservoir of knowledge that we acquire by simply partaking in the diverse language-driven social practices of a community. This is knowledge that is not directly or explicitly acquired but appropriated by being exposed to the regularities of the linguistic ecology that we live in. Chiu, Gelfand, Yamagishi, Shteynberg, and Wan (in press) advance a complementary view. They argue that culture is represented in the form of intersubjective perceptions. In this view, culture is constituted by beliefs and values that are believed to be widespread by members of the culture. The interesting interface between the perspective presented here and Chiu and colleagues' (in press) is that the linguistic ecology, which is the unintended consequence of social practices, may be sedimented in the form of intersubjective perceptions.

A number of interesting research questions arise in this context—questions that have remained unexamined to my knowledge. The first is differences across cultures in how different linguistic ecologies "represent" certain domains in language. I used the example of color earlier on in the context of comparing congenitally blind, color–blind, and normally sighted individuals (e.g., Shepard & Cooper, 1992) but also independently how color is represented in the linguistic ecology of the culture of the participants. This is but one example of a domain, but it can be extended to a number of significant domains, such as interpersonal predicates to examine how interpersonal relations are represented culturally, or simply an examination of male and female names in terms of their co-occurrence frequencies to find out how gender relationships are conceptualized in the linguistic ecology, and so on. Another fascinating issue is how such relationships that are found in the situated linguistic ecologies are actually appropriated. The acquisition of such patterns of knowledge must take place with repeated exposure over time and not direct experience of the patterns at once.

Finally, differences in the linguistic ecologies that people are exposed to not only between cultures but also within cultures must inevitably affect the knowledge structures of the respective linguistic communities.

The part of this contribution leading to an analysis of the unintended consequences of communication and social practices involving language in general focused on the minutiae of language use. What is the function of language examined from the perspective of "What is language for?" rather than merely "What is language?"—the traditional perspective? Having examined the attention-driving function of language and identified cognition in a triad of intersecting ways—as processes shaping communicative or production acts, as comprehension acts, and the entirety of communication itself as an emergent product of knowledge—we can see the connection between the two parts of this contribution. The last element, "cognition," supersedes individual productions and is the result of joint action, what some have termed "cognition in the wild' (Hutchins, 1996). In Hutchins' case, cognition is a dynamic product of joint action, is emergent, and is ephemeral due to its utterly situated and ever-changing qualities. Thus, the minutiae of language use gives rise to cognition that supersedes individual processes and products. There are, however, more lasting features resulting form the immediacy of language use and its emergent qualities, which is what I have referred to as the historically situated linguistic ecologies that are continuously reproduced by a wide variety of discourse forms in societies. Obviously, there is an intimate and recursive relationship between everyday discourse and linguistic ecologies both mutually contributing to the shape of human psychological functioning and varying as a function of linguistic communities.

ACKNOWLEDGMENTS

I would like to thank Margarida Garrido, Michele Gelfand, Cy Chiu, and Ying-Yi for their constructive comments on an earlier version of this paper.

Correspondence should be addressed to Gün R. Semin, Communication, Social Cognition, and Language Research Group, Faculty of Social and Behavioral Sciences, Utrecht University, the Netherlands. E-mail: G.R.Semin@uu.nl. (Web site: http://cratylus.org/)

REFERENCES

Bakthin, M. M. (1979). *The esthetics of verbal creativity*. Moscow: Iskusstvo.

Bargh, J.A., & Chartrand, T.L. (2000). The mind in the middle: A practical guide to prim- ing and automaticity research. In H.T. Reis & C.M. Judd (Eds.), *Handbook of research methods in social and personality psychology* (pp. 253–285). New York: Cambridge University Press.

Beaumont, J. G. (1985). Lateral organization and aesthetic preference: The importance of peripheral visual asymmetries. *Neuropsychologia, 23,* 103–113.

Bendix, E. H. (1966). *Componential analysis of general vocabulary: The semantic structure of a set of verbs in English, Hindu and Japanese*. The Hague, Netherlands: Mouton.

Boas, F. (1949). *Race, language, and culture*. New York: Macmillan.

Boroditsky, L. (2001). Does language shape thought? Mandarin and English speakers' conceptions of time. *Cognitive Psychology, 43,* 1–22.

Boroditsky, L., & Prinz, J. (2008). What thoughts are made of? In G. R. Semin & E. R. Smith (Eds.), *Embodied grounding: Social, cognitive, affective, and neuroscientific approaches* (pp. 98–118). New York: Cambridge University Press.

Boroditsky, L., Schmidt, L. A., & Phillips, W. (2003). Sex, syntax and semantics. In D. Gentner & S. Goldin-Meadow (Eds.), *Language in mind: Advances in the study of language and thought* (pp. 61–78). Cambridge, MA: MIT Press.

Brown, R. (1986). Linguistic relativity. In S. H. Hulse & B. F. Green (Eds.), *One hundred years of psychological research in America: G. Stanley Hall and the John Hopkins tradition*. (pp. 241–276). Baltimore: John Hopkins University Press.

Brown, R. & Fish, D. (1983). The psychological causality implicit in language. *Cognition, 14,* 237–273.

Chatterjee, A. (2001). Language and space: Some interactions. *Trends in Cognitive Sciences, 5,* 55–61.

Chiu, C. Y., & Hong, Y-Y. (2006). *Social psychology of culture*. New York: Psychology Press.

Chiu, C. Y., & Hong, Y-Y. (2007). Cultural processes: Basic principles. In A. W. Kruglanski & E. T. Higgins (Eds.), *Social psychology: Handbook of basic principles* (2nd ed., pp. 785–804). New York: Guilford.

Chiu, C., Lee, K., & Kwan L. (2007). *Handbook of cultural psychology*. New York: Guilford.

Chiu, C. Y., Gelfand, M., Yamagishi, T., Shteynberg, G., & Wan, C. (in press). Intersubjective culture: The role of intersubjective perceptions in cross-cultural research. *Perspectives on Psychological Science*.

Chokron, S., & De Agostini, M. (2000). Reading habits influence aesthetic preference. *Cognitive Brain Research*, *10*, 45–49.

Cousins, S. (1989). Culture and selfhood in Japan and the U.S. *Journal of Personality and Social Psychology*, *56*, 124–131.

Dehaene, S., Bossini, S., & Giraux, P. (1993). The mental representation of parity and number magnitude. *Journal of Experimental Psychology: General*, *12*, 371–396.

Fast, N. J., Heath, C., & Wu, G. (2009). Common ground and cultural prominence: How conversation reinforces culture. *Psychological Science*, *20*, 904–911.

Gertner, D., & Goldin-Meadow, G. (Eds.). *Language in mind*. Cambridge, MA: MIT Press.

Giddens, A. (1976). *New rules of sociological method*. London: Hutchinson.

Giddens, A. (1979). *Critical problems in social theory*. London: McMillan Press.

Glenberg, A. M. (2008). Toward the integration of bodily states, language, and action. In G. R. Semin & E. R. Smith (Eds.), *Embodied grounding: Social, cognitive, affective, and neuroscientific approaches*. New York: Cambridge University Press.

Gumpertz, J. J., & Levinson, S. C. (1996). *Rethinking linguistic relativity*. Cambridge, England: Cambridge University Press.

Heider, F., & Simmel, M. (1944). An experimental study of apparent behavior. *American Journal of Psychology*, *57*, 243–259.

Hofstede, G. (1980). *Culture's consequences*. Beverly Hills, CA: Sage.

Hutchins, E. (1996). *Cognition in the wild*. Cambridge, MA: MIT Press.

Isen, A. M., & Daubman, K. A. (1984). The influence of affect on categorization. *Journal of Personality and Social Psychology*, *47*, 1206–1217.

Jacobson, R. (1959). On linguistic aspects of translation. In R.A. Brower (Ed.), *On translation* (pp. 232–239). Cambridge, MA: Harvard University Press.

Ji, L. J., Zhang, Z., & Nisbett, R. E. (2004). Is it culture, or is it language? Examination of language in cross–cultural research on categorization. *Journal of Personality and Social Psychology*, *87*, 57–65.

Johnson-Laird, P. N., & Oatley, K. (1989). The language of emotions: An analysis of a semantic field. *Cognition and Emotion*, *3*, 81–123.

Kimchi, R., & Palmer, S. E., (1982). Form and texture in hierarchically constructed patterns. *Journal of Experimental Psychology: Human Perception and Performance*, *8*, 521–535.

Kitayama, S., Duffy, S., Kawamura, T., & Larsen, J. T. (2003). Perceiving an object and its context in different cultures. *Psychological Science*, *14*, 3, 201–207.

Lazarus, M. (1861). Über das Verhältnis des Einzelnen zur Gesamtheit. *Zeitschrift für Völkerpsychologie und Sprachwissenschaft*, *2*, 393–453.

Lazarus, M., & Steinhal, H. (1860). Einleitende Gedanken über Völkerpsychologie als Einladung zu für Völkerpsychologie und Sprachwissenschaft. *Zeitschrift für Völkerpsychologie und Sprachwissenschaft*, *1*, 1–73.

Lehman, D. R., Chiu, C-Y., & Schaller, M. (2004). Psychology and culture. *Annual Review of Psychology*, *55*, 689–714.

Lenneberg, E. H. (1953). Cognition in ethnolinguistics. *Language*, *29*, 463–471.

Levy, J. (1976). Lateral dominance and aesthetic preference. *Neuropsychologia*, *14*, 431–445.

Louwerse, M., & Benesh, N. (in press). Geography shapes language; Language shapes geographical thought. *Cognition*.

Louwerse, M. M., & Zwaan, R. A. (2009). Language encodes geographical information. *Cognitive Science*, *33*, 51–73.

Luria, A. R. (1976). *Cognitive development: Its cultural and social foundations*. Cambridge, MA: Harvard University Press.

Maass, A., Karasawa, M., Politi, F., & Suga, S. (2006). Do verbs and adjectives play different roles in different cultures? A cross-linguistic analysis of person representation. *Journal of Personality and Social Psychology*, *90*, 734–750.

Maass, A., & Russo, A. (2003). Directional bias in the mental representation of spatial events: Nature or culture? *Psychological Science*, *14*, 296–301.

Maass, A., Salvi, D., Arcuri, L., & Semin, G. R. (1989). Language use in intergroup contexts: The linguistic intergroup bias. *Journal of Personality and Social Psychology*, *57*, 981–993.

Majid, A., Bowerman, M., Kita, S., Haun, D. B. M., & Levinson, S. C. (2004). Can language restructure cognition? The case for space. *Trends in Cognitive Sciences*, *8*, 108–114.

Markus, H. R., & Kitayama, S. (1991). Culture and the self: Implications for cognition, emotion, and motivation. *Psychological Review*, *98*, 224–253.

Markus, H., & Kitayama, S. (1994). A collective fear of the collective: Implications for selves and theories of selves. *Personality and Social Psychology Bulletin*, *20*, 568–579.

Mauss, M. (1985/1938). A category of the human mind: The notion of person; The notion of self. (W. D. Halls, trans.). In M. Carrithers, S. Collins, & S. Lukes (Eds.), *The category of the person* (pp. 1–25). Cambridge, England: Cambridge University Press.

McBeath, M. K., Morikawa, K., & Kaiser, M. K. (1992). Perceptual bias for forward-facing motion. *Psychological Science*, *3*, 362–367.

McIntyre, A., Lyons, A., Clark, A., & Kashima, Y. (2004). The microgenesis of culture: Serial reproduction as an experimental simulation of cultural dynamics. In M. Schaller & C. Crandall (Eds.), *The psychological foundations of culture* (pp. 227–170). Hillsdale, NJ: Erlbaum.

Miller, G. A., & Johnson-Laird, P. (1976). *Language and perception*. Cambridge, England: Cambridge University Press.

Miller, J. G. (1984). Culture and the development of everyday social explanation. *Journal of Personality and Social Psychology*, *46*, 961–978.

Miller, J. G., & Bersoff, D. M. (1992). Culture and moral judgment: How are conflicts between justice and interpersonal responsibilities resolved? *Journal of Personality and Social Psychology*, *62*, 541–554.

Morris, M. W., & Peng, K. (1994). Culture and cause: American and Chinese attributions for social and physical events. *Journal of Personality and Social Psychology*, *67*, 949–971.

Nachshon, I. (1985). Directional preferences in perception of visual stimuli. *International Journal of Neuroscience*, *25*, 161–174.

Nachson, I., Argaman, E., & Luria, A. (1999). Effects of directional habits and handedness on aesthetic preference for left and right profiles. *Journal of Cross-Cultural Psychology*, *30*, 106–114.

Özgen, E. (2004). Language, learning, and color perception. *Current Directions in Psychological Science*, *13*, 95–98.

Pinker, S. (1994). *The language instinct: How the mind creates language*. New York: Harper Collins.

Regier, T., Kay, P., & Cook, R. (2005). Focal colors are universal after all. *Proceedings of the National Academy of Sciences*, *102*, 8386–8391.

Ricoeur, P. (1955). The model of the text: Meaningful action considered as text. *Social Research*, *38*, 530–547.

Saenger, P. (1997). *Space between words: The origins of silent reading*. Palo Alto, CA: Stanford University Press.

Sapir, E. (1951) *Selected writings of Edward Sapir in language, culture, and personality*. D. G. Mandelbaum (Ed.). Berkeley: California University Press.

Schaller, M., Conway, L. G. III, & Tanchuk, T. L. (2002). Selective pressures on the once and future contents of ethnic stereotypes: Effects of the communicability of traits. *Journal of Personality and Social Psychology*, *82*, 861–877.

Semin, G. R. (1998). Cognition, language. and communication. In S. R. Fussell & R. J. Kreuz (Eds.), *Social and cognitive psychological approaches to interpersonal communication* (pp. 229–257). Hillsdale, NJ: Erlbaum.

Semin, G. R. (2000a). Agenda 2000: Communication: Language as an implementational device for cognition. *European Journal of Social Psychology*, *30*, 595–612.

Semin, G. R. (2000b). Language as a cognitive and behavioral structuring resource: Question-answer exchanges. In W. Stroebe & M. Hewstone (Eds.), *European review of social psychology* (pp. 75–104). Chichester, England: Wiley.

Semin, G. R. (2007). Grounding communication: Synchrony. In A. Kruglanski & E. T. Higgins (Eds.), *Social psychology: Handbook of basic principles* (2nd ed., pp. 630–649). New York: Guilford Publications.

Semin, G. R. (2009). Language, culture, cognition—How do they intersect? In R. S. Wyer, C-Y. Chiu, & Y-Y. Hong (Eds.), *Understanding culture: Theory, research and application* (pp. 259–270). New York: Psychology Press.

Semin, G. R., & Fiedler, K. (1988). The cognitive functions of linguistic categories in describing persons: Social cognition and language. *Journal of Personality and Social Psychology*, *54*, 558–568.

Semin, G. R., & Fiedler, K. (1991). The linguistic category model: Its bases, applications, and range. *European Review of Social Psychology*, *2*, 1–30.

Semin, G. R., & Greenslade, L. (1985). Differential contributions of linguistic factors to memory based ratings: Systematizing the systematic distortion hypothesis. *Journal of Personality and Social Psychology, 49*, 1713–1723.

Semin, G. R., & Marsman, G. J. (1994). "Multiple inference inviting properties" of interpersonal verbs: Event instigation, dispositional inference, and implicit causality. *Journal of Personality and Social Psychology, 67*, 836–849.

Semin, G. R. & Rubini, M. (1990). Unfolding the concept of person by verbal abuse. *European Journal of Social Psychology, 20*, 463–474.

Semin, G. R., & Smith, E. R. (2002). Interfaces of social psychology with situated and embodied cognition. *Cognitive Systems Research, 3*, 385–396.

Semin, G. R., Görts, C., Nandram, S., & Semin-Goossens, A. (2002). Cultural perspectives on the linguistic representation of emotion and emotion events. *Cognition and Emotion, 16*, 11–28.

Sera, M.D., Berge, C., & del Castillo, J. (1994). Grammatical and conceptual forces in the attribution of gender by English and Spanish speakers. *Cognitive Development, 9*(3), 261–292.

Shepard, R. N., & Cooper, L. A. (1992). Representation of colors in the blind, color–blind, and normally sighted. *Psychological Science, 3*, 97–104.

Shweder, R. A., & Bourne, E. J. (1982). Does the concept of the person vary cross culturally? In A. J. Marsella & G. M. White (Eds.), *Cultural conceptions of mental health and therapy* (pp. 97–137). Dordrecht, Netherlands: Riedel.

Slobin, D. (1987). Thinking for speaking. *Proceedings of the Berkeley Linguistics Society, 13*, 435–444.

Slobin, D. (1996). From "thought and language" to "thinking for speaking." In J. J. Gumpertz & S. C. Levinson (Eds.), *Rethinking linguistic relativity* (pp. 70–96). Cambridge, England: Cambridge University Press.

Slobin, D. (2003). Language and thought online: Cognitive consequences of linguistic relativity. In D. Gertner & S. Goldin-Meadow (Eds.), *Language in mind* (pp. 277–312). Cambridge, MA: MIT Press.

Smith, E. R., & Semin, G. R. (2004). Socially situated cognition: Cognition in its social context. *Advances in Experimental Social Psychology, 36*, 53–117.

Spalek, T. M., & Hammad, S. (2005). The left-to-right bias in inhibition of return is due to the direction of reading. *Psychological Science, 16*, 15–18.

Sperber, D. (1996). *Explaining culture*. Oxford, England: Blackwell.

Srull, T. K., & Wyer, R. S. (1979). The role of category accessibility in the interpretation of information about persons: Some determinants and implications. *Journal of Personality and Social Psychology, 37*, 1660–1672.

Stahlberg, D., Sczesny, S., & Braun, F. (2001). Name your favorite musician: Effects of masculine generics and of their alternatives in German. *Journal of Language and Social Psychology, 20*, 464–469.

Stapel, D., & Semin, G. R. (2007). The magic spell of language. Linguistic categories and their perceptual consequences. *Journal of Personality and Social Psychology, 93*, 23–33.

Suga, S., & Karasawa, M. (in press). Jinbutsu no zokusei hyougen ni mirareru shakaiteki sutereotaipu no eikyou [Effects of social stereotypes on language use in the description of person dispositions]. *Japanese Journal of Social Psychology*.

Tanabe, Y., & Oka, T. (2001). Linguistic intergroup bias in Japan. *Japanese Psychological Research*, *43*, 104–111.

Tomasello, M. (2003). The key is social cognition. In D. Gertner & S. Goldin-Meadow (Eds.), *Language in mind* (pp. 47–58). Cambridge, MA: MIT Press.

Triandis, H. C. (1989). Cross-cultural studies of individualism and collectivism. In *Nebraska Symposium on Motivation, 1989* (pp. 41–133).

Triandis, H. C. (1994a). *Culture and social behavior*. New York: McGraw-Hill.

Triandis, H. C. (1994b). Major cultural syndromes and emotion. In S. Kitayama & H. Markus (Eds.), *Culture and emotion: Empirical studies of mutual influence* (pp. 285–305). Washington, DC: American Psychological Association.

Triandis, H. C. (1995). *Individualism and collectivism*. Boulder, CO: Westview Press.

Tversky, B., Kugelmass, S., & Winter, A. (1991). Cross-cultural and developmental trends in graphic productions. *Cognitive Psychology*, *23*, 515–557.

Whorf, B. L. (1956). *Language, thought, and reality*. Cambridge, MA: MIT Press.

CHAPTER 6

Micro–Macro Dynamics of the Cultural Construction of Reality

A Niche Construction Approach to Culture

TOSHIO YAMAGISHI

Department of Behavioral Science, Hokkaido University

I. INTRODUCTION

Cultural beliefs—beliefs shared by most members of a culture—differ from culture to culture. A good example of this is found between Western and East Asian construal of the self. Markus and Kitayama (Kitayama & Markus, 1994; Markus & Kitayama, 1991) argue that Westerners and East Asians have different beliefs about what human beings are like and how people perceive the nature of the self. Westerners construe the self as an independent entity. That is, they share the belief that human beings are internally driven agents operating independently from others, and they see themselves as unique entities endowed with unique goals, desires, emotions, and feelings, which differ from those of others. In contrast, East Asians share an interdependent construal of the self, a belief that human beings are elements of a larger system, and prefer to accommodate their internal states and behaviors to the needs of others. East Asians see the meaning and significance of themselves in their relations with others, and they feel happy when they are in a harmonious relation with others.

As exemplified by the fact that the aforementioned work by Markus and Kitayama has been cited more than 2800 times in various disciplines in psychology and related fields, their insight that cultural beliefs and the ways people think and behave are inseparably intertwined opened many psychologists' eyes to a new way of analyzing and understanding human psychology. The success of the research paradigm set up by Markus, Kitayama, and their associates, however, had an unintended effect of overly restricting the use of other approaches to analyzing how culturally shared beliefs shape the way people construct reality. The self-construal literature advocates that people think and behave in a way that is consistent with the culturally shared beliefs about humans. I call this view the "cultural agent" view of humans. According to this view of humans as cultural agents, personal values and preferences of a cultural agent are in harmony with the culturally shared beliefs and values. The cultural agents are also assumed to encourage each other to see the world in accordance with these views and to think and behave in accordance with their personal values and preferences.

However, I argue in this chapter that the cultural agent perspective is not the only perspective for analyzing the relationship between culturally shared beliefs and culture-specific behaviors. An alternative pathway that connects culturally shared beliefs with behaviors assumes that humans are "cultural game players" who pursue their goals in anticipation of others' actions. For the cultural game player, culturally expected responses of others to one's own action are at least as important as the goals per se in deciding (either consciously or through heuristics) one's behavior. In this chapter, I present an overview of the *niche construction approach* to analyzing culture-specific psychology and behavior that is based on the view of humans as cultural game players. I called the approach I present in this chapter the institutional approach in my other publications (Yamagishi, 2009a; Yamagishi & Suzuki, 2009). Since the audience of this volume is mostly psychologists who may not be familiar with the term "institution," I decided to call it the niche construction approach. I use the term "institution" practically in the same way as social niche, which refers to a collectively created and maintained set of constraints and incentives. The essence of the niche construction approach can be summarized in the following short sentence: Humans are social niche constructors, and culture may be conceived as a social niche.

A. Humans as Niche Constructors

I share the basic logic of the niche construction approach to culture with niche construction theory in evolutionary biology (Odling-Smee, Laland, & Feldman, 2003). Human as well as nonhuman individuals create, maintain, and alter through their actions the very environment to which they adapt. A beaver's dam is a good example. A beaver builds a dam to improve the safety of his nest and to increase food supply. Once built, the dam works as selection pressure for the beaver's body shape and behavioral traits such as a fin-like tail and waterproof fur. Beavers have evolved such traits to adapt to the environment that they themselves created.

Niche construction is much more widely practiced among humans. Humans make clothes, build houses, roads, bridges, automobiles, airplanes, and many other things, and they adapt to the environment mostly consisting of the artifacts of their own creation. The adaptive environment for humans is fundamentally social—a social niche or social ecology, in the sense that the presence of such ecology (e.g., presence of and reactions from other humans) would constrain and facilitate our own behaviors. For example, most individuals' behavior is regulated by social norms or the set of expectations about other individuals' responses. The social norms constrain and guide individuals' behavior. A social niche is a stable set of such constraints and incentives collectively created and maintained by individuals' behaviors. The niche construction approach to culture analyzes culture-specific psychology and behavior as an adaptation to a social niche or the set of constraints and incentives individuals collectively create.

Adaptation to the social niche takes the form of socially "wise" behaviors—behaviors that are likely to lead to the acquisition of resources valuable for one's fitness, survival, and procreation. These valuable resources are not limited to material resources such as food or money but also include social resources such as status, prestige, respect, friendship, love, and so on, which are more directly and instrumentally tied to the individuals' and their kin's survival and prosperity. The behavior that enhances the acquisition of such resources is a *socially wise behavior*. The core of the niche construction approach lies in the analysis of what makes a behavior socially wise. Sagacity of a particular behavior depends on the fitness value of the outcome of that behavior, and its outcome value depends mostly on how other individuals react to it. For example, to assert your ability and competence may be a socially wise behavior when applying for a job in North America, but it may not be wise when a schoolgirl wants to join a peer group in Japan.

B. Structure of the Chapter

Before presenting the theory and empirical studies advancing the niche construction approach, let me first briefly discuss the major contrasts between this approach and the mainstream cultural psychology approach. Their differences

TABLE 6.1: **Summary Contrasts between the Cultural Psychological Approach and the Niche Construction Approach**

Features	Cultural Psychological Approach	Niche Construction Approach
Model of humans	Cultural agent	Cultural game player
Nature of behavior	Voluntary expression of what humans are like	Means to acquire resources from others
Beliefs about the world and humans	Frame for understanding the world and humans	Sources of anticipating others' behavior
Aggregation mechanism	Mutual encouragement	Mutual production of incentives
Research agenda	How culturally shared frame of understanding of the world affects various psychological processes, including cognition, perception, and emotion	How people's socially adaptive behaviors collectively create (or alter) the very social environment
Audience	Mainstream psychology	Social sciences

are summarized in Table 6.1. I admit that such summary might be oversimplified since the table is designed to provide the reader with a bird's-eye view. More details will be found later in this chapter to exemplify these points.

As briefly discussed earlier, in the mainstream cultural psychology, typically represented by Markus and Kitayama (1991), humans are fundamentally cultural agents—creators and users of culturally shared meanings, whereas in the niche construction approach, humans are assumed as "cultural game players" who face various incentives and constraints in the process of acquiring resources for survival and procreation. For the cultural game players, behavior is a means to acquire resources. And, in the social world, acquiring resources means making others to provide the resources they control. How others would respond to one's behavior plays a critical role in this respect, and culturally shared beliefs about humans provide foundations for deriving expected responses from others. Cultural agents, in contrast, pay no particular attention to the consequences of their behavior they engage in. In other words, cultural game players live in a physical world in which they depend on various resources they acquire to survive and procreate, whereas cultural agents live in a world of *idea* where humans have no need to eat and have shelter to survive.

The most important difference between the two approaches lies in the assumed mechanism through which individuals' micro-level properties such as cognition, perception, emotion, motivation, and behavior are aggregated to form a macro property such as culturally shared beliefs, social norms, and institutions. The defining feature of the niche construction approach is in this aggregation mechanism—individuals' behaviors have externalities to function as incentives and constraints for others. This means that individuals provide incentives for each other as externalities (unintended consequences) of their behavior, and the aggregation of externalities collectively produces the social niche. The culturally shared beliefs are more or less an accurate reflection of the social ecology they live in. The mainstream cultural psychology is not explicit on this aggregation mechanism, but just generally suggests that people who share the same cultural beliefs encourage each other to hold onto the culturally shared beliefs and behave in accordance with what is "natural" in the shared beliefs.

Another important difference between the two approaches lies in the potential audience of their research. For the mainstream cultural psychology, the primary audience is the mainstream psychologists—students of cognition, perception, emotion, motivation, and the like. It aspires to inform the mainstream psychologists that the psychological processes they study are impossible to be fully understood unless they pay attention to the fact that human psychology is fundamentally culturally constructed. In contrast, the major audience for the niche constructionists is social scientists, especially those guided by game theory. Social sciences are fundamentally studies of why and how humans fail to achieve their own values and aims. We all prefer peace to war, but war occurs despite our hope for peace. We all prefer economic prosperity to recession, yet recession occurs. Social sciences study why and how we collectively create a macro phenomenon despite our own preferences and goals. The niche construction approach shares this fundamental view of human society and human social behavior with the rest of the social sciences, and it aspires to analyze how our beliefs and behavior collectively maintain the pattern we collectively create.

Interestingly, the niche construction approach is based on the Asian (i.e., holistic; Nisbett, 2003) view of the social world, according to which the world is made up with complex chains of unintended consequences of many individuals. In contrast, the mainstream cultural psychology seems to be based on the Western (i.e., analytic) view of the world, consisting of cultural agents, each endowed with particular inclinations toward perceiving, thinking, feeling, and behaving. I am advocating in this chapter the need to combine the two—Western and Asian—views of how humans and human society operate to advance the science of humans as social and cultural animals.

In the remaining sections of this chapter, I will first present in Section II a few examples of the niche construction approach in action to give the reader a general idea of what is meant by the niche construction approach. Then, in Section III, I will discuss the core concepts and theoretical ideas of the niche construction approach. Section IV is devoted to present empirical findings. In the concluding section, I will discuss how the two approaches—the mainstream cultural psychology approach and the niche construction approach—may inform each other to provide a fuller understanding of humans and human societies.

II. ILLUSTRATIONS: WHAT MAKES INDIVIDUALS IN A COLLECTIVIST CULTURE BEHAVE IN A COLLECTIVIST MANNER?

A. Within-Group Cooperation in a Social Vacuum

1. Group-Based Cooperation in Collectivistic Societies

Before presenting a more systematic and theoretical discussion of the niche construction approach, let me first present some examples of how this approach is used in explaining culture-specific behavior. The first example is the group-based cooperation in Japan. According to the widely accepted view that Japanese culture is a collectivistic culture (e.g., Dore, 1990; Hofstede, 1980; Nakane, 1970; Vogel, 1979), Japanese individuals are assumed to have preferences for group welfare over individual welfare, and they often behave in a way to promote group interests by sacrificing their self-interest.[1] Such preferences are considered to be a defining trait of collectivist cultures (Triandis, 1989). According to this view of Japanese culture, it is predicted that Japanese individuals will cooperate at a higher level than American individuals in a social dilemma situation in which individuals face a choice between doing an individually beneficial action and another action that enhances group welfare.

---

[1] The claim that Japanese are more collectivistic and less individualistic than Americans has been questioned by recent empirical studies. See Matsumoto (1999), Oyserman, Coon, and Kemmelmeier (2002), and Takano and Sogon (2008) on this issue.

Yamagishi (1988a, 1988b) challenged this prediction and argued that the seemingly voluntary, high-level group-based cooperation often reported as a characteristic of the Japanese culture is actually a product of the system of mutual monitoring and sanctioning (which he conceptualized as a social institution that monitors and ensures cooperation among group members), rather than individuals' internalized values and preferences for the group welfare. An important corollary of this argument is that group-based cooperation will not occur in a social vacuum in which the institutions that provide incentives for individuals to behave in a cooperative manner are absent. A typical example of such a social vacuum is found in the psychological laboratories where participants face situations that have no bearings on their "real" life outside the laboratory. Particularly relevant here are the social dilemma experiments conducted in the laboratory in which unrelated individuals are put together and asked to make choices in complete anonymity. What participants do in this type of experiment would have no bearings on their "real" life. If the Japanese inclination to work in a cooperative manner in a group setting is in fact the outcome of socioinstitutional arrangements (i.e., a social niche as a set of incentives and constraints), rather than internalized individual values and preferences, no cultural difference in the level of cooperation should be expected under such experimental settings of social vacuum. As presented later in this chapter, Yamagishi's (1988a, 1988b) cross-societal experiments on social dilemmas supported this prediction.

Yamagishi and colleagues (1988a, 1988b; Yamagishi, Cook, & Watabe, 1998; Yamagishi & Yamagishi, 1994) further argued that the presence of a strong social system providing institutional arrangements to curtail free-riding behavior would discourage trust in other individuals who are not controlled by such a system. Individuals who live under such social arrangements feel safe to deal with others insofar as the system effectively controls individuals. This gives an impression to naïve observers that a collectivist society, such as Japan, is a trust-based society in which people share the belief that humans are trustworthy to each other. In fact, the sense of security people experience in such a society when dealing with others is based on the assurance provided by the system that others are under control. When this system-based assurance is lacking, that is, in a social situation in which no control mechanism is provided—typically, in a one-shot, anonymous encounter with strangers—Japanese are expected to feel insecure. In other words, they would not trust other people in general beyond the limits of the security assurance provided by the social arrangements. Results of large-scale attitude surveys have repeatedly shown that the level of general trust in Japan is much lower than that in the Western countries. For example, according to the Pew Global Attitudes Survey (Wilke & Holzwart, 2008, conducted in 2007), 43% of the Japanese responders endorsed the statement that "most people in society are trustworthy," whereas the proportion of agreement with this statement was 78% in Sweden, 71% in Canada, 65% in Britain, and 58% in the United States. In the World Value Survey (http://www.worldvaluessurvey.org/), only 34% of Japanese responders (in 2000) answered, "Most people would try to be fair" to the question "Do you think most people would try to take advantage of you if they got a chance, or would they try to be fair?" whereas it was 87% in Sweden (in 1999), 67% in Canada (2000), and 62% in the United States (in 1999).

Based on the argument previously summarized, Yamagishi (1988a) predicted that the level of cooperation in a social dilemma experiment, in which participants' anonymity is guaranteed, would be lower among Japanese than North Americans. This prediction was supported in a cross-societal experiment conducted in Sapporo, Japan, and Seattle, Washington. In this experiment, each participant was provided with an endowment of 100 yen (approximately 50 cents according to the prevailing exchange rate of the time) and decided how much of it to contribute to their group. The contributed money was then doubled and equally allocated to the other three members of the group. The game was repeated 12 times. As shown in Figure 6.1 (black bars), the proportion of the endowment contributed to the group by the Japanese participants (44.4%) was smaller than that by the American participants (56.2%). This finding supports Yamagishi's prediction that Japanese would be less cooperative than Americans in a social vacuum.

2. Experimentally Setting up a Sanctioning System in the Laboratory

Another interesting finding in this experiment concerned the effect of a sanctioning system. In the control condition mentioned earlier (black bars in Fig. 6.1), Japanese participants cooperated at a lower level than Americans. In addition to this control condition, some of the participants in Japan and in the United States, respectively, were assigned to the sanctioning condition, and they were provided with an opportunity to voluntarily contribute their money to establish a sanctioning system (up to 100 yen or 50 cents from their cumulative earnings). The money contributed to the sanctioning system was used to punish the participant whose contribution level was the lowest among the four group members. Specifically, twice the total amount of money

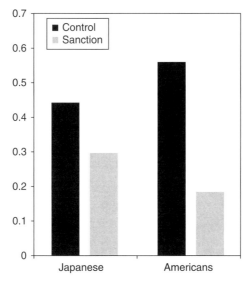

FIGURE 6.1: Cooperation levels among Japanese and American participants in Yamagishi's (1988a) social dilemma experiment. Black bars represent the proportion of the endowment (50 yen for the Japanese and $1 for the Americans) that participants contributed for the group. Gray bars represent the increase in the proportion of endowment provided for the group when a sanctioning system was introduced.

contributed by the four members was subtracted from the earnings of the target participant whose contribution level was the lowest. As shown in the gray bars in Figure 6.1, the introduction of this sanctioning system improved the Japanese participants' average contribution for the group by 29.6% of the endowment, whereas it increased the American participants' average contribution by only 18.3%.

These findings indicated, first, Japanese participants cooperated less than Americans in a social vacuum (i.e., in the control condition), and, second, Japanese participants' high level of cooperation required the presence of a social system to monitor and sanction their behavior. The Japanese participants' behavior (their contribution levels) was thus shown to represent their responses to a social niche (i.e., absence or presence of the sanctioning system) that was supported by the participants' own behavior, that is, their contribution to the sanctioning system.

3. Leaving the Group versus Staying in the Group

The dark side of social control is the distrust of other individuals in the absence of a sanctioning system. As Taylor (1976) pointed out, the existence of a strong monitoring and sanctioning system deprives people of their intrinsic motivation to cooperate (Lepper & Green, 1975; Lepper, Green, & Nisbett, 1973) and also of their belief that other people are internally motivated to cooperate (i.e., distrust of others who are not controlled by the system). The lack of trust in other individuals in a social vacuum (i.e., not controlled by the system) would make Japanese participants avoid being a member of a social dilemma group in which members are free to pursue their own self-interest. This is because they would expect others, the uncontrolled members, not to cooperate voluntarily. In another experiment, Yamagishi (1988b) provided evidence that supported this prediction. That is, he demonstrated that the absence of a social system to control free riding in the group led Japanese participants to leave a group where free riding is uncontrolled.

In this study, Yamagishi (1988b) predicted that participants' willingness to stay with the group should be higher for Americans than for Japanese. This prediction seems to contradict the view held by the mainstream cultural psychologists. According to the cultural agent view of humans, which assumes that people's collectivistic behaviors are a product of their culturally relished values and preferences, it predicts that collectivistic Japanese should prefer to stay with the group more than individualistic Americans. However, as shown in the experiment reported earlier (Yamagishi, 1988a), this view is valid only as long as the group members are mutually monitoring each other's behavior and providing sanctions against norm violators, that is, in a particular type of social niche. Once the monitoring and sanctioning system is eliminated, Japanese participants who do not trust others would be less willing to stay in the group where free riding is uncontrolled. That is, because Japanese participants do not trust other individuals in the absence of institutional assurance, they prefer to avoid risky situations in which they could be exploited by others.

A cross-societal experiment was conducted to test this prediction. In this experiment (Yamagishi, 1988b), Japanese and American participants performed tedious tasks of matching characters and were paid according to the total performance score in a three-person group, regardless of the individual's performance level. No arrangements were provided to monitor and sanction free riding in the group, and participants' anonymity was completely guaranteed. Those who did not like to work with "lazy" performers in the same group were provided with an option to exit the group and paid individually according to their individual performance level. This exit option took one of the two forms. In the no-cost condition, exiting the group did not cost them anything—individual performers were paid per unit of their performance at the same rate as that in the case of the group payment. In the high-cost condition, the pay rate per unit of performance was reduced to half when they were paid individually. In terms of individual earnings, it was not rational to exit in this condition unless the participant's performance was at least twice as high as the group average. No participant reached this level of high performance.

When exiting the group and getting paid individually was not costly (i.e., in the no-cost condition), about a third (i.e., most of the better-than-average performers in the three-person group) of the American and Japanese participants exited the group to get paid individually. In this no-cost condition, Japanese participants acted in a no less individualistic way than Americans. On the other hand, in the high-cost condition in which exiting the group and getting paid individually was economically irrational, practically no American participants chose the exit option. In sharp contrast, Japanese participants kept exiting the group despite a large economic loss they had to endure. In other words, Japanese participants chose to take the "individualistic" option of exiting the group and working individually even at the cost of getting paid less. When no assurance of curtailing free riders was present, Japanese participants did not want to stay in a "collectivistic" group in which rewards were shared equally. People in a collectivist culture may prefer an equal allocation of rewards as long as it promotes harmony among group members. However, such a "preference" for equal reward sharing was shown to be applied only to the situation in which defectors were controlled by an effective social system. In the absence of such a system, their "preferences" did not persist. Again, in this example, participants were responding to a social niche characterized by the presence or absence of mutual monitoring and sanctioning that they create (see Fig. 6.2).

III. THE CORE IDEA: INDIVIDUALS' BEHAVIORS COLLECTIVELY CREATE A SOCIAL NICHE

While the findings presented earlier capture one aspect of the niche construction view of culture-specific behavior, it is only half of the story. What these studies demonstrated was the power of the situational factors, compared to internal factors, in determining individuals' behavior. The seemingly internally driven behaviors, such as group-based cooperation and willingness to join and stay in the group, that have long been believed to characterize the Japanese collectivist culture, were shown to be actually driven by situational factors. That is, the cultural differences in such behaviors exist not in the

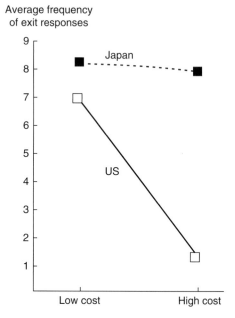

FIGURE 6.2: Average frequencies of the exit responses (out of 20 trials) by Japanese and American participants in the low exit cost condition and the high exit cost condition. (Reprinted from Yamagishi, T., Exit from the group as an individualistic solution to the public good problem in the United States and Japan. *Journal of Experimental Social Psychology, 24,* 530–542. Copyright 1988, with permission from Elsevier.)

minds of individuals but in the social arrangements that provide constraints and sanctions on behaviors.[2]

The power of the situation has long been acknowledged by social psychologists (Mischel, 1968, 1973), though researchers are not in total agreement on the relative importance of the situation and internal traits in determining individuals' behavior or how the two factors interact to produce a particular behavior (Bowers, 1973; Ekehammar, 1974; Mischel, 1968, 1973). While sharing the appreciation of the power of the situation with other social psychologists, the niche construction approach goes beyond this claim

---

[2] The situational view of human behavior is in accordance with the East Asian way of understanding human behavior—the belief that human behavior is externally induced and controlled rather than internally derived. By attributing this Asian behavior to their internal traits such as motivation, emotion, and cognition, the mainstream cultural psychologists seem to be imposing the Western view of humans as internally driven agents to understanding behavior of the Asians. In this sense, the niche construction approach represents the Asian way of theorizing about culture-specific behavior, whereas the mainstream cultural psychology approach represents the Western way of theorizing it.

and emphasizes *mutuality* of the relationship between situation and behavior. The situation, or the social niche, is not simply something given from the outside, such as culture or history. Rather, it is internally generated and sustained. A social niche is the sum of individuals' behaviors that collectively make it possible for each individual to anticipate the likely outcome of a particular action in a particular situation. Furthermore, it is a system of commonly shared beliefs about how people behave in a particular social situation, which more or less reflects the way other people who share the beliefs would actually behave. Using a phrase by the prominent comparative institutional economist Aoki (2001), an institution (which can be translated as a social niche) is a "self-sustaining system of shared beliefs" (p. 10). A set of shared beliefs makes it possible for the individuals to make educated guesses about other individuals' responses to their actions and makes it possible for them to take socially wise actions. At the same time, these individuals' adaptive or socially wise actions constitute the reality for the other individuals who are similarly anticipating and adjusting their behavior. The most important insight that the niche construction approach provides in this respect is that individuals adjust their behavior to the expected responses of others on the one hand, and such behavior collectively creates the foundation of such expectations on the other. This is fundamentally the logic of the self-fulfilling prophecy, especially in its sociological version, which will be explained shortly.

A. Social Niche Construction as a Self-Fulfilling Prophecy

1. The Subtle-Cue Theory of Self-Fulfilling Prophecy

A social niche is a state in which individuals responding to other individuals collectively constitute the "responses of other individuals." The emergence of a social niche in this sense closely resembles the process called the self-fulfilling prophecy. In fact, Spencer-Rogers and Peng (2005) described the relationship between culture and mind as a process of self-fulfilling prophecy. Although I use the same term "self-fulfilling prophecy," the micro-macro dynamics (or mutual construction of the mind and culture) assumed in the niche construction approach differs from that described in the standard cultural psychological approach. The niche construction approach sees the process of self-fulfilling prophecy in its original, sociological sense (Merton, 1957), rather than in its psychological interpretation (Rosenthal & Jacobson, 1968).

In psychology, the most well-known example of the self-fulfilling prophecy is "Pygmalion in the classroom" (Rosenthal & Jacobson, 1968). In this study, teachers' expectations that some of their students had high intelligence indeed substantially improved those students' actual test performances. This was because the teachers who expected high ability in those students signaled some subtle cues that encouraged the students to be more active and less restricted in the classroom. By labeling the students as competent, and helping students see themselves as competent, the cues provided by the teacher eventually improved the students' progress. Spencer-Rogers and Peng (2005) argued that this kind of self-fulfilling prophecy describes the process in which individuals encourage others to see, behave, and interpret their social reality in accordance with the culturally shared beliefs. For example, when those who share the independent self-construal face a situation in which they need to explain or predict another individual's behavior, they look into the individual's inner driving forces such as his/her motives, goals, emotions, personalities, and so on. As a result, they are more likely to find some internal driving forces for his/her behavior that could have been overlooked if they did not carefully scrutinize such inner traits. This experience of successfully finding internal driving forces further convinces them of their culturally shared belief that humans are internally driven agents. Their beliefs thus become a social reality. Similarly, those who share the interdependent self-construal would look into social relations as the cause of an individual's behavior and accordingly are convinced that the individual's behavior is driven by his/her social relations with others.

Kitayama and colleagues' (Kitayama, Markus, Matsumoto, & Norasakkunkit, 1997) situation sampling study illustrates this process. In this study, Kitayama and his colleagues asked Japanese and American participants to list the situations that enhanced or lowered their self-esteem. Then they showed those situations to another groups of Japanese and American participants and asked how they would feel when they faced these situations. Regardless of whether the situations were listed by Japanese or American students, American participants tended to show a greater self-enhancing tendency than Japanese participants when they read the self-enhancing scenarios. Americans also tended to show a weaker self-effacing tendency than Japanese participants when they read the self-effacing scenarios. At the same time, the self-enhancing situations listed by Americans had a stronger power than those listed by Japanese participants. These results suggested that Americans were not only more optimistic in assessing their own worth, but were also good at providing cues to encourage people around them to see themselves in an optimistic light. By mutually providing cues for seeing oneself in a positive light,

Americans collectively create a social reality of Lake Wobegon, where everyone is better than average. More generally speaking, in a culture in which a particular system of beliefs is shared, it is "natural" for people to think and behave in a particular way, and thus, they expect others to think and behave in such ways, and encourage them to think and behave in the ways they expect others to behave. This process makes cultural beliefs a social reality. A similar process has been documented by Gelfand and colleagues (2001) on how conflicts are perceived by Japanese and Americans. According to Gelfand and her colleagues, Americans perceive conflicts in terms of violations of individual rights and autonomy, whereas Japanese perceive the same conflicts as violations of duties and obligations. They also found that Americans perceive conflicts in terms of winning and losing, whereas Japanese perceive the same conflicts to be more about how to reach a compromise. Gelfand and her colleagues further conducted an analysis of newspaper accounts of conflicts in the United States and Japan. They found that newspaper articles reported conflicts that were consistent with these findings, suggesting that the way Japanese and Americans perceive conflicts actually makes them behave in accordance to the perceived reality of conflicts.

2. Self-Fulfilling Prophecy as the Process of Incentive Production

In contrast to this "subtle cue theory" of self-fulfilling prophecy, its sociological counterpart originally discussed by Merton (1957) involves less subtle processes of the production of incentives. Merton (1957) coined the term "self-fulfilling prophecy" to explain racial discrimination against black workers in the northern industrial areas of the United States. White workers in the 1940s and the 1950s in the industrial North shared the belief as summarized as follows:

> Thus our fair-minded white citizen strongly supports a policy of excluding Negroes from his labor union. His views are, of course, based *not upon prejudice, but upon the cold hard facts*. And the facts seem clear enough. Negroes, "lately from the non-industrial South, are undisciplined in traditions of trade unionism and the art of collective bargaining." The Negro, with his "low standard of living," rushes in to take jobs at less than prevailing wages. (Merton, 1957/1968, p. 478; italics added).

White workers' belief that a Black migrant from the South is "a traitor to the working class" convinced them that excluding Blacks from their labor unions was a necessary step to preserve their trade union. This more than subtle action by the White workers deprived Black migrants from getting opportunities to find regular jobs and thus forced them to "rush in to take jobs at less than prevailing wages" and often to work as strikebreakers. Hence, this created the reality that Black migrants were in fact traitors to the working class.

White workers in this example did not "encourage" Blacks to seek jobs as strikebreakers using subtle cues. Instead, they created constraints and incentives for Black migrants to seek jobs as "traitors to the working class." For the Black migrants such jobs are the only available ones because of the refusal by White workers to allow them to join labor unions. Black migrants faced the incentive to take such jobs because taking such jobs was better than starving. The belief that Blacks were traitors to the labor movement thus became the reality, not because they were encouraged through various cues to be traitors to the working class, but because of the constraints and incentives White workers collectively imposed on them. Furthermore, the reality of Blacks' working situations further convinced White workers that Blacks were in fact traitors to the working class.

The aforementioned logic of the sociological version of the self-fulfilling prophecy was later elaborated by a labor economist Thurow (1975) in his theory of statistical discrimination. Thurow argued that the presence of discrimination provides incentives for the discriminated group to invest in human capital in a manner that "justifies" the discrimination or makes the discrimination rational. That is, investment in human capital, such as higher education, yields differential returns to those who are and are not discriminated. The differential return rates from investment in human capital provide differential incentives for human capital development among those who are discriminated and those who are not. In short, the practice of discrimination itself creates incentives that discourage the discriminated from developing the proper human capital. Discrimination based on a particular belief collectively creates an incentive that discourages discriminated groups to acquire relevant human capital, thereby making the belief a reality. Thurow's analysis of statistical discrimination thus illustrates the presence of a social niche of discrimination in which the behavior of those who follow the incentives creates the very incentives they follow.

The essence of the self-fulfilling prophecy in its sociological tradition is the production of incentives that make certain actions socially wise and certain others socially unwise. In contrast, in the psychological version of the self-fulfilling prophecy, people come to think and behave in particular ways because they are encouraged to do so by people around them. People who share a cultural system of beliefs expect and encourage each other to think and behave in the way that is natural to them. It is natural because everyone else is doing so, and because it is natural they encourage others to do so.

B. Cultural Agents and Cultural Game Players

1. The Nail That Stands Out Gets Pounded Down

The difference between the cultural agent approach and the cultural game player approach is well captured by a Japanese saying, "the nail that stands out gets pounded down." This proverb can be interpreted in at least two different ways. First, this proverb can be considered as an indication of the Japanese preference for conformity, which characterizes the interdependent nature of the self-construal (Kitayama, 1998; Kitayama & Karasawa, 1995; Markus & Kitayama, 1991). Not to stand out represents a natural way of thinking and behaving for those who believe that humans are fundamentally relational, and that meanings and satisfaction of life depend on the harmonious relations with others. People who live in an interdependent culture and see the world through the lens of the interdependent self-construal would feel good and relaxed when they are well mixed with others and indistinguishable from others. Likewise, such interdependent individuals would feel uneasy when they stand out, since standing out from others does not fit well with their beliefs about human nature. Thus, people encourage others not to stand out so that they—both those who encourage and those who are encouraged—can feel happy and satisfied.

An alternative interpretation of this proverb is that it is a warning to people to avoid doing socially unwise behavior: "You may want to excel and stand out in front of admirers, but if you do, people around you will be jealous, and you will be hated and undermined. Thus, you'd better not stand out." The lesson here is that wanting to stand out may be a natural inclination, but to follow this natural inclination is socially unwise. This advice makes sense to those who share the belief that people are jealous of successful others and would like to undermine their success if given a chance.[3] Socially wise behavior

---

[3] People in collectivist cultures are reported to exhibit wary attitudes toward their close friends and acquaintances. They often believe that closely knit groups can be a place for exploitation by their neighbors (Adams, 2005). In other words, closely knit groups are where people are advised to be prudent and to behave in a socially wise manner.

is not necessarily behavior that people naturally want to do or voluntarily engage in. Oftentimes, socially wise behavior contradicts natural behavior that people are happy to engage in. Taking a strikebreaker's job would not be natural or preferred by Black migrants from the South in Merton's example, but it was certainly a wise action compared to not taking any job and letting oneself, and perhaps one's family, suffer from starvation.

2. Norms as Standards, Norms as Enforced Rules

Another way to contrast cultural game players to cultural agents is to compare the aspects of social norms that the two models assume humans respond to. Norms are shared standards of thoughts and behavior. Norms prescribe how to think, feel, and behave in the way normal people do. Those who do not observe the norms are regarded as "abnormal" or eccentric at best. Parents encourage their children, and adults encourage each other, to conform to those normal ways of thinking, feeling, and behaving. Norms in this sense are the driving force behind the process of the self fulfilling prophecy as it is understood in psychology. People jointly create a social reality in which the ways of thinking, feeling, and behaving "normally" are natural for them. Culture-specific behavior tends to be interpreted as normal or natural in the mainstream cultural psychology. An individual who lives in a particular culture where a particular way of thinking and behaving is regarded normal and natural, and who naturally thinks and behaves following such a way is a "cultural agent." An interdependent cultural agent is one who lives in an interdependent culture and sees the world through the lens of the interdependent self-construal. For the interdependent cultural agent, not standing out is a natural way of life. Similarly, an independent cultural agent is one who lives in an independent culture and sees the world through the lens of the independent self-construal. For such an independent cultural agent, not standing out would be unnatural.

Norms, however, are more than standards of thoughts and behaviors. They are also rules of behavior that are socially enforced. That is, norms tell people what would happen if they follow them and if they don't follow them. People use norms as a guideline for predicting the consequences of their behavior—how others would react to it. That is, norms set up constraints and incentives for behavior. Norms in this sense are the backbone of a social niche and the driving force of the process of the self-fulfilling prophecy as it is conceived in sociology. It is important to note that norms in this sense are not limited to formally enacted legal codes. They often take the form of cultural scripts, embedded in folk tales, proverbs, and common sense, telling people what the consequences of taking a particular action would be and how others would react to a particular action or to a particular type of people. To the degree that those expected responses of other people have relevance to the actor's own fitness, those cultural scripts would set up incentives for one's behavior and thus guide one's behavior.

The second interpretation of the stand-out nail proverb is based on the view that humans (or, in that sense, all individual organisms) are implicit (and sometimes explicit) game players as they are understood in game theory. The agents assumed in game theory (i.e., game players) are those who are endowed with a goal (often their own personal welfare, but not necessarily limited to it) and choose the option that will most likely attain the goal given the expected reactions by other players. Such a game player takes socially wise actions—choices that are instrumental for attaining their goals—as compared to cultural agents who are assumed to take natural or normal actions. In other words, the game player responds to incentives that are provided by the actual and expected behavior of others. Incentives are something that an individual desires to obtain. As humans are a social species, oftentimes what we desire (such as money, love, prestige, and so on) are provided by others. In this sense, incentives are inseparable from the actions taken by others to provide the desired object. An incentive-driven behavior, then, is a "strategy" to encourage the other individuals to elicit a behavior that provides the desired resources. I use the term "incentives" in this chapter to refer to the responses of other people that a game player expects. What constitutes incentives, or what makes a particular action socially wise, ultimately depends on the way how other people respond to the game player's behavior.

The cultural game player is not necessarily an *explicit* game player who consciously weighs relative merits of alternative actions. Rather, he or she can be an implicit game player who uses adaptive heuristics (Gigerenzer, Todd, & ABC Research Group, 1999) that work in most situations. Adaptive heuristics are the decision rules that are ecologically rational—that is, the decision rules that yield "wise" choices in a particular ecology on which they are originally established. Many of the cultural scripts (what would happen when one does this and that) embedded in cultural narratives such as proverbs, clichés, folk tales, dramas, novels, and so on constitute foundations of such adaptive heuristics. I use the term "default strategy" to refer to the adaptive heuristics to explain culture-specific behaviors from the perspective of the implicit game players.

C. Preferences and Strategies

1. Conformity as a Natural Way of Behaving

A good example of the cultural agent view of the culture-specific behavior is found in Kim and Markus' (1999) study of cultural preferences for conformity and uniqueness. From the perspective that humans are cultural agents, culture-specific ways of thinking and behaving are considered to be driven by the individual's values and preferences that are shared and encouraged by other members of a culture. Kim and Markus (1999) conducted experiments to demonstrate the validity of this view of humans as cultural agents, by comparing the preference for uniqueness and conformity among Westerners and East Asians. In one of these experiments (Experiment 3), their research team asked travelers in the waiting lounges of an airport to fill out a questionnaire. As a token of appreciation, they offered a pen to the traveler who filled out the questionnaire. The experimenter showed five pens and asked the traveler to choose one of them to take home. The pens came in two external (not ink) colors. The color combination of the five pens was either 1–4 or 2–3, with the first of the two numbers referring to the number of a "minority" or unique color and the second to a "majority" color. As they expected, Westerners showed a preference for uniqueness (that is, preference for a pen in the minority color), whereas East Asians showed a preference for conformity (that is, preference for a pen in the majority color). From the cultural agent view shared by Kim and Markus (1999), choosing a unique pen is natural from the Westerner's view of humans, whereas choosing a majority pen is natural from the East Asian's view of humans.

2. Conformity as a Socially Wise Behavior

Yamagishi and his colleagues (Yamagishi, Hashimoto, & Schug, 2008) replicated this pen-choice experiment from the view of humans as implicit game players, and they demonstrated that what may look like an expression of personal values and preferences may actually be a result of the heuristic decision making that reflected their use of a default strategy. Specifically, Yamagishi and colleagues posited that the differential "preferences" for the two types of pens were caused by the use of a particular heuristic or "default" strategy, which they termed the not-offend-others strategy.

A default strategy is a decision rule that people use by default when it is not clear what kind of decision rule should be used. When travelers in the original pen-choice experiment were presented with an opportunity to choose a pen, there was no strong need to use a particular decision rule. In the absence of cues indicating a need to use a particular decision rule appropriate in the situation, people often use a default strategy. Which strategy or decision rule is used as default would depend on its ecological fit—that is, the importance of the consequences of their choice to the fitness of the individual in his/her ecology. Yamagishi and colleagues reasoned that what decision rule to use when the nature of the situation is not clear would vary across societies, which also vary in the consequences of using particular decision rules.

One of the most notable differences in this respect is found in the importance of avoiding bad reputations as an irresponsible member of a community. In particular, the ecological fit of the strategy for avoiding a bad reputation varies between individualist societies and collectivist societies. This is because the ecological fit of such a strategy depends on the cost of accruing a bad reputation and being rejected from social relations. Ultimately, the cost of being excluded from the current social relations is a function of the opportunities available to individuals outside their current relations. To the degree that one's social life is circumscribed by the boundaries of the group or the social relations that one belongs to, a large cost is imposed on people who are excluded from that group. In a collectivist society in which groups are typically closed to outsiders, those who are excluded from the group they currently belong to have a hard time finding alternative groups that would accept them. The cost of being excluded, therefore, is much higher in collectivistic societies than in individualistic societies, in which individuals can more easily replace the lost opportunities (Greif, 1989, 1994; Yamagishi, 1998). Decision rules that minimize the risk of accruing bad reputations (i.e., the not-offend-others strategy) thus have a higher ecological fit in collectivist societies than in individualistic societies. The not-offend-others strategy is thus more likely to be the default strategy for interpersonal situations among East Asians, who live in a collectivist society, than for Americans who live in an individualist society, where "assert yourself when you want to gain something" is more likely to be the candidate of the default strategy.

3. Choosing a Majority Pen as a Default Strategy

To demonstrate that the choice for the majority pen by East Asians in Kim and Markus' (1999) study represented the use of the not-offend-others strategy rather than being driven by the preference for conformity, Yamagishi et al. (2008) conducted a vignette experiment, in which American and Japanese participants were presented with a set of scenarios. In each scenario, participants were asked to imagine that they had been asked to fill out a questionnaire and had been offered a pen as a token of appreciation. They were also asked to imagine that they had been offered five pens to choose from. Four of the five pens were of the same color, and the remaining one was of a different color. They were asked to indicate which pen they would choose. In the first, default scenario, they were simply told to choose a pen. In the second scenario, they were told that they were the *first* person in a group of five to choose the pen. In this latter scenario, participant's choice of a unique pen would restrict the opportunities for other people remaining in the group to obtain the unique pen. This manipulation was designed to exacerbate participants' concern for the social implications of their actions and thus to enhance their tendency to use the not-offend-others strategy. In the third scenario, participants were told that they were the *last* person to choose a pen. This manipulation was designed to eliminate participants' concern for the social implications of their action and thus to reduce their tendency to use the not-offend-others strategy, because choosing a unique pen had no implications to others who had already chosen their pens. These scenarios were manipulated as a within-participant factor.

In the default scenario, Kim and Markus's (1999) finding was replicated. A larger proportion of American participants (70%) than their Japanese counterparts (53%) chose a minority pen. However, when participants were the first to choose a pen and thus social implications of their choice were made salient, even Americans (47% chose a minority pen) acted like Japanese (45% chose a minority pen) and stopped choosing a minority pen. In the last-choice scenario in which it was clear that their choice would have no social implications, again, there was practically no difference between Japanese (71%) and American participants (72%)—both chose a minority pen more often than the majority pen.

These findings indicated, first, that the cultural difference emerged only in the default scenario in which the nature of the social constraints was unclear. The findings further suggested that the cultural difference found in the default scenario might be a result of how participants perceived the ambiguous situation. Japanese participants' propensity to choose a minority pen in the default situation (53%) was similar to that in the first-choice situation (45%), in which social implications of their choice were obvious (see the lower oval in Fig. 6.3). They seem to have regarded the default situation as if it had been in the first-choice situation, where avoiding negative social implications was socially wise, and thus applied the not-offend-others strategy accordingly. In contrast, American participants' propensity to choose a minority pen in the

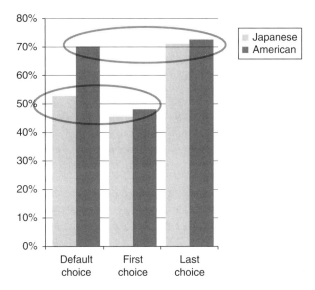

FIGURE 6.3: Percentages of Japanese and American respondents who chose a minority color pen in a scenario study by Yamagishi, Hashimoto, and Schug (2008). The lower oval indicates that the percentage of the Japanese participants' choice of the minority color pen in the default condition was similar to those in the first-choice condition among both Japanese and American participants. The upper oval indicates that the percentage of the American participants' choice of the minority pen was similar to those in the last-choice condition among both American and Japanese participants.

default situation (70%) was similar to that in the last-choice situation (72%), in which social implications of their choice were obviously absent (see the upper oval in Fig. 6.3). American participants seemed to have treated the default situation as if it had been the last-choice situation, in which they did not have to care about social implications of their actions. Although Americans also applied the not-offend-others strategy when its relevance was clear (the first-choice situation), they did not apply it when the nature of the social constraints was not apparent.

A recent study by Yamagishi, Hashimoto, Li, & Schug (2010) using a Japanese national sample replicated the earlier finding for the Japanese respondents, and it further demonstrated that the pattern of the Japanese responders shown earlier is not unique to Hokkaido University students used in the study. In this national sample study, 49% of the 821 respondents (51% in Hokkaido) chose a minority pen in the default condition, 44% (46% in Hokkaido) in the first-choice condition, and 57% (61% in Hokkaido) in the last-choice condition. While the choice of a minority pen in Hokkaido was slightly higher in Hokkaido than that in the other areas of Japan as suggested by Kitayama (2010), the difference was far from statistically significant. Furthermore, choice of a minority pen in Hokkaido was not different from that observed in metropolitan areas of Japan such as Tokyo, Osaka, and Nagoya (53% in the default condition, 46% in the first-choice condition, and 59% in the last-choice condition) that constitute more than half of the Japanese population. The percentage of the minority choice was lower in the rest of Japan (44% in the default choice, 37% in the first choice, and 51% in the last choice). In addition to the main effect of the situation (default, first choice, and last choice), the main effect of the area (Hokkaido, metropolitan areas, Kyoto, and the rest) was significant in the area (between-participant factor) by situation (within-participant factor) analysis of variance. These results suggest that the uniqueness-seeking behavior is more prevalent in metropolitan areas where people are less constrained by monitoring from people around them.

4. Pen Choice in the Laboratory

The study reported earlier was a scenario experiment, and thus its validity was debatable. Furthermore, participants might have thought that the unique pen in the last-choice scenario was a pen of popular color and had already been chosen by others. If this was the case, choosing a minority pen in the last-choice scenario actually conformed to the majority's choice. To deal with these potential problems in the interpretation of this earlier study, Hashimoto, Li, and Yamagishi (in press, Study 1), replicated the pen-choice study in the laboratory, in which participants were asked to choose a pen from a cup of five pens (one unique color and four majority color) in the waiting room to fill out a consent form.

In this experiment, there were five people in the waiting room sitting on one side of a long table facing an experimenter across the table. The first and the last ends of the line of the five people were real participants (Participants A and B), and the remaining three were confederate (Confederates 1, 2, and 3). The experimenter held a transparent cup with five pens in it and asked the participants to take a pen to use to sign the consent form and then to pass the cup to the next participant. The experimenter also announced that the participants could take the pen home. Then the experimenter handed the cup to Participant A and asked A to pick one pen and pass the cup with the remaining pens to the next person (Confederate 1). Confederate 1 also picked up a pen and passed the cup with the remaining three pens to the next person

(Confederate 2). Confederate 2 then pretended to take one pen, but secretly took two pens and passed the cup with only one pen left to Confederate 3. Confederate 3 picked up the last pen from the cup and informed the experimenter that the cup was empty. The experimenter received the empty cup from Confederate 3 and handed another cup with five pens to Participant B. This second cup contained one minority pen and four majority pens in the same configuration as that in the first cup. Thus, the first participant (the first chooser) and the second participant (the last chooser) had exactly the same option. Furthermore, it was clearly indicated that the minority pen was not a popular pen picked up by the majority. Thus, the alternative interpretation that the minority color pen had been chosen by the majority was ruled out.

Although only Japanese participants were used in this study, the results were astounding. All but two (93%) of the first choosers chose the majority color pen, whereas only about half (52%) of the last choosers took the majority color pen. The proportion of the majority choice was significantly greater than chance among the first choosers, and it was significantly less than chance among the last choosers. The "preference" for the majority pen emerged only in the initial choice situation where not choosing a unique pen implied a socially wise behavior.

The aforementioned three studies consistently show that Japanese participants chose a unique color pen in the last-choice situation where they did not have to worry about implications of their choice to other participants. This suggested that Japanese participants had a "preference for uniqueness," at least in the choice of the pen. Given this preference for uniqueness, the Japanese participants' choice of the majority pen in the first-choice situation and the default situation cannot be interpreted as a reflection of their preference for conformity. They took a socially wise action despite the fact that they personally preferred to have the unique color pen (and expected that others would also prefer the unique color pen).

5. Self-Effacement as a Socially Wise Behavior

Let me present another example of the default strategy as socially wise behavior. This time, it concerns the self-effacement tendency among the Japanese. Cross-cultural differences in self-enhancement and self-effacement have been reported in many studies (Bond, Leung, & Wan, 1982; Heine, Kitayama, & Lehman, 2001; Heine, Takata, & Lehman, 2000; Markus, & Kitayama, 1991). Their results showed that Westerners had a much stronger tendency to perceive themselves in a positive light than did East Asians. Furthermore,

East Asians were oftentimes shown to be self-effacing rather than self-enhancing, and they appeared to focus on their weaknesses rather than their strengths (Heine et al., 2001). This cultural difference has been interpreted as a reflection of the difference in self-construal discussed earlier (Markus & Kitayama, 1991).

Nevertheless, the self-effacement tendency among East Asians, and especially among Japanese, has also been interpreted as a result of conscious application of the not-offend-others strategy (Bond et al., 1982; Murakami & Ishiguro, 2005; Muramoto, 2003). These researchers argue that East Asians are more likely to choose to present themselves in a modest manner. One difficulty, however, with this alternative interpretation of self-effacement is the fact that the self-effacing tendency has been observed in completely anonymous settings such as in responses to anonymous questionnaire. When one's responses are unknown to others, one does not need to worry about social implications of one's behavior. This difficulty, however, does not prevent us from interpreting self-effacement as a *default* strategy. We argue that a default strategy should be used until its application to the situation becomes obviously irrelevant or inappropriate. When a Japanese individual is asked to reveal his or her self-evaluation, he or she is likely to use the not-offend-others strategy as a default option unless there is an obvious reason not to do so. As a result, this Japanese individual would present himself in a self-effacing manner as a default strategy. To demonstrate that this was actually the case, Suzuki and Yamagishi (2004) conducted a laboratory experiment.

In this experiment, participants first took a bogus intelligence test and then were asked to judge whether their performance would be above or below the average performance level in their university (Hokkaido University). In the control condition, in which no additional instructions were provided, 77% (43 of 56 participants) judged that their performance was below the school average. This result was in sharp contrast to the better-than-average effect often observed among Americans (Alicke, 1985; Alicke, Klotz, Breitenbecher, Yurak, & Vredenburg, 1995; Dunning, Meyerowitz, & Holzberg, 1989). A very clear self-effacement tendency of Japanese participants emerged in this condition, despite the fact that participants were assured of complete anonymity when reporting their judgment.

This self-effacing tendency, however, was completely reversed in the "bonus" condition. In the bonus condition, before making a judgment, participants were told that they would be paid 100 yen if their judgment was accurate. Through this manipulation, participants were provided with a reason for making the judgment—providing accurate judgments to earn extra money. This was in contrast to the control condition where participants were provided with no reason for making the judgment. This difference, Suzuki and Yamagishi (2004) predicted, would affect the use of the default strategy for self-presentation: Japanese should use the not-offend-others strategy by default in the control condition but not in the bonus condition where it was salient that the not-offend-others strategy was inappropriate for the purpose of expressing their judgment—that is, to express their true judgment to earn money. In the bonus condition, 69% (36 of 52) of the participants judged their performance above, not below, the school average, and the difference between the two conditions in the proportion of the above-average judgments was significant. These results demonstrated that the strong tendency toward self-effacement observed in the control condition under strict anonymity was not a straightforward reflection of participants' self-assessment. It was only when they lacked a reason to report their self-assessment that Japanese participants exhibited self-effacement.

This study by Suzuki and Yamagishi (2004) was later replicated by Yamagishi, Hashimoto, Cook, and Kiyonari (2010) using American participants. As was the case in the pen choice study reported earlier (Yamagishi, Hashimoto, & Schug, 2008), the cultural difference emerged only in the control condition where participants were not told of the reason for reporting their judgment. In this condition, 51.7% of American participants judged their performance to fall above the school mean, compared to 28.2% among Japanese participants (Suzuki & Yamagishi, 2004). However, this cultural difference almost completely disappeared in the bonus condition, where 65.6% of American participants judged as falling above the school mean, compared to 69.2% among Japanese participants.

6. Experiencing Mutual Monitoring Promotes Interdependent Self-Presentation

A study by Takahashi, Yamagishi, and Hashimoto (2009) further demonstrated that participants' responses to the interdependent self-construal scale was promoted after they experienced a collectivistic social system for monitoring and sanctioning (Greif, 1989, 1994; Yamagishi, 1998; Yamagishi & Yamagishi, 1994). Participants in this study took Singelis' (1994) independent and interdependent self-construal scales before and after they played a repeated social dilemma game. Each self-construal scale was broken into two halves.

Participants took one version of each scale before and the other version after a social dilemma game. The order of the two versions was counterbalanced. There were two conditions. In the control condition, participants completed the scales without further manipulations. In the public evaluation condition, participants were told that their responses to the scales would be revealed to another participant for mutual impression judgment. In each round of the repeated social dilemma game, each member of the six- or seven-person groups was given 60 yen and decided how much of the money to contribute to the group account. The money contributed to the group account was doubled in value and equally distributed among all group members. After each round of the game, the result—who contributed how much and earned how much—of that round was projected on a screen on the wall. Participants were identified by privately provided ID numbers, their desks were separated by partitions to provide privacy, and their anonymity was well protected. After the display of the result of each round, participants were provided with a chance to vote on whom they wanted to exclude from the group in the next round. Those who received three or more votes were excluded from the next round. However, the identities of those who were excluded were kept private and other participants were not informed except by the ID number. The game was repeated 15 rounds. After the final round, they completed the other version of each self-construal scale.

No significant change in the independent self-construal scores was observed in both conditions. However, participants' interdependent self-construal score in the public evaluation condition increased after they experienced the social dilemma games. This increase did not occur in the control condition. Furthermore, the number of times that a participant was excluded was strongly correlated with the increase in the interdependent self-construal score in the public evaluation condition ($r = .52$), but not in the control condition in which participants experienced exclusion but their responses in the self-construal scales would not be revealed to other participants ($r = .08$). Although participants were reminded that their responses would be revealed to another participant in the public evaluation condition, their personal identity was actually completely anonymous. They were identified only by a private ID number, and even the experimenter was unable to match this number back to the participant in person. Nonetheless, participants in this condition used a default self-presentation strategy to make themselves look acceptable to the others after experiencing the collectivistic system of mutual monitoring and sanctioning.

The aforementioned findings by Takahashi and her colleagues (2009) complement the findings by Gelfand and Realo (1999) that accountability enhanced cooperative behavior among collectivists and competitive behavior among individualists in intergroup negotiation. In their study, participants (Asian Americans and Caucasian Americans in Study 1, Estonians and Americans in Study 2) engaged in intergroup negotiations as representatives of their constituent group (Study 1) or responded to scenarios depicting the representative's position in such negotiations (Study 2), and they chose a set of negotiation strategies. Gelfand and Realo reasoned that the negotiators' behavior would reflect normative demands from their constituents more than their own personal preferences when they were held accountable for their behavior. The finding that collectivists behaved more cooperatively and individualists more competitively under high- than low-accountability situations suggests that their participants behaved more as cultural game players than cultural agents, who were adjusting their behavior to the expected demands from their constituents.

IV. RESEARCH AGENDAS

Having outlined the core ideas of the niche construction approach, I will present in this section the major research topics to be pursued, and what has been empirically demonstrated so far.

A. Individuals' Private Values and Preferences Do Not Always Coincide with their Perceptions of What Others Value and Prefer

I started this chapter with a discussion concerning the role of culturally shared beliefs in explaining culture-specific behavior, and with the assertion that cultural game players use culturally shared beliefs to predict other people's responses rather than to pursue their own values and preferences. This is in sharp contrast to the view of humans as cultural agents. Personal values and preferences of a cultural agent are assumed to be in harmony with the social norms prevalent in the culture. The cultural agents who share culturally relished values and preferences with others encourage each other to see the world in accordance with the culturally shared beliefs. In this perspective, no systematic conflict can exist between the intersubjectively constructed system of meanings on the one hand, and the intrasubjective values and preferences on the other. The first research agenda of the niche construction approach is to demonstrate that this harmonious relationship between the two—personal values and preferences on the one hand, and shared standards of what is normal and natural on the other—is often illusory.

Actually, the discrepancy between the two has been demonstrated by recent findings that individuals' personal values and preferences are not highly consistent with their perception about the values and preferences of the other members of a culture (Fischer, 2006; Hashimoto, in press; Kurman & Ronen-Eilon, 2004; Shteynberg, Gelfand, & Kim, 2009; Wan, Chiu, Tam, et al., 2007; Wan, Torelli, & Chiu, 2010; Zou et al., 2009). In particular, recent studies demonstrated the primacy of intersubjectivity over personal values and preferences in determining culture-specific cognition and behavior. Zou and her colleagues (2009), for example, argue that the fact that people perceive that others share particular beliefs, values, and preferences enables "us to use them to comprehend others' actions and expectations, to anticipate how they will evaluate and respond to our actions, and so on" (p. 582).

Cultural game players who pursue their goals in anticipation of others' actions and reactions can also be cultural agents at the same time, in the sense that their goals can be formed by culturally shared values. However, they differ from cultural agents who simple-mindedly pursue the internalized cultural values and preferences in that they adjust their behavior to the expected reactions of other people to achieve their goals (some of which may be internalized cultural values and preferences). For the cultural game player, expected responses of others to their own action are at least as important as the goals per se in determining what to do to achieve the goals. As shown in Yamagishi's (1988a) earlier study of group-based cooperation, an implicit game player would cooperate in the group only when a monitoring and sanctioning system exists, but not in a social vacuum.

B. Behavior Is Often More Strongly Related to the Perceived Consensus than Private Beliefs and Values

The second research agenda of the niche construction approach is to demonstrate the presence of the instrumental or strategic aspect behind the culture-specific behavior—that is, to demonstrate that cultural difference exists not necessarily in personal values and preferences but often in the beliefs about other people's values and preferences.

1. Cultural Differences Often Exist in Cultural Consensus, Not in Personal Values and Preferences

Zou and her associates (Zou et al., 2009) demonstrate that at least some of the cross-cultural differences in cognition and behavior are more strongly affected by "perceptions of broader societal or cultural consensus ('common sense')"—what people think others would think and do—than their own personal values and preferences. In their first study, Zou et al. demonstrated that Americans were no less collectivistic or no more individualistic than Poles in their personal values and preferences. However, Americans thought that other Americans were individualistic and Poles thought that other Poles were more collectivistic. They also replicated the cross-cultural difference in compliance with different persuasion principles such that Americans were more susceptible to consistency information and less susceptible to social proof than Poles—the difference originally found by Cialdini and his collaborators (Cialdini, Wosinska, Barrett, Butner, & Gornik-Durose, 1999). Finally, they showed that the cross-cultural difference in persuasion principles was mediated by perceived consensual collectivism (i.e., belief that others are collectivistic), but not by their own personal inclination toward collectivistic values and preferences.

Zou and her colleagues further found a similar pattern using different cultural beliefs and behavioral tendencies in their second and third studies. Specifically, they found that the cultural difference in attribution was mediated by perceived consensual belief in dispositionalism, and that the cultural difference in counterfactual thinking was mediated by perceived consensual belief in regulatory focus. In neither case were the cultural differences mediated by the participants' personal dispositionalism or regulatory focus. The meditational role of the perception of other people's beliefs was further demonstrated by a controlled experiment using bilingual/bicultural Chinese participants. In their fourth study, Zou and her colleagues (2009) reported that bicultural Chinese participants' consensual beliefs about dispositional and situational accounts of behavior were affected by the culture of the audience—either an American or Chinese experimenter. Furthermore, they reported that their participants exhibited culture-specific attribution styles (external attribution by Chinese, and internal attribution by Americans) depending on the culture of the audience (i.e., experimenter), implying that participants displayed attribution style that meets the expectations of the audience. Similar findings showed that perceived consensus is a more powerful predictor than personal values and preferences (Fischer, 2006; Fischer et al., 2009; Shteynberg et al., 2009; Wan, Chiu, Tam, et al., 2007; Yamagishi, Hashimoto, & Schug, 2008). Why is perceived consensus more important than personal values and preferences in determining cognition and behavior? Zou and her colleagues (2009) suggest that it is because people acquiesce to what the majority think and behave. For example, bicultural Chinese tend to make more external attributions when they face a Chinese audience than when they face an American audience because they expect that most Chinese expect other Chinese to exhibit more external attributions than Americans.

2. Taking the Role of the Generalized Other

The acquiescence to the perceived majority may look like conformity to the majority, but it is not necessarily so. It can be a result of taking the role of the majority or the *generalized other*, using G. H. Mead's (1934) famous concept. From this perspective, a cultural agent is also a cultural game player. He or she is someone who has internalized the role of the generalized other or the rule of the game. According to Mead (1934), those who have taken the perspective of the generalized other are the game players who adjust their actions to the anticipated actions of the other players who also follow the same rule. The individual who acquiesces to the consensual beliefs, values, and preferences is actually a cultural game player for whom anticipating the responses of the other people is the rule of the game.

The niche construction view of culture that I am advocating in this chapter is based on the understanding that all humans have the aspect of both the cultural agent and the cultural game player. They have more or less internalized culturally endorsed values and goals, and they pursue these goals in the social environment consisting of other people's actions and reactions. Beyond this basic understanding, the niche construction approach further postulates that the rule of the game is not something that is given from outside. The rule is a short hand of the incentive structure consisting of individuals' actions in response to the anticipated actions by others. The beliefs about how others would think and behave provide a foundation for the rule of the game, especially when these beliefs are shared and become self-sustained. The shared beliefs become self-sustained and come to constitute a social reality when the socially wise behavior that is guided by the rule of the game (i.e., the expected responses of others) collectively constitutes the set of incentives for their behavior.

A good (though, not in the moral sense) example is found in speeding, where the rules of the game are determined by how fast most drivers go. Not too many drivers observe a speed limit of 80 km/hr on a freeway when the majority of drivers are going at 120 km/hr. This may be conceptualized as conformity; drivers perceive that the real speed limit on which most drivers agree upon is 120 km/hr, rather than the legal speed limit of 80 km/hr, and so they conform to this agreed-upon speed limit. An alternative view of the same phenomenon is that the incentives for drivers to go over the legal speed limit increase as more and more drivers drive above the legal speed limit. This is because the chance of getting a ticket for driving at, say 100 km/hr, while most drivers are going at 120 km/hr becomes slim, whereas the same risk is much higher when most others are following the legal speed limit of 80 km/hr. In this example, drivers have collectively created incentives to drive above the speed limit, which would not have existed when everyone drove at 80 km/hr.

Another example is the situation represented by the proverb of the standing-out nail. As discussed earlier, this proverb is not simply a description of the normal way of life but also a piece of advice to those who are eager to display their excellence. It is too risky to display one's excellence when others are offended by this showing-off behavior and are likely to undermine those who do it. Furthermore, it is also too risky to praise or endorse someone who displays his excellence, since the admirer of the standing-out nail is also regarded as someone who wants to dominate others. The best strategy in such a situation is *(1)* not to be a standing-out nail, *(2)* to respond negatively to the standing-out nail, and *(3)* to respond negatively to the endorsers of the standing-out nail. To be accepted as a responsible member of a community, one has to join the crowd who despise the standing-out nails and their endorsers.

3. Those Who Choose the Majority Color Pen Are Concerned with Responses from Others

As presented earlier, Zou and her colleagues (2009) successfully demonstrated that some of the cross-cultural differences in cognition and behavior are mediated by perceived consensus of relevant beliefs. Yamagishi and his colleagues' studies of pen choice (Yamagishi et al., 2008; Hashimoto et al., in press, Study 2, in press) and self-effacement (Suzuki & Yamagishi, 2004; Yamagishi et al., 2010) also demonstrated that the seeming "preference" for conformity or self-effacement by the Japanese, at least some of them, may be conceived as socially wise responses to anticipated reactions by others—anticipation based on the culturally shared beliefs. To demonstrate the involuntary nature of the seemingly preference-based conformity among Japanese, Hashimoto, Li, and Yamagishi (in press, Study 2) conducted another study of the choice of the majority as compared to the minority color pen. A sample of 107 residents of Sapporo city in Japan who are over 20 years old and are nonstudents (mean age of 46.9, ranging from 21 to 68 years old; 51 males and 56 females) participated in this study. They were selected from a pool of applicants who responded to an advertisement posted at several major newspapers in Sapporo in the fall of 2007. Since then, they participated in five waves of studies (February, 2008; April, 2008; November, 2008; March, 2009; and November, 2009), each session of which lasted from 4 to 6 hours per day over a few weeks. They were liberally paid to encourage repeated participation (4,000 to 10,000 yen, depending on performance on some tasks). Since this study is still underway, I will present some of the findings from the preliminary data analysis.

Participants in this study responded to two versions of the self-construal scale. Specifically, they filled out Takata's (2000) independent and interdependent self-construal scales in the first and the second waves. The consistency of the participants' responses between the two waves was fairly high—the correlation between the first and the second waves of independence scale was $r = .79$, and the correlation was $r = .74$ for the interdependence scale. In the following analysis, I will present the average responses over the two waves. We also administered Uchida's (2008) interdependence and independence scales (in the fourth wave).

In addition to the self-construal scales mentioned earlier, we included Kramer's (1944) social paranoia scale and Yamagishi and Yamagishi's (1994) social prudence scale.[4] We included these scales because those who score high on these scales are considered to be chronically concerned about how they are perceived and evaluated by others. If the choice of the majority pen in the default situation among Japanese participants reflects their concerns that their choice may invite negative evaluations and responses from others, their tendency to choose a majority pen should be correlated with the degree that they are concerned with negative evaluations from others. Kramer's (1994) social paranoia scale was designed to measure respondents' tendency to construe other people's actions in overpersonalized terms, and their tendency to attribute greater negative intentionality of others' benign behavior directed toward them. We used a short (10-item version) instead of the full (20-item) version, and yet Cronbach's alpha of 0.83 was reasonably high. Yamagishi and Yamagishi's five-item social prudence scale (Cronbach's $\alpha = .72$) measures the responder's belief about the need for prudence in dealing with others, including such items as "One should better pay attention to the vicious side of other people to be successful in life" and "If we assume everyone has the capacity to be malicious, we will not be in trouble." Those who score high on this scale are socially prudent people who are sensitive to the implications of their actions.

---

[4]In Yamagishi and Yamagishi (1994), the scale was called the "caution scale." A better English translation of the original Japanese term *yojin* is prudence, and thus I used the term *social prudence* rather than *caution* in this chapter.

We suspected those who score high on the social paranoia and social prudence scales are the ones who have strong beliefs that they would suffer negative consequences unless they pay sufficient attention to how they would be assessed by others. They are also those who are likely to use the not-offend-other strategy to avoid putting themselves in a socially vulnerable position.

We also embedded a pen-choice study in an unobtrusive way. When participants first arrived at the reception desk for the first wave of the study, they were individually asked to pick up a pen from a cup containing five pens to use during the study and to take home after the study. There were one or two unique color pens and four or three majority color pens in the cup. The proportion of the majority color choosers in the 1:4 condition (39/56 or 70%) was not significantly different from that in the 2:3 condition (32/50 or 64%). Male participants chose the majority pen more frequently (39/51 or 76%) than female participants (32/55 or 58%; $\chi^2(1) = 4.00$, $p < .05$). The choice of the unique color pen was found not to be related to any of the other demographic factors, including age, income, marriage status, perceived social class, and house ownership. Since the proportion of the majority choosers was not significantly different between the two combination (1:4 and 2:3) conditions, I pool the two conditions in the following analyses.

Our data showed that whether the participants chose a minority pen or a majority pen was not related to any of the self-construal scores. We obtained the same result regardless of whether the effect of each scale was tested independently (regardless of whether gender of the participant was included as a control variable) in a logistic regression analysis, or all scales were included in a multiple logistic regression analysis. None of the effects in the series of analyses mentioned earlier came close to even a liberal significance level of .10. In contrast to this, both the social paranoia scale and the social prudence scale had significant effects on the choice of the minority versus majority pen. When social paranoia and social prudence were included separately in the logistic regression, both had a significant effect on the choice of the majority pen (regardless of whether gender was included as a control variable). When both scales were simultaneously included as independent variables, only the social prudence scale had a significant effect. When all six scales, including Takada's and Uchida's scales, social paranoia scale, and social prudence scale, were included as independent variables, only the effect of social prudence remained significant. The choice of the majority pen was particularly prevalent among participants whose social prudence scores were high (87% or 27 of 31 high-prudence participants chose the majority pen, compared to 60% or 27 of 45 medium-prudence participants, and 56%

or 17 of 30 low-prudence participants). The choice of the majority pen was thus shown to be a strategy adopted by socially prudent people.

C. People Anticipate Others' Responses based on the Perceived Consensus

The third research agenda concerns the central premise of the niche construction approach that cultural game players adjust their behavior to the expected responses of other players that are derived from the culturally shared beliefs.

1. Actual Self Is Closer to the Perceived Other's Self Than to the Ideal Self

Hashimoto's study (in press, Study 1) is an example of research pursuing this third agenda. In this study, Hashimoto demonstrated that his participants preferred to be independent rather than interdependent, yet they adjusted their self to meet expectations and evaluations from others, thus showing more interdependence than independence. This was demonstrated by prompting the participants to respond to the Takata's (2000) self-construal scales in two different ways. Participants responded to the scales first, by indicating how well the statements in the scale described themselves (actual self); and second, by indicating how a person whom they aspire to be would respond to those statements (ideal self). Their responses to these questions revealed that their ideal self was more independent (M = 5.35 on the seven-point response scale) than interdependent (M = 4.55). Yet they assessed that their actual self was more interdependent (M = 4.87) than independent (M = 4.15). The same pattern was observed in the second study with another 101 college students. In this second study, they used Uchida's (2008) scales rather than Takata's scales, and the results were almost completely replicated: Participants' ideal self was more independent (M = 3.87 on the five-point response scale) than interdependent (M = 3.31), whereas their actual self was more interdependent (M = 3.59) than independent (M = 3.21). In addition, they were asked to judge how other people would respond to the scale items (consensual self). The participants' perception of other people was more interdependent (M = 3.70) and less independent (M = 2.94) than the participants' actual self. In short, Hashimoto's (in press, Study 2) participants wanted to be an independent rather than interdependent person on the one hand, yet realized that other people were more interdependent than independent. Their actual self was closer to the consensual self than to the ideal self, and so the actual self seems

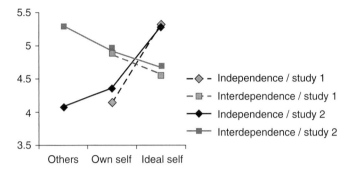

FIGURE 6.4: The average levels of independence and interdependence scales for the actual self, the ideal self, and the consensual self (expected responses by others) by Japanese participants (Hashimoto, in press). Takata's (2000) scales were used in Study 1, and Uchida's (2008) in Study 2. The consensual self was not measured in Study 1. Since Takata's used a seven-point response scale and Uchida used a five-point response scale, the average responses to Uchida's scales in the figure was adjusted to the seven-point scale.

to be a compromise between their ideal self and the consensual self (see Fig. 6.4).

2. I Compromise Because I Know That Others Would Evaluate an Independent Person Negatively

Why was Hashimoto's (in press) participants' actual self closer to the perceived others' self than to their ideal self? Hashimoto's third study provides a clue to this question. In that study, they presented 172 college students with a description of an ideal-typical independent person and an ideal-typical interdependent person, and asked them to judge how positively they would evaluate each person, and how other people would evaluate each person, on a nine-point scale ranging from 1 (= not so good) to 9 (= good). Below are the descriptions of the two types of person used in their study:

Ideal-Typical Independent Person: Person A has his/her own opinions on most issues and openly expresses them. He/she appreciates being independent, different from others, and unique. He/she expresses his/her ideas no matter how people around him/her would think of such ideas.

Ideal-Typical Interdependent Person: Person B often goes along with others when his/her opinions are in conflict with the others'. His/her priority is to preserve harmony with other people and to stay in his/her own place. He/she often changes his/her attitudes and behaviors in accordance with the nature of the situation and with whom he/she is interacting.

Participants in this study personally evaluated the independent person more positively ($M = 5.53$, $SD = 1.14$) than the interdependent person ($M = 4.49$, $SD = 1.51$). On the other hand, they thought that other people would evaluate the interdependent person more positively ($M = 5.05$, $SD = 1.22$) than the independent person ($M = 3.73$, $SD = 1.35$). Hashimoto (Study 3) further asked their participants whether certain characteristics would describe the ideal-typical interdependent person or the ideal-typical independent person on a seven-point scale that ranged from −3 (descriptive of the independent person) to +3 (descriptive of the interdependent person). Participants perceived that the independent person was more "honest" (−2.16) and "trustworthy" (−1.16), but he/she was more likely to be "disliked" (+1.67) by others than the interdependent person. Similarly, they perceived the interdependent person to be more "concerned about own reputation" (+2.34), "cunning" (+1.31), but more likely to "get along well with others" (+1.22), "have more friends" (+0.94), "receive help from others" (+0.92), and be "liked by others" (+0.80) than the independent person. In short, they personally admired the virtues of the independent person such as honesty and trustworthiness, but they were afraid that being independent would entice others to dislike them and be unfriendly toward them. These findings indicated that the Japanese participants in this study wanted to be independent but realized that being independent is not socially wise in a Japanese context. They expected others to be interdependent and believed that acting in an interdependent manner is the socially wise course of action in dealing with interdependent others around them who evaluate interdependence positively (see Fig. 6.5).

D. Default Strategies Depend on the Anticipated Responses of Others

Cultural game players adjust their behavior to the anticipated responses of others, but this process is often carried out automatically without requiring conscious calculations. The concept of "default strategy" emphasized this automatic nature of the decision making. The default strategy is adopted by cultural game players by default, until they face salient cues indicating the inappropriateness of using the default strategy. The fourth research agenda of

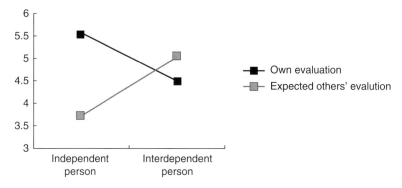

FIGURE 6.5: Evaluation of the typical-independent person and the typical-interdependent person by the participants themselves and the expected evaluation by others.

the niche construction approach is to demonstrate the operation of the default strategy.

1. Ingroup Favoritism in the Minimal Group

The concept of default strategy was first developed in the study of ingroup favoring behavior in minimal groups. Let me first review a series of studies by Yamagishi and his colleagues in which the concept was developed.

Group-based trust and cooperation are often believed to constitute a core aspect of collectivism (Chen, Brockner, & Chen, 2002; Triandis, 1995). Members of a collectivist culture are believed to cooperate more with members of the same group and to trust members of their own group more strongly than outgroup members. However, the studies by Yamagishi (1988a, 1988b) presented earlier in this chapter demonstrated that this is not necessarily true, especially in the context of a social vacuum. Those studies indicate that such behavior is supported by the assurance system that monitors and sanctions individuals, rather than by the individual's personal preferences for the welfare of the group members. In this section, I will present findings from a series of minimal group experiments by Yamagishi and his colleagues demonstrating that ingroup favoring behavior does not occur in a social vacuum, and that ingroup favoring behavior in minimal groups can be conceived as a response to what group members expect from other members.

Minimal groups are pure categorical groups devoid of interpersonal interactions of any kind. Most minimal groups are set up in the laboratory by assigning participants into two groups based on a trivial criterion such as the preference of paintings. Despite the lack of interpersonal interactions or interdependence of interests, participants often treat members of their own group more favorably than outgroup members (Tajfel, Billi, Bundy, & Flament, 1971). Social identity and self-categorization theorists argued that identification with a social category is the underlying psychological mechanism for the ingroup favoritism observed in this "social vacuum." In this tradition, ingroup favoritism is argued to reflect a motivation to create and maintain positive distinctiveness for the group with which one is identified (Brewer, 1981; Brown, 2000; Tajfel & Turner, 1986; Turner, 1985). Furthermore, categorization of self with others leads to perceptions of the self as an interchangeable exemplar of the group (Turner, Hogg, Oakes, Reicher, & Wetherell, 1987). Through this process of depersonalization, others' interests become one's own interests (Bourhis, Moise, Perreault, Perreault, & Senecal, 1997), and one is motivated to evaluate positively, to bestow favors on, and cooperate with other ingroup members.

An alternative view of ingroup favoritism in the minimal group situation has been proposed by Yamagishi and his colleagues (Foddy, Platow, & Yamagishi, 2009; Jin & Yamagishi, 1997; Jin, Yamagishi, & Kiyonari, 1996; Karp, Jin, Yamagishi, & Shinotsuka, 1993; Kiyonari, Tanida, & Yamagishi, 2000; Kiyonari & Yamagishi, 2004; Mifune, Hashimoto, & Yamagishi, 2010; Yamagishi, 2007, 2009b; Yamagishi, Jin, & Kiyonari, 1999; Yamagishi, Jin, & Miller, 1998; Yamagishi & Kiyonari, 2000; Yamagishi & Mifune, 2008, 2009; Yamagishi, Terai, Kiyonari, Mifune, & Kanazawa, 2007; Yamagishi et al., 2005; Yamagishi et al., 2008), according to which ingroup favoritism observed in minimal groups is a default strategy designed to enhance individuals' fitness in the group situation. They argue that the collectivistic practice of ingroup favoritism is generated and supported by the shared understanding that people generally expect others to favor ingroup members, and that violating this expectation would endanger one's reputation within the group.

In support of this argument, Yamagishi and his colleagues demonstrated that in a social vacuum, ingroup favoring behavior would disappear. They argued that the original minimal groups unwittingly included indirect reciprocity, which worked as a cue for a collectivistic group. The first of this series of studies was an experiment by Karp et al. (1993) in which they successfully replicated the ingroup favoring reward allocation reported in Tajfel et al.'s (1971) original study. In addition to this replication condition, they added another, truly minimal group condition that they termed the "unilateral dependency" condition. In this new condition, the participant allocated a fixed amount of money between one ingroup member and one outgroup member as in the replication condition. The purpose of this condition was to eliminate the possibility that the participant would be a recipient of reward allocation by other ingroup members—the possibility that existed in Tajfel et al.'s (1971) original study. Karp and his colleagues (1993) reasoned that the expectation that they are treated by other ingroup members favorably would prompt participants to reciprocate in a generalized manner. When this possibility was eliminated by paying the participant a predetermined amount of money, the ingroup favoring reward allocation completely disappeared. The same finding was replicated by Jin, Yamagishi, and Kiyonari (1996). What induced participants in these studies to behave in a collectivistic manner, treating ingroup members more favorably than outgroup members, was shown to be the expectation that other ingroup members would behave in the ingroup-favoring manner, rather than the intrinsic preference for the welfare of their own group members.

A similar conclusion was drawn from a series of prisoner's dilemma game (Jin & Yamagishi, 1997; Kiyonari, 2002; Yamagishi & Kiyonari, 2000) and dictator game (Yamagishi & Mifune, 2008) studies utilizing the minimal group setting. In those studies, the game player cooperated more with an ingroup member than an outgroup member *only when* he/she knew that his/her partner was also aware of their respective group membership. Whether the game partner was an ingroup member or an outgroup member per se did not affect the player's cooperation level when the partner was not aware of it. If the higher level of cooperation with the ingroup is based on preference for the ingroup (i.e., intrinsic love of the ingroup), whether the partner identifies the player as an ingroup member or an outgroup member should not matter. Contrary to this identity-theoretic prediction, participants in these studies cooperated with an ingroup member more than outgroup member when and only when they expected that the ingroup partner would recognize them as an ingroup member and treat them favorably. When the partner does not know that the player is an ingroup member, the player cannot expect a favorable treatment from the ingroup partner. In short, results of these studies demonstrated that the ingroup favoritism often observed in the minimal group experiments can be conceived as a default strategy for reciprocating a favorable treatment expected from other ingroup members.

The same pattern was replicated when the participant's nationality, instead of the minimal group, was used as groups (Yamagishi et al., 2005), and when participants were Australians (Yamagishi et al., 2005) and New Zealanders (Yamagishi et al., 2008) rather than Japanese. Furthermore, in a similar trust game experiment, Suzuki, Konno, and Yamagishi (2007) demonstrated that participants trusted ingroup members more than outgroup members in the common knowledge condition in which their partner (trustees) knew that the participant knew that the trustee was a member of their own group. The same result was successfully replicated by Foddy, Platow, and Yamagishi (2009) using Australians as participants and by using colleges and academic departments as groups.

In all of these studies, participants cooperated more with an ingroup member than with an outgroup member, or trusted an ingroup member more than an outgroup member, only when both the participants and their partner mutually shared the knowledge of their respective group membership. No ingroup favoring behavior occurred when participants knew that their partner was an ingroup member, yet their partner did not know which group they belonged to. Yamagishi and his colleagues argue that the ingroup-favoring behavior often observed in minimal groups (and only in the common knowledge condition in which both participants and their partner mutually knew their respective group membership) was produced by their default strategy designed to minimize the risk of incurring a bad reputation among members of their own group.

Such default strategy is used mainly when participants are identified by their partners as a member of the same group. When they are not identified by their partners as members of the same group, their concern for reputation diminishes and so does the ingroup-favoring behavior. The shared belief that others would appreciate ingroup-favoring behavior and expect everyone to engage in this collectivistic practice was critical for participants to actually engage in ingroup-favoring behavior.

Yamagishi and his colleagues' conclusion was further supported by a recent experiment by Mifune, Hashimoto, and Yamagishi (2010). Haley and Fessler (2005) demonstrated that display of stylized eyes on a computer screen enhanced the altruistic behavior of a dictator toward his recipient in a dictator game, and they argued that the stylized eyes enhanced altruism through enhanced concern for reputation. Based on this finding, Mifune and his colleagues (2009) speculated that the presence of stylized eyes would have the same effect on ingroup-favoring behavior as the effect of the commonality of knowledge—they both enhance participants' concerns for reputation. They thus predicted that the presence of stylized eyes would engender ingroup-favoring behavior even in the private knowledge condition in which no ingroup-favoring behavior was observed in the earlier studies. This prediction was clearly supported by their dictator game experiment with minimal groups.

Eyes had the same within-group cooperation-enhancing effect as that of the knowledge commonality manipulation.

These findings consistently demonstrated that the collectivistic practice of ingroup favoritism is generated and supported by the shared understanding that people generally expect others to favor ingroup members, and that violating this expectation would endanger one's reputation within the group, rather than by the intrinsic preference for the welfare of the ingroup members, as commonly understood in the collectivism-individualism literature.

2. Culture of Honor as a Social Niche

The findings presented in the earlier section indicate that Japanese participants expected others to be more interdependent than themselves. Furthermore, participants expected others to expect people to be interdependent. These beliefs provided them with incentives to present themselves as an interdependent person and behave in an interdependent manner. And their actions following these incentives would constitute the same incentives for others. This cycle of incentive-following behaviors producing the incentives for others is the mechanism through which socially wise behaviors generate the environment under which the very behaviors are maintained as socially wise behaviors. Demonstrating this circular relationship between incentive-following behaviors and the production of incentives—that is, niche construction—constitutes the core of the research activities by the niche construction approach.

One example of such niche construction processes is found in the formation and maintenance of "culture of honor" discussed by Nisbett and Cohen (1996). Culture of honor is found in various parts of the world where people have to defend themselves, their family, and their livelihood on their own without much help from the government, such as in the areas where people depend on herding for their livelihood (Daly & Wilson, 1988; Nisbett & Cohen, 1996). The central theme of the culture of honor is to earn a reputation for being tough and determined to defend one's property and integrity. For this purpose, one has to send costly signals of his or her determination and toughness. That is, "to maintain credible power of deterrence, the individual must project a stance of willingness to commit mayhem and to risk wounds or death for himself" (Nisbett & Cohen, 1996, p. xv). Being sensitive to insults and responding violently to challenges to one's integrity is an adaptive strategy in the ecology of herding.

Nisbett and Cohen (1996) traces the origin of the culture of honor in the contemporary American South to the tradition of herdsmen who immigrated from Scotland and Ireland. These herdsmen brought the culture of honor originally developed in the herding societies when they immigrated to the South. A question still remains: How does the culture originating from the ecology of herding still remain and prevail in a new ecology of the contemporary American South? One possible answer to this question is that it is through the process of psychological self-fulfilling prophecy, as discussed earlier. Once honor became a culturally endorsed virtue, people encouraged each other to hold onto the virtue. People were praised for being tough and acting violently, and they despised those who were weak and yielded to the demands of others. Children raised in the South still internalize such virtues of toughness and find pride in being tough.

Five years after the publication of Nisbett & Cohen (1996), Cohen (2001) expanded his explanation of the continued prevalence of the culture of honor in the contemporary South to include the sociological version of the self-fulfilling prophecy. In short, he claimed that the culture of honor continued beyond the original ecology of herding because it formed an equilibrium in the game theoretic sense. That is, culture of honor provides a shared belief that people are tough and that the weak will be taken advantage of. This shared belief convinces the Southerners that they will be taken advantage of if they do not act firmly. And, insofar as the majority of people act on the belief, those who are more rational and agreeable are regarded as wimps and are victimized by the majority. This creates the reality in which the tough people prevail and the more accommodating people are exploited, further strengthening the belief that one has to be tough to prevail in the society. The belief and the incentives sustain each other. In other words, culture of honor prevails through an equilibrium of shared beliefs and incentives.

Vandello, Cohen, and Ransom's (2008) study points to the sociological nature of the self-fulfilling prophecy of violence in the South. They argue that the Southern men tend to act in a violent manner as a means of impression management (i.e., as a socially wise way of presenting oneself to others). In their study, Vandello and his colleagues first demonstrated that Southerners and Northerners were not different in their responses to scenarios in which they faced a challenge from others, but Southern men tended to overestimate aggressiveness of others. They further found that Southern men were more likely than Northern men to perceive others as provoking aggression when witnessing interpersonal conflicts. Based on these findings, Vandello and his colleagues argued that the consensual beliefs of the Southern men that other men are aggressive encourage them to behave in an aggressive manner, thus perpetuating the belief and the aggressive behavior that individual Southern men do not personally prefer. They concluded that "Through a self-fulfilling prophecy, expectations of violence can create violence even if neither side had any private aggressive inclinations to begin with" (Vandello et al., 2008, p. 174).

E. Default Strategies Collectively Create the Incentives that Encourage People to Follow the Same Strategies

So far, we have demonstrated *(1)* that individuals' private values and preferences do not always coincide with their perception of what others value and prefer, *(2)* behavior is often more strongly related to the perceived consensus than private beliefs and values, *(3)* people anticipate others' responses based on the perceived consensus, and *(4)* the use of default strategies such as the not-offend-others strategy is based on the (often implicitly) anticipated responses of others. These lead us to the last of the five assertions I proposed earlier: People who respond to expected responses of others jointly create the incentives or the rule of the game that they individually follow. We need evidence of the last assertion to complete the process of niche construction—the use of default strategies such as the not-offend-others strategy collectively creates incentives that encourage people to follow the same strategies.

To provide empirical evidence for the last assertion is difficult, since it requires us to demonstrate the fact that the individuals' micro cognitions and behaviors collectively generate the macro, social niche as a set of self-sustaining incentives. This process constitutes the core of the niche construction approach, or the analysis of micro-macro dynamics of the cultural construction of reality. Yamagishi's (1986) study of group-based cooperation is one of the few studies that are directly addressing this last step. Yamagishi argued and demonstrated, first, that the presence of a monitoring and sanctioning system reduces the level of individuals' general trust and promotes the belief that people are not willing to cooperate unless controlled by an institution. This belief that people are not willing to cooperate unless others' cooperation is guaranteed by a social system, in turn, motivates them to set up the social system to monitor and control behaviors. In the experiment conducted by Yamagishi (1986), low-trusters (as identified by their responses to the general trust scale) in fact invested more money in setting up such a monitoring system. This completes the cycle of the belief that people are not trustworthy (lack of trust) and thus spending the effort to establish a monitoring system. That is, those who do not trust people work harder to establish a monitoring and sanctioning system, and the presence of such a system further reduces their level of trust to those who are not under control of the system.

Yamagishi, Cook, and Watabe's (1998) study as well as Yamagishi's other earlier studies (e.g., Yamagishi, 1988a, 1988b, 1988c; Yamagishi & Yamagishi, 1994) provide further examples of the micro-macro dynamics. In Yamagishi, Cook, and Watabe's (1998) study, they first asserted that societies characterized by the prevalence of strong social control enforced by strong commitment relations prevent general trust from developing beyond those relations. As shown earlier, this assertion was supported by the results of large-scale cross-national attitude surveys, and of the cross-societal experiments by Yamagishi (1988a, 1988b) reported earlier. Using our terminology, a collectivist social niche engenders a set of beliefs of low general trust, represented by a well-known Japanese proverb, "everyone is a thief"—the belief that we are safe when we are surrounded by strong ties, but once we get out of this safe port, the outer world is a social jungle. This belief that others are not trustworthy outside the closed relations makes people further stick with such closed relations and groups. That is, the closed nature of groups in the collectivist society prevents general trust from developing beyond such closed groups on the one hand, and the lack of general trust prevents people from leaving the closed groups into the social jungle outside on the other hand. Both the closed nature of social groups and the beliefs of low general trust give support to each other and produce collectivist social niche—closed groups in which people monitor each other and control each other's behavior.

What Yamagishi and his colleagues (1998) demonstrated is the micro to macro link in the whole cycle; the lack of trust makes individuals establish and stick with a closed circle of people bound by strong commitment relations. In their first study, Yamagishi and his colleagues (1998) demonstrated through a trading experiment that both Japanese and American participants formed committed relations with past trading partners who had never cheated before. That is, participants in this study tended to keep trading with their previous trading partners even when they received a better offer from a new partner whose trustworthiness had not been established, especially when the risk of being cheated is high. In the second study, they further demonstrated that the tendency to form strong ties with safe partners was stronger among low-trusters who scored below average on Yamagishi and Yamagishi's (1994) general trust scale than among high-trusters. The findings are examples of the micro processes (i.e., differences in general trust) that generate the macro structure characterizing the East Asian type of society consisting of the network of strong ties as compared to the more loosely connected Western social structure.

V. CONCLUSION: MUTUAL CONSTRUCTION OF MIND AND ECOLOGY

Humans think, communicate, and behave in particular manners to adapt to a particular social ecology; by doing so, they collectively create, maintain, and change the ecology that I call a social niche. The social niche consists of behaviors of people who are responding to others' behaviors, directly or indirectly. One important feature of a social niche is that it determines the consequences—others' responses—of individuals' behavior. Furthermore, it gives rise to a set of beliefs (or a network of knowledge, using Hong's (2009) terminology) about human nature and how the world functions. And, most importantly, a social niche is a total set of observable regularities in the way people actually behave. These regularities become stabilized when they provide incentives for people to behave in the way consistent with the regularities.

In short, the niche construction approach analyzes how people induce each other by behaving in particular ways themselves. I have presented a few examples of how this approach explains cultural differences in behavior, but how successfully this approach can be applied to other differences has to be empirically demonstrated in future research. The best strategy for testing the success of the niche construction account of cultural differences is to examine whether the cultural differences persist in a social vacuum—in a situation in which participants can choose their behavior free of any social concern. When the difference disappears in a social vacuum (as in the case of the last-choice condition in the pen-choice experiment), the next step is to identify the consequences (actual or expected) of the behavior that work as incentives. The final stage is to logically specify, and empirically test, the ways the consequences function to induce people to take (or avoid) particular behaviors.

It should be noted that the niche construction approach presented in this chapter does not aim to provide a comprehensive understanding of culture. Instead, it aims to provide a new perspective that might enrich our understanding of culture-specific psychology and behavior. It hopes to provide the arsenal of cultural psychology a new and potentially powerful weapon to analyze how humans create culture on the one hand, and are influenced by culture on the other. One noteworthy advantage of adding the niche construction approach to the arsenal of cultural psychology is its capacity to connect with the social sciences, particularly social sciences informed by game theory, which is on the road to the theoretical backbone for the mainstream social sciences, including economics and political science.

The niche construction approach shares the understanding with the mainstream cultural psychology that even some of the "fundamental" psychological functioning is shaped by culturally shared beliefs. It seems natural, for example, for those who have the belief that humans are independent agents driven by internal factors such as motivations, values, and beliefs to direct their attention to such internal factors of the target person when they explain or predict that person's behavior. This will lead them to overlook external factors as the driving force of the target's behavior, resulting in a cognitive bias such as the fundamental attribution error. In contrast, those who have a different belief that humans seek to have harmonious relations with others will direct their attention to the expectations and wishes of people around them, and not to the internal factors of the target, when they explain and predict the target's behavior; this will make them less vulnerable to the fundamental attribution error.

Having agreed on these points, a question still remains: Where do these beliefs come from? Mainstream cultural psychologists posit that the beliefts came from the ecology of the area in which a particular culture emerged. For example, Nisbett and Cohen (1996) argue that culture of honor emerged as an adaptation to the ecology of herding. Similarly, Nisbett (2003) argues that the holistic thinking characteristic of East Asians has its root in the ecology of rice cultivation in ancient China that required collective effort to maintain irrigation systems, whereas the analytic thinking characteristic of Westerners has its root in the ecology of fishing and trading among ancient Greeks. Here, Nisbett seems to agree with the niche constructionist that the mind is a tool for adapting to the particular ecology.

Nevertheless, Nisbett (2003) argues that the mind developed as a tool for adaptation to the ecology in an ancient time, and that was the only time it occurred. Once the mind acquired the basic architecture useful for adaptation in the ancient ecology, the mind has stayed in captivity since then within the prison of culture. Changes in ecology since that time failed to affect the basic architecture of the mind. In contrast to this "imprinting" theory of adaptation to ecology, the niche construction approach assumes that the process of adaptation to ecology has always taken place throughout human history.

Ancient Chinese and Greeks are not the only people who faced challenges of ecology for their survival and procreation. There is no reason to assume that people who live in the contemporary world of globalization are free of the challenges to adapt to this ever-changing world. An interesting example of the contemporary challenges to new ecology is illustrated by Chen, Cen, Li, and He (2005), who found that shy school children were more adaptive than expressive children in China in 1990, whereas this relationship between shyness and adaptation was completely reversed by 2002, ostensibly reflecting the need for being expressive in the age of globalization.

It is noteworthy that the similar criticism is being directed to the mainstream evolutionary biologists and evolutional psychologists by niche constructionists in biology (Olding-Smee et al., 2003). Olding-Smee and colleagues, for example, criticize that the mainstream evolutionary biologists assume that the environment to which organisms adapt is static—evolution is considered a one-way street, in which organisms adapt to the environment, which is not affected by the organisms. Niche constructionists consider this a two-way street; organisms adapt to the environment, and the evolved features of the organisms affect the very environment they face, as illustrated in the example of a beaver's dam. They argue that evolution is a dynamic process through which both organisms and the environment interact to constitute a niche. Here, I would repeat my argument presented in the introduction section of this chapter that the process of niche construction plays a much more central role among humans. Dynamic constructivists in cultural psychology (Hong, 2009; Hong & Chiu, 2001; Hong, Morris, Chiu, & Benet-Martinez, 2000) who define culture as networks of knowledge (which I call "beliefs") share a similar view about the dynamic construction of culture and social ecology. For example, Hong (2009), citing historian Ray Huang's (1997) work, argues that Confucian teachings were adopted and disseminated to consolidate Chinese solidarity against the fierce northerners, who posed threats of invasion to the ancient Chinese kingdoms and empires. A belief system (or networks of knowledge) such as Confucian teachings thus was developed to consolidate the Chinese empire against fierce enemies from the north. At the same time, it contributed to the construction of a particular political system, under which Confucius scholars-bureaucrats played critical roles. The belief system and the political system helped sustain each other to constitute a social niche.

The dynamic nature of adaptation to ecology, however, does not imply that the adaptive behavior (and the nature of the mind that produces adaptive behavior) is in the state of constant change. A social niche can be in equilibrium. Equilibrium is a situation in which people have no incentives to change. Since people who follow the incentives do not change their behavior, the incentives themselves (consisting of their behavior) stay the same. As a result, the niche is maintained over time. Such a stability of beliefs and behavior seems to imply that the system of beliefs sustains itself by its own internal consistency. From the niche constructionist perspective, the stability of the belief system has its ultimate foundation in the stability of the incentives. Insofar as the incentives stay intact, attempts to change beliefs will often be futile. Once the incentives have changed, it is difficult to keep the belief system intact; this is what numerous people currently facing a globalizing world are experiencing.

Let me end this chapter by repeating my argument about how cultural agents and cultural game players construct social reality. Cultural agents encourage each other to feel, think, and behave in the way that they believe natural and normal—that is, through the psychologically construed process of self-fulfilling prophecy. We encourage others to feel, think, and behave in the culturally endorsed way and, at the same time, we are encouraged by other members of the culture to feel, think, and behave in the same manner. Cultural agents feel, think, and behave in accordance with the shared beliefs about how humans should and do feel, think, and behave because they mutually encourage each other to do so. Through this process, shared beliefs become a social reality.

For cultural game players, the perception that the beliefs are shared makes it possible for them to anticipate other people's responses to their own behavior. When the anticipated responses are negative, they would refrain from engaging in that behavior. When the anticipated responses are positive, they would seek to engage in that behavior. The anticipated responses thus function as incentives for engaging in or not engaging in that behavior. By behaving in accordance with these incentives, we provide incentives for others to take certain actions, resulting in another form of social reality—that is, a social niche.

These two processes are undoubtedly not mutually exclusive, and one process is likely to facilitate the other. First, the likelihood that others will respond in a particular manner increases when people encourage each other to feel, think, and behave in a culturally endorsed way. Second, people would be more encouraged to endorse a certain way of feeling, thinking, and behaving as being proper and natural when the consequences of feeling, thinking, and behaving in such a way are more positive than negative. The harmonious relationship between the two processes, however, could be disrupted particularly in the period of cultural and/or social transitions. Changes in one process may facilitate or hinder changes in the other. Analytically separating the two processes will help cultural psychologists to identify important issues that have not been discovered when the two were not clearly distinguished. The huge gap between the ideal self and the actual self among the Japanese participants reported earlier in this chapter (Hashimoto, in press) suggests that Japanese people are currently facing a new set of incentives that are conducive to the independent lifestyle, yet the shared beliefs that others are still thinking and behaving in the collectivistic manner discourage them from being and acting in the way that they personally prefer and value. Japanese people dream of being standing-out nails, but they are still afraid of the shadow of the hammer hitting standing-out nails. The macro change will take place in the form of an equilibrium shift when and only when they realize that the hammer does not exist anymore.

ACKNOWLEDGMENTS

I would like to express my deep appreciation to Michele Gelfand, Chi-Yue Chiu, and Ying-Yi Hong for their encouragement and valuable suggestions for writing this chapter; Victoria Yeung and Joanna Schug for their comments and suggestions on earlier drafts; my young collaborators, including Hirofumi Hashimoto, Yang Li, Nobuhiro Mifune, Yutaka Horita, Haruto Takagishi, Mizuho Shinada, Chisato Takahashi, Toko Kiyonari, Naoto Suzuki, Shigehito Tanida, and many others who helped me develop ideas and conduct experiments; and my colleagues in various departments at Hokkaido University for letting me recruit participants for some of the studies reported in this chapter.

REFERENCES

Adams, G. (2005). The cultural grounding of personal relationship: Enemyship in North American and West African worlds. *Journal of Personality and Social Psychology*, *88*, 948–968.

Alicke, M. D. (1985). Global self-evaluation as determined by the desirability and controllability of trait adjectives. *Journal of Personality and Social Psychology*, *49*, 1621–1630.

Alicke, M. D., Klotz, M. L., Breitenbecher, D. L., Yurak, T. J., & Vredenburg, D. S. (1995). Personal contact, individuation, and the better-than-average effect. *Journal of Personality and Social Psychology*, *68*, 804–825.

Aoki, M. (2001). *Toward a comparative institutional analysis*. Cambridge, MA: MIT Press.

Bond, M. H., Leung, K., & Wan, K. C. (1982). The social impact of self-effacing attributions: The Chinese case. *Journal of Social Psychology*, *118*, 157–166.

Bourhis, R. Y., Moise, L. C, Perreault, S., Perreault, S., & Senecal, S. (1977). Towards an interactive acculturation model: A social psychological approach. *International Journal of Psychology*, 32, 369–386.

Bowers, K. (1973). Situationism in psychology: An analysis and a critique. *Psychological Review*, 80, 307–3036.

Brewer, M. B. (1981). Ethnocentrism and its role in interpersonal trust. In M.G. Brewer & B. Collins (Eds.), *Scientific inquiry in the social sciences* (pp. 214–231). San Francisco: Jossey Bass.

Brown, R. (2000). Social identity theory: Past achievements, current problems and future challenges. *European Journal of Social Psychology*, 30, 745–778.

Chen, Y., Brockner, J., & Chen, X. (2002). Individual-collective primacy and ingroup favoritism: Enhancement and protection effects. *Journal of Experimental Social Psychology*, 38, 482–491.

Chen, X., Cen, G., Li, D., & He, Y. (2005). Social functioning and adjustment in Chinese children: The imprint of historical time. *Child Development*, 76, 182–195.

Cialdini, R. B., Wosinska, W., Barrett, D. W., Butner, J., & Gornik-Durose, M. (1999). Compliance with a request in two cultures: The differential influence of social proof and commitment/consistency on collectivists and individualists. *Personality and Social Psychology Bulletin*, 25, 1242–1253.

Cohen, D. (2001). Cultural variation: Considerations and implications. *Psychological Bulletin*, 127, 451–471.

Daly, M., & Wilson, M. (1988). *Homicide*. Hawthorne, NY: Aldine de Gruyter.

Dore, R. P. (1990). *Will the 21st century be the age of individualism?* Tokyo: Simul Press.

Dunning, D., Meyerowitz, J., & Holzberg, A. D. (1989). Ambiguity and self-evaluation: The role of idiosyncratic trait definitions in self-serving assessments of ability. *Journal of Personality and Social Psychology*, 57, 1082–1090.

Ekehammar, B. (1974). Interactionism in personality from a historical perspective. *Psychological Bulletin*, 81, 1026–1048.

Fischer, R. (2006). Congruence and functions of personal and cultural values: Do my values reflect my culture's values? *Personality and Social Psychology Bulletin*, 32, 1419–1431.

Fischer, R., Ferreira, M. C., Assmar, E., Redford, P., Harb, C., Glazer, S., Cheng, B. S., Jiang, D. Y., Wong, C., Kumar, N., Kärtner, J., Hofer, J., & Achoui, M. (2009). Individualism-collectivism as descriptive norms: Development of a subjective norm approach to culture measurement. *Journal of Cross-Cultural Psychology*, 40, 187–213.

Foddy, M., Platow, M., & Yamagishi, T. (2009). Group-based trust in strangers: The roles of stereotypes and expectations. *Psychological Science*, 20, 419–422.

Gelfand, M. J., Nishii, L. H., Holcombe, K., Dyer, N., Ohbuchi, K., & Fukumo, M. (2001). Cultural influences on cognitive representations of conflict: Interpretations of conflict episodes in the U.S. and Japan. *Journal of Applied Psychology*, 86, 1059–1074.

Gelfand, M. J., & Realo, A. (1999). "Individualism-collectivism and accountability in intergroup negotiation." *Journal of Applied Psychology*, *84*, 721–773.

Gigerenzer, G., Todd, P. M., & ABC Research Group. (1999). *Simple heuristics that make us smart*. New York: Oxford University Press.

Greif, A. (1989). Reputation and coalitions in Medieval trade: Evidence on the Maghribi traders. *The Journal of Economic History*, *49*, 857–882.

Greif, A. (1994). Cultural beliefs and the organization of society: A historical and theoretical reflection on collectivist and individualist societies. *The Journal of Political Economy*, *102*(5), 912–950.

Haley, K. J., & Fessler, D. M. T. (2005). Nobody's watching? Subtle cues affect generosity in an anonymous economic game. *Evolution and Human Behavior*, *26*, 245–256.

Hashimoto, H., Li, Y., & Yamagishi, T. (In Press). Beliefs and preferences in cultural agents and cultural game players. *Asian Journal of Social Psychology*.

Hashimoto, H. (In Press). Interdependence as a set of self-sustaining beliefs. Japanese Journal of Experimental Social Psychology. (In Japanese with an English abstract).

Heine, S., Kitayama, S., & Lehman, D. (2001). Cultural differences in self-evaluation: Japanese readily accept negative self-relevant information. *Journal of Cross-Cultural Psychology*, *32*, 434–443.

Heine, S. J., Kitayama, S., Lehman, D. R., Takata, T., Ide, E., Leung, C., & Matsumoto, H. (2001). Divergent consequences of success and failure in Japan and North America: An investigation of self-improving motivation. *Journal of Personality and Social Psychology*, *81*, 599–615.

Heine, S. J., Takata, T., & Lehman, D. R. (2000). Beyond self-presentation: Evidence for self-criticism among Japanese. *Personality and Social Psychology Bulletin*, *26*, 71–78.

Hofstede, G. (1980). *Culture's consequences*. Beverly Hills, CA: Sage.

Hong, Y. (2009). A dynamic constructivist approach to culture: Moving from describing culture to explaining culture. In R. Wyer, C.-y. Chiu, & Y. Hong (Eds.), *Understanding culture: Theory, research and application* (pp. 3–23). New York: Psychology Press.

Hong, Y-y., & Chiu, C-y. (2001). Toward a paradigm shift: From cross-cultural differences in social-cognition to social-cognitive mediation of cultural differences. *Social Cognition*, *19*, 181–196.

Hong, Y. Y., Morris, M. W., Chiu, C. Y., & Benet-Martinez, V. (2000). Multicultural minds: A dynamic constructivist approach to culture and cognition. *American Psychologist*, *55*, 709–720.

Huang, R. (1997). *China: A macro history*. New York: M. E. Sharpe.

Jin, N., & Yamagishi, T. (1997). Group heuristics in social dilemma. *Japanese Journal of Social Psychology*, *12*, 190–198.

Jin, N., Yamagishi, T., & Kiyonari, T. (1996). Bilateral dependency and the minimal group paradigm (In Japanese). *The Japanese Journal of Psychology*, *67*, 77–85.

Karp, D., Jin, N., Yamagishi, T., & Shinotsuka, H. (1993). Raising the minimum in the minimal group paradigm. *Japanese Journal of Experimental Social Psychology*, *32*, 231–240.

Kim, H., & Markus, H. R. (1999). Deviance or uniqueness, harmony or conformity? A cultural analysis. *Journal of Personality and Social Psychology*, *77*, 785–800.

Kitayama, S. (1998). *Self and emotion: An approach from cultural psychology* (In Japanese). Tokyo: Kyoritsu Shuppan.

Kitayama, S. (2010). Frontiers in social and behavioral sciences: Toward the new history of frontiers (In Japanese). In H. Ishiguro & T. Kameda (Eds.), *Culture and practice: Looking for the fundamental sociality of the mind* (pp. 199–244). Tokyo: Shinyosha.

Kitayama, S., & Karasawa, M. (1995). Self: A cultural psychological perspective (In Japanese). *Japanese Journal of Experimental Social Psychology*, *35*, 133–163.

Kitayama, S., & Markus, H. R. (Eds.). (1994). *Emotion and culture: Empirical studies of mutual influence*. Washington, DC: American Psychological Association.

Kitayama, S., Markus, H. R., Matsumoto, H., & Norasakkunkit, V. (1997). Individual and collective processes in the construction of the self: Self-enhancement in the United States and self-criticism in Japan. *Journal of Personality and Social Psychology*, *72*, 1245–1267.

Kiyonari, T. (2002). Expectations of a generalized exchange system and ingroup favoritism: An experimental study of bounded reciprocity. *Japanese Journal of Psychology*, *73*, 1–9.

Kiyonari, T., Tanida, S., & Yamagishi, T. (2000). Social exchange and reciprocity: Confusion or a heuristic? *Evolution and Human Behavior*, *21*(6), 411–427.

Kiyonari, T., & Yamagishi, T. (2004). Ingroup cooperation and the social exchange heuristic. In R. Suleiman, D. V. Budescu, I. Fischer, & D. M. Messick (Eds.), *Contemporary psychological research on social dilemmas* (pp. 269–286). Cambridge, England: Cambridge University Press.

Kramer, R. M. (1994). The sinister attribution error: Paranoid cognition and collective distrust in organizations. *Motivation and Emotion*, *18*, 199–230.

Kurman, J., & Ronen-Eilon, C. (2004). Lack of knowledge of a culture's social axioms and adaptation difficulties among immigrants. *Journal of Cross-Cultural Psychology*, *35*, 192–208.

Lepper, M. R., & Green, D. (1975). Turning play into work: Effects of adult surveillance and extrinsic rewards on children's intrinsic motivation. *Journal of Personality and Social Psychology*, *31*, 479–486.

Lepper, M. R., Green, D., & Nisbett, R. E. (1973). Undermining children's intrinsic interest with extrinsic rewards: A test of the "overjustification" hypothesis. *Journal of Personality and Social Psychology*, *28*, 129–137.

Markus, H. R., & Kitayama, S. (1991). Culture and the self: Implication for cognition, emotion, and motivation. *Psychological Review*, *98*, 224–253.

Mastumoto, D. (1999). Culture and self: An empirical assessment of Markus and Kitayama's theory of independent and interdependent self construal. *Asian Journal of Social Psychology*, 2, 289–310.

Mead, G. H. (1934). *Mind, self and society*. Chicago: University of Chicago Press.

Merton, R. K. (1957/1968). *Social theory and social structure: Toward the codification of theory and research*. New York: Free Press.

Mifune, N., Hashimoto, H., & Yamagishi, T. (2010). Altruism toward ingroup members as a reputation mechanism. *Evolution and Human Behavior, 31*, 109–117.

Mischel, W. (1968). *Personality and assessment*. New York: Wiley.

Mischel, W. (1973). Toward a cognitive social learning reconceptualization of personality. *Psychological Review*, 80, 252–283.

Murakami, F., & Ishiguro, I. (2005). The effects of the communication target on self-effacement. *Japanese Journal of Social Psychology*, 21, 1–11.

Muramoto, Y. (2003). An indirect self-enhancement in relationship among Japanese. *Journal of Cross-Cultural Psychology*, 34, 552–566.

Nakane, C. (1970). *Japanese society*. Berkeley: University of California Press.

Nisbett, R. E. (2003). *The geography of thought: How Asians and Westerners think differently . . . and why*. New York: Free Press.

Nisbett, R. E., & Cohen, D. (1996). *Culture of honor*. Boulder, CO: Westview Press.

Olding-Smee, F. J., Laland, K. N., & Feldman, M. W. (2003). *Niche construction: The neglected processes in evolution*. Princeton, NJ: Princeton University Press.

Oyserman, D., Coon, H. M., & Kemmelmeier, M. (2002). Rethinking individualism and collectivism: Evaluation of theoretical assumptions and meta-analyses. *Psychological Bulletin*, *128*, 2–37.

Rosenthal, R., & Jacobson, L. (1968). *Pygmalion in the classroom: Teacher expectations and pupils' intellectual development*. New York: Holt, Rinehart, and Winston.

Shteynberg, G., Gelfand, M. J., & Kim, K. (2009). Peering into the "magnum mysterium" of culture: The explanatory power of descriptive norms. *Journal of Cross-Cultural Psychology*, *40*, 46–69.

Singelis, T. M. (1994). The measurement of independent and interdependent self-construal. *Personality and Social Psychological Bulletin*, *20*, 580–591.

Spencer-Rogers, J., & Peng, K. (2005). The dialectical self: Contradiction, change, and holism in the East Asian self-concept. In R. M. Sorrentino, D. Cohen, J. M. Olson, & M. P. Zanna (Eds.), *Culture and social behavior: The Ontario Symposium* (Vol. 10, pp. 227–250). Mahwah, NJ: Erlbaum.

Suzuki, N., & Yamagishi, T. (2004). An experimental study of self-effacement and self-enhancement among the Japanese (In Japanese). *Japanese Journal of Social Psychology*, 20, 2004, 17–25.

Suzuki, N., Konno, Y., & Yamagishi, T. (2007). In-group bias in trusting behavior: A choice of allocator experiment with minimal groups. *Japanese Journal of Psychology*, 78, 17–24.

Tajfel, H., Billig, M., Bundy, R., & Flament, C. (1971). Social categorization in intergroup behaviour. *European Journal of Social Psychology*, 1, 149–178.

Tajfel, H., & Turner, J. C. (1986). The social identity theory of intergroup behavior. In S. Worchel & W. G. Austin (Eds.), *Psychology of intergroup behavior* (pp. 7–24). Chicago: Nelson Hall.

Takahashi, C., Yamagishi, T., & Hashimoto, H. (2009). Interdependent self as a form of self presentation in response to a threat of exclusion from the group. *Japanese Journal of Social Psychology*, 25, 113–120.

Takano, Y., & Sogon, S. (2008). Are Japanese more collectivistic than Americans? Examining conformity in in-groups and the reference-group Effect. *Journal of Cross-Cultural Psychology*, 39, 237–250.

Takata, T. (2000). Scales to measure the independent and interdependent self-construal. *Proceedings of the Nara University Institute of General Studies*, 8, 145–163.

Taylor, M. (1976). *Anarchy and cooperation*. New York: Wiley.

Thurow, L. C. (1975). *Generating inequality: Mechanisms of distribution in the U.S. economy*. New York: Basic Books.

Triandis, H. C. (1989). The self and social-behavior in differing cultural contexts. *Psychological Review*, 96, 506–520.

Triandis H. C. (1995). *Individualism and collectivism*. Boulder, CO: Westview Press.

Turner, J. C. (1985). Social categorization and the self concept: A social cognitive theory of group behavior. *Advances in Group Processes*, 2, 77–121.

Turner, J. C., Hogg, M. A., Oakes, P. J., Reicher, S. D., & Wetherell, M. S. (1987). *Rediscovering the social group: A Self-categorization theory*. Oxford, England: Blackwell.

Uchida, Y. (2008). Contingencies of self-worth in Japanese culture: Validation of the Japanese contingencies of self-worth scale (In Japanese). *Japanese Journal of Psychology*, 79, 250–256.

Vandello, J. A., Cohen, D., & Ransom, S. (2008). U. S. Southern and Northern differences in perceptions of norms about aggression: Mechanisms for the perpetuation of a culture of honor. *Journal of Cross-Cultural Psychology*, 39, 162–177.

Vogel, E. F. (1979). *Japan as number one: Lessons for America*. Cambridge, MA: Harvard University Press.

Wan, C., Chiu, C., Tam, K. P., Lee, S. L., Lau, I. Y. M., & Peng, S. Q. (2007). Perceived cultural importance and actual self-importance of values in cultural identification. *Journal of Personality and Social Psychology*, 92, 337–354.

Wan, C., Torelli, C. J., & Chiu, C. (2010). Intersubjective consensus and the maintenance of normative shared reality. *Social Cognition*, 28, 422–446.

Wike, R. & Holzwart, K. (2008, April 15). Where trust is high, crime and corruption are low: Since communism's fall, social trust has fallen in Eastern Europe. *Pew Research Center*. Retrieved June 12, 2010, from http://pewresearch.org/pubs/799/global-social-trust-crime-corruption

Yamagishi, T. (1986). The provision of a sanctioning system as a public good. *Journal of Personality and Social Psychology*, 51, 110–116.

Yamagishi, T. (1988a). The provision of a sanctioning system in the United States and Japan. *Social Psychology Quarterly, 51,* 265–271.

Yamagishi, T. (1988b). Exit from the group as an individualistic solution to the public good problem in the United States and Japan. *Journal of Experimental Social Psychology, 24,* 530–542.

Yamagishi, T. (1988c). Seriousness of social dilemmas and the provision of a sanctioning system. *Social Psychology Quarterly, 51,* 32–42.

Yamagishi, T. (1998). *The structure of trust: The evolutionary game of mind and society* (In Japanese). Tokyo: University of Tokyo Press.

Yamagishi, T. (2007). The social exchange heuristic: A psychological mechanism that makes a system of generalized exchange self-sustaining. In M. Radford, S. Ohnuma, & T. Yamagishi (Eds.), *Cultural and ecological foundations of the mind* (pp. 11–37). Sapporo, Japan: Hokkaido University Press.

Yamagishi, T. (2009a). An institutional approach to culture (In Japanese). In H. Ishiguro & T. Kameda (Eds.), *Culture and practice* (pp. 141–170). Tokyo: Shinyosha.

Yamagishi, T. (2009b). Intra-group cooperation and inter-group aggression: Implications of minimal group studies (In Japanese). *Leviathan, 44,* 22–46.

Yamagishi, T., Cook, K. S., & Watabe, M. (1998). Uncertainty, trust and commitment formation in the United States and Japan. *American Journal of Sociology, 104,* 165–194.

Yamagishi, T., Hashimoto, H., Cook, K. S., & Kiyonari, T. (2010). Modesty in Self-Presentation: A Comparison between the U.S. and Japan. *Center for the Study of Cultural and Ecological Foundations of the Mind Working Paper Series* (No. 116). Sapporo, Japan: Hokkaido University.

Yamagishi, T., Hashimoto, H., Li, Y., & Schug, J. (2010). City air brings freedom. *Center for the Study of Cultural and Ecological Foundations of the Mind Working Paper Series* (No. 115). Sapporo, Japan: Hokkaido University.

Yamagishi, T., Hashimoto, H., & Schug, J. (2008). Preference vs. strategies as explanations for culture-specific behavior. *Psychological Science, 19,* 579–584.

Yamagishi, T., Jin, N., & Miller, A. S. (1998). In-group bias and culture of collectivism. *Asian Journal of Social Psychology, 1,* 315–328.

Yamagishi, T., Jin, N., & Kiyonari, T. (1999). Bounded generalized reciprocity: Ingroup favoritism and ingroup boasting. *Advances in Group Processes, 16,* 161–197.

Yamagishi, T., & Kiyonari, T. (2000). The group as the container of generalized reciprocity. *Social Psychology Quarterly, 63,* 116–132.

Yamagishi, T., Makimura, Y., Foddy, M., Matsuda, M., Kiyonari, T., & Platow, M. (2005). Comparisons of Australians and Japanese on group-based cooperation. *Asian Journal of Social Psychology, 8,* 173–190.

Yamagishi, T., & Mifune, N. (2008). Does shared group membership promote altruism? *Rationality and Society,* 20, 5–30.

Yamagishi, T., & Mifune, N. (2009). Social exchange and solidarity: In-group love or out-group hate? *Evolution and Human Behavior, 30,* 229–237.

Yamagishi, T., Mifune, N., Liu, J. H., & Pauling, J. (2008). Exchanges of group-based favors: Ingroup bias in the prisoner's dilemma game with minimal groups in Japan and New Zealand. *Asian Journal of Social Psychology*, *11*, 196–207.

Yamagishi, T., & Suzuki, N. (2009). An niche construction approach to culture. In M. Schaller, A. Norenzayan, S. Heine, T. Yamagishi, & T. Kameda (Eds.), *Evolution, culture, and the human mind* (pp. 185–203). New York: Psychology Press.

Yamagishi, T., Terai, S., Kiyonari, T., Mifune, N., & Kanazawa, S. (2007). The social exchange heuristic: Managing errors in social exchange. *Rationality and Society*, *19*, 259–298.

Yamagishi, T., & Yamagishi, M. (1994). Trust and commitment in the United States and Japan. *Motivation and Emotion*, *18*, 129–166.

Zou, X., Tam, K. P., Morris, M. W., Lee, S., Lau, I. Y., & Chiu, C., (2009). Culture as common sense: Perceived consensus versus personal beliefs as mechanisms of cultural influence. *Journal of Personality and Social Psychology*, *97*, 579–597.

CHAPTER 7

Horizontal and Vertical Individualism and Collectivism
Implications for Understanding Psychological Processes

SHARON SHAVITT
University of Illinois at Urbana-Champaign

CARLOS J. TORELLI
University of Minnesota

HILA RIEMER
Ben-Gurion University of the Negev

I. INTRODUCTION

The constructs of individualism (IND) and collectivism (COL) have dominated the discourse on the psychological impacts of culture over the last 20 years of cross-cultural research (Oyserman, Coon, & Kemmelmeier, 2002). The conceptualizations of IND and COL have historically been broad and multi-dimensional, summarizing a host of differences in focus of attention, self-definitions, motivations, emotional connections to in-groups, as well as belief systems and behavioral patterns (Bond, 2002; Ho & Chiu, 1994; Hofstede, 1980; Oyserman et al., 2002; Triandis, 1995; Triandis, Chen, & Chan, 1998; Triandis, Leung, Villareal, & Clack, 1985). Although the breadth and power of these constructs have profoundly advanced the field, critiques of their multifaceted nature and debates about the "core" essence of IND and COL limit the insights afforded by these broad dimensions (Briley & Wyer, 2001;

Maheswaran & Shavitt, 2000; Oyserman et al., 2002). In this chapter, we review evidence supporting the value of a horizontal (valuing equality) and vertical (emphasizing hierarchy) cultural distinction nested within the broader IND-COL classification. Together with our colleagues (Alokparna Basu Monga, Sergio Carvalho, Chi-yue Chiu, Timothy Johnson, Andrew Kaikati, Hean Tat Keh, Ashok Lalwani, Natalia Maehle, Aysegul Ozsomer, Jimmy Wong, and Jing Zhang), we have investigated this distinction and its implications for the understanding of cultural processes. Our findings underscore the value of the horizontal and vertical distinction for uncovering novel cultural patterns. This work and others' work highlight several sources of value for a vertical/horizontal distinction—as a predictor of new phenomena not anticipated by a broader focus on IND-COL, and as a basis for refining the understanding of existing phenomena linked to the IND-COL distinction. In this chapter, we describe the horizontal-vertical distinction and its measurement, and we review several lines of research that show how it can contribute to predicting the role of culture in shaping perceptions, motives, values, and social relations. Our coverage is structured around a core set of questions: Who am I and what do I value? How should I present myself to others? How do I perceive the social environment? We close by discussing implications for understanding consumer psychology and suggest future directions for research on the horizontal-vertical distinction.

II. HORIZONTAL AND VERTICAL INDIVIDUALISM AND COLLECTIVISM

Describing a delineation of different "species" of individualism and collectivism, Triandis and his colleagues (Singelis, Triandis, Bhawuk, & Gelfand, 1995; Triandis, 1995; Triandis et al., 1998; Triandis & Gelfand, 1998) noted that, nested within each IND-COL category, some societies are *horizontal* (valuing equality), whereas others are *vertical* (emphasizing hierarchy). The horizontal-vertical distinction emerges from the observation that American or British individualism differs from, say, Swedish or Danish individualism in much the same way that Korean or Japanese collectivism differs from the collectivism of the Israeli kibbutz.

In vertical-individualist (VI) societies or cultural contexts (e. g., United States, Great Britain, France), people tend to be concerned with improving their individual status and standing out—distinguishing themselves from others via competition, achievement, and power. In contrast, in horizontal-individualist (HI) societies or cultural contexts (e. g., Sweden, Denmark, Norway, Australia), people prefer to view themselves as equal to others in status and eschew status differentiation (e. g., Feather, 1994; Nelson & Shavitt, 2002). Rather than standing out, the focus is on expressing one's uniqueness and establishing one's capability to be successfully self-reliant (Triandis & Singelis, 1998). In vertical-collectivist (VC) societies or cultural contexts (e. g., Korea, Japan, India), people focus on complying with authorities and on enhancing the cohesion and status of their ingroups, even when that entails sacrificing their own personal goals. In horizontal-collectivist (HC) societies or cultural contexts (exemplified histori-cally by the Israeli kibbutz), the focus is on sociability and interdependence with others, within an egalitarian framework (see Erez & Earley, 1987). These distinct psychological characteristics are summarized in Table 7. 1.

Thus, although individualist societies share a focus on self-reliance, independence, and hedonism, Scandinavians and Australians (societies characterized as HI) show aversion to conspicuously successful persons and to braggarts, emphasizing instead the virtues of modesty (e. g., Askgaard, 1992; Daun, 1991, 1992; Feather, 1994; Nelson & Shavitt, 2002; Triandis & Gelfand, 1998). In contrast, people in the United States (VI) have been shown to aspire to distinction, achievement, success, and being or having "the best"

TABLE 7.1: **Psychological Characteristics of Each Cultural Orientation**

Psychological Domain	Cultural Orientation			
	HI	VI	HC	VC
Major motivational concern	Self-reliance	Power and status-seeking	Interdependence and helping others	Duties and obligations toward in-groups
Nature of person-person relations	As needed with equal others	Dominance of low-status others	Nurturing, undifferentiated relations with equal others	Close-knit with in-groups of different status levels
Nature of self-society relations	Individual rights	Upward mobility	Social responsibility	Established hierarchy
Self-presentation goals and means of achievement	Self-deceptive enhancement	Self-aggrandizing, status symbols	Impression management, benefiting others	Being dutiful, Ingroup distinction
Perception and information processing	Undetermined	Stereotyping	Individuating	Context-dependent

(e. g., Markus & Kitayama, 1991; Triandis & Gelfand, 1998; Weldon, 1984). In fact, in the United States, "success is communicated, shared and displayed because it is natural to show off" (de Mooij, 1998, p. 195).

Similarly, although collectivists share an interdependent worldview, Koreans and other East Asians (VC) emphasize deference to authority and preservation of harmony in the context of hierarchical relations with others. Indeed, the status of one's family and other key ingroups establishes one's individual social standing in VC cultures. In contrast, in the Israeli kibbutz (HC), the emphasis is neither on harmony nor status. Instead, honesty, direct-ness, and cooperation are valued, within a framework of assumed equality (Gannon, 2001; Kurman & Sriram, 2002; Triandis & Gelfand, 1998).

The horizontal-vertical distinction resembles the culture-level dimension of *power distance* (Hofstede, 1980, 2001), although there are important con-ceptual and structural distinctions (see Shavitt, Lalwani, Zhang, & Torelli, 2006). For instance, power distance is conceptualized in unipolar terms (high to low). The horizontal-vertical classification is nested within individualism and collectivism to yield four distinct categories.

This four-category typology fits with Fiske's (1992) categories of sociality: communal sharing (corresponding to collectivism), market pricing (corre-sponding to individualism), equality matching (horizontal relationships), and authority ranking (vertical relationships; Triandis & Gelfand, 1998). A recent study by Vodosek (2009) provides some support for these relations. In his study, members of chemistry research groups at U. S. universities completed a scale to assess the relational models they apply to their group members (Haslam 1994, 1995; Haslam & Fiske 1999) and a scale to assess cultural ori-entations of horizontal and vertical IND and COL (Triandis & Gelfand, 1998). Results revealed associations between communal sharing and collectivism, between authority and vertical orientation, and between equality matching and horizontal collectivism (albeit not horizontal individualism). These results underscore the role of both IND-COL and horizontal-vertical cultural distinc-tions in explaining preferences for certain relational models of sociality.

The horizontal-vertical distinction is also conceptually linked to personal value categories such as power, achievement, and conformity values (vertical), as contrasted with self-direction, benevolence, and universalism values (hori-zontal; e. g., Schwartz & Bilsky, 1987, 1990).

Most cross-national comparisons in the psychology and consumer behav-ior literatures contrast people in the United States (VI) with those in East Asian countries (VC; see Oyserman et al., 2002; and Shavitt, Lee, & Torelli, 2009, for reviews). Therefore, established differences between IND and COL societies may be more reflective of vertical forms of these syndromes and may not generalize to comparisons between horizontal cultures. As one example, conformity in product choice, as studied by Kim and Markus (1999), may be a tendency specific to VC cultures, in which deference to authority figures and to ingroup wishes is stressed. Much lower levels of conformity may be observed in HC cultural contexts, which emphasize cooperation, solidarity, and sociability but not deference or hierarchy (Triandis & Gelfand, 1998). Thus, observed differences in conformity in consumer choices between Korea (VC) and the United States (VI; Kim & Markus, 1999; see also Choi, Lee, & Kim, 2005) cannot be ascribed solely to the role of IND-COL because such conformity patterns might not be expected when comparing HI and HC societies.

Oyserman et al. (2002), in their comprehensive meta-analysis and review of the psychological implications of IND-COL, suggested that values of hierarchy and competition function independently of IND and COL. They found that when measures of IND and COL cultural orientation included items tapping hierarchy and competition themes, cross-national patterns in IND-COL orientation changed. For example, "when competition was included in the scale, the difference between Americans and Japanese in IND disappeared, suggesting that competitiveness is a construct unrelated to IND" (p. 16). Such findings are consistent with a view of both the United States and Japan as vertical societies. According to this interpretation, when IND-COL cultural orientation scales emphasize themes relevant to vertical orientations, responses across these societies appear more similar. The findings also illustrate the aforementioned limitation in studying IND and COL primarily within vertical cultural contexts. It is difficult to determine which differences are associated with the broader IND-COL distinction and which reflect patterns of judgment or behavior mostly relevant to specific comparisons of VI versus VC contexts (rather than HI vs. HC contexts).

Before reviewing consequences associated with horizontal versus vertical cultural categories, we describe current methods for measuring horizontal and vertical individualistic and collectivistic orientations.

III. MEASURING HORIZONTAL AND VERTICAL FORMS OF INDIVIDUALISM AND COLLECTIVISM

Triandis and his colleagues have developed and refined a scale for measuring the HI, VI, HC, and VC cultural orientations within-culture (e. g., Singelis et al., 1995; Triandis et al., 1998; Triandis & Gelfand, 1998). People with a

VI orientation are more likely to agree with such items as "competition is the law of nature," "winning is everything," and "it is important that I do my job better than others," whereas people with an HI orientation are more likely to agree that "I often do 'my own thing,'" "I'd rather depend on myself than others," and "my personal identity, independent of others, is very important to me." People with a VC orientation are more likely to agree with such items as "parents and children must stay together as much as possible," "it is my duty to take care of my family, even when I have to sacrifice what I want," and "it is important to me that I respect the decisions made by my groups," whereas people with a HC orientation are more likely to agree that "I feel good when I cooperate with others," "to me, pleasure is spending time with others," and "the well-being of my coworkers is important to me" (Singelis et al., 1995; Triandis & Gelfand, 1998).

Several studies have explored the cross-cultural generality of these orientation categories and the dimensionality of the scale. Triandis and Gelfand (1998) provided evidence for the convergent and divergent validity of these four constructs and reported interrelations between their cultural-orientation measure and other measures that fit the conceptual definitions of these categories. They also showed that their 16-item cultural-orientation measure shares the same factor structure in Korea as was previously identified in the United States (see also Chiou, 2001; Gouveia, Clemente, & Espinosa, 2003; Robert, Lee, & Chan, 2006; Soh & Leong, 2002, for additional evidence for cross-national structural equivalence of various versions of these scales). However, comparability across published studies is limited by the fact that different subsets of items have been used across some of the studies to classify cultural orientation (e. g., Kurman & Sriram, 2002). More recently, Sivadas, Bruvold, and Nelson (2008) tested a 14-item reduced version of the scale in several countries and provided evidence that it outperforms the longer versions (e. g., Singelis et al., 1995; Triandis & Gelfand, 1998). Current work has also focused on measures of culture that capture intersubjective norms (Zou et al., 2009), including horizontal and vertical categories (Shteynberg, Gelfand, & Kim, 2009), indicating that these categories can be represented as culturally consensual norms.

Next, we review key consequences associated with horizontal versus vertical cultural categories. As we shall show, our program of research and others' have not only established that these distinctions are well replicated but also that they have far-reaching implications for personal values, identities, self-presentational tendencies, and perceptions of the social environment.

These implications go beyond those that would be anticipated by a focus on the broad IND and COL cultural categories.

IV. WHO AM I AND WHAT DO I VALUE?

A. Personal Values

Although most comparisons of cultural values contrast broader IND versus COL categories, a number of studies have pointed to differences in hierarchical or status-oriented values within IND or COL categories. For instance, our cross-national research in the United States (viewed as a VI society) and Denmark (viewed as an HI society) showed clear differences in the importance that people place upon achievement, the display of success, and the gaining of influence (Nelson & Shavitt, 2002), even though both societies are Western and individualistic cultures (Hofstede, 1980). Denmark is characterized by benevolent social welfare policies designed to help the least fortunate in society, coupled with a ubiquitous social modesty code (the *Janteloven*) that frowns on showing off. In contrast, in the United States the notion of equality is "equal *opportunity*," as opposed to equivalence of outcomes. Popular culture themes of rags-to-riches emphasize individual social mobility up the ladder of success, and these are reinforced by tax and social welfare policies that allow for relatively high income disparities within the society (Nelson & Shavitt, 2002; Triandis, 1995).

We reasoned that this would manifest in different values being articulated when people reflected on their goals and hopes for the future. Indeed, in open-ended interview responses, we found that Americans discussed the importance of achieving their goals as something that makes them happy, whereas Danes did not (58% vs. 0%, respectively). When Americans were asked about their future, their responses reflected career options first, often with an interest in entrepreneurship, a theme that was completely lacking from Danes (Nelson & Shavitt, 2002, Study 1). As one informant, a Danish attorney, explained, "There's no incentive to achieve more or work harder here. My taxes are so high that it's actually cheaper for me to take the afternoon off work and go golfing" (p. 445). The hierarchical nature of U. S. society rewards those who set goals and achieve them, whereas the same course of action is frowned upon in Denmark's HI society.

Moreover, in another study (Nelson & Shavitt, 2002, Study 2), self-ratings showed a similar pattern indicating that the cultural orientations and values of Americans were more vertical and more achievement oriented than those of

Danes—more oriented toward success, ambition, and gaining influence. In contrast, we found that the values of Danes were more universalistic than those of Americans—that is, more oriented toward social justice, nature, and equality (see Schwartz & Bilsky, 1987, 1990). Moreover, endorsement of achievement values was correlated with a VI cultural orientation in both countries.

Other research has also shown positive relationships between a VI cultural orientation and achievement and power values, as well as negative relationships between those values and an HC cultural orientation (Oishi, Schimmack, Diener, & Suh, 1998). Further, self-direction was positively correlated with HI orientation but negatively correlated with VI orientation. In contrast, a focus on social relationships correlated positively with HC orientation, but not VC orientation. Along similar lines, Triandis and Gelfand (1998) reported that an HC orientation was predicted by interdependence and sociability. Confirming this cross-nationally, our results showed in both the United States and Denmark that HC (but not VC) orientation correlated with sociable and benevolent values (Nelson & Shavitt, 2002). In line with this, Chen, Meindl, and Hunt (1997) found that, in China, those with an HC orientation preferred an egalitarian reward system, which fosters shared responsibility and interpersonal interdependence, whereas those with a VC orientation preferred a differential reward system, which fosters hierarchy. Soh and Leong (2002) reported in both the United States and Singapore that HC orientation was best predicted by benevolence values, VC by conformity values, VI by power values, and HI by self-direction values.

In sum, although the broad definition of COL has focused on interdependence and the maintenance of social relationships, several studies suggest that it is people with an HC orientation who are particularly oriented toward sociability and are motivated to maintain benevolent relationships. Similarly, although independence and a focus upon self-direction and uniqueness have been key to the definition of IND, it appears that it is those with an HI orientation who are especially motivated to maintain their self-image as being separate from others and are capable of self-reliance.

B. Gender Differences in Horizontal and Vertical Cultural Orientations

The relationship between gender and cultural orientation may also depend on whether VI or HI (or VC or HC) is considered. Males are generally seen as more

IND or independent than females, whereas females are seen as more COL or interdependent than males (e. g., Cross & Madson, 1997; Gilligan, 1982, 1986; Kitayama, Markus, Matsumoto, & Norasakkunkit, 1997; Markus & Kitayama, 1991; Wood & Eagly, 2002). Several studies have pointed to such gender differences, although the specific nature of these differences varies across studies (see Cross & Madson, 1997; Kashima et al., 1995). Some research has shown no differences on broad IND-COL indicators. For instance, Gabriel and Gardner (1999) reported that whereas women are more relational and less group-oriented than men in their patterns of interdependent judgments and behaviors, there were no gender differences on behaviors relating to independent ones (see also Baumeister & Sommer, 1997; Kashima et al., 1995).

Our findings suggest that taking the horizontal-vertical distinction into account sheds light on the nature of the gender differences to be expected. In studies conducted with U. S. participants (see Shavitt, et al., 2006), men scored consistently higher in VI than women (see also Chirkov, Ryan, Kim, & Kaplan, 2003; Nelson & Shavitt, 2002 for similar patterns replicated cross-nationally). The pattern for HI was much less consistent, with females sometimes scoring directionally higher than males (see also Kurman & Sriram, 2002, for cross-national evidence consistent with this). In other words, robust gender differences in IND only emerged in our results for the vertical form. The results also showed that women scored consistently higher in HC than men (see also Kurman & Sriram, 2002; Nelson & Shavitt, 2002). However, women are not broadly more collectivistic than men and did not score higher in VC (if anything, men scored higher in VC than women did, a pattern also observed by Chirkov et al., 2003, and Kurman & Sriram, 2002). Thus, gender differences in COL were specific to HC.

In another study, when responding to a variety of behavioral scenarios (Triandis et al., 1998), men were more likely than women to endorse choices that characterize vertical forms of individualism (e. g., splitting a restaurant bill according to how much each person makes) but not horizontal forms (e. g., splitting the bill according to what that person ordered). In contrast, women were more likely than men to endorse choices that characterize horizontal forms of collectivism (e. g., splitting a restaurant bill equally, without regard to who ordered what) but not vertical forms (e. g., having a group leader pay the bill or decide how to split it) (Lalwani & Shavitt, unpublished data).

Additional studies examined whether the links between gender and VI and HC that were observed reflect distinct masculine and feminine cultural value orientations (Lalwani & Shavitt, unpublished data). To address this, subjective measures of masculinity and femininity were included (Spence & Helmreich, 1978; Stern, Barak, & Gold, 1987). For instance, in one study, U. S. participants completed the scale of horizontal and vertical IND-COL (Triandis & Gelfand, 1998), as well as Spence and Helmreich's (1978) Personal Attributes Questionnaire on which they rated themselves on a series of five-point semantic differential items to measure masculinity and femininity. Feminine items included "Not at all emotional—Very emotional," "Very rough—Very gentle," and "Not at all kind—Very kind." Masculine items included "Very passive—Very active," "Gives up very easily—Never gives up easily," and "Goes to pieces under pressure—Stands up well under pressure."

If a feminine focus is associated with a type of collectivism that emphasizes cooperation and social relationships (HC), and a masculine focus is associated with an individualism that emphasizes status, power, and prestige (VI), then one would expect a distinct pattern of correlations between VI and self-rated masculinity on the one hand, and HC and self-rated femininity on the other. This is the pattern that was observed across different subjective gender measures (Lalwani & Shavitt, unpublished data).

These patterns would not be anticipated in the broader literature on gender and cultural self-construal. For instance, whereas some have concluded that men and women do not differ in dimensions of self-construal relevant to IND (Baumeister & Sommer, 1997; Gabriel & Gardner, 1999), we found that males consistently score higher than females on one type of IND. That is, IND in males appears especially focused on status, power, and achievement through competition (VI). Traditional masculine social roles that emphasize achievement and power gained through work outside the home may contribute to the robust gender differences that were observed.

Results also shed light on the motivational underpinnings of gender differences that have been proposed and observed in other studies. Specifically, COL in females appears to emphasize benevolence, sociability, common goals, and cooperation (HC). This may parallel the relational interdependence identified in previous studies (Cross, Bacon, & Morris, 2000; Gabriel & Gardner, 1999; Kashima et al., 1995; see also Wang, Bristol, Mowen, & Ckakraborty, 2000). However, women do not appear always to be higher in COL or interdependence. If anything, men report a somewhat greater emphasis on familial duties and obligations and on deference to authority (VC). That is, they are more likely to endorse the values of family integrity and in-group deference.

In sum, our results and those of other researchers indicate that the horizontal-vertical distinction is useful in predicting or qualifying the nature of gender differences in cultural orientation, as well as in understanding the motivational underpinnings of the differences observed.

V. HOW SHOULD I PRESENT MYSELF?

A. Self-Presentation and Response Styles

These observations about the values associated with horizontal and vertical orientations have implications for understanding self-presentational patterns across cultures. Self-presentation pervades all aspects of human behavior. However, what constitutes desirable self-presentation may differ as a function of cultural variables. As a result, we have argued that distinct self-presentational patterns should emerge for people of different cultures (Lalwani, Shavitt, & Johnson, 2006). The foregoing discussion suggests that self-presentational tendencies of people with different cultural orientations or backgrounds should correspond to two response styles associated with socially desirable responding: impression management (IM) and self-deceptive enhancement (SDE) (Gur & Sackeim, 1979; Paulhus, 1991; Sackeim & Gur, 1979). The Paulhus Deception Scales (Paulhus, 1984, 1991, 1998b) comprise two subscales measuring these dimensions of socially desirable responding. Impression management refers to an attempt to present one's self-reported actions in the most positive manner to convey a favorable image (Paulhus, 1998a; Schlenker & Britt, 1999; Schlenker, Britt, & Pennington, 1996). It is an effort to control the images that one projects to others. This construct is often associated with dissimulation or deception (Mick, 1996), and it is tapped by such items as "I have never dropped litter on the street" and "I sometimes drive faster than the speed limit" (reverse scored; Paulhus, 1998a). Self-deceptive enhancement refers to the tendency to describe oneself in inflated and overconfident terms. It is a predisposition to see one's skills in a positive light, and it has been described as a form of "rigid overconfidence" (Paulhus, 1998a). Self-deceptive enhancement is assessed by agreement with such items as "My first impressions of people usually turn out to be right" and "I am very confident of my judgments."

We first review evidence on self-presentation as a function of the broad IND-COL distinction, as well as the related contextual distinction in independent versus interdependent salient self-construal. Then we demonstrate how a consideration of horizontal-vertical distinction further enhances our understanding of the links between culture and self-presentation.

Our research has demonstrated that INDs, compared to COLs, scored higher in self-deceptive enhancement and lower in impression management

(Lalwani et al., 2006). In line with this, we further argued that people may highlight different qualities in their self-presentations, and that what is considered desirable will vary from one culturally relevant context to another (Lalwani & Shavitt, 2009). Across several studies, we showed that when an independent versus interdependent cultural self-construal is made salient, distinct self-presentational goals are activated. Thus, when the independent self-construal is salient, people strive to present themselves as self-reliant, confident, and skillful. However, when the interdependent self-construal is salient, people strive to present themselves as sensitive and socially appropriate (Markus & Kitayama, 1991; Sackheim & Gur, 1979; Taylor & Brown, 1988; van Baaren, Maddux, Chartrand, De Bouter, & Van Knippenberg, 2003). Indeed, in multiple studies, we showed that salient self-construal leads to an increased likelihood of choosing to perform tasks that could showcase culturally valued skills: Participants with a salient interdependent self-construal were more likely to choose to take a test that could showcase their social sensitivity, whereas those with a salient independent self-construal were more likely to choose to take a test that would showcase their self-reliance (Lalwani & Shavitt, 2009). Moreover, participants proved to be more effective at showcasing culturally appropriate skills. Thus, as shown in Figure 7. 1, people with a salient independent (vs. interdependent) self-construal actually scored higher on a test of general-knowledge trivia. In contrast, people with a salient interdependent (vs. independent) self-construal were more effective at portraying themselves in a socially sensitive manner, for instance by scoring

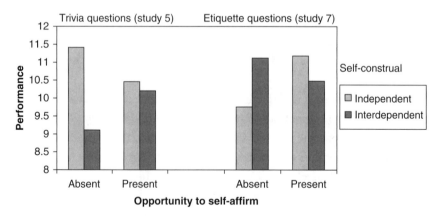

FIGURE 7.1: The effects of salient self-construal on performance on general trivia knowledge and etiquette questions. (Adapted from Lalwani & Shavitt, 2009, studies 5 and 7. Reprinted with permission of American Psychological Association. Copyright 2009.)

higher on a test of etiquette. Importantly, these effects were not observed when participants were first given the opportunity to engage in self-affirmation (Johnson & Stapel, 2007; Steele & Liu, 1983), allowing them to fulfill their self-presentational goals before choosing or participating in tests (Lalwani & Shavitt, 2009).

Additional studies also supported the role of self-presentational goals underlying the effects of salient self-construal. For instance, when participants were led to doubt their upcoming performance on tests, by first trying to solve very difficult GRE test problems, the effects of salient self-construal on test choice were eliminated or reversed (Lalwani & Shavitt, 2009). Apparently, facing the possibility that they might fail a test of social appropriateness led people with a salient interdependent (vs. independent) self-construal to be *less* likely to choose that test. Taken together, these findings indicate that salient self-construal activated a readiness to pursue self-presentational goals, rather than the semantic activation of beliefs or concepts.

The findings just described demonstrated important IND and COL cultural differences in self-presentations. However, examination of horizontal versus vertical categories yielded more nuanced insights into the motives being served by these self-presentations. Indeed, when examined in U. S. participants as a function of cultural orientation, self-presentation patterns were contingent on the horizontal versus vertical orientation distinction (Lalwani et al., 2006). As already noted, research on personal values indicates that people with an HI orientation are especially motivated to view themselves as separate from others, self-reliant, and unique. Similarly, people with an HC orientation are especially motivated to maintain strong and benevolent social relations and, therefore, to appear socially appropriate in their responses. Thus, we reasoned that an HI (but not a VI) orientation should foster a response style characterized by SDE because such responses help to establish a view of oneself as capable of being successfully self-reliant. However, an HC (but not a VC) orientation should foster a response style characterized by IM because such responses help to maintain cooperative social relationships through conveying a socially appropriate image. That is, SDE and IM responding addresses the distinct self-presentational motives associated with horizontal individualism or horizontal collectivism, respectively.

Indeed, in multiple studies with U. S. participants, we showed that the relations observed between cultural variables and self-presentational patterns were specific to HI and HC orientations (Lalwani et al., 2006). HI (but not VI) reliably predicted SDE, whereas HC (but not VC) reliably predicted IM on the

Paulhus Deception Scales (Paulhus, 1991, 1998b). These distinctions also emerged for responses to specific behavioral scenarios relevant either to motives of self-reliance or motives of normative appropriateness. For instance, people who were high versus low in HI orientation expressed more confidence that they could make the right decision about whether to accept a future job, and they were more likely to anticipate performing well on the job. People who were high versus low in HC orientation were more likely to deny that they would gossip about coworkers on a job, plagiarize a friend's paper for a course, or damage someone's furniture without telling them. We also found (Lalwani et al., 2006, Study 3) that high HC people were more likely to engage in deceptive responding, as assessed by Eysenck's Lie Scale (Eysenck & Eysenck, 1964).

Overall, these findings underscore the value of the horizontal-vertical distinction for delineating self-presentation goals and for predicting cultural differences in the tendencies to pursue them. The studies converge on the conclusion that people with an HC cultural orientation, who emphasize sociability, benevolence, and normative appropriateness, are characterized by a tendency to engage in impression management, regardless of how this self-presentational response style is assessed. However, people with a VC orientation, who emphasize stature, duty, and conformity, are less likely to be concerned with impression management. One might speculate that the VC orientation would instead be more predictive of desirable self-presentations concerning one's deference, sense of duty, and fulfillment of obligations. Our studies also establish that people with an HI orientation, who emphasize self-competence, self-direction, and independence, have a tendency to engage in SDE. On the other hand, those with a VI orientation, who put emphasis on status, power, and achievement, are less likely to exhibit SDE. Instead, one may speculate that the VI orientation would be more predictive of desirable self-presentations concerning one's achievements and competitive success.

B. Self-Presentation Mechanisms

In another line of work, we examined cultural differences in the mechanism by which self-presentation via impression management occurs (Riemer, 2009). As previously described, collectivists are more motivated than individualists to engage in impression management (Lalwani et al., 2006). Thus, collectivists receive more frequent practice in adjusting to normative constraints to maintain harmonious relations with others (e. g., Lalwani et al., 2006; Triandis & Suh 2002; van Hemert, Van De Vijver, Poortinga, & Georgas, 2002).

According to research on automaticity, this frequent practice, in turn, should lead to more routinized, automated processes (Bargh 1994, 1997; Smith & Lerner, 1986), such that the process of adjusting to norms would require little or no deliberation. Combining research on automaticity with evidence about differences in the frequency with which collectivists and individualists engage in impression management, we proposed that collectivists' adjustment to social norms in responding to attitude questions takes place through a relatively automatic process. Therefore, it does not require significant cognitive resources. In contrast, individualists' adjustment to social norms is more effortful, and thus it will take place only when cognitive resources are available (Riemer, 2009).

Across a number of studies, we demonstrated that collectivists were able to adjust responses to the norm regardless of their cognitive busyness. Individualists, on the other hand, were able to do so only when they had the cognitive capacity to adjust or edit their responses. In these studies, we asked people to report their attitudes regarding social issues and led them to expect an upcoming discussion with other participants about their responses. This was done to motivate them to impression manage. Participants' tendencies to engage in impression management were measured using a modified version of the IM subscale (Paulhus 1984, 1988), in which participants reported attitudes toward target behaviors instead of actual behaviors (e. g., "I think it is bad to damage a library book or store merchandise without reporting it" instead of "I have never damaged a library book or store merchandise without reporting it"). The expression of normatively appropriate attitudes should result in higher scores on this scale. In another study, we asked respondents about their attitude toward an environmentally friendly but very expensive hybrid car. Respondents perceived that the normative attitude was to favor the car. Thus, we expected that impression management would be manifested in more favorable expressed attitudes.

In all of our studies, we examined differences in the degree to which, when motivated to impression manage, collectivists and individualists would differ in their ability to express normative attitudes effortlessly. To do so, we manipulated cognitive load. Reduction of impression management tendencies under cognitive load (vs. no load condition) would suggest the operation of effortful processes that require cognitive resources, whereas impression management tendencies under cognitive load would point to automatic processes that can be enacted with little or no effort. Cognitive load was manipulated either by high versus low time pressure or by asking half of the participants to memorize an eight-digit number (e. g., Gilbert & Osborne, 1989).

Indeed, across our studies, cognitive load and cultural orientation or background interacted to influence impression management tendencies. Collectivists engaged in impression management to the same degree regardless of their cognitive busyness, suggesting a relatively effortless process. In contrast, individualists did so only when not cognitively busy, suggesting a relatively effortful process. These effects were consistent when assessing cultural orientation on individual bases, and when using nationality as an alternative operationalization of culture—with East Asian participants representing collectivists and U. S. participants representing individualists.

The predictions we proposed for cultural differences in impression management processes may be extended to consider horizontal and vertical categories of culture. One issue to consider is what motivates people to adjust their responses to the norm. As described earlier, in our studies all participants were induced to be motivated to impression manage using an anticipated discussion technique. Future research may examine whether there are cultural differences in the nature of anticipated interactions that would motivate such impression management, as we suggested earlier (Lalwani et al., 2006). Because in vertical cultures people value social status and hierarchy, people high in VC may be motivated to impression manage when their responses will be visible to people of higher status (e. g., their boss), but they may be less concerned about self-presentation when their responses will be visible to their peers (e. g., their friends). The reverse may be true for people high in HC.

Second, the type of norms people would tend to adjust to would be related to their cultural orientation across both individualism-collectivism and horizontal-vertical categories. Because people high in VC tend to focus on complying with authority, they should tend to adjust to norms associated with people of higher status (e. g., respecting one's teacher). People high in HC, on the other hand, focus on sociability with ingroups, and therefore they may tend to adjust to norms associated with benevolent peer interactions (e. g., helping one's classmate).

Finally, the process by which people engage in impression management may also vary with horizontal versus vertical cultural categories. Our studies have addressed the automaticity of adjusting to norms for collectivists versus individualists with a focus on the cognitive demands of the process (i. e., the extent to which the process takes place effortlessly; Riemer, 2009). Other characteristics of the process may distinguish impression management processes for people with horizontal versus vertical orientations. For instance, the ability to control adjustment to norms may vary for horizontal and vertical collectivists. Consider the following common instruction on a survey: "Please answer candidly. There are no right or wrong answers; all we are interested in is your own opinion." Research reviewed earlier has suggested that an HC orientation is sometimes associated with honesty and directness, whereas a VC orientation is associated with a tendency to preserve harmony in the context of hierarchical relations with others (Gannon, 2001; Kurman & Sriram, 2002; Triandis & Gelfand, 1998). Therefore, people high in HC may tend to answer honestly when it appears appropriate to do so. However, people high in VC may be reluctant to do so, due to their focus on maintaining harmony. Therefore, whereas horizontal collectivists may be able to control their tendency to shift their attitudinal self-reports to impression manage, vertical collectivists may be less able to do so.

VI. HOW DO I PERCEIVE THE SOCIAL ENVIRONMENT?

A. The Meaning and Purpose of Power

Thus far, our review indicates that horizontal and vertical cultural orientations pattern personal values and self-presentational goals. These ongoing motivational concerns should require continued mustering of resources toward goal fulfillment. Because power is instrumental for achieving culturally desirable goals, cultures foster normative standards for its legitimate use (Chiu & Hong, 2006). Because those goals differ for people with vertical versus horizontal orientations, views of power as a tool for achieving culturally specific goals should differ as well. Our research suggests that people with vertical and horizontal cultural orientations differ in their views about the meaning and purpose of power (Torelli & Shavitt, in press).

Building on past research pointing to individual differences in the way in which people use power (Chen, Lee-Chai, & Bargh, 2001; Howard, Gardner, & Thompson, 2007), we linked people's cultural orientations to their distinct associations with power. As reviewed earlier, people high in VI (but not HI) orientation tend to be concerned with improving their individual status and distinguishing themselves from others via competition and achievement (Nelson & Shavitt, 2002). In contrast, people high in HC tend to focus on sociability and interdependence with others within an egalitarian framework, whereas those high in VC emphasize duties and obligations to ingroups (Triandis, 1995). Accordingly, we reasoned that VI (and not HI), either measured as a chronic cultural orientation or inferred from ethnic group membership, is associated with tendencies to interpret power in *personalized* terms (i. e., power is for status and personal advancement; Winter, 1973), whereas HC (and not VC) is associated with tendencies to interpret power in *socialized* terms (i. e., power is for benefiting and helping others). Although individuals high in VC orientation may associate power with the well-being of ingroups (as captured by scale items such as "It is my duty to take care of my family, even when I have to sacrifice what I want"; Triandis & Gelfand, 1998), a VC orientation can also predict high levels of prejudice and hostile treatment of outgroups (particularly among high-status VC individuals; Triandis, 1995). Because for people high in VC, power associations may depend on their place in the hierarchy and on other contextual factors, we did not expect them to exhibit the general associations between power and prosocial endstates anticipated among high HC individuals. Indeed, as shown in Table 7. 2, across multiple studies we observed distinct and systematic power conceptualizations only for VI and HC cultural orientations, as reflected in self-reported beliefs about appropriate uses of power, episodic memories about power, attitudes in the service of power goals, and intentions to use power in particular ways (Torelli & Shavitt, in press).

Specifically, when studying distinct beliefs endorsing a personalized or a socialized view of power, we found support for the cultural patterning of power representations using both individuals' cultural orientations and ethnic group as alternative operationalizations of culture (Torelli & Shavitt, in press). By sampling for ethnicities that tend to foster a given cultural orientation (e. g., VI orientation among European Americans, Triandis & Gelfand, 1998, compared to an HC orientation among Hispanics, Penaloza, 1994), we examined the independent contribution of individual and ethnic cultural variables on power associations (see Chiu & Hong, 2006; Lalwani et al., 2006; Lalwani, Shrum, & Chiu, 2009). As shown in Table 7. 2, panel A, a VI (and not an HI) orientation was associated with personalized power beliefs, including favoring the abuse of power for one's own benefit (misuse of power, Lee-Chai, Chen, & Chartrand, 2001) and believing in the inequalities of social groups and in the appropriateness of maintaining one's highstatus by dominating others (social dominance orientation; Pratto, Sidanius, Stallworth, & Malle, 1994). At the same time, as shown in Table 7. 2, panel B, a VI orientation was uncorrelated with inclinations to exercise socialized power by helping others (helping power motivation; Frieze & Boneva, 2001). In contrast, an HC orientation was positively associated with a motivation to exercise socialized power by helping others. These effects also emerged at the group level when contrasting

TABLE 7.2: **Summary of Relations between Cultural Orientation and Power Concepts**

		PANEL A - Measures that Reflect a Personalized Power Concept		Relationship with Cultural Orientation			
Study	Psychological Domain	Type of Measure	DV	HI	VI	HC	VC
1	Beliefs	Self-report	Misuse of Power	–.05	.24***	–.29***	–.07*
1	Beliefs	Self-report	Social Dominance Orientation	–.08	.28**	–.27***	–.11
2	Episodic Memory	Independent Rating	Vividness of Recall of Personalized Power Events	–.07	.32**	–.03	.01
3	Attitudes	Self-Report	Liking for brands that embody personalized power	.02	.41***	.02	.05
4	Goal Oriented Responses	Projective Self-Report Behavioral Intention	Thematic Apperception Test Evaluation of a status target Likelihood to restore status	.03	.32***	–.19**	.02

*p < .10   **p < .05   ***p < .01

(Continued)

TABLE 7.2: **Summary of Relations between Cultural Orientation and Power Concepts** (Cont'd)

PANEL B - Measures that Reflect a Socialized Power Concept

Study	Psychological Domain	Type of Measure	DV	Relationship with Cultural Orientation			
				HI	VI	HC	VC
1	Beliefs	Self-report	Helping Power Motivation	.05	–.03	.51***	.14***
2	Episodic Memory	Independent Rating	Vividness of Recall of Socialized Power Events	–.11	–.05	.48**	.06
3	Attitudes	Self-Report	Liking for brands that embody socialized power	.09	–.17***	.32***	.05
4	Goal Oriented Responses	Self-Report Self-Report Behavioral Intention	Perception of a Power holder Evaluation of a helpful target Likelihood to help others	.02	.07	.49***	.00
5	Behavior	Behavior	Amount to be paid[1]	.10	–.44***	.30***	.04

*p < .10 **p < .05 ***p < .01

[1] The positive relationship with HC means a more benevolent behavior consistent with a socialized view of power, whereas the negative relationship with VI signifies a more exploitative behavior consistent with a personalized view of power

European Americans (high-VI group) and Hispanics (high-HC group). Furthermore, individual VI and HC cultural orientation scores mediated the differences in power beliefs between European American and Hispanic participants. Results across multiple studies also highlighted differences between individuals high in VC and HC. An HC (but not a VC) orientation was negatively correlated with tendencies to abuse power, with beliefs in the inequalities of social groups, and with a self-reported willingness to dominate others (see Table 7. 2, panel A). Thus, a consideration of the horizontal-vertical distinction significantly enhanced understanding of the relation between cultural variables and power beliefs.

Culturally patterned associations with power were also evident when studying memory for events associated with the pursuit of culturally relevant power goals. To the extent that ongoing personalized (socialized) power representations impact the encoding of experiences in memory and facilitate the accessibility of goal-relevant episodes, we hypothesized that a VI (HC) orientation would be associated with strong and vivid mental representations of personalized (socialized) power. We asked an ethnically diverse sample of participants (e. g., Hispanics or European Americans) to think about situations in which one acquired status over others or in which one helped others. As expected, a VI (and not an HI) measured cultural orientation was positively related to the vivid recall of experiences in which one acquired status. In contrast, an HC (and not a VC) orientation was positively related to the vivid recall of experiences in which one helped others. Again, evidence for this cultural patterning of power representations was supported at both the individual and the cultural group levels. Hispanic (high-HC group) participants' episodic recall was significantly more (less) vivid for socialized (personalized) power events than the recall of European American participants (high-VI group). Moreover, individual VI and HC cultural orientation scores mediated the differences in vividness ratings between the two ethnic groups.

In another set of studies, we extended the findings to attitudes toward brands that may assist in the pursuit of distinct power goals. In these studies (Torelli & Shavitt, in press; Torelli, Ozsomer, Carvalho, Keh, & Maehle, 2009), cross-national samples of participants rated the extent to which they liked brands that symbolize personalized or socialized power concerns. As expected, a VI orientation was positively associated with liking for brands that symbolize personalized power concerns (e. g., sunglasses described as "an exceptional piece of adornment that conveys your status and signifies your exquisite taste"). In contrast, an HC orientation was positively associated with liking for brands that symbolize socialized power concerns (e. g., a shopping bag with which "you're doing your part to save the environment"). These effects also emerged at the group level when contrasting Americans (high-VI group) and Brazilians (high-HC group). A mediation analysis further suggested that individual-level VI and HC cultural orientations mediated nation-level differences in liking for such brands (Torelli & Shavitt, in press).

Our studies also suggest that VI versus HC cultural orientation predicts less liking of brands associated with actions that are incongruent with one's power concepts. Evidence for this comes from studies investigating attitudes toward status (prosocial) brands engaged in incongruent actions—that is, socially responsible (high-status) actions (Torelli, Basu-Monga, & Kaikati, unpublished data). Our predictions were based on the distinctive associations with power demonstrated so far, as well as the opposition between status-oriented and prosocial-oriented endstates documented in past research (e. g., power and benevolence values; Schwartz, 1992) and revealed in some of the studies reported earlier. In short, we reasoned that high-VI versus low-VI people would evaluate less favorably status brands engaged in socially responsible actions (e. g., BMW engaged in prosocial efforts). We also expected that high-HC versus low-HC people would evaluate less favorably nurturing brands engaged in status-oriented actions. A series of studies provided support for these propositions. Moreover, as expected, the effects were driven by greater perceptions among high versus low-VIs (high vs. low-HCs) that the socially-responsible (status-oriented) actions negatively affected the status (nurturing) image of the brand (Torelli, Basu-Monga, & Kaikati, unpublished data).

In another set of studies, we show how VI and HC cultural orientations can be used to predict behaviors in situations with different power affordances (Torelli & Shavitt, in press). We presented participants with situations that promote the attainment of personalized or socialized power objectives (e. g., behavioral scenarios or simulated negotiation tasks) and measured their behavior in such situations. Results indicated that a VI (HC) orientation, measured at the individual level, predicted greater exploitative (benevolent) behavior in a negotiation, and also greater intentions to behave in ways aimed at impressing (helping) others.

In combination, the findings just described shed light on the core elements of the horizontal and vertical versions of individualism and collectivism, and they further our understanding of the ways in which these constructs influence basic psychological processes (see Brewer & Chen, 2007; Oyserman et al., 2002). Current theorizing has focused on the role of competition in characterizing vertical individualists. Our findings suggest that the understanding of VI may be advanced by expanding our definition beyond competition to encompass the different facets of personalized power, particularly the notion of power as status (see Triandis & Gelfand, 1998, for a similar suggestion). Although vertical individualists may be concerned with competing and winning out over others, they may do so mainly to achieve the status that satisfies their personalized power goals. The use of status symbols may fulfill the same goals. On the other hand, the core elements of individualism identified by Oyserman et al. (2002), independence and uniqueness, may specifically describe horizontal individualism. The lack of power concerns among people high in HI may be the key factor that distinguishes them from those high in VI. Thus, an HI (compared to VI) orientation may predict a distinct set of outcomes in which self-reliance is focal, as noted earlier (Lalwani et al., 2006).

Current theorizing has defined horizontal collectivism in terms of interdependence and sociability. Our findings suggest that understanding HC requires acknowledging its multiple associations with power. People high in HC may have mental representations of both desirable prosocial goals and undesirable status-enhancing goals (see Winter, 1973, for a similar discussion about people high in *fear of power*), and they may therefore have ambivalent feelings toward exercises of power. Thus, they do not submit easily to authority (Triandis, 1995), and they oppose social inequalities (Strunk & Chang, 1999; Torelli & Shavitt, in press, study 1).

Although our findings to date do not speak directly to the power concerns of vertical collectivists, we speculate that vertical collectivists' perceptions of personalized or socialized power are likely to be context dependent. Vertical collectivists may share with vertical individualists a concern with personalized power in relation to outgroups, yet they may have prosocial concerns toward ingroups of a lower status. Indeed, the emphasis on duties and obligations toward lower status ingroup members and the filial piety toward higher status ingroup members, which previous research has linked to collectivism (Oyserman et al., 2002), may specifically describe VC rather than collectivism more broadly.

In summary, our findings show that the horizontal-vertical distinction predicts systematic variations in the perceived meaning and purpose of power. These distinct tendencies to conceptualize power in personalized versus socialized terms by people high in VI versus HC should affect the way they perceive others and the world when power is salient. We turn to these issues next.

B. Mindset Activation

1. Stereotyping and Individuating Processes

Horizontal and vertical cultural orientations should also be associated with distinct cognitive processes that facilitate the fulfillment of culturally relevant power goals. Previous research suggests that having power triggers inward-focused information processing. Briñol and colleagues (2007) showed that priming power concepts prior to processing a message about a topic leads people to try to validate their initial views and impressions on the topic, which results in reduced information processing. Rucker and Galinsky (2009) indicate that inducing a feeling of powerfulness (compared to powerlessness) creates an internal focus in processing product information that produces an emphasis on the utility that a product offers the individual. Fiske and colleagues (Fiske 1993, 2001; Goodwin, Gubin, Fiske, & Yzerbyt, 2000) further demonstrate the inward focus of powerful individuals who use their own stereotypes when evaluating low-status others. These individuals attend more to information congruent with their prior expectations about the other person (e. g., category-based information) and attend less to incongruent information (e. g., category-inconsistent information). Cognitive processes aimed at confirming prior expectations about low-status others facilitate defending one's powerful status by reasserting control (Fiske, 1993).

The stereotyping mindset just described seems more congruent with a personalized view of power for status and personal advancement than with a socialized view of power for benefiting and helping others. Thus, we reasoned that people high in VI, who view power in personalized terms, should more easily activate a stereotyping mindset for interpreting the environment than other people (Torelli & Shavitt, 2008). For such people, their frequent and consistent experience activating a stereotyping mindset in social situations would give rise to the routinizing of these processes (Bargh, 1984). Thus, for these high-VI individuals, cueing with power should trigger this mindset, even when processing information about nonsocial targets. In contrast, people high in HC, who view power in socialized terms, should process information via an outward-focused approach, rather than an inward-focused one, when cued with power. We advance this proposition based on the other-centered nature of socialized power. Indeed, findings suggest that power-holders induced to feel responsible for others evaluate low-status others by attending carefully to information that is incongruent with their prior expectations about the target

(Goodwin et al., 2000), presumably because such cognitive processes facilitate forming an accurate impression instrumental for helping the other person. By extension, we argued that cueing with power should trigger such an individuating mindset in people high in HC, even when processing information about nonsocial targets.

In a series of studies using products and brands as targets, we found that cueing with power leads people of different cultural orientations to process information via different mindsets (Torelli & Shavitt, 2008). People high in VI activate cognitive processes that facilitate defending their power, such as reasserting control by confirming prior expectations (stereotyping processes; Fiske, 1993). In contrast, people high in HC activate cognitive processes that facilitate helping others, such as forming accurate, careful impressions (individuating processes; Goodwin et al., 2000). Specifically, cueing with personalized power led people high (vs. low) in a VI orientation to engage in more stereotyping. That is, they recognized better the product information that was congruent with their prior expectations relative to their recognition of the incongruent information. In contrast, activating socialized power goals led people high (vs. low) in an HC orientation to engage in more individuating processes, improving their recall and recognition of incongruent product information.

In a first study, we cued participants with either personalized or socialized power concepts by having them read initial information about one of two products. For one of the products, the initial information contained status features aimed at cueing personalized power (e. g., a prestigious and exclusive financial advisory company), whereas the information for the other product contained nurturing features aimed at cueing socialized power (e. g., pet food designed to light up your dog's face). Participants were then presented with additional information congruent and incongruent with the initial product information. We assessed the use of stereotyping and individuating processing by measuring, in a subsequent task, participants' recognition for the congruent and incongruent information. Congruent (incongruent) information was defined as arguments that were (not) congruent with the status or nurturing qualities of the product. Recognition results were consistent with past research suggesting more stereotyping when personalized power is made salient and more individuating when concerns for others are made salient (Goodwin et al., 2000). More importantly, we found evidence for culturally patterned effects of the power cues on the use of information processing mindsets.

High-VI (vs. low-VI) participants stereotyped more when cued with personalized power. That is, they recognized better the information congruent with the initial description of the status product, relative to their recognition of the incongruent information. In contrast, high-HC (vs. low-HC) participants cued with socialized power individuated more, as evidenced by their better recognition of information incongruent with the initial description of the nurturing product.

Another study examined stereotyping and individuated processing regarding a well-established brand (McDonald's; Torelli & Shavitt, 2008, study 3). Stereotyping (individuating) was assessed based on the delayed recognition of congruent (incongruent) arguments. Personalized or socialized power cues, in the form of power words, were embedded in a separate task prior to the presentation of the product information. For instance, "wealth" or "ambitious" were paired with "power" to cue with personalized power, and "helpful" or "caring" were paired with "power" to cue with socialized power. Results confirmed our predictions that participants high (vs. low) in VI cued with personalized power stereotyped more. That is, they recognized better the information congruent with the McDonald's stereotype of unhealthiness and convenience relative to their recognition of the incongruent information. In contrast, participants high (vs. low) in HC cued with socialized power individuated more. That is, they were more likely to recognize information incongruent with the McDonald's stereotype.

In combination, these studies establish that the horizontal-vertical distinction predicts distinct information processing mindsets. People with a VI cultural orientation, who have an elaborated "power-as-status" self-schema, readily activate a stereotyping mindset. In contrast, people with an HC orientation, who have an elaborated "power-as-helping" self-schema, readily activate an individuating mindset in information processing. People with other cultural orientations did not exhibit these mindsets in response to power cues, supporting the value of the horizontal-vertical distinction in understanding the relation between culture and power-related processes. We speculate that, in general, the unelaborated power-as-status self-schema of people high in HI should make them unlikely to engage in stereotyping processes in response to power cues. However, we suggest that among people high in VC, either stereotyping or individuating in power situations may occur depending on the context. In situations involving outgroups, high-VC individuals cued with power may engage in stereotyping, whereas individuating processes may be more likely in an ingroup situation.

2. Readiness to Perceive Power Threat and to Restore Power

More evidence that specific cultural identities can trigger the readiness to think and act consistently with cultural representations of power comes from our recent research on responses to power threats (Wong & Shavitt, 2009, 2010). These studies specifically examined the role of vertical individualism in the context of service encounters that implicate hierarchical relationships. Participants read scenarios in which they either imagined receiving rude service from a low-rank (e. g., hotel receptionist) or a high-rank (e. g., hotel vice president) service provider. We reasoned that being disrespected by another person should be interpreted differently depending on one's culturally based power associations, as well as the power of the other. Specifically, for people with a VI cultural orientation, power is particularly likely to be associated with status and personal advancement. Thus, the rude receptionist's behavior should be likely to be interpreted as a threat to their sense of status and power, triggering a readiness to act to restore one's power. However, the rude vice president's behavior poses less of a threat to one's own power and could instead trigger deferential responses to the high-ranking individual.

Indeed, in the low-rank (i. e., receptionist) condition, the higher one's VI cultural orientation the greater the dissatisfaction and the more negative emotions one reported (Wong & Shavitt, 2009). Other studies (Wong & Shavitt, 2010) provided direct evidence for the role of power motivation in these relations. For instance, the VI level of participants who read the low-rank scenario predicted higher scores on projective measures assessing fear of power loss and hope for power gain (see Sokolowski, Schmalt, Langens, & Puca, 2000). Moreover, high (versus low) VI participants who read the low-rank scenario indicated a greater willingness to pay for status products such as cuff links and expensive pens; this effect was not observed for nonstatus products such as sofas and minivans. This greater desire for status items presumably emerged because status products afford a method for restoring one's sense of power when it is threatened (Rucker & Galinsky, 2008).

Importantly, a VI cultural orientation did not predict these responses when individuals had first been given an opportunity to engage in self-affirmation. This supports the role of motivational processes to restore power in driving these responses. Finally, the high-rank condition in which a hotel vice president provided rude service was not interpreted in terms of power threat. Instead, a VI orientation was sometimes associated with greater acceptance of rude treatment from a high-ranking person. These findings indicate that one's specific cultural identity (VI) can shape mindsets and action tendencies in pursuit of relevant power goals.

C. Content and Persuasiveness of Message Appeals

Further evidence that the vertical-horizontal distinction offers novel predictions about perceptions of the social environment comes from several lines of research on attitudes and persuasion. For instance, in a study about country-of-origin effects (i. e., the extent to which the country of manufacture affects the evaluation of a product), Gürhan-Canli and Maheswaran (2000) demonstrated that the tendency to favor products from one's own country over foreign products emerged more strongly in Japan (a VC culture) than in the United States (a VI culture). Broadly speaking, this fits well with a conceptualization of collectivists as oriented toward their ingroup, perhaps even to the point of chauvinism in product evaluations. However, mediation analyses using consumers' measured cultural orientations indicated that only the vertical aspect of COL and IND explained country-of-origin effects. For instance, the COL tendency to favor one's own country's products appeared to be driven by cultural values that emphasize deference to the ingroup, hierarchy, and status concerns (VC), and not by values that stress cooperation and sociability (HC).

In line with this, our research suggests that advertising messages with themes that emphasize status, prestige, and hierarchy may be persuasive for those with a vertical cultural orientation but may be inappropriate for those with a horizontal one. When U. S. respondents were asked to write advertisements that they personally would find persuasive, the extent to which the ad appeals they wrote emphasized status themes was positively (negatively) correlated with the degree to which they had a vertical (horizontal) cultural orientation (see Shavitt, et al., 2006).

Additional evidence for the horizontal-vertical cultural patterning of brand evaluations comes from our recent cross-national research on brand symbolism (Torelli et al., 2009). Based on the core motivations underlying HI, VI, HC, and VC orientations outlined earlier (e. g., self-direction for HI or power for VI), we predicted liking for brands that symbolize these core motivations from individuals' cultural orientations. Participants from the United States and China evaluated brand messages for four different brands. The four messages were designed to distinctively position each of the brands on one of four different value domains: self-direction, power, universalism, and tradition. For instance, the "self-direction" brand was described as a t-shirt for which you could "pick your color, pick your message, and pick your style." The "power" brand referred to sunglasses described as "an exceptional piece of adornment that conveys your status and signifies your exquisite taste." The "universalism" brand was described as a shopping bag with which "you're doing your part to save the environment." Finally, the "tradition" brand referred to a "patriotic decoration company making flags since 1820" (In China, this was changed to a traditional restaurant dating to the Ming Dynasty). Participants also completed the 16-item cultural orientation scale (Triandis & Gelfand, 1998). As predicted, the higher the HI orientation of participants, the more favorable the evaluations of a brand positioned on "self-direction" values. Similarly, VI (HC, VC) positively predicted evaluations of a brand positioned on "power" ("universalism," "tradition") values. These results were consistent across the two countries.

More extensive evidence for the horizontal-vertical patterning of persuasive appeals comes from a content analysis of 1211 magazine advertisements in five countries representing VI (United States), HI (Denmark), and VC (Korea, Russia, Poland) cultural contexts (Shavitt, Johnson, & Zhang, in press). This analysis revealed patterns in the benefits emphasized in the ads that supported expectations about the prevalence of appeals in vertical versus horizontal cultures. In particular, the observed emphasis on status in ad appeals—including depictions of luxury, or references to prestige, impressing others, prominence, membership in high-status groups (e. g., ivy league graduates), endorsements by high-status persons (e. g., celebrities), or other distinctions (e. g., "award-winning")—corresponded to the cultural profiles of the countries. Ads in all three VC societies (Korea, Russia, Poland) and the VI society (the United States) evidenced a greater emphasis on status benefits than did ads in the HI society (Denmark). Indeed, status appeared to be a dominant ad theme in all of the vertical societies we examined (relative to appeals that emphasized pleasure, uniqueness, or relationships). In contrast, pleasure appeals dominated in the HI society.

Also as expected, the emphasis on uniqueness in ad appeals—including depictions of differentiation, self-expression, self-reliance, and novelty—was greater in HI versus VI (and VC) cultures (Shavitt, Johnson, & Zhang, in press). These types of appeals frame the product as a form of self-expression, appropriate in cultural contexts that emphasize being distinct and self-reliant (rather than better than others). Thus, although the United States and Denmark are both considered IND societies, their advertisements differed significantly in their emphasis on uniqueness and in their emphasis on status in ways that were consistent with their vertical versus horizontal cultural values. These patterns would not have been anticipated by analyses based on the broader IND-COL classification.

In addition to generating novel hypotheses, a consideration of vertical and horizontal cultural values offers refinements to predictions about the kinds of appeals that distinguish IND and COL cultures. For instance, past research suggests that U. S. appeals are more focused on being unique than are Korean appeals (Kim & Markus, 1999), but uniqueness was defined broadly in that research, incorporating themes of choice and freedom. Our analysis suggests that appeals that more specifically emphasize uniqueness and self-expression (e. g., being different, not better than others) may be especially relevant to an HI (but not a VI) cultural context. Thus, in our study, ads in VI versus VC societies did not differ in their focus on the specific uniqueness themes we examined (Shavitt et al., in press). Future research could address whether, for instance, status appeals in VI societies such as the United States are more focused on "sticking out" and being admired, whereas those in VC societies such as Korea are more focused on fitting in or being included in successful groups. This would be congruent with findings indicating that in the United States (VI) celebrity endorsers are frequently identified by name or profession and their credentials are used to pitch the product directly to the audience, whereas in Korea (VC) celebrities are not often identified by name and they frequently play a character embodying a family or traditional role (Choi et al., 2005).

In sum, although appeals promising to enhance a consumer's status and impress others seem commonplace in our society, cultural factors should play a role in the degree to which such ads speak to consumers' motivations. In this regard, a consideration of horizontal-vertical cultural distinctions stimulates predictions not anticipated by prior cross-cultural research on persuasive communication.

VII. FUTURE DIRECTIONS AND IMPLICATIONS FOR CONSUMER PSYCHOLOGY

We have argued for the importance of the distinction between horizontal and vertical forms of individualism and collectivism for understanding the psychological effects of cultural differences. The review of the findings underscores the value of the horizontal-vertical distinction for uncovering novel cultural patterns, as described in Table 7. 1. We reviewed the impact of these distinct orientations on the values that people endorse, their self-presentation styles, their major motivational concerns and preferred means of attaining their goals, and their perceptions of their social environment.

Our review included many studies on consumer psychology, which allowed us to illustrate some of the substantive implications that emerge from the horizontal/vertical distinction. As marketing efforts become increasingly globalized, understanding cross-cultural consumer psychology has become a mainstream goal of consumer research. Our review indicates that brands that are advertised in a way that better reflects the major motivational concern associated with a given cultural orientation are more likely to resonate among consumers high in this orientation. To the extent that people in a particular market share this cultural orientation, such brands are likely to enjoy widespread acceptance and might even become cultural icons. For instance, brands such as Nike and Harley Davidson, commonly perceived as icons of the vertical individualistic American culture, have built their images around notions of power and status (Torelli, Chiu, & Keh, 2010). Although these brands could successfully penetrate a foreign market with different cultural values (e. g., a horizontal collectivistic society), it might be difficult for them to reach an iconic status in such markets. Doing so may require a change in brand image to better reflect prevailing cultural values and norms.

A. Attitude Functions Across Cultures

Some of the cultural differences reviewed earlier in this chapter (e. g., in impression management and self-presentation patterns) may be linked to differences between INDs and COLs in the nature and functions of their attitudes.

The traditional conceptualization of attitudes posits that an attitude is an enduring disposition toward an object that is stable, consistent, aids in making decisions, guides behavior, and may be used for self-expression. However, the appropriateness of this conceptualization may depend on cultural variables. In contrast with the traditional view of attitudes and their functions, we suggest that collectivists' attitudes are less consistent and stable, less likely to serve as guides to behavior, and less likely to be used as a means for self-expression.

Based on this research on cross-cultural differences in relation to contradictions, we argue that collectivists (i. e., Easterners) would be more likely to form evaluatively ambivalent attitudes, compared to individualists (i. e., Westerners) (Choi & Choi 2002; Choi, Koo, & Choi 2007; Nisbett, Peng, Choi, & Norenzayan, 2001; Peng & Nisbett 1999; Wong, Rindfleisch, & Burroughs, 2003). Several lines of research support this reasoning. For instance, according to Peng and Nisbett (1999), the philosophies underlying Eastern and Western cultures are associated with distinct views on contradictions.

Eastern philosophy is based on Confucian and Buddhist views that conceive of the world as complex and holistic, and stress that everything needs to be assessed within its context. This view encourages compromise and suggests that many beliefs can be both true and false. Western philosophy is based on Aristotelian logical thinking, which stresses that there can only be one truth. Hence, Westerners are likely to regard contradictions as unacceptable, whereas Easterners are relatively comfortable with them.

Studies on emotions provide further evidence that supports this notion. Bagozzi, Wong, and Yi (1999) show that Westerners experience emotions in a bipolar way such that they exhibit a strong negative correlation between reported negative and positive emotions. Easterners, on the other hand, exhibit weak correlations between reported negative and positive emotions. Williams and Aaker (2002) show that Easterners' propensity to accept mixed emotions leads them in turn to express more favorable attitudes towards appeals containing mixed emotions, compared to messages containing either purely happy or purely sad emotions. Westerners, on the other hand, express greater discomfort when exposed to appeals containing mixed emotions, compared to messages containing pure emotions. These cross-cultural differences may also apply to attitudes, such that one might expect more ambivalent attitudes among COLs (vs. INDs) and higher internal consistency in attitudes among INDs (vs. COLs).

These different dispositions toward contradiction imply not only that collectivists' attitudes compared to individualists' attitudes may be more ambivalent but also that they may be less stable over time. Because collectivists pay more attention to the context, they may place greater importance on situational influences when evaluating targets of judgment. Indeed, research has shown that collectivists' attributions, personality descriptions, and judgment tend to be context dependent, whereas individualists' tend to be more context general (Ji, Peng, & Nisbett, 2000; Knowles, Butler, & Linn, 2001; Markus & Kitayama, 1991; Masuda, Ellsworth, Mesquita, Leu, Tanida, & van de Veerdonk, 2008; Masuda & Nisbett, 2001; Miller, 1984; Morris & Peng, 1994; Norenzayan, Choi, & Nisbett, 2002; Rhee, Uleman, Lee, & Roman, 1995). The observed cultural differences in self-presentations in responding to attitude questions, reviewed earlier in this chapter, may be viewed as an instance of this tendency. That is, collectivists tend to report normative attitudes when motivated to impress. Thus, when the context requires adjustment to the norm, their attitude responses shift accordingly.

Fazio (2000) suggests that accessible attitudes assist individuals in coping with the multitude of objects they encounter in their daily lives (see also

Katz, 1960; Smith, Bruner, & White, 1956). Having accessible attitudes serves as knowledge to guide one's behavior and decision making. However, this may be more the case for individualists, who make decisions based on their personal preferences, than for collectivists, who are motivated also to consider norms and others' preferences. This is in accord with the findings of Savani, Markus, and Conner (2008), who suggested that preferences and choice have different functions for people from India compared with North Americans, and thus Indians take more time to choose and exhibit weaker relationships between their personal preferences and choices (see also Savani, Markus, Naidu, Kumar, & Berlia, 2010).

The horizontal versus vertical dimension may also predict cultural variations in the functions of attitudes. As noted earlier, people high in VC are particularly focused on maintaining harmony. Thus, people high in VC (compared to HC) may be more practiced at adjusting their attitude expressions to fit in, and they may be more likely to do so in deference to high-status others. In contrast, harmony is less of a concern for HCs. They are more likely to value cooperation in the context of honesty and direct self-expression. This may predict greater candor in their attitudinal responses in general. However, an HC orientation has both an emphasis on appropriateness and cooperation. Therefore, when behavioral norms that involve cooperation and interpersonal appropriateness are salient, people high in HC may adjust their behavior expressions to those norms. Indeed, Lalwani et al. (2006) found that the HC (vs. VC) orientation was more predictive of the appropriateness of self-reported behaviors.

In other words, the nature of the norm and the degree to which the context requires cooperation and appropriateness versus harmony and deference may determine whether horizontal collectivists or vertical collectivists show greater tendency toward, and automaticity in, their normative adjustments.

VIII. CONCLUSION

The constructs of individualism and collectivism have dominated the research discourse on the psychological impacts of culture for many years. Although the breadth and power of these constructs have profoundly advanced the field, we argue that future research should move beyond the broad IND and COL dichotomy. In particular, recent research supports the need to distinguish between horizontal and vertical forms of individualism and collectivism. In this chapter, we have reviewed several lines of work establishing the value of the horizontal and vertical cultural distinction nested within the broader

IND-COL classification. Several lines of evidence indicate that these specific cultural orientations or categories are associated with distinct mental representations and trigger specific cognitive processes and action tendencies that facilitate the fulfillment of culturally relevant goals. Attending to the cultural patterning of hierarchy, status, and power motivations offers several important directions for future research to enhance cross-cultural theorizing.

REFERENCES

Askgaard, H. (1992). As Denmark sees herself and is seen by others. In P. Himmelstrup, K. Hegelund, & H. Askgaard (Eds.), *Discover Denmark-On Denmark and the Danes: Past, present and future*. Herning, Denmark: Danish Cultural Institute, Copenhagen and Systime Publishers.

Bagozzi, R. P., Wong, N., & Yi, Y. (1999). The role of culture and gender in the relationship between positive and negative affect. *Cognition and Emotion*, *13*(6), 641–672.

Bargh, J. A. (1984). Automatic and conscious processing of social information. In R. S. J. Wyer & T. K. Srull (Eds.), *Handbook of social cognition* (Vol. 3, pp. 1–43). Hillsdale, NJ: Erlbaum.

Bargh, J. A. (1994). The four horsemen of automaticity: awareness, intention, efficiency, and control in social cognition. In R. S. Wyer, Jr. & T. K. Srull (Eds.), *Handbook of social cognition* (pp. 1–40). Hillsdale, NJ: Erlbaum.

Bargh, J. A. (1997). The automaticity of everyday life. In R. S. Wyer (Ed.), *Advances in social cognition* (Vol. 10, pp. 1–61). Mahwah, NJ: Erlbaum.

Baumeister, R. F., & Sommer, K. L. (1997). What do men want? Gender differences and two spheres of belongingness: Comment on Cross and Madson (1997). *Psychological Bulletin*, *122*(1), 38–44.

Bond, M. H. (2002). Reclaiming the individual from Hofstede's ecological analysis–A 20-year odyssey: Comment on Oyserman et al. (2002). *Psychological Bulletin*, 128(1), 73–77.

Brewer, M. B., & Chen, Y. -R. (2007). Where (Who) are collectives in collectivism? Toward conceptual clarification of individualism and collectivism. *Psychological Review*, *114*(1), 133–151.

Briley, D. A., & Wyer, R. S. Jr. (2001). Transitory determinants of values and decisions: The utility (or non-utility) of Individualism-Collectivism in understanding cultural differences. *Social Cognition*, *19*(3), 198–229.

Brinol, P., Petty, R. E., Valle, C., Rucker, D. D., & Becerra, A. (2007). The effects of message recipients' power before and after persuasion: A self-validation analysis. *Journal of Personality and Social Psychology*, *93*(6), 1040–1053.

Chen, C. C., Meindl, J. R., & Hunt, R. G. (1997). Testing the effects of vertical and horizontal collectivism: A study of reward allocation preferences in China. *Journal of Cross-Cultural Psychology*, *28*(1), 44–70.

Chen, S., Lee-Chai, A. Y., & Bargh, J. A. (2001). Relationship orientation as a moderator of the effects of social power. *Journal of Personality and Social Psychology*, *80*(2), 173–187.

Chiou, J-S. (2001). Horizontal and vertical individualism and collectivism among college students in the United States, Taiwan, and Argentina. *Journal of Social Psychology*, *141*(5), 667–678.

Chirkov, V., Ryan, R. M., Kim, Y., & Kaplan, U. (2003). Differentiating autonomy from individualism and independence: A self-determination theory perspective on internalization of cultural orientations and well-being. *Journal of Personality and Social Psychology*, *84*(1), 97–110.

Chiu, C-y., & Hong, Y-Y. (2006). *Social psychology of culture*. New York: Psychology Press.

Choi, I., & Choi, Y. (2002). Culture and self-concept flexibility. *Personality and Social Psychology Bulletin*, *28*(11), 1508–1517.

Choi, I., Koo, M., & Choi, J. A. (2007). Individual differences in analytic versus holistic thinking. *Personality and Social Psychology Bulletin*, *33*(5), 691–705.

Choi, S. M., Lee, W. N., & Kim, H. J. (2005). Lessons from the rich and famous: A cross-cultural comparison of celebrity endorsement in advertising. *Journal of Advertising*, *34*(2), 85–98.

Cross, S. E., Bacon, P. L., & Morris, M. L. (2000). The relational interdependent self-construal and relationships. *Journal of Personality and Social Psychology*, *78*(4), 791–808.

Cross, S. E., & Madson, L. (1997). Models of the self: Self-construals and gender. *Psychological Bulletin*, *122*(1), 5–37.

Daun, A. (1991). Individualism and collectivity among Swedes. *Ethnos*, *56*(3–4), 165–172.

Daun, A. (1992). Modern and modest: Mentality and self-stereotypes among Swedes. In A. Sjoegren & L. Janson (Eds.), *Culture and management* (pp. 101–111). Stockholm, Sweden: Institution for International Business.

de Mooij, M. (1998). *Global marketing and advertising*. Thousand Oaks, CA: Sage.

Erez, M., & Earley, P. C. (1987). Comparative analysis of goal-setting strategies across cultures. *Journal of Applied Psychology*, *72*(4), 658–665.

Eysenck, S. B. G., & Eysenck, H. J. (1964). An improved short questionnaire for the measurement of extraversion and neuroticism. *Life Sciences*, *3*(10), 1103–1109.

Fazio, R. H. (2000). Accessible attitudes as tools for object appraisal: Their costs and benefits. In G. Maio & J. Olson (Eds.), *Why we evaluate: Functions of attitudes* (pp. 1–36). Mahwah, NJ: Erlbaum.

Feather, N. T. (1994). Human values and their relation to justice. *Journal of Social Issues*, *50*(4), 129–151.

Fiske, A. P. (1992). The four elementary forms of sociality: Framework for a unified theory of social relations. *Psychological Review*, *99*(4), 689–723.

Fiske, S. T. (1993). Controlling other people: The impact of power on stereotyping. *American Psychologist*, *48*(6), 621–628.

Fiske, S. T. (2001). Effects of power on bias: Power explains and maintains individual, group, and societal disparities. In A. Y. Lee-Chai & J. A. Bargh (Eds.), *The use and abuse of power: Multiple perspectives on the causes of corruption* (pp. 181–193). New York: Psychology Press.

Frieze, I. H., & Boneva, B. S. (2001). Power motivation and motivation to help others. In A. Y. Lee-Chai & J. A. Bargh (Eds.), *The use and abuse of power: Multiple perspectives on the causes of corruption* (pp. 75–89). New York: Psychology Press.

Gabriel, S., & Gardner, W. L. (1999). Are there "his" and "hers" types of interdependence? The implications of gender differences in collective versus relational interdependence for affect, behavior, and cognition. *Journal of Personality and Social Psychology, 77*(3), 642–655.

Gannon, M. J. (2001). *Understanding global cultures: Metaphorical journeys through 23 nations* (2nd ed.). Thousand Oaks, CA: Sage.

Gilbert, D. T., & Osborne, R. E. (1989). Thinking backward: some curable and incurable consequences of cognitive busyness. *Journal of Personality and Social Psychology, 57*(6), 940–950.

Gilligan, C. (1982). New maps of development: New visions of maturity. *American Journal of Orthopsychiatry, 52*(2), 199–212.

Gilligan, C. (1986). On In a different voice: An interdisciplinary forum: Reply. *Signs, 11*(2), 324–333.

Goodwin, S. A., Gubin, A., Fiske, S. T., & Yzerbyt, V. Y. (2000). Power can bias impression processes: Stereotyping subordinates by default and by design. *Group Processes and Intergroup Relations, 3*(3), 227–256.

Gouveia, V. V., Clemente, M., & Espinosa, P. (2003). The horizontal and vertical attributes of individualism and collectivism in a Spanish population. *Journal of Social Psychology, 143*(1), 43–63.

Gur, R. C., & Sackeim, H. A. (1979). Self-deception: A concept in search of a phenomenon. *Journal of Personality and Social Psychology, 37*(2), 147–169.

Gürhan-Canli, Z., & Maheswaran, D. (2000). Cultural variations in country of origin effects. *Journal of Marketing Research, 37*(3), 309–317.

Haslam, N. (1994). Categories of social relationship. *Cognition, 53*, 59–90.

Haslam, N. (1995). Factor structure of social relationships: An examination of relational models and resource exchange theories. *Journal of Social and Personal Relationships, 12*, 217–227.

Haslam, N., & Fiske, A. P. (1999). Relational models theory: A confirmatory factor analysis. *Journal of Personal Relationships, 6*, 241–250.

Ho, D. Y. F., & Chiu, C-y. (1994). Component ideas of individualism, collectivism, and social organization: An application in the study of Chinese culture. In U. Kim, H. C. Triandis, C. Kagitçibasi, G. Choi & G. Yoon (Eds.), *Individualism and collectivism: Theory, method and applications* (pp. 137–156). Thousand Oaks, CA: Sage.

Hofstede, G. H. (1980). *Culture's consequences: International differences in work-related values*. Newbury Park, CA: Sage.

Hofstede, G. H. (2001). *Culture's consequences: Comparing values, behaviors, institutions and organizations across nations*. Thousand Oaks, CA: Sage.

Howard, E. S., Gardner, W. L., & Thompson, L. (2007). The role of the self-concept and the social context in determining the behavior of power holders: Self-construal in intergroup versus dyadic dispute resolution negotiations. *Journal of Personality and Social Psychology*, *93*(4), 614–631.

Ji, L. J., Peng, K., & Nisbett, R. E. (2000). Culture, control, and perception of relationships in the environment. *Journal of Personality and Social Psychology*, *78*(5), 943–955.

Johnson, C. S., & Stapel, D. A. (2007). No pain, no gain: The conditions under which upward comparisons lead to better performance. *Journal of Personality and Social Psychology*, *92*, 1051–1067.

Kashima, Y., Yamaguchi, S., Kim, U., Choi, S. C., Gelfand, M. J., & Yuki, M. (1995). Culture, gender, and self: A perspective from individualism-collectivism research. *Journal of Personality and Social Psychology*, *69*(5), 925–937.

Katz, D. (1960). The functional approach of the study of attitudes. *Public Opinion Quarterly*, *24*(2), 163–204.

Kim, H. S., & Markus, H. R. (1999). Deviance or uniqueness, harmony or conformity? A cultural analysis. *Journal of Personality and Social Psychology*, *77*(4), 785–800.

Kitayama, S., Markus, H. R., Matsumoto, H., & Norasakkunkit, V. (1997). Individual and collective processes in the construction of the self: Self-enhancement in the United States and self-criticism in Japan. *Journal of Personality and Social Psychology*, *72*(6), 1245–1267.

Knowles, E. S., Butler, S., & Linn, J. A. (2001). Increasing compliance by reducing resistance. In J. Forgas & K. Williams (Eds.), *Social influence: Direct and indirect processes*. New York: Psychology Press.

Kurman, J., & Sriram, N. (2002). Interrelationships among vertical and horizontal collectivism, modesty, and self-enhancement. *Journal of Cross-Cultural Psychology*, *33*(1), 71–86.

Lalwani, A. K., & Shavitt, S. (2009). The "Me" I claim to be: Cultural self-construal elicits self-presentational goal pursuit. *Journal of Personality and Social Psychology*, *97*(1), 88–102.

Lalwani, A. K., Shavitt, S., & Johnson, T. (2006). What is the relation between cultural orientation and socially desirable responding? *Journal of Personality and Social Psychology*, *90*(1), 165–178.

Lalwani, A. K., Shrum, L. J., & Chiu, C-y. (2009). Motivated response styles: The role of cultural values, regulatory focus, and self-consciousness in socially desirable responding. *Journal of Personality and Social Psychology*, *96*(4), 870–882.

Lee-Chai, A. Y., Chen, S., & Chartrand, T. L. (2001). From Moses to Marcos: Individual differences in the use and abuse of power. In A. Y. Lee-Chai & J. A. Bargh (Eds.), *The use and abuse of power: Multiple perspectives on the causes of corruption* (pp. 57–74). New York: Psychology Press.

Maheswaran, D., & Shavitt, S. (2000). Issues and new directions in global consumer psychology. *Journal of Consumer Psychology*, 9(2), 59–66.

Markus, H. R., & Kitayama, S. (1991). Culture and the self: Implications for cognition, emotion, and motivation. *Psychological Review*, 98(2), 224–253.

Masuda, T., Ellsworth, P. C., Mesquita, B., Leu, J., Tanida, S., & Veerdonk, E. (2008). Placing the face in context: Cultural differences in the perception of facial emotion. *Journal of Personality and Social Psychology*, 94 (3), 365–381.

Masuda, T., & Nisbett, R. E. (2001). Attending holistically versus analytically: Comparing the context sensitivity of Japanese and Americans. *Journal of Personality and Social Psychology*, 81(5), 922–934.

Mick, D. G. (1996). Are studies of dark side variables confounded by socially desirable responding? The case of materialism. *Journal of Consumer Research*, 23(2), 106–119.

Miller, J. G. (1984). Culture and the development of everyday social explanation. *Journal of Personality and Social Psychology*, 46(5), 961–978.

Morris, M. W., & Peng, K. (1994). Culture and cause: American and Chinese attributions for social and physical events. *Journal of Personality and Social Psychology*, 67(6), 949–971.

Nelson, M. R., & Shavitt, S. (2002). Horizontal and vertical individualism and achievement values: A multimethod examination of Denmark and the United States. *Journal of Cross-Cultural Psychology*, 33(5), 439–458.

Nisbett, R. E., Peng, K., Choi, I., & Norenzayan, A. (2001). Culture and systems of thought: Holistic versus analytic cognition. *Psychological Review*, 108(2), 291–310.

Norenzayan, A., Choi, I., & Nisbett, R. E. (2002). Cultural similarities and differences in social inference: Evidence from behavioral predictions and lay theories of behavior. *Personality and Social Psychology Bulletin*, 28(1), 109–120.

Oishi, S., Schimmack, U., Diener, E., & Suh, E. M. (1998). The measurement of values and individualism-collectivism. *Personality and Social Psychology Bulletin*, 24(11), 1177–1189.

Oyserman, D., Coon, H. M., & Kemmelmeier, M. (2002). Rethinking individualism and collectivism: Evaluation of theoretical assumptions and meta-analyses. *Psychological Bulletin*, 128(1), 3–72.

Paulhus, D. L. (1984). Two-component models of socially desirable responding. *Journal of Personality and Social Psychology*, 46(3), 598–609.

Paulhus, D. L. (1988). *Assessing self-deception and impression management in self-reports: The balanced inventory of desirable responding.* Unpublished manual, University of British Columbia.

Paulhus, D. L. (1991). Measurement and control of response bias. In J. P. Robinson & P. R. Shaver (Eds.), *Measures of personality and social psychological attitudes* (pp. 17–59). San Diego: Academic Press, Inc.

Paulhus, D. L. (1998a). Interpersonal and intrapsychic adaptiveness of trait self-enhancement: A mixed blessing? *Journal of Personality and Social Psychology*, 74(5), 1197–1208.

Paulhus, D. L. (1998b). *Paulhus deception scales: User's manual*. North Tonawanda, NY: Multi-Health Systems.

Penaloza, L. (1994). Atravesando fronteras/border crossings: A critical ethnographic exploration of the consumer acculturation of Mexican immigrants. *Journal of Consumer Research*, 21(1), 32–54.

Peng, K., & Nisbett, R. E. (1999). Culture, dialectics, and reasoning about contradiction. *American Psychologist*, 54(9), 741–754.

Pratto, F., Sidanius, J., Stallworth, L. M., & Malle, B. F. (1994). Social dominance orientation: A personality variable predicting social and political attitudes. *Journal of Personality and Social Psychology*, 67(4), 741–763.

Rhee, E., Uleman, J. S., Lee, H. K., & Roman, R. J. (1995). Spontaneous self-descriptions and ethnic identities in individualistic and collectivistic cultures. *Journal of Personality and Social Psychology*, 69(1), 142–152.

Riemer, H. (2009). Automatic and effortful processes in socially desirable responding: A cross-cultural view. In A. L. McGill & S. Shavitt (Eds.), *Advances in Consumer Research, Vol. 36*, (p. 915). Duluth, MN: Association for Consumer Research.

Robert, C., Lee, W. C., & Chan, K. Y. (2006). An empirical analysis of measurement equivalence with the indcol measure of individualism and collectivism: Implications for valid cross-cultural inference. *Personnel Psychology*, 59(1), 65–99.

Rucker, D. D., & Galinsky, A. D. (2009). Conspicuous consumption versus utilitarian ideals: How different levels of power shape consumption. *Journal of Experimental Social Psychology*, 45, 549–555.

Sackeim, H. A., & Gur, R. C. (1979). Self-deception, other-deception, and self-reported psychopathology. *Journal of Consulting and Clinical Psychology*, 47(1), 213–215.

Savani, K., Markus, H. R., & Conner, A. L. (2008). Let your preference be your guide? Preferences and choices are more tightly linked for North Americans than for Indians. *Journal of Personality and Social Psychology*, 95(4), 861–876.

Savani, K., Markus, H. R., Naidu, N. V. R., Kumar, S., & Berlia, N. (2010). What counts as a choice? U. S. Americans are more likely than Indians to construe actions as choices. *Psychological Science*, 21(3), 391–398.

Schlenker, B. R., & Britt, T. W. (1999). Beneficial impression management: Strategically controlling information to help friends. *Journal of Personality and Social Psychology*, 76(4), 559–573.

Schlenker, B. R., Britt, T. W., & Pennington, J. (1996). Impression regulation and management: Highlights of a theory of self-identification. In R. M. Sorrentino & E. T. Higgins (Eds.), *Handbook of motivation and cognition, Vol. 3: The interpersonal context* (pp. 118–147). New York: Guilford.

Schwartz, S. H. (1992). Universals in the content and structure of values: Theoretical advances and empirical tests in 20 countries. In M. P. Zanna (Ed.), *Advances in experimental social psychology* (Vol. 25, pp. 1–65). San Diego, CA: Academic Press.

Schwartz, S. H., & Bilsky, W. (1987). Toward a universal psychological structure of human values. *Journal of Personality and Social Psychology*, *53*(3), 550–562.

Schwartz, S. H., & Bilsky, W. (1990). Toward a theory of the universal content and structure of values: Extensions and cross-cultural replications. *Journal of Personality and Social Psychology*, *58*(5), 878–891.

Shavitt, S., Johnson, T. P., & Zhang, J. (in press). Horizontal and vertical cultural differences in the content of advertising appeals. *Journal of International Consumer Marketing*.

Shavitt, S., Lalwani, A. K., Zhang, J., & Torelli, C. J. (2006). The horizontal/vertical distinction in cross-cultural consumer research. *Journal of Consumer Psychology*, *16*(4), 325–356.

Shavitt, S., Lee, A. Y., & Torelli, C. J. (2009). Cross-cultural issues in consumer behavior. In M. Wanke (Ed.), *Social psychology of consumer behavior* (pp. 227–250). New York: Psychology Press.

Shteynberg, G., Gelfand, M., & Kim, K. (2009). Peering into the "magnum mysterium" of culture: The explanatory power of descriptive norms. *Journal of Cross-Cultural Psychology*, *40*(1), 46–69.

Singelis, T. M., Triandis, H. C., Bhawuk, D., & Gelfand, M. J. (1995). Horizontal and vertical dimensions of individualism and collectivism: A theoretical and measurement refinement. *Cross-Cultural Research: The Journal of Comparative Social Science*, *29*(3), 240–275.

Sivadas, E., Bruvold, N. T., & Nelson, M. R. (2008). A reduced version of the horizontal and vertical individualism and collectivism scale: A four-country assessment. *Journal of Business Research*, *61*(3), 201–210.

Smith, E. R., & Lerner, M. (1986). Development of automatism of social judgments. *Journal of Personality & Social Psychology*, *50*(2), 257–267.

Smith, M., Bruner, J., & White, R. (1956). *Opinions and personality*. New York: John Wiley & Sons, Inc.

Soh, S., & Leong, F. T. (2002). Validity of vertical and horizontal individualism and collectivism in Singapore: Relationships with values and interests. *Journal of Cross-Cultural Psychology*, *33*(1), 3–15.

Sokolowski, K., Schmalt, H-D., Langens, T. A., & Puca, R. M. (2000). Assessing achievement, affiliation, and power motives all at once: The Multi-Motive Grid (MMG). *Journal of Personality Assessment*, *74*(1), 126–145.

Spence, J. T., & Helmreich, R. L. (1978). *Msaculinity and femininity: Their psychological dimensions, correlates, & antecedents.* Austin: University of Texas Press.

Steele, C. M., & Liu, T. J. (1983). Dissonance processes as self-affirmation. *Journal of Personality and Social Psychology*, *45*, 5–19.

Stern, B. B., Barak, B., & Gould, S. J. (1987). Sexual identity scale: A new self-assessment measure. *Sex Roles*, *17*(9–10), 503–519.

Strunk, D. R., & Chang, E. C. (1999). Distinguishing between fundamental dimensions of individualism-collectivism: Relations to sociopolitical attitudes and beliefs. *Personality and Individual Differences*, *27*(4), 665–671.

Taylor, S. E., & Brown, J. D. (1988). Illusion and well-being: A social psychological perspective on mental health. *Psychological Bulletin*, *103*(2), 193–210.

Torelli, C. J., Chiu, C-y, & Keh, H. T. (2010). Cultural symbolism of brands in a globalized economy. Paper presented at the Global Brand Management Conference, Istanbul Turkey (June, 2010).

Torelli, C. J., Ozsomer, A., Carvalho, S., Keh, H. T., & Maehle, N. (2009). A measure of brand values: Cross-cultural implications for brand preferences. *Advances in Consumer Research*, *36*, 41–44.

Torelli, C. J., & Shavitt, S. (in press). Culture and concepts of power. *Journal of Personality and Social Psychology*.

Torelli, C. J., & Shavitt, S. (2008). Culture and mental representations of power goals: Consequences for information processing. *Advances in Consumer Research*, *35*, 194–197.

Triandis, H. C. (1995). *Individualism & collectivism.* Boulder, CO: Westview Press.

Triandis, H. C., Chen, X. P., & Chan, D. K. (1998). Scenarios for the measurement of collectivism and individualism. *Journal of Cross-Cultural Psychology*, *29*(2), 275–289.

Triandis, H. C., & Gelfand, M. J. (1998). Converging measurement of horizontal and vertical individualism and collectivism. *Journal of Personality and Social Psychology*, *74*(1), 118–128.

Triandis, H. C., Leung, K., Villareal, M. J., & Clack, F. L. (1985). Allocentric versus idiocentric tendencies: Convergent and discriminant validation. *Journal of Research in Personality*, *19*(4), 395–415.

Triandis, H. C., & Singelis, T. M. (1998). Training to recognize individual differences in collectivism and individualism within culture. *International Journal of Intercultural Relations*, *22*(1), 35–47.

Triandis, H. C., & Suh, E. M. (2002). Cultural influences on personality. *Annual Review of Psychology*, *53*, 133–160.

Van Baaren, R. B., Maddux, W. W., Chartrand, T. L., De Bouter, C., & Van Knippenberg, A. (2003). It takes two to mimic: Behavioral consequences of self-construals. *Journal of Personality and Social Psychology*, *84*(5), 1093–1102.

Van Hemert, D. A., Van De Vijver, F. J. R., Poortinga, Y. H., & Georgas, J. (2002). Structural and functional equivalence of the Eysenck Personality

Questionnaire within and between countries. *Personality and Individual Differences, 33*(8), 1229–1249.

Vodosek, M. (2009). The relationship between relational models and individualism and collectivism: Evidence from culturally diverse work groups. *International Journal of Psychology, 44*(2), 120–128.

Wang, C. L., Bristol, T., Mowen, J. C., & Chakraborty, G. (2000). Alternative modes of self-construal: Dimensions of connectedness-separateness and advertising appeals to the cultural and gender-specific self. *Journal of Consumer Psychology, 9*(2), 107–115.

Weldon, E. (1984). Deindividualization, interpersonal affect, and productivity in laboratory task groups. *Journal of Applied Social Psychology, 14*(5), 469–485.

Williams, P., & Aaker, J. L. (2002). Can mixed emotions peacefully coexist? *Journal of Consumer Research, 28*(4), 636–649.

Winter, D. G. (1973). *The power motive.* New York: Free Press.

Wong, N., Rindfleisch, A., & Burroughs, J. E. (2003). Do reverse-worded items confound measures in cross-cultural consumer research? The case of the material values scale. *Journal of Consumer Research, 30,* 72–91.

Wong, J., & Shavitt, S. (February, 2009). The impact of cultural orientation on service experiences: When does the status of the service staff matter? Paper presented at the conference of the Society for Consumer Psychology, San Diego, CA.

Wong, J., & Shavitt, S. (2010). Be rude to me and I will buy a Rolex: Effects of cultural orientation on responses to power threat in a service setting. *Advances in Consumer Psychology, Vol. 2,* 95.

Wood, W., & Eagly, A. H. (2002). A cross-cultural analysis of the behavior of women and men: Implications for the origins of sex differences. *Psychological Bulletin, 128*(5), 699–727.

Zou, X., Tam, K. P., Morris, M. W., Lee, S. L., Lau, Y. M., & Chiu, C-y. (2009). Culture as common sense: Perceived consensus vs. personal beliefs as mechanisms of cultural influence. *Journal of Personality and Social Psychology, 97*(4), 579–597.

INDEX

Note: Page numbers followed by "*f*" and "*t*" refer to figures and tables, respectively.